CLOTH
AND HUMAN
EXPERIENCE

Smithsonian Series in Ethnographic Inquiry
Ivan Karp and William L. Merrill, Series Editors

Ethnography as fieldwork, analysis, and literary form is the distinguishing feature of modern anthropology. Guided by the assumption that anthropological theory and ethnography are inextricably linked, this series is devoted to exploring the ethnographic enterprise.

ADVISORY BOARD

CLOTH
AND HUMAN
EXPERIENCE

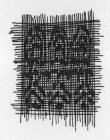

Edited by
Annette B. Weiner & Jane Schneider

Smithsonian Institution Press
Washington and London

Cover image: From Chelna Desai, *Ikat Textiles of India* (San Francisco: Chronicle Books, 1988), p. 76.

This book is published with the assistance of the Wenner-Gren Foundation for Anthropological Research

Edited by Allan Forsyth
Designed by Linda McKnight

05 04 03 02 01 00 99   10 9 8 7 6 5

Library of Congress Cataloging-in-Publication Data
Weiner, Annette B., 1933–
    Cloth and human experience.
    (Smithsonian series in ethnographic inquiry)
    Bibliography: p.
    Includes index.
    1. Costume—Social aspects.   2. Textile fabrics—
Social aspects.   I. Schneider, Jane, 1938–
II. Title.   III. Series.
GT525.W45   1989   391   88–32696
ISBN 0–87474–986–7   ISBN 0–87474–995–6 (ppb).

British Library Cataloguing-in-Publication Data available

∞The paper used in this publication meets the minimum requirements of the American National Standard for Permanence of Paper for Printed Library Materials Z39.48-1984

For permission to reproduce illustrations appearing in this book, please correspond directly with the owners of the works, as listed in the individual captions. The Smithsonian Institution Press does not retain reproduction rights for these illustrations or maintain a file of addresses for photo sources

Contents

Preface

During many years of field research in Western Sicily, Jane Schneider became increasingly impressed by the dedication, time, and effort that Sicilian women direct towards the preparation of their cloth trousseau. Less evident in today's world than in the past, this tradition seemed to call out for study. At about the same time but in another part of the world, Annette Weiner confronted the political importance that Trobrianders and Samoans still attach to "cloth" wealth woven from banana- and pandanus-leaf fibers. These particular experiences convinced us that on a world-wide scale, complex moral and ethical issues related to dominance and autonomy, opulence and poverty, political legitimacy and succession, and gender and sexuality, find ready expression through cloth. Therefore, we organized an interdisciplinary conference, attended by art historians, historians, textile experts, and anthropologists.

The conference, held in 1983 at Troutbeck, New York, was funded by the Wenner-Gren Foundation for Anthropological Research. We are deeply grateful to the participants: Lisa Aaronson, Monni Adams, Susan Bean, Bernard Cohn, Louise Cort, Patricia Darish, Joanne Eicher, Gillian Feeley-Harnik, Diane Owen Hughes, Billie Jean Isbell, H. Leedom Lefferts, Jr., Kathryn March, Matthew Mines, Linda A. Stone, Maude Wahlman, and Ronald Waterbury; to the discussants, T. O. Beidelman, Maurice Bloch, James Boon, Warren D'Azevedo, Shirley Lindenbaum, and Richard C. Trexler; and to the rapporteurs, Ivan Karp and Jason Williams. Each person's particular research interests and intellectual vitality enhanced the conference with a variety of important insights and perspectives. We are particularly grateful to Lita Osmundsen, who was Director of Research for the Wenner-Gren Foundation. Her generous counsel, organizational skills, dedicated staff, and financial support were essential to the conference's success. Her continued assistance with the publication of this volume has enabled us to bring the recognition of cloth's significance before a wider audience.

In preparation for this book, we selected specific themes that would reveal the properties of cloth that underlie its social and political contributions within broad historical time periods. Because we wanted to sharpen our focus in these directions, the volume neither replicates the conference papers nor encompasses the work of all those who participated. Moreover, some essays not presented at the conference have been included in the book. We thank Ivan Karp for his guidance during the publication process. Daniel Goodwin, Editorial Director, and Ruth Spiegel, Managing Editor, of the Smithsonian Institution Press, were splendid working colleagues as was Allan Forsyth, who edited the manuscript. Finally, we are most grateful to the volume contributors, whose enthusiasm for the project made our own endeavors so much more meaningful.

Annette B. Weiner
Jane Schneider

Contributors

SUSAN S. BEAN is Chief Curator and Curator of Ethnology at the Peabody Museum of Salem. Her analyses of the language of social life in south India have appeared in a book, *Symbolic and Pragmatic Semantics: A Kannada System of Address* and in numerous articles. In 1981–82, she was a Mellon Fellow at the Metropolitan Museum of Art. Among the outcomes of her research on Indian textiles are her contribution to this volume and a new permanent exhibit at the Peabody Museum of Salem, "Yankee Traders and Indian Merchants: 1785–1865," created for the 1985–86 Festival of India.

BERNARD S. COHN is Professor of Anthropology and History at the University of Chicago. His primary research interest has been the study of colonial societies, with particular reference to South Asia. His book, *An Anthropologist Among the Historians and Other Essays*, has recently been published.

LOUISE ALLISON CORT is a Museum Specialist for Ceramics at the Freer Gallery of Art and Arthur M. Sackler Gallery within the Smithsonian Institution. She is interested in craft production in Asia and has done extensive research on ceramics and textiles in Japan and India. Her book, *Shigaraki, Potters' Valley* was published in 1979; she is presently preparing for publication her studies of the temple potters of Puri and Orissa, and a seventeenth-century Japanese potter's diary.

PATRICIA DARISH is completing her dissertation in the School of Fine Arts at Indiana University. Her main interest is Central African art traditions. She conducted research among the Kuba of south-central Zaire during 1981 and 1982 and is currently a Research Associate at the University of Missouri–Kansas City, in the department of fine arts.

GILLIAN FEELEY-HARNIK is Professor in the Anthropology Department at The Johns Hopkins University. Her publications include *The Lord's Table: Eucharist and Passover in Early Christianity* (Univ. of Pennsylvania Press, 1981) and a forthcoming book *Death and Development in Madagascar* as well as many articles based on ethnographic and archival research in Madagascar and on research in biblical studies.

JANET HOSKINS is Assistant Professor of Anthropology at the University of Southern California. She has done extensive field work in Kodi, West Sumba, Indonesia and has published articles on traditional poetics, ritual, art, conversion, and emerging historical consciousness among the Kodi people. She has served as a Research Fellow in the Gender Relations Research Group, Research School of Pacific studies, Australian National University, and has collaborated on several films on Sumbanese rituals.

JOHN V. MURRA is President of the Institute of Andean Research. He has taught at Cornell University, the Universidad Nacional de San Marcos (Lima, Peru), Yale University, and Vassar College. He has published *Formaciones economicas y politicas en el mundo andino* (Instituto de Estudios Peruanos, Lima, 1975) and "The Economic Organization of the Inca State" (JAI Press, 1980). He is a corresponding member of the Peruvian Academy of History.

JANE SCHNEIDER is Professor in the Ph.D. Program of Anthropology of the City University of New York. Her long-term fieldwork in Sicily has led to several publications, co-authored by Peter Schneider, including the book, *Culture and Political Economy in Western Sicily*. She has also written about European cloth traditions and is the author of "The Anthropology of Cloth" in the *Annual Review of Anthropology*.

LINDA STONE-FERRIER is currently Associate Professor in the Kress Foundation Department of Art History at the University of Kansas. Her publications include *Images of Textiles: The Weave of 17th-Century Dutch Art and Society*, and an exhibition catalogue, *Dutch Prints of Daily Life: Mirrors of Life or Masks of Morals?* in which she examined the interpretative problems raised by seventeenth-century Dutch everyday scenes.

RONALD WATERBURY, Associate Professor of Anthropology at Queens College, CUNY, has carried out research in Oaxaca, Mexico intermittently since 1965, with an emphasis on economic and political matters. He has also researched, lived, or traveled in many other countries of Latin America, and, in the bargain, has accumulated a considerable collection of popular artisanry.

ANNETTE B. WEINER is David Kriser Distinguished Professor of Anthropology and Chair at New York University. She has conducted ethnographic field research for over a decade in Papua New Guinea and most recently in Western Samoa, Polynesia. She is the author of *Women of Value, Men of Renown: New Perspectives in Trobriand Exchange* and *The Trobrianders of Papua New Guinea*.

1. *Introduction*

JANE SCHNEIDER AND ANNETTE B. WEINER

 Throughout history, cloth has furthered the organization of social and political life. In the form of clothing and adornment, or rolled or piled high for exchange and heirloom conservation, cloth helps social
groups to reproduce themselves and to achieve autonomy or advantage in interactions with others. This book brings to light the properties of cloth that underlie its social and political contributions, the
ritual and social domains in which people acknowledge these properties and give them meaning, and the transformations of meaning
over time.

Malleable and soft, cloth can take many shapes, especially if
pieces are cut for architectural assembly. Cloth also lends itself to
an extraordinary range of decorative variation, whether through the
patterned weaving of colored warps and wefts, or through the embroidery, staining, painting, or dyeing of the whole. These broad
possibilities of construction, color, and patterning give cloth an almost limitless potential for communication. Worn or displayed in an
emblematic way, cloth can denote variations in age, sex, rank, status, and group affiliation. As much as cloth discloses it can conceal,
however, homogenizing difference through uniforms or sackcloth,
or superimposing disguised identities through costumes and masks.
Cloth can also communicate the wearer's or user's ideological values
and claims. Complex moral and ethical issues of dominance and au-

tonomy, opulence and poverty, continence and sexuality, find ready expression through cloth.

In addition to its seemingly endless variability and related semiotic potential, cloth is a repository for prized fibers and dyes, dedicated human labor, and the virtuoso artistry of competitive aesthetic development. As such, it attracts the attention of power holders, including those who would build chiefdoms and states. Throughout history, the architects of centralizing polities have awed spectators with sartorial splendor, strategically distributed beautiful fabrics among clients, and exported the textile output of royal and peasant workshops to earn foreign exchange. Cloth has often become a standard of value, circulating as money, so it should come as no surprise that cloth wealth has enriched the treasuries of many kingdoms and chiefdoms, conferring credibility on political elites along with gold, silver, jewels, and exotic shells.

Another characteristic of cloth, which enhances its social and political roles, is how readily its appearance and that of its constituent fibers can evoke ideas of connectedness or tying. Wrapping individuals to protect them from the malevolent forces of their cultural or natural environment, bark cloths and woven textiles can also envelop more than one person, as in an Indonesian marriage ceremony where a tubular, uncut fabric binds the bride to the groom. A moment's reflection brings to mind any number of instances in which a cloth or thread metaphor illuminates similarly "tied" relations—for example, Anaîs Nin's portrait of love in one of her novels: "She was weaving and sewing and mending because he carried in himself no thread of connection . . . of continuity or repair. . . . She sewed . . . so that the warmth would not seep out of their days together, the soft interskin of their relationship" (1959: 57–58).

Indeed, cloth metaphors echo from many parts of the world, today and in the past. Social scientists and laypersons regularly describe society as fabric, woven or knit together. Cloth as a metaphor for society, thread for social relations, express more than connectedness, however. The softness and ultimate fragility of these materials capture the vulnerability of humans, whose every relationship is transient, subject to the degenerative processes of illness, death, and decay. Weiner (this volume) recalls Homer's description of Penelope, weaving Laertes's shroud by day but then unraveling the same fabric each night, seeking thereby to halt time, neither burying her husband nor marrying a suitor in his absence, and thus preserving the balance between the gods and humans.

To seek the symbolic potentialities of cloth in its material properties is, however, but a preliminary step, and only partially compelling. Equally important are the human actions that make cloth politically and socially salient. The papers in this volume identify various domains of meaning in which people use cloth to consolidate social relations and mobilize political power.

First is the domain of cloth manufacture itself, as spinners, weavers, dyers, and finishers harness the imagined blessings of ancestors and divinities to inspire or animate the product, and draw analogies between weaving or dyeing and the life cycle of birth, maturation, death, and decay. The ritual and discourse that surround its manufacture establish cloth as a convincing analog for the regenerative and degenerative processes of life, and as a great connector, binding humans not only to each other but to the ancestors of their past and the progeny who constitute their future.

A second domain in which cloth acquires social and political significance is that of bestowal and exchange. Participants in life-cycle celebrations in general, and rituals of death in particular, frequently make of cloth a continuous thread, a binding tie between two kinship groups, or three and more generations. The cloth-givers on such occasions generate political power as well, committing recipients to loyalty and obligation in the future.

In a third domain of meaning—ceremonies of investiture and rulership—powerholders or aspirants to power declare that particular cloths transmit the authority of earlier possessors or the sanctity of past traditions, thus constituting a source of legitimacy in the present. A fourth domain involves manipulations of cloth as clothing, the uses of dress and adornment to reveal or conceal identities and values.

The actors who manipulate cloth in one or another domain of meaning vary according to gender. Women are by no means the universal producers of cloth, but in many societies they monopolize all or most of the manufacturing sequence, giving them a larger role than men. Many societies also assign women, rather than men, to exchange or give the cloths that tie the living to the dead, the bride's family to the groom's family, the politically dominant to their dependent clients. In ceremonies of rulership, cloth is generally in the hands of the men, but here, too, women may participate as producers or handlers of sanctified materials. Emblematic and communicative uses of cloth are, finally, as common among women as men; in the fashion system of contemporary Western capitalism, women's dress is elaborated to a uniquely high degree. As this volume suggests, the study of cloth can illuminate women's contributions to social and political organization that are otherwise overlooked.

One can imagine people imbuing cloth with social and political meanings in domains other than the ones just outlined. The domains we describe, however, illuminate with particular precision a theoretical problem posed in a variety of ways by the papers in this book. Capitalist production and its associated cultural values reordered the symbolic potential of cloth in two interrelated ways. First, altering the process of manufacture, capitalism eliminated the opportunity for weavers and dyers to infuse their product with spiritual value and to reflect and pronounce on analogies between reproduction and production. Second, by encouraging the growth of fashion—a consumption system of high-velocity turnover and endless, ever-changing variation—capitalist entrepreneurs vastly inflated dress and adornment as a domain for expression through cloth. Despite these shifts of emphasis and the worldwide expansion of capitalist manufacturing and fashion, ancient cloths and traditions of making them continue to reemerge with political—indeed often subversive—intent, above all in societies emerging from colonial domination. Exploring the domains of manufacture, exchange, and the legitimation of rule, as well as the domain of dress, helps one understand this continuing role of cloth in the reproduction of social life and power.

PART I: CLOTH IN SMALL-SCALE SOCIETIES

Annette B. Weiner's paper, "Why Cloth? Wealth, Gender, and Power in Oceania" introduces Part I, which considers the political significance of cloth in small-scale societies. Focusing on succession to authority, Weiner compares the relatively unstratified Trobriand Islands with Western Samoa, where ranked chiefly titles prevail. In the Trobriands, women gather banana leaves, scrape, dry, and bind them into bundles, or intricately tie them around waist cords to make skirts. At mortuary ceremonies, the female kin of a deceased person amass and distribute these "cloths," valued at hundreds of

U.S. dollars. In Trobriand society, people characteristically attribute death to sorcery, interpreting the loss of a person as a direct attack on the vitality and continuity of his or her kin group as a whole. The more cloth the group's women bestow on others, the better they protect themselves and their kin against continued enmity and political danger. Their distributions simultaneously "untie" the deceased from former social and political obligations.

Where Trobriand women process banana leaves to create a rudimentary form of cloth, women in Samoa soak and dry pandanus, plaiting the narrow fibers into large mats that, when carefully made, feel as soft as linen. Of the two, Samoan "cloth" has more permanence, with some fine mats lasting for as long as 200 years. The oldest mats carry the highest value. Often possessed of individuated histories, these mats are exchanged in all life-cycle ceremonies and at the investitures of chiefs. Relying on these mats to emphasize their associations with ancestors and mythical events of the past, living political actors legitimatize their claims to titles and ranks. In contrast, recently produced wealth circulates at Trobriand mortuary distributions, and new bundles and skirts are considered far more valuable than old ones. A similar contrast separates the ancient polities of Fiji from those of the Hawaiian Islands. Upon the death of a predecessor, the Fijian chief wrapped himself in magnificent rolls of barkcloth, including a train 100 yards long (Kooijman 1972). Although exemplifying the authority of his newly acquired position, these rolls also betrayed the underlying weakness of his succession for, unlike the dynastic cloaks of the substantially more stratified islands of Hawaii, they were not themselves heirlooms.

According to Weiner, the relationship between a greater degree of permanence in cloth and a greater elaboration of political hierarchy is not coincidental. The two go together because a hierarchy depends in part upon sumptuary paraphernalia to objectify rank and, more importantly, to constitute a physical bond between the past and the present. In some Polynesian societies such as Hawaii and Tahiti, it was historically the custom when rulers died to destroy their personal belongings as potentially polluting. But inaugural regalia, in the form of feathered cloaks and girdles, passed from generation to generation as the very substance of dynasty (Henry 1928; Valeri 1985). As Graham Clark (1986) noted for Medieval and Renaissance Europe, the regalia of office transmit ideas of sanctity and majesty as well as social status. Replete with cosmological referents and believed to be seats of spiritual power, such objects have even been said to "rule" in lieu of humans (Heine-Gildern 1956:10).

Weiner observes that once cloth attains a degree of permanence, absorbing value from the passage of time, political elites attempt to hoard and store it, not as capital for eventual deployment or merely for display, but as treasure to be saved in the face of all exigencies that force its dissipation. More than an economic resource or an affirmation of political status, treasure facilitates claims to the past—its names, legends, and events—that justify the transactions and extend the power of living actors. Treasure, of course, also includes valuables of stone, bone, and precious metals with which dynastic elites fill the vaults of state. Hard where cloth is soft, and far more durable, these objects would seem a better vehicle for expressing continuity through time. Weiner argues, however, that all social groups experience contradictory yearnings—for circulation and permanence, for expansion through alliance and conquest, and for rootedness through an internal deepening of authority. Precisely because it wears thin and disintegrates, cloth becomes an apt medium for communicating a central problem of power: Social and political relationships are necessarily fragile in an impermanent, ever-changing world.

The second chapter of Part I, Gillian Feeley-Harnik's "Cloth and the Creation of Ancestors in Madagascar," similarly emphasizes the tendency for cloth to legitimatize power while suggesting the fragility of relationships. The case concerns the Sakalava people of coastal Madagascar, who wrap their dead royalty in cotton cloth, place them in wooden coffins, and bury them in a royal tomb located on a small, offshore island. Unlike the Merina and other peoples of highland Madagascar, the Sakalava do not practice secondary burials in which, as Bloch has described for the Merina (1971), corpses are disinterred to be rewrapped for placement in ancestral tombs. Rather, in Sakalava belief, the dead remain social beings only by returning to possess the living, whom they make ill. In possession episodes, returning spirits disclose their identity by demanding cloths appropriate to their status—cloths that friends and relatives must wrap around the person who is possessed. Most of the returning spirits are of royal ancestry; their high position leads them to ask for *lamba* cloths that, because of age and authenticity, are among the most expensive and difficult to procure. A *lamba* is a rectangular length of silk that also serves as "a common form of dress, a marker of social status, and a valued medium of exchange." Reincarnated through the aid of such fabrics, deceased royalty can pronounce on events of current interest, offering prophesy and vital talk in voices that disguise the politics of the living.

The voices, however, are tenuous. The *lamba* wrapping that clothes a spirit and makes it audible is also like a shroud, demanding silence. Drawing attention to the ambiguity of speech and quiet, revelation and concealment, Feeley-Harnik reflects on the relationship of hard to soft objects in other Sakalava rituals. Besides possession, whose episodic occurence mirrors the distribution of individual illnesses, are events of regional significance, staged collectively at the ancestral tomb. In one such event, a kind of reburial, guardians of the cemetery and the royal capital, assisted by spirit mediums, lead the populace in cleaning the tomb, replacing the fence around it, and weeding the grounds. The activities, Feeley-Harnik suggests, establish an analogy between the skeleton and fleshy corpse, the dead body and its shroud, the tomb and its surrounding greenery, the hardwood fencing and its "wrapping" of leafy branches, hard valuables and the soft silk *lambas*—an interplay of concepts suggesting durability and decay.

Whereas in Madagascar the dead demand cloth from the living after they have been buried, possessing them to make their wishes known, elsewhere negotiations of the deceased for cloth precede burial, constituting a focus of the funeral ritual. Patricia Darish's essay (Chapter 4), "Dressing for the Next Life: Raffia Textile Production and Use among the Kuba of Zaire," illustrates this alternative. Considering a corpse to be nude unless adorned with elaborately embroidered raffia textiles, the Kuba make costly prestations to the dead as a way of ensuring their peaceful transition to an afterlife. The dead, they believe, wish to be buried with cloth of sufficient quantity and quality to facilitate a continued existence as social beings. If disappointed in this request, they will interfere malevolently in the lives of the living.

Darish traces the complexity of fulfilling the sartorial demands of the dead in funerary rituals. The members of the deceased's clan section will have collectively prepared raffia cloth over the years; men weave small squares of it, to which women add a plush-pile embroidery and then assemble the squares into larger garments. At a formal meeting during the mortuary celebration, section members decide which of the various cloths wrapped up in the clan treasury are worthy of bestowal, taking note of the past associations of individual pieces of cloth. Finally, close kin of the deceased observe, evaluate, and criticize or praise the textiles placed on the corpse by more distant relatives and friends. Spousal offerings are especially scrutinized for appropriateness of quantity and workmanship, spouses of course being of a different clan. According to Darish, although the Kuba are an otherwise modern people, who have substantially abandoned raffia cloth in favor of Western dress, their funerals continue to highlight the capacity of cloth to mediate between past and present, the dead and the living, ancestral authority and contemporary political claims.

Janet Hoskins' contribution (Chapter 5), "Why Do Ladies Sing the Blues? Indigo Dyeing, Cloth Production, and Gender Symbolism in Kodi," shifts our attention from death and investiture rituals to textile manufacture and the reproduction of children as domains for attending to the meaning of cloth. Living in western Sumba the Kodi, like other rural Indonesians, give pattern to cloth through the resist dyeing of warp yarns prior to weaving them with plain wefts on the backstrap loom. Known as ikatting, the patterning of the yarns is done by specialists, instructed in the manipulation of various earth tones and indigo. Older Kodi women, past their childbearing years and likely practitioners of herbal medicine, midwifery, tatooing and, more covertly, witchcraft, are the ikat dyers. In communication through sacrificial offerings with the ancestral spirit who introduced indigo to Sumba from the nearby island of Savu, these women alone are in a position to manipulate the color blue.

According to Hoskins, Kodi indigo dyeing involves rituals, songs, laments, and sayings that establish an analog with another process of creation: the conception and birth of a child. Cloth, the Kodi reason, is patterned through the "quickening" and "dampening" of dyestuffs in the blueing bath, whereas children are conceived by the "quickening" of men's sperm and fetuses are nurtured by the "dampening" of the mother's blood. Not only are the most respected and powerful women simultaneously midwives and dyers; they make strikingly parallel ritual offerings on behalf of both dyepot and womb. Fittingly, expectant mothers and older female dyers use the same herbs and barks to enhance their respective forms of productivity, while women's laments compare miscarriages to imperfectly dyed cloths.

Analogous to birth and regeneration, Kodi textile dyeing is also vulnerable to the cycle of death and decay. Hoskins records that practitioners associate the unpleasant smell of the dyebath with the putrefaction of rotting flesh, and consider the bath polluting to gestation. Pregnant women should not look at the dye pots, lest the sight of the dark and churning liquid dissolve the contents of their wombs. Reciprocally, menstruating women are kept from the pots, as the flow of their blood is believed to disrupt the dyeing process. The dependence of birth upon death, gain upon loss, creation upon destruction, is acknowledged by the Kodi in other ways: They model their weddings and funerals after each other, using the same indigo-dyed fabrics to wrap both bride and corpse, and associating blue with the sadness of either separation. Visions of blue add symbolic fuel to both birth and the ikatting process, imbuing them with sacred qualities. From this, Hoskins implies, it is but a short step to the belief that cloth enhances fertility and protects humans from harm.

Kodi rituals and proscriptions are reminiscent of peoples elsewhere who, in the process of making cloth, mythically relate the creation of fabrics to the creation of social progeny. Exemplifying the train of thought that makes one set of processes an analog for the other are taboos that exclude menstruating women from weaving as well as dyeing, and forbid sexually active or pregnant women from seeing or handling the loom (e.g., Emmons 1907; Gustafson 1980; Kent 1983; Messick 1987; Rattray 1927). Also common is the tendency for cloth makers to interact with the spirits and divinities of their homelands and their ancestral pasts, hoping thereby to perfect their skills, acquire inspiration for new motifs, and animate their product with a blessing (e.g., Davis 1982; Tedlock and Tedlock 1985). Besides the Kodi dyers, many peoples believe that weaving skills derive from a mythical diety or ancestor, and are transmitted through dreams or revelations (e.g., Aronson 1983; March 1983). By careful attention to ritual and taboos, the weaver not only demonstrates respect for these sacred sources, but also reactivates the spiritual connection, consecrating the raw materials, the techniques, and the emerging cloth (e.g., Best 1898; Mead 1969; Weiner 1985).

Acknowledging sacred associations in the process of cloth manufacture is like acknowledging historical and mythical past events in the process of cloth bestowal and exchange. Both enhance the affective qualities that are lodged in objects of value. Anthropologists have long puzzled over these qualities. In 1922, for example, Malinowski wrote a poignant account of Trobrianders dangling prized *kula* shells over a dying man as if the shells could inspire him with life (1922: 512–13). Perceiving the power in such objects, Marcel Mauss (1954) emphasized that, in the Trobriands, people encoded *kula* shells with highly significant names and past histories. Ultimately, Malinowski (1926) opted for a rational explanation that equated *kula* valuables with the intense interest of customary exchange, but Mauss held to the idea that the affect elicited by the shells indicated a spiritual force. "One gives away what is in reality a part of one's nature and substance, while to receive something is to receive a part of someone's spiritual essence" (1954:10). The papers in Part I of this book support Mauss's view. Examining the domains of succession, gift exchange, and manufacturing, they show how cloth comes to symbolize such fundamental processes of human experience as biological and social reproduction, the transmittal of authority or legitimation of power, and the vulnerability of people and their relationships to illness and death.

PART II: CAPITALISM AND THE MEANINGS OF CLOTH

On reflection, anyone who lives in a large-scale, industrial capitalist society will agree that cloth is far more than a means to profit in the textile and garment industries and a means to status among fashion-conscious consumers. People under capitalism continue to mark sacred and ceremonial moments with banners, hangings, shrouds, and robes that they carefully conserve from year to year and often over generations. They also acknowledge the birth and maturation of children with gifts of clothing or bedding that are chosen to evoke security, if not a protective power, and they marry with trousseaux of lingerie and linens. Nor do the citizens of capitalist societies refrain from collecting treasured fabrics in heirloom chests, as antiques, or in museums, where they gain in value. Granted, many textile treasures grow threadbare under capitalism, abandoned or abused by owners who see no return—either monetary or sentimental—in them. Equally common, however, is the rediscovery of both sorts of value in one's grandmothers' quilts, or in the hand-crafted cloth of formerly colonized peoples. Finally, notwithstanding the spread of capitalism, political and religious elites still depend upon cloth to mobilize human emotions in support of such large-scale institutions as the nation-state. Flags and military uniforms are two powerful examples.

Yet the roles of cloth have also changed under capitalism. A central difference flows from the vastly expanded scope of fashion that capitalist production and merchandizing encourage. Although not new to the Early Modern period of Western European expansion, the hegemony of fashion in that time and place went so far as to marginalize the idea that cloth constitutes a binding tie to authorities and sacred sources of the past. As Roland Barthes has argued (1967), obsolescence and rapid turnover are the essence of the fashion system, with the result that a disproportionate volume of cloth ends up in the ragbag or as hand-me-downs when compared to non-capitalist circulation.

The changing funeral ceremonies of the seventeenth-century English aristocracy might be seen as heralding a related transformation. As they became increasingly expressive of private loss, these funerals no longer allowed kin groups, through spectacular cloth prestations, to channel death into regeneration and political gain. In earlier times, the mourners had received black drapes from the kin of the deceased; now, to accompany the funeral cortege, they had to supply their own. Cloth no longer expressed the continuity of the groups with ancestral authority and their reproduction through time (Gittings 1984).

The three papers that make up Part II highlight a second difference between the meanings of cloth in capitalist and non-capitalist societies. Under capitalism, the domain of cloth manufacture seems incapable of generating or sustaining ideas of benevolent spiritual or ancestral involvement in the production process, or analogies between this process and the reproduction of offspring. Even when, as in each of the papers, manufacturing is organized through home industries and involves considerable handwork—even when, as in two of the papers, factory production has yet to emerge—market pressures to cheapen and streamline labor prevent spinners and weavers, dyers and finishers, from thinking about or ritually acknowledging the transmission of a sacred ancestry through cloth.

From its inception, capitalist manufacture elevated entrepreneurs whose goals emphasized profit to positions of strategic importance. Merchants or merchant-manufacturers procured the raw materials, structured the production process, supplied equipment or credit for equipment, and arranged for eventual marketing and distribution. Above all, they pressured workers so as to reduce the cost of labor in production. Although factories and well-capitalized machinery represent the extreme of pressure on labor, they were not historically or even today the only alternative. Also common is "putting-out." Where the organization of guilds or unions renders labor more costly, entrepreneurs place textile orders with non-organized producers in rural homes. Here, no less than in factories, the impact of the market is felt. Homeworkers typically experience low piece rates, the fragmentation of the production process among different categories of operatives, the introduction of labor-saving machinery, and the employment of women for less remuneration than men (see Goody 1982; Medick 1981; Schlumbohm 1981).

Entrepreneurs are hardly the only non-producers to have controlled production in the course of textile history. Political and religious elites sponsored the specialized workshops of luxury cloth manufacture in the large-scale agrarian civilizations of Asia, Africa, and the Americas. Here, too, spinners, weavers, and dyers depended upon others to procure their raw materials, organize the labor process, supply equipment, and manage distributions. Luxury industries, however, competed with each other less in the domain of cost than in the domain of aesthetic elaboration, and cloth artisans retained control of aesthetic decisions (see Schneider 1987). Indeed, the luxury cloth of centralized workshops characteristically incorporated not only exotic materials but intensive and highly skilled craftsmanship as well.

Capitalist entrepreneurs sometimes organize productive activity in which aesthetic elaboration is a more salient goal than cutting labor costs. In these situations, the aesthetic judgments, skills, and time of the workers are protected, making possible a continuing role for ritual. But capitalism historically has focused on the manufacture of commodities, defined not simply as goods for sale (for luxury cloth was frequently merchandized), but also as "commodious"— useful, advantageous, beneficial. Such goods strike a middle ground between luxury and deprivation, indulgence and necessity and, if inexpensive enough, permit non-elites to enrich their patterns of consumption. Commodities in the form of commodious textiles, produced in cottages under a putting-out system and eventually in factories, illustrate most dramatically the decline of manufacturing as an arena for imbuing cloth with sacred and ancestral referents, relevant for enhancing its social and political symbolism. As Marx observed, under capitalism it is consumers and not producers who make commodities into fetishes, and in ways that have nothing to do with their manufacture.

Jane Schneider's essay (Chapter 6), "Rumpelstiltskin's Bargain: Folklore and the Merchant Capitalist Intensification of Linen Manufacture in Early Modern Europe," captures an initial phase of what might be called the "disenchantment" of cloth manufacture under capitalism. Schneider outlines how a burgeoning transatlantic trade and domestic fashion market gave an unprecedented spur to linen production in Northern Europe in the seventeenth and eighteenth centuries, leading to the formation of rural "proto-industries" as an alternative to the urban guilds. In some of the industries, peasant households performed all stages of manufacture, selling a finished or nearly finished product to itinerant buyers or at regional fairs. More commonly, merchant-entrepreneurs divided the stages of manufacture, putting out raw materials and semifinished goods to different laboring households, remunerating them by the piece. Either way, entrepreneurs manipulated peasant spinners and weavers by offering premiums for extra work, advancing credit and equipment selectively, and promising opportunities for marriage through participation in manufacture. They also employed women at lower piece rates than men.

In addition to tracing how linen entrepreneurs reshaped cottage industry in Early Modern Europe, Schneider examines a changing folklore of flax and linen production. She describes a new tendency for animistic spirits to take on demonic qualities, as exemplified by the Rumpelstiltskin tale in which a poltergeist offers assistance to a poor spinner, but only at the price of her firstborn child. The negative, malevolent message implicit in such a devil-pact contrasts with the previously widespread idea that spirits impart socially binding protective powers to cloth. There is another transformation as well. In the cloth-making contexts of non-capitalist societies such as that described by Hoskins, women's reproduction is often represented as an analog to dyeing or weaving. The Rumpelstiltskin-type tale, by contrast, pits the goals of production against the goals of reproduction, suggesting that they are inherently contradictory rather than related. Schneider speculates on the possible connections between the merchant capitalist intensification of linen production in seventeenth- and eighteenth-century Europe, and the folkloric transformation of spirit helpers into demons, hostile to women's fertility and reproduction. The transformation, she thinks, was part of the process through which cloth manufacturing ceased to be a setting for thinking about, and articulating, the regenerative power of cloth.

Chapter 7 by Linda Stone-Ferrier, "Spun Virtue, the Lacework of Folly, and the World Wound Upside-Down: Seventeenth-Century Dutch Depictions of Female Handwork," looks at a similar transformation from a different angle, that of the seventeenth-century Dutch artists who interpreted linen cloth production in oils and woodcuts. Painting and drawing at a time when Haarlem and other Dutch cities were becoming centers of linen manufacture for the Atlantic economy, these masters frequently included textile motifs in their art, above all images of spinners and winders of yarn. As Stone-Ferrier points out, in real life the Dutch did not support much flax cultivation or spinning, concentrating instead on the more lucrative stages of the manufacturing process, the weaving and especially the bleaching of imported yarn and cloth. The images of spinners in paintings and prints must therefore be read not as depictions of reality, but as a moral commentary on the subjects as their activities became enmeshed in proto-industry.

According to Stone-Ferrier, seventeenth-century Dutch oils portrayed individual spinners and winders, always female, as proper and virtuous, but poked fun at women who indulged in, or produced for, fashion. Thus, embroiderers and lacemakers were made to appear licentious, as was the fashionably dressed woman, painted with a lover under her skirt. Oil paintings of spinning rooms, as distinct from individual spinners, depicted a raucous and sexually promiscuous world in which women, devoid of all reference to their reproductive role, cavorted with demons and dominated men—a newly intrusive element. This theme of unbridled sexuality and devilish play also typified the spinning rooms shown in woodcuts, a cheaper medium of communication than oils. Popular among the expanding ranks of bourgeois consumers, woodcuts portrayed even individual spinners not as virtuous, but in erotic poses. In their overall effect they, even more than the oils, undermined associations between yarn production and the continuous re-creation of a moral order, promoting instead the lewd and antisocial symbolism of a world turned upside-down by pending change.

The final paper of Part II, "Embroidery for Tourists: A Contemporary Putting-Out System in Oaxaca, Mexico," offers an ironic twist on the problem of cloth manufacture as a symbolic domain under capitalism. In this essay (Chapter 8), Ronald Waterbury examines the traditional Zapotec Indian wedding dress, once offered by grooms to their brides but made today for boutique and tourist markets whose buyers live in, or come from, the industrial United States and Europe. Decorated with colorful inserts of hand-embroidered birds and flowers, the dress is laden with sentiment. To the young Oaxacan women who traditionally received it, the embroidery conferred a religious blessing; to many contemporary North American and European consumers, it represents a nostalgia for lost arts, for the people and crafts that industrial capitalism so brutally pushed aside. Yet the present conditions of manufacture, structured through putting-out, allow no opportunity for reflection or action on these meanings. According to Waterbury, peasant women in the poorest outlying areas embroider the designs on swatches for merchant entrepreneurs, who assemble the pieces using sewing machines. Neither the entrepreneurs, for the most part local women, nor the embroiderers, view their labor as imparting a social meaning to the product, understanding it only in relation to its monetary return in profits or piece rates.

Part I considered domains of meaning in small-scale societies, where political actors attempt to legitimatize their power through displays or transfers of cloth believed to embody associations with authoritative persons of the past, and thus with sacred or ancestral sources. We might wonder whether the changes in manufacturing and the hegemony of fashion that accompanied the emergence of capitalism interfered with this legitimating role of cloth in a substantial way. Diane Owen Hughes (personal communication) has observed that the reliance of fashion on cutting and tailoring challenges the idea that continuous weaving transmits a spiritual force. In relatively uncommercialized areas of the world, taboos on cutting cloth still make this point. Some Indonesians, for example, continue to distinguish between cloth for wearing and cloth for bridewealth, the former being cut and sewn, the latter's endless warp representing "the continuous threads of kinship and descent" (Barnes 1983:17). Similarly the Yoruba (Drewal 1979:198) permit the use of tailored and purchased cloth in Ege/Gelede cult performances that emphasize alliance-making, but insist on "tied, bound or wrapped" fabrics for the Egungun cult in which lineage ancestry and solidarity are celebrated.

Characterized by perpetual mutations, rapid obsolescence, and high-velocity turnover, fashion is propelled through the interaction of designers or "tastemakers" and the changing wants of consumers. Not so the cloth that in small-scale societies binds brides to grooms, the living to the dead, ancestors to heirs, the past to the present and future. At times such binding material is of foreign provenance. According to Feeley-Harnik, many of the expensive *lamba* cloths coveted by Sakalava ancestors in possession episodes are imported silk fabrics that arrived long ago through the precolonial trading networks of the Indian Ocean. But as a rule, the ritual manipulation of particular cloths as symbols of continuity and closeness gains power from the realization that, in their making, they absorbed ancestral authority as well as fibers and dyes. The early ethnographer, Rattray, in his 1929 book on the Ashanti, recorded how kings in investiture rites discarded their luxurious royal robes to don bark cloth, the earliest cloth of their people. It seems fair, in other words, to conclude that the breakthrough to capitalism challenged cloth as a medium of political power. It is the overcoming of this challenge that concerns us in Part III.

PART III: CLOTH IN LARGE-SCALE SOCIETIES

Three large-scale, class-stratified societies, all historically in tension with the expanding markets and institutions of Euro-American industrial capitalism, draw our attention in the final part of this book. Each of them—Peru, India, and Japan—boasts a deep past of interacting textile traditions, some at the level of peasant households, others at the level of state. Identifying these interactions, the papers of Part III also examine the still broader processes that were set in motion by the local appearance of commercial and factory cloth. In each case, certain indigenous handmade cloths persisted despite this pressure, or have been revived, not merely to satisfy boutique and tourist markets as in Waterbury's case study of Oaxaca, but as aspects of the consolidation of cultural identities and the mobilization of political power. By detailing the past meanings and values of cloth in societies of the scale of India or Japan, Part III offers insights into these emotionally charged revivals.

Leading off is Chapter 9, John Murra's revision of his 1962 article, "Cloth and Its Function in the Inka State." Facilitating our comprehension of large-scale contexts, Murra disaggregates the peasant and state levels. Woven with "magical precautions," peasant cloth was the main ceremonial good, the preferred gift for reciprocal exchanges among kin at funerals and weddings, and a seminal offering, sometimes in diminuitive form, to the dead and to religious idols. Peasant women, the preeminent weavers, also produced a surplus for the state. Mobilized through the Inka tribute system, the cloth of Andean peasant populations was piled so high in the royal warehouses as to stagger the Spanish conquerors. Although destined for many uses, military attire was among the most important, soliders being rewarded for distinction in battle and made to feel ritually protected through grants of clothes.

In addition to the peasant surplus, the Inka state relied for cloth on weavers at court and in administrative centers, including the well-known cloistered women called *aqlla*. These specialists were the source of exquisitely fine tapestries, woven from a mixture of cotton and wool and dyed in many colors. Coveted as items of diplomacy and foreign exchange, tapestries could not be worn or displayed in the absence of royal approval, while kings offered them to attract the loyalty of lords in newly incorporated peripheries. Most valued for this overtly political purpose were cloths from the royal wardrobe, steeped with associations of past rulers and deeds. An "initial pump primer of dependency," suggests Murra, cloth of this sort was hoarded and treasured by the lords of the provinces for four or more generations, symbolizing at once their obligations to Cuzco, and Cuzco's bestowal of citizenship in return. Even today, Murra notes, peasants of the Andean highlands celebrate ancestral tapestries as the standard for beauty and value—a value emphasized by the pirated dispersal of many ancient weavings into the art markets of the industrialized world.

In Chapter 10, "Cloth, Clothes, and Colonialism: India in the Nineteenth Century," Bernard S. Cohn notes a parallel between the uses of cloth at the state and the domestic levels. Indian village families and the Mughal court both stored gifts of cloth as "emblems of honor for posterity," letting them mark the events of history and the cycles of life over several generations. In both rural households and the royal palace, trunks and chests conserved the textile tracers of bygone social and political relations. Even more varied than in the Inka state was the production of cloth at different levels, with specialized industries responsible for renowned traditions in wool, silk, sheer, and painted cotton. Peasant manufacture articulated women's household spinning with the weaving castes. As among the Inka, the Mughal court thrived on cloth accumulated from distant producers, whether as tribute or through markets. According to Cohn, Akbar stockpiled a collection from Indian, European, and other Asian sources, classifying the multitude of textiles in his midst by their weight, color, and day of arrival at court.

Focusing on the nineteenth century, Cohn's paper highlights the misunderstandings that ensued from British rule. As in the small-scale societies analyzed in Part I of this book, the Mughals believed that their garments, handed down through a continuous succession of donors and receivers, served as a medium for the transfer of essential substances, thus constituting political authority, the unity of rule. When British colonial overlords, culturally prepared to anticipate contracts, treated gifts of cloth as bribes, the Mughals were offended. Nor was this the biggest disjuncture. The various constituencies of the Indian population had to negotiate between three conflicting pressures regarding dress. These were their own rules of propriety in relation to social rank, the hegemonic British presence that tempted some to enter the fashion system of Westerners, and the contradictory and changing body of British sumptuary requirements governing what Indians should and should not wear. Although the British disdained "Oriental" clothing, they recognized its capacity to demarcate hierarchically ordered social statuses and, according to Cohn, encouraged its perpetuation, "Orientalizing" the ruled. An especially striking manifestation of this tendency was the turban that the Sikh regiment was urged to adopt as an "Oriental" symbol of military prowess, covering yet harnessing the fierceness of uncut hair.

Complementing Cohn's essay is Susan Bean's Chapter 11, titled "Gandhi and *Khadi*, the Fabric of Indian Independence," in which we follow Gandhi as he arrived at homespun cotton cloth and the peasant woman's spinning wheel as the central, unifying symbols of the national struggle for liberation from British rule. By the late 1880s, Manchester cottons had penetrated much of India, creating a severe trade deficit and artisan unemployment (Bayle 1986:307–09,212). Gandhi's campaign for the renewed production and use in dress of a handspun and handwoven textile is testimony to the potentiality of cloth to unify large-scale societies. Not only did *khadi* displace the trousers, hats, shoes, and tailored coats that English manufacturers were dumping, along with machine-loomed fabrics, on Indian markets; it also challenged British rule and its arrogant imposition of sumptuary codes. Most important, through its ascetic imagery and identification with the poor, *khadi* dissolved the boundaries that divided Indian society. Distinctions of region, religion, gender, and rank were overcome by a simple and colorless textile as Gandhi, the renouncer, summoned up the oldest and most humble traditions of the subcontinent.

In the final essay of this book, "The Changing Fortunes of Three Archaic Japanese Textiles," Louise Cort analyzes rustic and ancient fabrics made from the long fibers of mulberry, *kuzu* vine, and thread-banana leaf. Difficult to collect and necessitating a lengthy soaking, rotting, boiling, and beating process to render them pliable for weaving, these fibers long ago surrendered to the cultivated "grass basts" like ramie and flax, in turn superseded by cotton and, in the famous urban workshops, by silk. Notwithstanding their lowly position in this evolving textile hierarchy, the long-vegetable fibers survived in two "extreme situations,"—in Japan's poorest, most remote regions and as the preferred cloth for sacred state rituals, above all the installation of new emperors. An expression of the "ancient core of Japanese culture," according to Cort, the cloths of rough, uncultivated fibers entered court circles through a process reciprocal to that of royal bestowals. Historically, an expanding Japanese Empire incorporated them as it subdued their producers, seeking not only tribute but a unity of disparate cultural elements in the interest of pacification.

Examining the three "rough" or "thick" cloths of peripheral Japan, Cort addresses themes important to the earlier chapters of this book: The centrality of cloth to gift exchange at marriage and death, the beliefs in its affective, spiritual powers—its capacity to bless and protect—and its evocation of continuities, however fragile, with the past. As a political center of gravity for the Ryukyu island chain, Okinawa even elevated banana leaf cloth to be a courtly textile. Only after the Japanese takeover in the seventeenth century did silk displace this fabric, reducing it to the role of an export to Japan. "Thick" brown cloth of mulberry fiber, woven in the remote mountains of Japan's main island, had long since undergone a parallel transformation, becoming a ritual mainstay of the imperial court.

Like the Ashanti ruler donning bark cloth for ancestral rites, like Gandhi adopting *khadi* in the struggle for Independence, the emperors of Japan forwent their fine silks on occasions of death and investiture, seeking legitimacy from a master symbol of "neolithic" ancestral ties.

Cort's account spans new uses of rustic cloth under modern conditions. Already in the late nineteenth century, mulberry textiles ceased to be used for clothing and ritual purposes. Instead, poor women manufactured food and storage bags from this sturdy material, selling their output for cash. More recently still, an urban movement of craft revival has defined mulberry as a fiber of choice for studio weavers. Comparable but different is cloth of the banana-leaf fiber, promoted today by an Okinawan folk-art movement seeking to establish a cultural identity for the Ryukyu islands independent of Japan—and in competition with the Japanese government's claim that this cloth belongs to the "Living National Treasure." In these and related examples, we see the whole range of cloth symbolism in a complex society, from its ancient beginnings to its myriad uses in rituals of continuity and legitimation, to its mobilization for tribute and, despite the competition of fashion and factory, its contested retention as an anchoring point, a link to real and imagined roots of the past.

CLOTH AND GENDER

The division of labor between men and women in cloth manufacture and distribution, and the assignment of gender symbolism to cloth, emerge as issues in virtually all of the papers in this book. These papers leave us with the impression that, in many societies, cloth is more closely connected with women than with men. As a warning against universalizing this impression, but also as a way to consider its implications, we conclude with a discussion of gender and cloth.

To analyze the gender relations of cloth production, it is essential to acknowledge the multiplicity of steps involved in the manufacture of most fabrics, from the harvesting or collecting of fibers, to soaking, drying, softening, cleaning, and spinning them, to their reconstitution through weaving and their further elaboration through dyeing, bleaching, embroidery, appliqué, and so on. In many cloth traditions, especially those where textiles are associated with ancestral histories, production demands not only technical and artistic skills, but rigorous attention to ritual as well. Men and women may take on some of these tasks in complement to each other, each participating in different stages of the production process, or the preponderance of technical, artistic, and ritual tasks may fall to one gender, excluding the other.

The ethnographic record includes many social groups in which cloth is manufactured wholly or largely by men. In much of Africa, men rather than women, or men as well as women, work at the looms. Among the Lele of Central Africa, women are responsible for food cultivation, leaving men to weave the fine raffia textiles so important to the politics of acquiring wives, settling disputes, and participating in exchange (Douglas 1965:197; 1967). As Darish's paper (this volume) shows, neighbors of the Lele, the Kuba, also assign men to the weaving of raffia, although women add the plush-pile embroidery that gives the material its aesthetic form. In the characteristic "men's" cloths of West Africa, men brocade imported silk or woolen yarn into their weavings but rely on women to spin for the cotton ground. Historically, among the Pueblo Indians, men spun as well as wove and embroidered, all of these activities taking place in the male ritual center, the *kiva*. The weavers and dyers of many urban or courtly textile traditions in large-scale societies were also men. Nevertheless, on a world scale and over several centuries, women have played a larger role than men in cloth production.

It does not necessarily follow that the producers of cloth are the controllers of its distribution. In the Lele case, where men do all of the weaving, women control some raffia exchanges as recipients of especially fine pieces (Douglas 1967:107–09). Yet women's role in production often gives them a larger say in distribution than one might expect. In Samoa, as Weiner (this volume) reports, it was more common for men than for women to hold the highest-ranking titles—but as producers of important textiles, women influenced decisions about bestowals regardless of their rank. Elsewhere, women not only make cloth but also preside over its allocation at major rituals of death and regeneration, marriage and the establishment of new families, investiture and the transmission of ancestral authority.

The predominance of women in cloth production and distribution in many parts of the world is linked to the widespread symbolic systems in which cloth evokes female power. The Kodi of western

Sumba typify this pattern. As Hoskins (this volume) shows, although Kodi women do not participate directly in men's political affairs, their role as skilled dyers renders them fearful, even polluting, to men and gives them command of their own destinies. Like people throughout Indonesia and much of Southeast Asia, they also adhere to symbolic categories that identify cloth with women and "hard" wealth, above all metal, with men. Each set of objects acquires gender-associated values that relate to sexuality, kinship, marriage alliances, and politics.

Upon a Kodi marriage, the groom's kin present gold ornaments along with buffalo and horses to the bride's family, while the kin of the bride give pigs and cloth to the relatives of the groom. Reinforcing the binary code of male and female oppositions are permutations internal to each category. Motifs on Kodi marriage cloths depict the wife-takers' bridewealth offerings, for example buffalos' eyes and horses' tails, while the gold ornaments that grooms offer resemble female genitalia. Both signify the loss of a daughter to her natal lineage and the transfer of her sexuality to her husband's group, a separation that Kodi women compare to death. Yet, according to Hoskins, the secrets of indigo dyeing redress women's subjugation after marriage. Indeed, one finds married women adorning themselves in beautiful ikats as a warning to their in-laws that outstanding bridewealth debts must still be paid.

The Kodi elaboration of a symbolic opposition between cloth and metal, related to each other as "women are to men" and differentially produced by each gender, has parallels among the Iban of Borneo, whose myths juxtapose textiles to sacred traditions of headhunting. "Even in this century," writes Gittinger, "no man's prowess was confirmed until he had taken the head of an enemy, and no woman was fully recognized until she had woven a *pua*" (an elaborate ikat blanket). During the preparation of mordants for the ikat dyeing of yarns, Iban women, like the Kodi, observe the same taboos as those imposed for childbirth and, comparing the laying out of warps for the loom with the taking of heads, call this activity "the warpath of women" (Gittinger 1979:218–19).

Other Southeast Asian symbolic systems balance cloth against writing—the textile and the text. Among the Temang in Nepal (March 1983), women make cloth for bridewealth and funerals, and are depicted as the horizontal weft threads of the loom in contrast to men, symbolized by the vertical warp threads. Whereas the men's texts record the divine oaths that give continuity to ancestral lineages, exchanges of women's cloth at marriage bind the disruptive breaks in lineage solidarity. The contrast extends to an association of men with the right hand, women with the left and, in a mythic past, men with hunting and women with the loom (March 1983; see also Lefferts 1983; Messick 1987).

In societies where women are the main producers of cloth and control its distribution at marriage and death, their contribution to social and political life is considerable. Unfortunately, as Weiner details for one famous instance, ethnographers often overlook this possibility, whether from a disinterest in women's activities, or in fibers and fabrics (as distinct from food), or both. The famous instance is that of Malinowski, whose field research in the Trobriand Islands began in 1915 and led to publications that subsequently influenced theories of "primitive" exchange (notably Firth 1967; Lévi-Strauss 1969; Polanyi 1944; Sahlins 1972). The Trobriand wealth that formed the basis for Malinowski's discussions was produced and exchanged by men. Women's wealth, in the form of banana-leaf bundles and skirts, was obscured by men's production of yams, aesthetically displayed at harvest, and by the shells that men circulated in *kula* exchanges.

As Weiner (1976) asked, would Malinowski have ignored banana-leaf wealth if men had produced it? He did photograph women distributing this "cloth" and in his fieldnotes recorded the Kiriwina term for it as well as its role at death. Yet he overlooked its economic and ritual importance in relation to men's wealth, missing how women leveled the wealth of men (Weiner, this volume). Obligated to contribute to their sisters' accumulations for mortuary payments, men were constrained in the accumulation of "male" wealth, hence in their ability to create and sustain political alliances. Taking a comparative view of the differences between chieftaincy in Melanesia and Polynesia, Weiner (this volume) points out that as political hierarchies gained support from cloth wealth in Polynesian societies, some women achieved political prominence equal to that of men.

What about political formations that transcend chieftaincy, integrating or attempting to integrate a large-scale class society? The cases of Japan, India, and Inka Peru presented in this book are suggestive. In each instance, locally produced cloth, in addition to being the substance of kinship, became a basis for tribute or taxation and an element to be stored in dynastic treasuries. Although women produced this cloth in the Andes and the mountainous peripheries of Japan, in India they often spun for male weavers. In all three societies, courtly and urban textile traditions made use of male artisans, for example the weavers of silk in Japan or the Inka weavers of feathered cloth. Highly skilled female specialists could also play a role in urban or court workshops, however, the cloistered *aqlla* of the Inka state being an outstanding example.

Perhaps the most important conclusion to be drawn from the large-scale societies introduced in this book concerns women's continued affinity for the sacred values that local and rural people historically invested in cloth. These values, derived from concerns about continuity with the past and about transcending the disjunctures of death and marriage, were appropriated, distorted, and at times suppressed as classes and states emerged. Yet they did not go away. Revived during struggles for independence against impinging colonial powers, both the values and the women associated with them enjoyed an elevation of status, at least temporarily. The independence movement of Okinawans against Japanese hegemony (Cort, this volume), and of India against British rule (Bean, this volume), symbolically characterized both women and their role in cloth production as mainstays of the claim to an authentic past and a politically autonomous future.

It is against this backdrop that one might consider the impact on gender of capitalist production and culture. As suggested by the papers in this volume, market pressures to reduce labor costs made women vulnerable to loss of recognition for their contribution to textile wealth. Heavily recruited into the cottage industries of early modern Europe and subsequently into factories, female spinners and weavers were systematically paid at lower piece rates or wages than men. In Europe and perhaps elsewhere, these developments coincided with ideological changes such as those detailed by Stone-Ferrier and Schneider, in which women's manufacturing roles, earlier linked to sexual continence and domestic virtue, were increasingly portrayed as lascivious, demonic, at odds with reproduction. In contrast, the Kodi dyers, although guardians of industrial secrets considered polluting and possessors of such occult powers as witchcraft, command attention; some of these women become priests and even important leaders.

Women's involvement with cloth production exposes in complex ways the complementarity, the domination, and the subversive tactics that together comprise gender relations, forcing us to rethink women's roles in kinship, economic, and political domains. The sacred qualities historically associated with cloth express sexuality as they also transmit notions of biological and social reproductive capabilities, all attributes associated with women. As a master symbol proclaiming the legitimacy of ancestors and succession, the cloth that circulates at births, marriages, and deaths establishes obligations and legitimacy. Such cloth gives women a measure of economic autonomy and even, in some cases, political authority. From these cloth-related perspectives, the analytical categories used to define oppositions between women and men, such as domestic versus public and nature versus culture, are simplistic and inadequate.

CONCLUSION

Perhaps there is a kind of *hubris* in picking up threads from societies so separated in time and space and drawing them together into a meaningful portrayal of the social and political implications of producing and controlling cloth. But the analytical and historical perspectives represented in this book are, by their variety, a powerful testimony to the role of cloth in social transformation. In Part I we saw how, despite the presence of national currencies in societies such as those of Oceania, traditional cloth wealth not only remains an integral part of social and political life, but the continual demand for its presence also integrates its economic value with each nation's inflationary trends. In areas of Madagascar, imported silk textiles, replacing traditional ones, mediate death and relations with ancestors while also constituting symbols of national political importance. Even when vast public displays of cloth are subsequently buried with the dead, as among the Kuba, the continuation of these ancient rituals can subvert the local chiefly ranking system, drawing attention to an economy of equality that levels wealth in contradiction to the hierarchy of regional nobles and chiefs. The attribution to cloth of such a range of symbolic and economic roles reflects more than the labor invested in its production; the connections of its threads and weaving patterns with ancestral or mythical knowledge ultimately make it a political vehicle for transmitting legitimacy, authority, and obligation.

Like language, cloth in its communicative aspect can be used to coerce. In Parts II and III, we see this coercion in situations of complex, socially stratified, capitalist and colonial societies. Whether we view the merchant capitalist cloth manufacturing in early modern Europe or the contemporary Mexican putting-out system, meanings in cloth and the gender division of labor were transformed by those in dominant positions. One society's representations of cloth were misread and misused by another, as the British colonial rule in India so incisively demonstrates. Yet, especially in the examples from India and Japan, we see the political power to be gained through the possession of cloth that symbolizes a sacred past. Cloth as an expression of "keeping while giving" does not articulate the ranking and hierarchy among groups and their chiefs only in small-scale societies. These same principles emerge in different times and places as rallying points for national legitimization. Valued as currency, shroud, ancestor, royalty, or fashion, cloth represents the key dilemmas of social and political life: How to bring the past actively into the present. Ultimately, the opposing properties of cloth—its inalienability and its fragilty—exemplify these universal needs and their contradictions.

REFERENCES CITED

Aronson, Lisa
   1983   Legends, History and Identity Among Akwete Weavers.
           Wenner-Gren Conference, Cloth and Human Experience.

Barnes, Ruth
   1983   Cloth in Lamalera, Indonesia and the Adoption of Patola Patterns. Wenner-Gren Conference, Cloth and Human Experience.

Barthes, Roland
   1967   Système de la Mode. Paris: Seuil.

Bayle, C.A.
   1986   The Origins of Swadeshi (Home Industry): Cloth and Indian Society. In The Social Life of Things. A. Appadurai, ed. Cambridge: Cambridge University Press.

Best, Elsdon
  1898   The Art of the Whare Pora: Clothing of the Ancient Maori.
          Transactions of the New Zealand Institute 31:625–58.

Bloch, Maurice
  1971   Placing the Dead: Tombs, Ancestral Villages, and Kinship Organ-
          ization in Madagascar. London: Seminar Press.

Clark, Graham
  1986   Symbols of Excellence. Cambridge: Cambridge University Press.

Davis, Natalie Zemon
  1982   Women in the Crafts in Sixteenth-Century Lyons. Feminist Stud-
          ies 8:47–80.

Douglas, Mary
  1965   The Lele Resistance to Change. *In* Markets in Africa.
          P. Bohannan and G. Dalton, eds. New York: Anchor Books.
  1967   Raffia Cloth Distribution in the Lele Economy. *In* Tribal and
          Peasant Economies: Readings in Economic Anthropology. G.
          Dalton, ed. New York: American Museum of Natural History Press.

Drewel, H.J.
  1979   Pagentry and Power in Yoruba Costuming. *In* From the Fabrics
          of Culture. The Anthropology of Clothing and Adornment.
          J.M. Corwell and R.A. Schwartz, eds. the Hague: Mouton.

Emmons, G.T.
  1907   The Chilkat Blanket. Memoirs of the American Museum of Natu-
          ral History, Vol. III:329–409.

Firth, Raymond
  1967   Introduction. *In* Themes in Economic Anthropology. R.Firth, ed.
          ASA Monograph No. 6. London: Tavistock.

Gittinger, Mattiebelle
  1979   Splendid Symbols: Textiles and Tradition in Indonesia. Washing-
          ton, D.C.: The Textile Museum.

Gittings, C.
  1984   Death, Burial and the Individual in Early Modern England. Lon-
          don: Croom Helm.

Goody, Esther N.
  1982   Introduction. *In* From Craft to Industry. The Ethnography of
          Proto-Industrial Cloth Production. E.N. Goody, ed. Cambridge:
          Cambridge University Press.

Gustafson, Paula
  1980   Salish Weaving. Vancouver: Douglas and McIntyre.

Heine-Geldern, R.
  1956   Conceptions of State and Kingship in Southeast Asia. Data Paper
          #18. Ithaca: University of Cornell, Southeast Asia Program.

Henry, Tevira
    1928   Ancient Tahiti. Honolulu: Bernice P. Bishop Museum Bulletin 48.

Kent, Kate Peck
    1983   Pueblo Indian Textiles: A Living Tradition. Albuquerque: University of New Mexico Press.

Kooijman, Simon
    1972   Tapa In Polynesia. Honolulu: Bernice P. Bishop Museum Bulletin 234.

Lefferts, Leedon H., Jr.
    1983   Textiles, Buddhism, and Society in Northeast Thailand. Wenner-Gren Conference, Cloth and Human Experience.

Lévi-Strauss, Claude
    1969   The Elementary Structures of Kinship. Boston: Beacon Press.

Malinowski, Bronislaw
    1922   Argonauts of the Western Pacific. London: Routledge & Kegan Paul.
    1926   Crime and Custom in Savage Society. New York: International Library of Psychology, Philosophy, and Scientific Method. [Patterson: Littlefield, Adams. 1962]

March, Katherine
    1983   Weaving, Writing, and Gender. Man (n.s.) 18:729–44.

Mauss, Marcel
    1954   The Gift. Ian Cunnison, transl. Glencoe,Il: Free Press.

Mead, Sidney M.
    1969   Traditional Maori Clothing. Wellington: A.H. & A.W. Reed.

Medick Hans
    1981   The Proto-Industrial Family Economy. In Industrialization Before Industrialization. P.Kriedte, H. Medick, and J. Schlumbohm, eds. Cambridge: Cambridge University Press.

Messick, Brinkley
    1987   Subordinate Discourse: Women, Weaving and Gender Relations in North Africa. American Ethnologist 14:210–26.

Murra, John V.
    1962   Cloth and Its Function in the Inca State. American Anthropologist 64:710–28.

Nin, Anaïs
    1959   Ladders to Fire. Chicago: Swallow Press.

Polyani, Karl
    1944   The Great Transformation. New York: Rinehart.

Rattray, R.S.
    1927   Religion and Art in Ashanti. London: Oxford University Press.

Sahlins, Marshall
    1972   Stone Age Economics. Chicago: Aldine.

Schlumbohm, Jürgen
    1981   Relations of Production—Productive Forces—Crises in Proto-
            Industrialization. *In* Industrialization Before Industrialization.
            P.Kriedte, H. Medick, and J. Schlumbohm, eds. Cambridge:
            Cambridge University Press.

Schneider, Jane
    1987   The Anthropology of Cloth. Annual Review of Anthropology
            16:409–48.

Tedlock, Barbara and Dennis Tedlock
    1985   Text and Textile: Language and Technology in the Art of the
            Quiché Maya. Journal of Anthropological Research 41:121–47.

Valeri, Valerio
    1985   Kingship and Sacrifice: Ritual and Society in Ancient Hawaii.
            Chicago: University of Chicago Press.

Weiner, Annette B.
    1976   Women of Value, Men of Renown: New Perspectives on Trobri-
            and Exchange. Austin: University of Texas Press.
    1985   Inalienable Wealth. American Ethnologist 12(2): 210–27.

PART I. *Cloth in Small-Scale Societies*

2. *Why Cloth?*

Wealth, Gender, and Power in Oceania

ANNETTE B. WEINER

 Poets long ago recognized the power of cloth to symbolize the binding together of social relations. Spinning and weaving form a major theme in Homer's epics, as human destinies are expressed through the threads which gods or fates bind around a person at birth. Poignantly, we remember Penelope weaving Laertes's shroud by day but unraveling her work each night to halt time so she would not be forced to choose a waiting suitor. Hesiod gave women the following advice: "Weave closely; make good cloth, with many woof-threads in a short length of warp." According to the classics scholar Onians (1951:325–26), these references are not metaphoric; they represent explicit imperatives for all manner of fastenings and constructions that sustain the social and cosmological order. Hesiod's advice is echoed in many other societies, past and present. The Tongans of Western Polynesia say that "Humankind is like a mat being woven."[1] This is not only a metaphor for social relations; it is as literal a directive about the nature and complexity of the Tongan social and cosmological order as any expressed in ancient Greece.

In this essay, I take such prescriptions about cloth seriously and analyze cloth as the agent through which kinship identities are translated into political authority. My purpose is to demonstrate that in South Pacific societies with ranked lineages, titles, and chiefs, cloth serves as a major source of wealth and underwrites the political hierarchy. I explore the social and historical conditions in which cloth circulates as wealth in two such societies: the Trobriand Islands of Papua New Guinea and the Samoan Islands of Western Polynesia. Although Samoa and the Trobriands are not the only societies in Oceania where forms of cloth wealth play a central role, they are the societies that I know best through my field research.[2] Because they represent different levels of political organization, they make excellent benchmarks for examining the relation between cloth, rank, and hierarchy in Oceania. Although I take my examples from this part of the world, I believe these relationships have global importance. In general terms, I pursue the issues raised by John Murra (1962; this volume) in his analysis of the significance of Andean cloth production to the rise of Inka civilization. To illustrate my premise that cloth wealth plays a central role in the evolution of political hierarchy,[3] I examine the indigenous understandings about the properties and powers attributed to cloth.

Unlike most Melanesian societies, the Trobriands have a political system in which certain matrilineages are ranked higher than others and where chiefs, by right of birth, are members of such ranking lineages.

In Samoa, too, the rankings of chiefly titles are associated with specific descent groups, but individual access to titles is not necessarily a birthright. Samoan descent groups and the political order differ considerably from those of the Trobriands and these differences are reflected in the cultural and material properties of cloth wealth. By examining cloth wealth as the expression of these differences, I also point out important similarities, establishing a gradient rather than an analytical separation between ranked societies in Melanesia and Polynesia.

For Samoans, as several of my informants told me, fine mats made from pandanus fibers are "more important to us than your gold."[4] The finest of these mats are so delicately plaited that they are soft and pliable as fine linen. "Cloth" of a totally different style is found in the Trobriands, where bundles of banana leaves and women's fibrous skirts are distributed following a person's death. Their importance is apparent; according to an informant, they "show where you belong."

Although mats, bundles and skirts have not been thought of as "cloth," they can and should be analyzed within this category. The technologies of preparing fibers and then plaiting, tying, and binding them together in standardized ways are similar in kind, if not in degree, to weaving. Once we recognize strips of dried leaves as cloth wealth, we find that Oceanic societies with cloth traditions value such wealth not only as a form of currency, but also as a major exchange object, presented to others at births, marriages, deaths, and the inauguration of chiefs. Yet this wealth cannot be understood in all its dynamic properties if it is regarded only as an object eliciting reciprocal returns, for in its circulation it is never a neutral counter.

For example, in Samoa and the Trobriands, women are the producers of cloth wealth and they control its distribution in part or in full.[5] Because the circulation of cloth wealth has political consequences and because women figure in the public aspects of its distribution, cloth and women are an inherent part of political affairs. But though cloth wealth expresses ongoing political actions, such events are rooted in kinship relations, especially between sisters and brothers.[6] While the incest taboo separates a brother and his sister sexually, their relationship remains economically and politically central even after they marry, so that their reproductive potentials are not lost to their natal group. The roots and the importance of this relationship are expressed in major cloth transactions. These efforts to maintain relationships with sisters are reflected in the way some valued cloths are kept rather than given to others.

When an object such as cloth lasts for generations and is identified with the same lineage or descent group, it becomes a treasure that is kept rather than given away. In this sense it becomes inalienable, hidden away and protected from circulation. Even when the treasured cloth must be given to others on loan, or is lost in warfare or some other form of political default, the idea that it should be kept as "the capital stock of substance belonging to a family" (Granet 1975:89), makes keeping the primary locus of value. To keep objects rather than give them to others strengthens an individual's or a group's integrity, but it seriously reduces the value associated with circulation, such as gains in economic and political currency. Conversely, to give and not keep destroys the regenerative potential that brings the force of ancestors, mythological beginnings, and complex genealogies into present concerns. Thus, cloth is not only the means through which rank and hierarchy are expressed in these societies; it also communicates in powerful ways the constraints and limitations on how these relations are regenerated and transformed through time.

Other perceptions about cloth's sacredness add even further to its critical political role. In his classic essay on "value" in Greek myth, Louis Gernet (1981) observed that the legends surrounding precious objects "originate more or less directly in the thematic of magical kingship . . . the well-spring . . . of the different aspects of authority" (p. 144). It is here that we see how deeply the cosmological realm is tied to the economic, as the most sacred cloths are associated with mythical or ancestral events, located in a domain outside daily life. In varying degrees immortal, these ancestors are endowed with an authority that the members of the society respect or hold in awe. Valued cloths demonstrate that their owners have rights to the power of this past and thus they convey authority that is greater than that of the owners themselves. In its association with the past, cloth brings the external, the immortal, into everyday life.[7]

This cosmological connection possessed by certain cloths makes these objects a focal point for this study. How to keep-while-giving is as difficult a societal problem as how death can be transcended or how rank can be preserved. The same problem is reflected in kinship relations, where sisters marry, yet still remain attached to their brothers in important ways. Understanding how societies cope with these never-ending problems of social, political, and cosmological loss, how they attempt to transcend time, to gain permanence when nothing is permanent, to keep sisters and to create treasures, gives us a vital analytical perspective. And this perspective enables us to conjoin categories usually thought of as opposed, such as the material and the ideal, infrastructure and superstructure, the ceremonial and the utilitarian. We can see the political world clearly without losing sight of its cosmological referents, or see the economic necessities amid their context of kinship and gender relationships. Consequently, this perspective enables us to map out and compare how cloth wealth provides the underpinnings of political authority and how this affects the social and political relations between women and men.

To pursue these points I focus closely on significant ethnographic details of the production, exchange, and control of cloth wealth, as these events intersect with gender relations that have political consequences. I begin with a discussion of Trobriand and Samoan kinship from the perspective of the relations between a brother and his sister. Although channeled by the incest taboo and the rules of marrying "out," their combined relationships are central to each others' political successes. In both societies, women as sisters draw on cosmological connections that infuse positions of rank with stability and ultimately, power. Yet at the same time, their actions illuminate the vulnerability of such power for women and men. In structuralist analyses, Polynesian women are often described as playing ambiguous roles, such as symbolizing both fertility and pollution (cf. Sahlins 1985; Shore 1981; Valeri 1985). Unfortunately, these views ignore the ways in which women's roles limit men's power and also give rise to their own political and economic authority.

Because women and cloth form the nexus for this authority, my second section describes the processes of cloth production for both societies, to show how the material objects themselves take on meanings that make them expressions of a range of political alignments. The material properties of cloth, such as its soft yet durable texture and the complexity of its manufacture, illustrate how Samoan fine mats and Trobriand banana-leaf bundles operate as indicators of the level of rank that can be sustained in each society. In the third section, I compare the way differences in the brother-sister relationship enable Samoan women as well as men to achieve power in public politics, in contrast to the Trobriand situation where women's power, also gained through their control over cloth wealth, ultimately undercuts men's power in day-to-day political and economic competition. After presenting these two ethnographic examples, I consider the implications of cloth wealth as an object whose circulation indicates how rank can be meaningfully compared.

WOMEN AND THEIR BROTHERS: THE TROBRIAND SOLUTION

In Samoa and the Trobriands, the social bond between women and their brothers is extremely strong. Although affinity is important, it is made more complex by the vital and never-ending associations and demands within the natal group. For Lévi-Strauss (1969: 12–25), the prohibition of incest was the rule that created the separation between a woman and her brother, thereby establishing a new order of things. Yet in this new order, Lévi-Strauss perceived women's reproductive power as sexual and biological only. The rule of incest was to be understood through the fact that women leaving their brothers, physically and sexually, lost any reproductive role within their own descent or kinship group. The role of women in society became like the role of many objects: to move between men. If, however, we consider the incest prohibition between women and their brothers from the perspective of keeping-while-giving, we find that the incest taboo transforms sexuality into a reproductive force that is expressed in the production of women's wealth. In many societies, even though women marry outside their natal group, their presence and power within it remain essential, tying men's productive work to that of their sisters. Elsewhere I have shown (Weiner 1982) that even in a society where descent is reckoned patrilineally, the significance of sisters to the regeneration of their own patrilineage is critical to the stability of men's sacred rituals.

In the Trobriands, although the incest prohibition between a woman and her brother separates them as sexual partners, the lifelong relationship between them demonstrates the strength of their natal matrilineage—that is, the brother's group. Through their own economic endeavors, and through the processes of giving and transmitting resources to their respective children, brother and sister maintain their natal matrilineage as a forceful social and political presence. For example, when a woman gives things of importance to her brothers' children (see Weiner 1976:133), she is helping to strengthen the lifelong associations and to encourage contributions of those children in their work for her (and her brother's) matrilineage.

The role of women as sisters enters even more profoundly into the reproduction of the matrilineage. Biological reproduction is perceived through a complex set of beliefs that collapse the distinctions we make between biological fact and cultural assumption. After death, a person's spirit continues its existence on an island close enough to the Trobriands to be within sight of Kiriwina, the largest Trobriand Island.[8] At some undesignated time, the spirit is transformed into a spirit child. In this state, it returns to the Trobriands to enter a woman's body, causing conception. Traditional Trobriand belief assumes that the combination of a woman's blood and this ancestral spirit transmits to the infant full identity in its mother's matrilineage and matriclan, and full inheritable rights to the property of its mother's matrilineage.

Although a man's children are not identified through birthright with his matrilineage, he attends to them and lends them things so that from birth, they begin to build up obligations to him and the other members of his matrilineage. Trobrianders claim that a woman's husband plays no part in conception, but they believe that he contributes to the growth of the fetus through repeated sexual intercourse. After the birth of his child, a father continues to provide for its growth by giving the child things from his own matrilineage, such as an ancestral name, decorations, food, and later, use rights to land. Men as fathers take things from their own matrilineage and give them to their children, expanding the potential resources for their children while temporarily depleting the resources of their own matrilineage. But when children become adults they, in turn, support their fathers in economic ways that directly benefit their father and the members of his matrilineage. Through successive generations, those things once given as loans are returned to the members of the father's matrilineage.

Because of these loans, complex sets of exchanges that take place throughout each person's life occur as one's potential for the use of property and access to wealth is augmented by others who are members of different lineages. One's father makes the first effort at these expanding possibilities, followed by one's father's sister, and later one's spouse (see Weiner 1976:123–27; 1988a:51–64 for details). The vast numbers of exchanges made by a person's matrilineage when she or he dies are directed toward the replacement of all that has been given by members of other matrilineages to the dead person during her or his life (see Weiner 1980). During the person's life, she or he had rights to the use of matrilineal properties such as land, ancestral names, and body decorations from the father's matrilineage. Through mortuary exchanges, these properties are incorporated back into the original matrilineage. Although through time, some property may be lost to others, this process of replacement generally makes certain property inalienable within the matrilineage.

Bundles of dried banana leaves and women's fibrous skirts secure the return of some inalienable property, such as lineage (ancestral) names. But even more importantly, this wealth is used by women as sisters in a major distribution each time someone in their natal matrilineage dies. In this one distribution, they disperse thousands of bundles (in total equivalent to several hundred dollars or more) to members of other matrilineages who gave things of value to the dead person during his or her life. In this way, women as sisters expose and reclaim for their own matrilineage all that went into making the dead person more than she or he was at conception. From a societal perspective, these distributions reinforce the relations created through marriages between one matriclan and another, even as they regenerate the purity of matrilineal identity.

In the beliefs associated with conception and in the exchange events at a death, women stand as the controllers of matrilineal identity, in two ways claiming for their brothers and themselves the autonomy and authority of matrilineal regeneration. First, the incest taboo is circumvented by the continued reproductive support a woman gives to her own natal lineage. Incest itself, however, is not totally subverted for it is the ancestral *baloma* spirit that is thought to impregnate a woman. Villagers believe that the spirit child that enters a woman's body has come from a deceased male ancestor of the women's matrilineage, even though its specific identity remains unknown. The notion that women conceive in this way masks an incestuous reproductive cycle that continually creates the essential element of "true" matrilineal identity, dependent upon unnamed ancestors who as classificatory brothers represent a subversive form of incest. The beliefs supporting what anthropologists have called Trobriand "virgin birth" (see e.g., Leach 1966; Spiro 1968; but cf. Delaney 1986) have been interpreted as an attempt to disguise the biological contribution of men as fathers, but in fact they are the means through which the basic problem created by the incest taboo—how to keep while giving—is resolved.

Second, at each death, women's cloth wealth serves as the anchoring matrilineal force, demonstrating the success of regeneration in the face of death and the continued inalienability of matrilineal identity for ranking and non-ranking lineages alike. The numbers of bundles and skirts distributed reveal the strength of members of a lineage as well as the political importance of their relationships with members of other lineages. In purely economic terms, a vast amount of cloth wealth is necessary to make these political statements and, as we will see, therein lie the limitations of Trobriand chiefly rank.

WOMEN AND THEIR BROTHERS: THE SAMOAN SOLUTION

In the Trobriands, the beliefs and practices associated with matrili-
neality serve to keep lineage identity intact while incorporating the
work and support of those from another lineage, such as a man's
children. The Samoan situation is more complex, both in actual
practice and in terms of the histories of kin connections. In Samoa,
the basic unit of descent is not a lineage but rather a multi-branching
group (*'āiga*) with genealogies traced back for ten or fifteen generations.[9] The members of a descent group trace their ancestry
either to a founding woman whose descendants, both male and
female, comprise the *tamafafine* branches, or to a founding man,
usually thought to be the brother of the female founder, whose
descendants comprise the *tamatane* branches (see Shore 1982:
33,91–94). The branches within each descent group own titles,
with specific ones traced through the *tamafafine* lines as well
as the *tamatane* lines. All titles vary in rank, status, and historical
depth.[10]

Titleholders are selected by members of a descent group and
a person may simultaneously hold titles from several branches. Marriage, changes in residence, and adoption all allow individuals to
join or work for several descent groups at the same time and gain
chiefly titles from each of them. With so many possibilities for gaining titles, competition is endemic. The highest titles usually are
traced specifically to the founders of the original title. Titles of lower
rank can be created at any time; one title can be split among several
holders, and some titles are even destroyed. Rights to titles and the
power associated with the bestowal of specific titles shift through
time depending upon the political demands of the moment. Unless
an individual holding a title, even one of the highest rank, receives
the support of the members of his or her descent group, the title
is "empty" and the chief has no power at all.

Despite the complexity that surrounds individual membership
and rights in one or more descent groups, at the very base of *'āiga*
relationships we find a division of interests and duties between a
woman and her brother that is not so different from the Trobriand
brother and sister relationship. To fully understand these similarities
and differences as they apply to the value and meaning of cloth
wealth, we must explore the Samoan relationship between those

who count themselves as *tamatane* and those who are related as
tamafafine. *Tamatane* members are the primary contenders for the in-
heritance of descent group property and for the highest titles, although some titles traced through the *tamafafine* are of equally high
rank. Those who belong to the *tamafafine* category are treated with
the utmost respect by those who identify themselves as *tamatane*.
As in the Trobriands, the relationship between those who are
tamatane and those who are *tamafafine* centers on the continuing relationship between a woman and her brother. Although a growing girl
and her brother are isolated from each other within the household
in terms of living arrangements and division of labor, a grown man
is expected to provide his sister with anything that she needs. A
brother is the protector of his sister and he should always treat her
with respect throughout her life. A woman has the right to demand
this attention from her brother and to aggressively berate him if he
is remiss in his duties toward her and her children. Shore (1982:235)
points out that when a man is with his sister, he acts shyly and controls the assertive behavior that he usually displays when he is with
his male peers. Following his sister's marriage, a man also must ac-
cord her husband the same highest respect (see Stuebel 1896:89;
Krämer [1902] 1930,II:98).[11]

The force of the brother-sister relationship in Samoa is formally
expressed through the roles played by the oldest sister and her oldest brother. Samoans call the oldest sister the *feagaiga* or "sacred"
sister. The word *feagaiga* means "perpetual kinship" between the
two, which is extended to include their position as *tamatane* and
tamafafine to each other. *Feagaiga* also means "covenant" or "agreement," and as a verb, it means "to stand opposite" or "to face
each other" (Milner 1966:8). A woman's sacred relationship to her
brother and his children extends to the sacredness of her son, called
tamasā, "the sacred child," and to all those who stand as *tamafafine*
to her brother. At the same time, the woman's daughter will become
the sacred sister to her brother. At every important event in a person's life, the sacred sister, as the representative of those reckoning
their ancestral identities back to the founding female, is accorded
the highest respect. For example, when a marriage, birth or death
occurs, a woman's brother first makes a presentation to her. Called
a *sua*, it includes one sample of all the major foods, such as a coco-
nut, a small pig and a yam, plus an exceptionally valuable fine mat.
These objects, especially the fine mat, publicly symbolize the respect

of the *tamatane* side for this line of *tamafafine* titles, relationships, and ancestors.

The revered position of the oldest sister also indicates her individual power to affect the descent group's affairs. She has the right to veto any decision concerning the conferring of a title on someone within the descent group and she also has the right to arbitrate disagreements within the descent group and to defy her brother.[12] A sacred sister can "throw her weight around the *'āiga* and tell off her brother even if he has a high title," a Samoan informant emphatically told me.[13] The "curse" of the oldest sister is feared because traditionally it was thought that such a curse could destroy those who have the highest priority to titles, especially her brother and his children.

If the sacred powers of a woman as sister give her the potential to cause sickness and death among those kin who stand as *tamatane* to her, these powers also enable her to assist in preventing such calamities. As Huntsman and Hooper (1975:424) point out, too often the cursing power of the sacred sister is emphasized by anthropologists while the other "mystical" powers, which enable her to bless and assist her brother and his children, are seldom noted. Following up on this point, Schoeffel (1981) makes a convincing case for the political importance of Samoan women before missionary influences. She demonstrates that the sacredness surrounding Samoan women as sisters was anchored in cosmological beliefs regarding their sacred powers. Samoans trace this power to the original sister-brother founders, so that when a woman took on the *feagaiga* title she traditionally was thought to assume the sacredness associated with the *mana* (sacred potency) attributed to the original female founder (see Krämer [1902] 1930). By weakening beliefs in the notions of *mana*, the Church effectively weakened the once awesome role of women as sisters. In Schoeffel's view, women who were *feagaiga* not only assisted their brothers who held high titles and were chiefs, but also provided them with *mana* and thereby ensured that the chiefly titles themselves carried a moral, sacred force.

This sacred power associated with the titles and actions of a sacred sister and the chief is equally associated with the best fine mats. Many ancient stories reveal how *mana* was thought to be embedded in fine mats. For example, when a woman was to be married, members of her descent group came without fine mats to the groom's village, where the groom's relatives had a thousand fine mats assembled. When only one fine mat was finally presented by the bride, thunder and lightning ensued. This one fine mat, extremely old yet made just like the thousand others, was far more valued because of its sacred history (Krämer [1902] 1930,I:54).[14] An informant whom I was questioning once stopped and challenged me: "Why do you think Samoans attribute so much significance to strips of pandanus? They have no use at all." It was then that he told me, "A fine mat is protection for life." This sacred value associated with cloth, also seen elsewhere in Polynesia,[15] indicates the vital importance of women and cloth to the political process.[16]

In the past, the sacred sister provided for the well-being of her descent group and she also had the power to destroy it. Today, her role still is vital as she brings together the *tamatane* and *tamafafine* divisions within each descent group. In any generation a sacred sister, in relation to her brother as chief, can weaken or strengthen the status and power of the descent group. This view of sacred protection is a basic value deeply associated with fine mats. Even in contemporary Western or American Samoa, where all commercial enterprises are conducted with national currencies, the economic and symbolic values of fine mats still are of vital consequence. Contemporary events involving violence and potential retribution illustrate the continuing strength of Samoan people's perceptions about a fine mat's sacred power. For example, when a murder occurs, the highest title holder of the murderer's descent group covers himself with a valued fine mat, called for this purpose, *'ie ifoga*, and hurries to the house of the highest title holder of the dead person's descent group in order to forestall vengeance. He then sits outside covered in fine mats (*'ie ifoga*), waiting to be granted forgiveness (see Shore [1982:19] for an actual account). At least one fine mat must be of the highest rank, valued because of its age and aesthetic beauty; by first wearing it and then giving it up to the victim's group, the chief of the guilty man and the other members of his descent group receive "protection for life."

As we have seen, the principles of Samoan descent differ significantly from Trobriand descent principles, yet the basic brother-sister relationship reveals similarities about how the descent group is regenerated through time. In Samoa, despite the vast complexity of ways in which individuals attach themselves to a descent group and the enormous competition to hold a title, the autonomy of the descent group traditionally was maintained by the regenerative, sa-

cred power of women as sisters. So close were the connections between the sacred sister and her brother the chief, that it is not
surprising to find tales of incest among the myths and stories associated with certain ancient sister-brother descent-group founders.
Here again we are reminded of the Trobriand pattern, where the inalienability of matrilineal descent includes the notion that the regeneration of matrilineal identity is achieved by masking the incestuous
relations between a woman and her deceased kinsman.

By contrast, in Samoa the notion of incest is not completely disguised, for at certain times it is given political relevance. Even today,
ancestral cases of brother-sister incest are used as powerful kinds
of knowledge that, when spoken about publicly in political debate,
prove that a chief is the proper and rightful title-holder. In fact,
some of the most powerful spirits (*āitu*) are still believed to return
to the living and are thought to have come into being through
brother-sister incest (Cain 1971:174). Similarly, incest between a
woman and her brother figures in origin stories associated with the
ancient names of the most revered fine mats, giving these mats,
when presented, enormous political advantage. Even the names of
certain fine-mat exchanges evoke the recognition of brother-sister incest. The importance of keeping a sister united with her brother is
enacted through cosmological connections to ancestors, through ongoing political controls, and through the subversive yet powerful
notion of incestuous relations. Elements of each of these features are
transferred to cloth wealth, giving the cloth object power in its own
right and making women an inherent part of that power.

CLOTH AND WOMEN'S PRODUCTION

We must now look critically at the way women are involved in cloth
production. Because the labor involved in cloth production endows
that cloth with certain values, it is important to know the details of
how bundles and fine mats are made. In the Trobriands, although
women may plant yam gardens, men are primarily responsible for
yam production, while only women produce cloth wealth.[17] Bundles, the form of cloth wealth used in the largest quantities, are
made through a long process in which segments of banana leaves
are bleached and dried in the sun and then tied together at one end.
To make skirts to be used as wealth, strips of dried banana leaves

are fringed and dyed red before they are woven between three pieces of cord that form the belt. Decorations of pandanus, cut into geometric designs, are woven into the waist band.[18] While walking through a village, I would often see girls as young as five or six, working on the first stages of scraping the fibers from the recently picked banana leaves. Once the leaves are dried, further work is done by married women and their adolescent unmarried daughters. New bundles have no use value and the technology of their manufacture is hardly complex, yet the labor involved in bundle-making is intricate. After scraping and drying the strips of banana leaves, a woman places about twenty-five strips in a bunch, then tightly ties them together at one end and trims the tied ends into a neat point. Holding the tied end in one hand, she pulls each individual strip outward, as though stretching crepe paper. Then each stiffened strip is pulled back in place to make the bundle's leaves slightly puffed out. The final stage of shaping the bundle takes about fifteen minutes and then it resembles a whisk broom made with flat strips rather than thin bristles.

This final process of puffing out the bundle is important; the extensive labor gives specific value to the newly fabricated object. Without the puffy center, the bundle is considered "old" or "dirty" and it can only be used in inconsequential exchanges (see Weiner 1976:94–95). New cloth bundles and skirts are the most highly valued, and a woman needs thousands of new bundles and as much as twenty to fifty skirts when someone dies in her matrilineage.[19] Even though the distributions following a death are a lineage affair, women work alone at their production, competing with other women who are members of the same matrilineage to be "first" and have the most wealth to give away on the day of a women's mortuary distribution.

In Samoa, making fine mats is infinitely more demanding than producing bundles and skirts, although like bundles, fine mats have no utilitarian value. Preparation of the threads from the pandanus plant requires that the leaves be trimmed and then baked in an earth oven. Next the material is bleached, first by soaking in seawater for a week and then by drying in the sun. Strips of millimeter-wide fibers are separated and the finished plaiting takes from six months to a year. In contemporary Samoa, women sometimes meet together as a group (*fale lalaga*) to work on fine mat production. Men pool their agricultural resources to provide the women with food each

Figure 1. A Trobriand woman counting her new bundles in preparation for the women's mortuary distribution. Photo by Annette B. Weiner

day.[20] While plaiting, women are also relieved of child care and as they work together they gossip, sing, and entertain each other. Although certain women achieve renown for their ability to make exceptionally beautiful fine mats, production does not require unique skills.

The organization of these women's groups remains part of the ranking system, for the woman with the highest title in the village or the wife of the highest title holder controls the group's organization and activities. In contemporary Samoa, this woman has the right to levy fines for lack of attention to work or for disrespectful behavior (see Shore 1982:105–06). Before missionaries inflicted changes on the status of women, the responsibilities and power of high-ranked women were even more of a monopoly. They controlled the activities of the *aualuma* village groups, comprised of women and girls who were related by descent or adoption to the men of a village (Schoeffel 1977). One of their major responsibilities was the production of fine mats.[21] Women who married into the village came under the authority of the highest woman title-holder, who generally would be the sacred sister; if widowed, women always returned to live with their natal *aualuma* groups. After the establishment of the first missionary station in 1830, these groups came under attack and gradually were disbanded. Other women's organizations have taken their place but now many women work alone. Because so many fine mats are needed, especially at a death, Samoans often are forced to buy new ones, which are sold by these women at the local market in Apia, the capitol of Western Samoa, for upwards of $150.00.

The fine mats produced by groups rather than women alone are thought of as *'āiga* property. Each woman stores her own fine mats and has the right to refuse requests from the chief, although most informants agreed that this would rarely happen. But the decisions about which fine mat to give are made by women. Grades are distinguished by the fineness of the pandanus threads, the evenness of plaiting, and the size and softness of the finished product. The most important have specific names associated with historical and mythic events and are carefully, sometimes secretly, saved for important political occasions.[22]

Like the organization of the descent group itself, control of property is a complex issue. A woman's fine mats go to support her husband when he needs such wealth, but they also support her brother's needs. In addition, she brings fine mats herself to all events associated with her natal descent group or one from which she has a title or some other affiliated association. The respect accorded women is further emphasized when a number of fine mats are completed. At that time, a large celebration is held to which people from many other villages come. The fine mats are paraded through the village by the women workers, and large quantities of food are presented by the men whose wives or sisters produced this wealth. The participation of both husbands and brothers in these exchanges points up an important contrast with the Trobriand situation where, at the end of the women's mortuary distribution, when women have given away all their bundles and skirts, they receive gifts of food only from their brothers. While the brother-sister relationship in both the Trobriands and Samoa is well-defined, in Samoa fine mat production and the food exchanges that "thank" women for their work involve both brothers and husbands. The inclusion of the husband reflects the nonexclusivity of Samoan descent groups as compared with the exclusivity of Trobriand descent groups. These examples of men's food production and women's cloth production, however, are only intimations of how, in both societies, the economic roles of men are tied to cloth production and circulation.

CLOTH AND MEN'S PRODUCTION

In the Trobriands, production of cloth wealth and control over its distribution remain exclusively within the household. Whatever a woman produces belongs to her. She has full rights to sell bundles, but in the selling, men enter into the domain of women's wealth. Because a woman needs many more bundles than she can produce herself, her husband becomes her major source for more cloth wealth. A man takes his own resources, such as yams, pigs, or carved goods, and sells them to other villagers for a specified amount of bundles. Today, men also purchase trade store foods with money and then sell the imported items for bundles. In the circulation of these foods and goods, bundles act as a limited currency, increasing in economic value as inflation raises trade store prices.

A man reduces his own holdings, including money, which is much needed for other things and always in short supply, in order to help his wife accumulate objects with no use value. Yet the exchange value of cloth wealth is essential to maintain the prestige and power of a woman's matrilineage and her brother's political position within that lineage. Thus, men as brothers are equally involved in the cloth exchanges between a woman and her husband. Each year a man makes a special yam garden for his married sister (see Weiner 1976:195–210). He gives the yams to his sister's husband who is obligated, in turn, to contribute to her cloth accumulation as needed.[23] The garden labor of a woman's brother insures that her husband will expend his wealth in ways that ultimately increase her wealth. The obligations a man establishes through his own children are fulfilled after they marry, as they, too, add to his sister's accumulation of wealth. From a societal perspective, the necessity for bundles at each death acts as a leveling device, periodically depleting the wealth of men when gardening, pig raising, craft production and now cash, go toward the support of women's cloth wealth.

In Samoa, anywhere from 500 to 1000 or more fine mats may circulate at births, marriages, deaths, the inauguration of title holders, even the building of a new church or school. In these events there are forty major named categories of distributions, each one referring to the kinship or political relation between the giver and receiver. During these distributions, gifts called 'oloa, which traditionally included food, pigs, and crafted goods, are distributed by the major receivers of fine mats. Today, men present cases of biscuits, bread, tinned meat, pigs, cattle, and cash as 'oloa.[24] In historical sources and even in recent ethnography, Samoan exchanges of fine mats and 'oloa are described as reciprocal returns. For example, Shore (1982:203–08) reported that at marriages or the births of children, the members of a woman's descent group presented fine mats to the members of the groom's descent group who then gave 'oloa in repayment for the fine mats as "balanced reciprocity."

The actual transactions are more complicated; most people who come to the event with fine mats return home with fine mats comparable to those they gave away. Women organize and present the fine mats which are collected from both women and men, and both women and men receive them. At the distribution, a person may receive a better one than she or he brought or even an additional one, which is why a woman rarely refuses her husband's or a chief's request. In each distribution, depending upon the strategies of those who redistribute them, individuals have the possibility of getting back better ones, although sometimes they receive one of lesser value or none at all. Decisions are based on who attends with the highest titles and the kinds of fine mats that are presented. In this way, each distribution is an example of the negotiation and validation of rank and power.

When an event is to take place, the highest title-holder of the descent group collects fine mats from all the other members and also from the members of his wife's descent group. His sister collects fine mats in the same way, calling for support from her husband's relatives and those who are related to her through the tamafafine category. A chief remains indebted to all those who brought fine mats and only the later return of other fine mats cancels the debt. The direction in which the fine mats are given varies with the kind of event as well as where the participants are living.

A few examples will illustrate the procedures. In the exchanges of fine mats and *'oloa* that occur following a murder, the members of the victim's descent group and those from the killer's descent group all bring both *'oloa* and fine mats; they all receive *'oloa* and fine mats in return. At the birth of a child, fine mats are brought by members of the mother's parents' descent groups, if she is living with her husband's relatives, whose responsibility it will be to provide *'oloa*. But if she resides with her own kin, then the responsibility for fine mats falls to those from her husband's descent group. For a funeral, the same conditions of residence apply. If we examine the entire distribution of fine mats at a death, we find that the relationships being defined through each category in which fine mats are presented encompass a huge range of people including kin and in-law relations, branches of the deceased mother's and father's descent groups, the in-laws of the deceased's siblings, title holders within all the descent groups represented, and those holding high titles from all neighboring villages and districts. Who attends, and the value of the fine mats presented, depend upon how high the titles are for the people involved. Within these categories, some fine mats will be presented from members of descent group A to members of descent group B. In other categories, the direction of giving fine mats is reversed.[25]

In contrast, *'oloa* distributions are made expressly to thank people for the work of bringing fine mats and for travelling to the event. In the Trobriands, the response is similar though much less elaborated; when the women's mortuary distribution of bundles and skirts ends, men enter the center of the village and distribute yams to the women who attended the distribution from other villages.[26] The yams thank the women for participating in the event. This example shows that the relationship between *'oloa* and fine mats is not one of "balanced reciprocity" at all. *'Oloa* never cancels the debt of fine mats, for food and fine mats can never be equated.[27] In both societies, the exchanges that define and act on kinship in the most fundamental way are those of cloth wealth. Food, livestock, material goods, and money contribute to the scope and intensity of the circulation of cloth wealth, but they cannot replace such wealth. In the Trobriands, men's garden production increases cloth accumulation.

In Samoa, men's production, by repaying the work of accumulating fine mats, also increases accumulation.

In other Melanesian societies, yams, taro, and pigs take on properties that associate them with ancestral spirits, human relationships, and ritual paraphernalia (see e.g., Young 1971; Kahn 1986; Rappaport 1984 respectively). But these exchanges of food, so immediately consumable, are not durable enough to support the constitution of ranking clans. To view the exchanges of fine mats and 'oloa only as reciprocal elements in an exchange ignores how attempts to create inalienable relationships are rooted in certain kinds of objects, and how the objects themselves express the success of these attempts. As my Samoan informant said, fine mats are statements "for life."

CLOTH AND ITS INALIENABLE PROPERTIES

Cloth wealth not only operates as a defining agent of "life," it also reveals the constraints and limitations within which individuals must negotiate their relations with each other. In traditional Fiji, to mark the end of mourning for a high-ranking chief, enormous quantities of barkcloth, including a train one hundred yards long, were worn by the chief's successor (Kooijman 1972:412). While the billows of cloth added volume to his presence, the cloth's role in masking the chief's vulnerability called attention to it as well, for this barkcloth was not considered a durable heirloom. Thus, while cloth wraps a person with an object that symbolizes the regeneration of authority, it also signals the difficulties of keeping that authority and its history sacrosanct. Because cloth is subject to physical disintegration, keeping an old cloth despite all the ravages of time and the pressures to give it to others adds immeasurably to its value. Old cloths carry the histories of past relationships, making the cloth itself into a material archive that brings the authority of the past into the present. Such objects, which become treasures, are not accumulated for a future investment as capital. Although their owners may need to divest themselves of their most prized possessions, they do so at great loss, regardless of what they gain.

For example, the Maori considered objects made from nephrite as well as flax cloaks (both called taonga) essential for payments for land, peace treaties, services, marriages, and deaths. But certain prized cloaks and jade objects remained inalienable, never to be given to other tribes. "*Taonga* captured history and showed it to the living, and they echoed patterns of the past from first creation to the present" (Salmond 1984:118) as they were passed down from one generation to another. Cloaks no less then nephrite occupied this "fixed point" in the tribal histories because they belonged to specific ancestors and were inherited through specific descent lines. Such inalienability was never achieved in the Trobriands but, in certain circumstances, does occur in Samoa.

In Western Samoa, the fine mats sold in Apia's main market are extremely expensive. But a new fine mat, regardless of the price paid, cannot replace the value of an old mat, even if the old one is patched and faded or brown with age. Ancient fine mats are difficult to find, since the most valued ones remain stored away for years or even generations. In the hundreds of fine mats that circulate for an event, only those presented in certain categories, such as the fine mat of "farewell" when someone dies (see n.25) are extremely valuable. As already noted, Samoans deliberately save special fine mats for important occasions, even for a particular exchange (see n. 22). So important are the strategies in keeping and giving that at times, a person decides to hold his own funeral distributions of fine mats before he dies, thereby insuring that the valuable ones are given to the appropriate people. One man explained his own strategies to me and said that when he dies after the distributions, he will be buried simply without further exchanges.

In all important distributions, when the oldest and, therefore, the most prized fine mats are presented, they are given names that refer to specific legends and historical or mythical events involving the ancestors of a descent group. These names are only used among people with high titles and the stories associated with the names, like the histories of chiefly titles, are considered the secret property of the descent group. When such a fine mat is presented, usually at the death of a high title-holder or at the taking of a high title, as one of my informants said, it is "a kingly event."[28]

In these important exchanges, reciprocity is vital. After a valuable fine mat is given, those who receive it must find one of equivalent or higher value to return, unless they want to belittle the authority of the giver. If the receivers do not have an equivalent fine mat, they must return the very one they just received. In this instance, a fine mat that cannot be replaced by another becomes inalienable and demonstrates the authority of high rank. Today, when especially important fine mats are sent to Samoans living in New Zealand, Hawaii, or the United States for occasions such as marriages and deaths, Samoans usually attach to the fine mat a written history of its previous owners and the dates and places that the fine mat has traveled (Meleisea, personal communication). Without the presence of those who know such histories and can recognize the name of a famous fine mat, a written record is essential to validate its rank.

Trobriand cloth wealth is not associated with individual histories and new bundles are far more valuable than old ones. These differences reflect the dissimilar ways of genealogical reckoning in relation to rank. In the Trobriands, women reproduce lineage identity in direct association with ancestral spirits, without the necessity for long genealogical accounting. The right to chieftaincy comes from being born a member of the appropriate lineage and not, as in the Samoan case, from the competition to gain titles. In Samoa, titles are conferred by members of a descent group through consensus that then must be agreed upon by the sacred sister—or in disputed choices, through her veto. Indeed such controversy now ends in lengthy court cases (see e.g., Tiffany 1974). Conversely, Trobriand chiefs select their successors themselves among members of their matrilineage without consensus or veto rights by others. What changes over time is the actual power of particular Trobriand matrilineages and these shifts are what distributions of cloth wealth expose. Here cloth is not valued because it is an heirloom nor is it imbued with protective and dangerous powers. Yet we can hardly discount the economic and political power of Trobriand cloth since it continually absorbs men's money, pigs, and yams. Although men benefit from the cloth exchanges, their obligations in this respect set limits on how autonomous they can be in using their wealth for more personal political advantage.[29] Trobriand rank remains tied to kinship and death, because even the autonomy of chiefs is curtailed by the necessity to support wives and sisters. While Samoan rank is rooted in kinship, political power shifts constantly, and these changes are revealed and confirmed by extensive exchanges of fine mats. As a result, gender relations regularly shift too, with some men and some women attaining greater political authority at the expense of others.

CLOTH WEALTH, CHIEFS, AND GENDER

Each time someone dies in the Trobriands, the circulation of cloth marks the current state of relationships between the members of one matrilineage and those related primarily through spouses and fathers. On this one day, bundles and skirts are distributed in seventeen categories defined by the specifics of these relationships (see Weiner 1976:103–16). If we could document these events historically, we would see the flux in the strength and weakness of lineages. More or less wealth is given to larger or smaller numbers of people, by the full complement of members of a matrilineage or by those who belong to competitive segments of a matrilineage or only by a few surviving members of a matrilineage that is dying out. Since all deaths, except those of very old people who die in their sleep, are thought to occur through sorcery, each death is seen as a political attack on the growth and stability of a matrilineage. Therefore, the women's distribution of wealth is a defiant act against the reality of aggression—a public assertion that the established political order at that time has not been undermined.

With the help of husbands, brothers, and brothers' children, women counter the threat to the regeneration of matrilineal identity by their ability to show through cloth where each person belongs.[30] For chiefs who are polygynous, the display is essential to maintain connections with the members of their wives' matrilineages and other extended ties. Therefore, men's economic ties to women and their cloth wealth are determined as much by the need for political support as by kinship. Yet, as this support is given, it depletes men's accumulations of their own wealth, so these obligations keep men, including chiefs, economically dependent on women.

Women are not chiefs but their control over cloth wealth supports the strength of matrilineal identity when it is under the most dangerous threat. Even though these distributions are organized around death, they give women their own public domain that is inherently political. But if Trobriand women hold a degree of political power, the use of that power still restricts how much ranking and political autonomy are possible. New wealth must be produced at each death, for genealogical histories are not condensed in cloth.

The shallowness of genealogies is affirmed in the notion of

Figure 2. At the end of the women's mortuary distribution, Trobriand women march with the skirts that they will present to the spouse and father of the deceased. Photo by Annette B. Weiner

anonymous conception, vaguely linked to the reproduction of the lineage through brother-sister incest. Unlike Samoa, Trobriand banana-leaf bundles never become heirlooms that make them the agent and symbol of high rank or, as elsewhere in Polynesia, dynastic hierarchies. The histories of matrilineages remain secret knowledge, only revealed publicly in dangerous disputes over land rights (see Weiner 1976:156–67). No objects used in exchange, except bundles and skirts, validate lineage histories (see n.29). Yet unlike Samoan fine mats, Trobriand bundles and skirts do not serve as historical documents or genealogies. Thus, although Trobriand cloth wealth enables women to participate fully in the politics brought into play at a death, ownership of cloth does not entitle them to direct participation in other political affairs. In the same way, while cloth provides the economic base for a level of ranking that gives some men more authority and power over others, it ultimately checks the level of ranking and the scope of men's political engagement.

In contrast, Samoan fine mats are necessary, not only at deaths, but for all major kinship events, such as births and marriages. Moreover this cloth figures centrally in situations that are more singularly political. In traditional warfare, peace could only be declared with a fine mat distribution. In fact, if an acclaimed fine mat was withheld from an expected presentation, this decision alone could precipitate a war (Krämer [1902] 1930,I:377). Fine mats used in these political situations were called *'ie o le malo*, "the fine mat of state" and today they are still presented at the bestowal of a very high title or at the death of a distinguished title-holder.[31]

Yet Samoan political events are still grounded in the internal organization of the descent group. The bestowal of high-ranking titles necessitates approval from major branches of the descent group, measured in fine mats. In the last century, a contender for one of the highest titles defeated another "lawful antagonist" because he had the support of two strong branches, "owing to their wealth in fine mats" (Krämer [1902] 1930,I:26). Another account describes how succession to one of the four highest titles only occurred when eight branches of the descent group came forward with huge piles of fine mats (Krämer [1902] 1930,I:387). When the histories of these special fine mats are read, it becomes clear, as Krämer ([1902] 1930,I:57) emphasized, why certain descent groups and specific titles became so powerful over the last two hundred years.

Marriages are also significant political affairs if they involve high title-holders or the possibility of important alliances. For example, in the 1970s, a young woman from American Samoa married a Western Samoan man and at the wedding, 3,000 fine mats were distributed. These huge presentations occurred not because the couple had especially high titles, but because the marriage consolidated a tie between traditional political districts that had long been separated. According to Krämer ([1902] 1930,I:24), in the last century, not only were the polygynous marriages of chiefs important, but "[m]arriages of daughters of the great chiefs were always affairs of state, which were considered very deliberately." But a marriage was politically important only if the girl's mother was of "noble descent" and came from a descent group wealthy in fine mats.

The political history of Samoa is expressed through fine mats, as these objects demonstrate the economics of wealth, alliances, the

histories of titles, and political support. Fine mats are the underpinnings of titles, making kinship negotiations essential for the highest
levels of political office. Fine mats not only trace the dynamics of
these histories and the statuses of certain titles, but as with Trobri-
and bundles and skirts, they equally reveal the limits of ranking. Although chiefs eagerly seek out the best fine mats, they cannot keep
them for they must give many to those who originally brought
them, repay their orators (tulāfale) for their services during the distributions, and give the very best ones to their sacred sisters.[32] The
complementary roles of the orator and the sacred sister, at least in
the past centuries, indicate how much a chief's autonomy still remains dependent on others. A chief and his orator "sit opposite
each other" just as the chief "sits opposite" his sacred sister. The
sister surrounds the chief's title with sacred mana, while the secular
power of a title depends on the orator's skill and strategic command
of situations (see Schoeffel 1981). The orator's importance is his defense of the chief's title in public debates; he must have extensive
knowledge of past circumstances and genealogical histories in addition to the proper linguistic form and etiquette involved in speaking
for chiefs (see Duranti 1981). The secular power of chiefs can be undermined by other title-holders and their orators. Although a sister
no longer keeps her brother's sacred powers intact as she did traditionally, she still is responsible for his support within the internal
branches of the descent group. Both the sacred and secular (or internal and external) roles of sisters and orators are sustained with fine
mats.

Chiefs' economic demands and obligations never cease and
they may hold titles from several descent groups, multiplying their
commitments. A man with aspirations for a title has first priorities
to the members of his father's descent group, but because his
mother, her brother, and her brother's sons give him respect and
fine mats, he should support them as well. In doing so, he may
eventually succeed to their titles (see Shore 1982:61).[33] This tension
between a woman, her children and her brother lies at the core of
kinship relations—how to keep a woman's children a strong part of
her kin connections despite the importance of their father's kin relations. A statement made to Stuebel in the nineteenth century illustrates the internal politics of descent group organization and the
way the political ranking that constitutes its base depends upon
these relations.

When a chief is dying he says to his sons: "If one of your children takes a wife, the . . . girdle [fine mat] of the bride is to be
brought to my sister and her son. Also you must continue the
agreement [*feagaiga*] with her son. You are to have a special reverence for him, and your children also. Barkcloths and whatever
you obtain you are to take first to my sister and her son!" A
chief makes presents to his sister's daughters also, who are
called *tamafafine*, but only if they have no brothers . . . (quoted
in Krämer [1902] 1930,II:110,112).

Through fine mats, a man defines his relationship to his sister and
her children. By keeping the very best fine mats flowing to his sister's son as well as her daughter, a man also secures the allegiance
of the next generation, so that they will continue to keep those who
are *tamafafine* (related through the sacred sister) closely allied with
those who are *tamatane* (related through her brother). It now should
be apparent why at a woman's marriage and at the birth of her first
daughter, the very best fine mats are presented in her honor by her
brother; in other events, the woman's sons receive fine mats from
her brother or his sons. When a married woman dies, her brother
presents an exceptionally valued fine mat to her husband's relatives.[34] Usually this is a fine mat that he has kept for many years,
reserving it for an occasion of importance. The fine mat is called,
'ie o le measā. The word, *measā*, according to my informants, means
genitals of either sex and it signifies the fine mat of respect from a
man to his sister. This final element of incest speaks directly to the
importance of the sacred sister in relation to her own and to her
brother's position as the conserving and regenerating links between
the two sides of the descent group.[35]

The fine mats that go between a woman and her brother are the
signs of the convenant between them and all those who stand as
tamatane and *tamafafine* to each other. In compressed form, the fine
mat represents the actions necessary to hold the internal organization of the descent group or some of its branches together. The sacred sister always sits opposite the chief, just as her connection to
those who are *tamafafine* is opposite those who are *tamatane*. From
the perspective of individual relationships and the formal descent
group as a whole, the threads of the fine mat keep these divisions
together. Herein lies the political force behind titles. Unlike the Trobriand case, where men cannot escape from the demands of death
and the drain of their own wealth for accumulations of cloth wealth,

Figure 3. Western Samoan women carry fine mats to the house where the funeral distribution will take place. Photo by Annette B. Weiner

Samoan fine mats are the wealth of women and men. In Samoa, the political domain is not completely encumbered by death as it is in the Trobriands, even though ranking still is constituted by the relations between women as sisters and men as brothers.

Because of their political power, some Samoan women have access to the highest titles and political office. In A.D. 1500, one woman, Salamasina, held the four highest titles in Samoa, an achievement that for the first time united the major traditional political districts (see Krämer [1923] 1958). Although women's major political roles have diminished since colonization, some women still gain very high titles. Krämer writing at the turn of the century, recognized the key feature in relation to gender and the political domain. He noted that although girls from lower-ranked descent groups were often treated oppressively, "girls and women of rank enjoyed an almost godlike veneration. It is not only through their prestige that they have great influence over their husbands and relatives and through them, over affairs of state, but titles and offices, even the throne are open to them . . . "([1902] 1930,I:68–69).

Untitled men and women are forbidden participation in village political events, just as they are unable to accumulate fine mats of distinction. Therefore, any discussion of Samoan oppression and domination of women must take into account the oppression and domination of all untitled Samoans. The focus cannot be on gender; it must be on differences created by rank. The politics of titles encompasses gender in its priorities and gives to some women political power that is equal to, and at times greater than, the political power of some men. As rank is equated with greater authority and possibilities for power, gender criteria no longer exclude women from the privileges of political office. In Samoa, we see the beginning outlines of the disengagement of kinship and politics, supported by the ancestral validations that fine mats produce. Samoan women, the symbols and agents for the power believed to be embedded in those sacred heirlooms, the fine mats, provide support for strong titles as some women gain access to these titles themselves.

WHY CLOTH?

The cultural processes surrounding Samoan and Trobriand cloth clearly illustrate how a woman remains a reproductive force within her own natal group even after she marries outside the group. The sexual loss of women as sisters is transcended by the transformation of women's reproductive capacity into an object that maintains the links between kinship and political power. The Samoan fine mat called "genitals" is illuminating; it symbolizes the relationship between sisters and brothers in their efforts to regenerate the most important relationships within their own descent group, despite competing demands and choices. The problem that these societies confront is not how one gives up a sister to obtain a wife, as Lévi-Strauss would have it, for a wife and sister are not equivalents. Rather the dilemma to be resolved is much more existential, yet deeply connected to the practical considerations of economic and political affairs: How is sexuality transformed into social action that remains culturally reproductive for the woman's kin group?

Marriage and death disrupt personal relationships and property, making loss an inherent part of all social action. How these losses are overcome so that a descent group retains its prominence and force through time is the same problem as how titles or dynasties remain sovereign over others. In Oceania, women, death, and cloth come together as the key variables in the regeneration of descent-group identity and by extension, the political authority invested in titles and rank. Cloth is culturally enhanced so that it represents the union of a man and his sister and by extension, kinship solidarity. With this value accorded cloth, it operates as a powerful economic and cosmological resource that symbolizes the abilities of individuals to transcend time, loss, death, and the results of the incest taboo. And because it can be made to last for generations, cloth also exhibits some semblance of immortality.

Cloth is by no means the only object that can outlast a person's life. Bones, stones, and shells (Weiner 1982, 1985) also serve as the material form through which past histories are incorporated into the present. In these Pacific societies, however, "hard wealth" is made by experts, often with imported materials, and thus it is rare. Cloth is locally produced and as "soft wealth," far more abundant. Where the technologies for making it become more complex and where the cloth itself becomes an heirloom, as in Samoa, its preparation becomes highly organized. Not only in Samoa, but elsewhere in Polynesia, certain cloths are thought of as treasures; they are endowed with sacred qualities[37] which enable them to represent the histories and legends associated with important ancestors and mythical dieties. Presentation of such a cloth reveals a person's right to claim the prerogatives and powers evoked by this conjunction of past and present. Although cloths are economic resources, essential to political endeavors, the best ones—the heirlooms—are, if possible, kept out of circulation as inalienable possessions.

To create inalienable possessions is a difficult achievement, yet the need to have something that can last beyond a person's lifetime, and thus allows claims to be made on the past, is a major cultural undertaking. Hocart's (1954:77) well-known dictum, "the first king was a dead king" is pertinent to my point. Inauguration consecrates the past ruler as it transfers sanctions based on the past to the new ruler. A grave site, the bones of the deceased, and even the wealth exchanged at the time of burial, all objectify the sanctity accorded the successor by anchoring her or his newly defined claims to power in objects associated with former power. But where kinship is still the means for political succession, these affinities with the past must incorporate the kin group itself. Objects of cloth can serve these functions because of their profound connections to women, the kinship relations between brothers and sisters, and the sacredness of their ancestors.

In evaluating the differences between Samoan and Trobriand cloth, we find how difficult it is to achieve true inalienability in cloth. Sometimes, as in the Trobriands, cloth never becomes inalienable. Yet bundles and skirts do provide a foundation that regenerates matrilineal identity through successive generations and thereby, this cloth supports a degree of political rank. Samoan cloth has much greater longevity, giving it a measure of inalienability and historical authority which can support more formal levels of rank. These differences in cloth reflect significant differences in gender roles and political influence between Samoa and the Trobriands. While Trobriand women greatly influence the political dynamics surrounding a death, Samoan women's power enters directly into every aspect of political life. Indeed, rights to titles are claimed by some Samoan women, giving titled women and sisters far greater potential for political preeminence. In ancient Hawaii and Tahiti, where cloth production was even more complex and diversified, women ruled over districts, even entire islands.

Throughout Polynesia, cloth wealth provided the economic and cosmological foundation for rank and hierarchy. The Trobriands and Samoa illuminate how difficult this achievement was by showing the centrality of problems associated with death and inalienability. Women and cloth make kinship into a regenerating force that creates a partial solution to the sustainment of rank. Thus, their connections with cloth enable women to enter the political domain. In comparison with men, their roles are limited, but men's participation in both societies is curtailed as well. With all the exchanges, strategies, and investments that people make with cloth, this object reveals the fragile nature of the very relationships deemed by the societies themselves to be of the highest order. The physical characteristics of cloth as it is plaited or woven, unraveled or torn, as it rots and disintegrates, bring to the histories of persons and lineages the reality of life's ultimate incompleteness.

The question for Oceania, "Why Cloth?" exposes the transformations that occur as cloth is culturally imbued with the inalienability of the social group and therefore, the authority attached to rank. The social and political relationships that the use of cloth supports or suppresses are, fundamentally, attempts to make something permanent in a world of change. Defeat through strategy and manipulation, death through human and natural causes, and the loss of women as sisters constitute the continuing degenerative processes inherent in any social system. Keeping an object even for ten years or over a generation demonstrates some success in sustaining permanence. Cloth absorbs time, giving it a visible form, but cloth does not merely describe or circumscribe time. Rather, for these two Oceanic societies, cloth gives to time a range of possibilities while keeping the political world anchored in kinship.

ACKNOWLEDGMENTS

Field research for this paper was supported by the John S. Guggenheim Foundation and an early draft was completed while I was a Member, The Institute for Advanced Study, Princeton. I am grateful to both institutions. This research would not have been possible without the cooperation of the Prime Minister's Department, Western Samoa, the Institute for Papua New Guinea Studies, and the Milne Bay Provincial Government, Papua New Guinea. I am especially grateful to Dr. Horst Cain, Suya and Liki Crichton, Tuala F. Tiresa Malietoa, Leota Pepe, and the Hon. Nomumalo Leulumwenga for their assistance in Samoa and to the many people in Kwaibwaga and Omarakana villages, Kiriwina, Trobriand Islands, who helped me during the years of my research there. I thank T.O. Beidelman, Deborah Battaglia, Gillian Feeley-Harnik, Judith Huntsman, William E. Mitchell, and Jane Schneider for their comments on earlier drafts of this paper and very special thanks to Malama Meleisea and Penelope Schoeffel for sharing information with me.

NOTES

1. This quotation is cited in Rogers 1977.

2. My field work was done on the island of Upolu in Western Samoa during part of 1980 and on northern Kiriwina Island in the Trobriand group in 1971, 1972, 1976, 1980, and 1982.

3. The role of cloth wealth in Oceania has been ignored in studies focusing on gender and hierarchy (e.g., Ortner 1981; Shore 1981) and in two major studies

of Polynesian social stratification (Sahlins 1958; Goldman 1970); more recently, women chiefs and queens have been excluded from studies of Hawaiian divine rulers (Sahlins 1985; Valeri 1985; but cf. Weiner 1987, 1988b). Even the importance of exchange in Polynesia has not been given full recognition, nor have archaeologists considered the importance of cloth in this part of the world (see e.g., Kirch 1984; Terrell 1986). But Leacock (1972), writing from a global perspective, noted that textile production was one of the areas that gave decision-making power to women in precapitalist societies prior to colonization. A recent dissertation focuses on the contemporary importance of Fijian women's economic status, achieved through their production of barkcloth (Teckle 1986). Also see Gailey (1980) on precolonial Tongan women's production of barkcloth.

4. Traditionally, barkcloth was also used as wealth in association with fine mats, but production stopped with colonization and the use of European cloth.

5. Throughout traditional Polynesia, women were the producers of most cloth that was considered wealth. But in special cases, men also produced cloth. For example, in ancient Tahiti, when large quantities of barkcloth were needed, men helped women with production (Henry 1928) and in Hawaii, men made the valued feathered cloaks, but women produced the sacred barkcloths necessary for the most important temple ceremonies, including the installation of the divine king (e.g., Kooijman 1972; Weiner 1987).

6. Margaret Mead (1930) called attention to the importance of Samoan women who, as sisters, had sacred and dangerous powers over their brothers. Huntsman and Hooper (1975) noted the similarity between the sacred sister in Samoa and the covenant between a woman and her brother in the Tokelau Islands. Garth Rogers (1977) analyzed the role of Tongan women, illustrating the significant sacred and political power women had over their brothers. Rogers (1977) suggested that the weaver in the Tongan proverb at the beginning of the essay was the father's eldest sister. See also Hocart (1915;1952) and Mabuchi (1964) on the role of the sacred sister throughout Polynesia.

7. Indonesian textiles, when wrapped around the body, are believed to restrain the natural and cosmological world in the name of social order; when exchanged at marriages or deaths, these same cloths convey a blessing for vitality, fertility, and regeneration (Adams 1980; Fox 1977; Gittinger 1979).

8. Kiriwina also is the most heavily populated island in the Trobriand group and is the ancestral and contemporary home of the highest-ranking chiefs. Unless noted, all references to Trobriand cloth wealth pertain only to Kiriwina, where such wealth is more elaborated than on the other islands.

9. For ease of reading, I translate "*āiga*" as "descent group," but in actuality, the group at any one time or event may only be represented by certain branches rather than the entire unit.

10. See Krämer [1923] 1958 on the histories of high titles before Samoa was colonized.

11. But as Shore (1982:235) notes, if a woman is caught with a lover her

brother will react violently. In the same way, if a man squanders his money or is lazy, his sister will berate him publicly for not attending to her and the needs of the family.

12. See Schoeffel 1981 for contemporary examples.

13. Of course, the power of individual women varies; if a woman does not care to enforce her rights, the rights disappear.

14. Krämer ([1902] 1930,I:20) also gives an example of how a title became so powerful that the holder threatened to become dangerous even to his own descent group because the title was thought to have increased in power through the efforts of Nafannu, the goddess of war.

15. The entwined importance of cloth, *mana*, and women also occurs elsewhere in Polynesia, e.g., among the Maori (Weiner 1985); ancient Tahiti and Hawaii (e.g., Kooijman 1972; Weiner 1987) and Fiji (Kooijman 1977).

16. I do not discuss the circumstances of traditional overseas trade in fine mats with Fijian and Tongan chiefs (but see Kaeppler 1978; Hjarnø 1979/80). See Buck (1930) for details on the technology of fine mat production; also Krämer [1902] 1930,II:521–23; and Stair 1897.

17. In the southern Massim, Sabarl women make baskets which are distributed at each death as women's "bulk wealth." (Battaglia 1981) and on Sudest, women's skirts are used in mortuary exchanges (Lepowsky 1981), but only Kiriwina women in the Trobriands make banana-leaf bundles and only here does the general distribution of cloth wealth reach such elaborate proportions.

18. See Weiner 1976:237–41 for additional details on the technology of skirts and bundles.

19. Clean bundles are remade from old ones by untying the bundle and stretching out each leaf. Although they are not equivalent in value to new bundles, clean ones have more value than old ones.

20. Traditionally and in contemporary Western Samoa, men always do the cooking in earth ovens and do all garden work as well. Now that many Samoan households have Western kitchen appliances, women do the stove cooking, but men are still responsible for the yams, taro, and pig roasted in outdoor traditional ovens.

21. Ella (1899:169) observed that "The manufacture of the '*ie* [fine mat] is the work of women and confined to ladies of distinction, and common people dare not infringe the monopoly, which is *sā* [tabu or sacred]."

22. Women also exercise control over fine mats that belong to their husbands. One informant told me that no one else in her family knew that her mother had two very old fine mats. Years later she told her daughter how she had received them when her husband took a chiefly title and periodically, she would air them early in the morning so that no one would see them. Her plans were to keep them for an important event in her own family.

23. Because Malinowski (e.g., 1935) never took women's cloth wealth into account in his studies of Trobriand exchange, he could not understand why men made gardens for their sisters rather than their wives.

24. Krämer ([1902] 1930,II:158) lists all objects made by men as *'oloa*, including anything foreign. The category of fine mats (*ie toga*) traditionally included everything made by women, such as barkcloth, sleeping mats, fans, oil, combs, baskets, etc., as well as fine mats. Even in Kramer's account, nothing is as important and valued as fine mats.

25. For example, if a man dies, the members of his mother's and his father's descent groups present fine mats under the category called *'ie mavaega*, the fine mat of "farewell" to the deceased. When they are presented to members of the dead man's descent group, these people now must respond by presenting other fine mats to each person who originally presented an *'ie mavaega*.

26. The hamlet's name is called out and the senior woman who resides there gathers the yams and then divides them among the other women who live there and attended the distribution.

27. Mauss (1923/4) recognized these differences when he wrote at the beginning of *"Essai sur le Don"* that Samoan fine mats were "feminine" property, "bound up with land, the clan, the family and the person" making them *"immeuble"* ("things that cannot be alienated"; my translation) (see also Weiner 1985).

28. Through marriages between high-ranking Tongan men and Samoan women, many fine mats have become part of Tongan wealth. In the Tongan King's palace today, there are Samoan fine mats stored away that are over three hundred years old (Hau'afa, personal communication).

29. In Kiriwina, stone axe blades, the "hard" wealth of men, are also exchanged at deaths, but this wealth carries the histories of individual men who have owned the blades previously. Here I am only concerned with wealth that symbolizes the kin group and ancestral histories, but see Weiner (1983, 1988a) for a discussion of Trobriand "hard" and "soft" wealth.

30. Even though a man's children are not members of his matrilineage, they still support these people by accumulating wealth for them to give away. In the same way, a man's daughter's husband helps her to get bundles for her father's matrilineage.

31. Even though pigs and other foods as well as money will also be given as *'oloa*, the fine mats are the most valued.

32. The *tulāfale* titles are ranked and each high ranked chief has more than one orator. According to Krämer ([1902] 1930), chiefs themselves often took *tulāfale* titles in addition to their own so they could receive fine mats themselves.

33. In addition, a man must support members of his wife's descent group as well as those from his father's sister's husband's descent group.

34. If the woman is widowed or has never married, then her brother who is

the chief will not present fine mats in her name because the members of her descent group will sponsor her funeral. If she is living with her husband, then the members of her husband's descent group are the sponsor and her brother presents the fine mat (Schoeffel, personal communication).

35. Certain important titles from the *tamatane* and *tamafafine* branches are themselves *feagaiga* to each other, as Schoeffel (1981) has demonstrated. Each title-holder stands as brother and sister to each other with the obligations that a brother and sister have to each other, even though the two chiefs may both be men. When a death occurs, one branch as the "brother" will bring fine mats to the "sister", those who are *tamafafine* (also see Krämer [1902] 1930,I:52 for a similar example).

36. As of 1981, untitled men were not even permitted to vote in the national elections.

37. See e.g., Kooijman 1972; Mead 1969; Weiner 1985.

REFERENCES CITED

Adams, M.
    1980   Structural Aspects of East Sumbanese Art. *In* The Flow of Life: Essays on Eastern Indonesia. J.J. Fox, ed. Cambridge: Harvard University Press.

Battaglia, D.
    1981   Segaya: Commemoration in a Massim Society. Ph.D. thesis. Cambridge University.

Buck, Sir P.H.
    1930   Samoan Material Culture. Honolulu: Bernice P. Bishop Museum Bulletin 75.

Cain, H.
    1971   The Sacred Child and the Origins of Spirit in Samoa. Anthropos 66:173–81.

Delaney, C.
    1986   The Meaning of Paternity and the Virgin Birth Debate. Man 21(3):494–513.

Duranti, A.
    1981   The Samoan Fono: A Sociolinguistic Study. Canberra: Pacific Linguistics.

Ella, Rev. S.
    1899   Polynesian Native Clothing. The Journal of the Polynesian Society 8:165–70.

Fox, J.J.
    1977   Roti, Nada and Savu. *In* Textile Traditions of Indonesia. M.H.
            Kahlenberg, ed. L.A.: County Museum.

Gailey, C.
    1987   Kinship to Kingship: Gender Hierarchy and State Formation in
            the Tongan Islands. Austin: University of Texas Press.

Gernet, L.
    1981   "Value" in Greek Myth. *In* Myth, Religion and Society. R.L. Gor-
            don, ed. London: Cambridge University Press.

Gittinger, M.
    1979   Splendid Symbols: Textiles and Tradition in Indonesia. Washing-
            ton D.C.: The Textile Museum.

Goldman, I
    1970   Ancient Polynesian Society. Chicago: University of Chicago Press.

Granet, M.
    1975   The Religion of the Chinese People. New York: Harper & Row.
            (First published 1922).

Hau'afa, E.
    1980   Personal communication.

Henry, T.
    1928   Ancient Tahiti. Honolulu: Bernice P. Bishop Museum Bulletin 48.

Hjarnø, J.
    1979–80 Social Reproduction: Towards an Understanding of Aboriginal
            Samoa. Folk:21–22.

Hocart, A.M.
    1915   Chieftainship and the Sister's Son in the Pacific. American An-
            thropologist 17(4):631–46.
    1954   The Life-Giving Myth and Other Essays. New York: Harper &
            Row.

Huntsman, J. and A. Hooper
    1975   Male and Female in Tokelau Culture. The Journal of the Polyne-
            sian Society:84(4)415–30.

Kaeppler, A.
    1978   Exchange Partners in Goods and Spouses: Fiji, Tonga and
            Samoa. Mankind:11(2) 246–52.

Kahn, M.
    1986   Always Hungry, Never Greedy: Food and the Expression of
            Gender in a Melanesian Society. Cambridge: Cambridge Univer-
            sity Press.

Kirch, P.
    1984   The Evolution of Polynesian Chiefdoms. Cambridge: Cambridge
            University Press.

Kooijman, S.
    1972   Tapa in Polynesia. Honolulu: Bernice P. Bishop Museum Bulletin
            234.
    1977   Tapa on Moce Island, Fiji. Leiden: E.J. Brill.

Krämer, A.
    1930   The Samoan Islands. 2 volumes. Stuttgart. English translation,
            D.H. & M. DeBeer. (Original German publication, 1902).
    1958   Salamasina. Stuttgart. English translation, Assn. of the Marist
            Brothers. (Original German publication, 1923).

Leach, E.R.
    1966   Virgin birth. Proceedings of the Royal Anthropological Institute,
            pp. 39–50.

Leacock, E.
    1972   Introduction In The Origin of the Family, Private Property and
            the State. F. Engels. New York: International Publishers. pp. 7–67.

Lévi-Strauss, C.
    1969   The Elementary Structures of Kinship. Boston: Beacon Press.

Lepowsky, M.
    1981   Fruit of the Motherland: Gender and Exchange on Vanatinai,
            Papua New Guinea. Ph.D. thesis. University of California,
            Berkeley.

Mabuchi, T.
    1964   Spiritual Predominance of the Sister. In Ryukyan Culture and
            Society: A Survey. 10th Pacific Science Congress. Honolulu: Uni-
            versity of Hawaii Press.

Malinowski, B.
    1935   Coral Gardens and Their Magic. 2 vols. Bloomington: Indiana
            University Press.

Mauss, M.
    1923–24 Essai sur le Don: Form et Raison de l'Echange dans les So-
            ciétés Archaîques. In Année Sociologique. Nouvelle Série 1.
    1979   Sociology and Psychology, Essays by Marcel Mauss. London:
            Routledge & Kegan Paul.

Mead, M.
    1930   Social Organization of Manu'a. Honolulu: Bernice P. Bishop Mu-
            seum Bulletin 76.

Mead, S.
    1969   Traditional Maori Clothing. Wellington: A.H. and A.W. Reed.

Milner, G.
  1966   Samoan Dictionary. Oxford: Oxford University Press.

Murra, J.
  1962   Cloth and Its Function in the Inca State. American Anthropologist 65:710–28.

Onians, R.B.
  1951   The Origins of European Thought About the Body, the Mind, the Soul, the World, Time, and Fate. Cambridge: Cambridge University Press.

Ortner, S.
  1981   Gender and Sexuality in Hierarchical Societies: The Case of Polynesia and Some Comparative Implications. *In* Sexual Meanings, the Cultural Construction of Gender and Sexuality. S. Ortner and H. Whitehead, eds. Cambridge: Cambridge University Press.

Rappaport, R.
  1984   Pigs for the Ancestors. New Haven: Yale University Press. Second edition.

Rogers, G.
  1977   "The Father's Sister is Black," A Consideration of Rank and Power in Tonga. The Journal of the Polynesian Society 86:158–82.

Sahlins, M.
  1958   Social Stratification in Polynesia. Seattle: University of Washington Press.
  1985   Islands of History. Chicago: University of Chicago Press.

Salmond, A.
  1984   Nga Muarahl O Te Ao Maori: Pathways in the Maori World. *In* Te Maori, Maori Art from New Zealand Collections. S. Mead, ed. New York: Harry N. Abrams, Inc.

Schoeffel, P.
  1977   The Origin and Development of Contemporary Women's Associations in Western Samoa. Journal of Pacific Studies 3:1–22.
  1981   Daughters of Sina, A Study of Gender, Status and Power in Western Samoa. Ph.D. thesis, Australian National University.

Shore, B.
  1981   Sexuality and Gender in Samoa: Conceptions and Misconceptions. *In* Sexual Meanings, The Cultural Construction of Gender and Sexuality. S. Ortner and H. Whitehead, eds. Cambridge: Cambridge University Press.
  1982   Sala'ilua. A Samoan Mystery. New York: Columbia University Press.

Spiro, M.
    1968   Virgin Birth, Parthenogenesis, and Physiological Paternity: an
            Essay in Cultural Interpretation. Man, n.s., 3:242–61.

Stair, Rev. J.B.
    1897   Old Samoa, or Flotsam and Jetsam From the Pacific Ocean. Lon-
            don: The Religious Tract Society.

Stuebel, O.
    1896   Samoanische Texte. Berlin: Geographische Verlagshandlung
            Dietrich Reimer.

Teckle, B.
    1986   The Position of Women in Fiji. Ph.D. thesis, University of Sydney.

Tiffany, S.
    1974   The Land and Titles Court and the Regulation of Customary
            Title Successions and Removal in Western Samoa. The Journal of
            the Polynesian Society 83:35–57.

Weiner, A. B.
    1976   Women of Value, Men of Renown: New Perspectives in Trobri-
            and Exchange. Austin: University of Texas Press.
    1980   Reproduction: A Replacement for Reciprocity. American Ethnolo-
            gist 7:71–85.
    1982   Sexuality Among the Anthropologists, Reproduction Among the
            Informants. Social Analysis 12:52–65.
    1983   "A World of Made is Not a World of Born"—Doing Kula in
            Kiriwina. In J.W. Leach and E.R. Leach, eds. The Kula: New
            Perspectives on Massim Exchange. Cambridge: Cambridge Uni-
            versity Press. pp. 147–70.
    1985   Inalienable Wealth. American Ethnologist 12:210–27.
    1987   Towards a Theory of Gender Power: An Evolutionary Perspec-
            tive. In The Gender of Power: A Symposium. M. Leyenaar et.al.,
            eds. Leiden: Vakgroep Vrouwenstudies FSW. pp. 41–77.
    1988a   The Trobrianders of Papua New Guinea. New York: Holt,
            Rinehart and Winston.
    1988b   Dominant Kings and Forgotten Queens. Oceania 58:157–60.

Young, M.
    1971   Fighting With Food. Cambridge: Cambridge University Press.

Valeri, V.
    1985   Kingship and Sacrifice: Ritual and Society in Ancient Hawaii. Chi-
            cago: University of Chicago Press.

3. Cloth and the Creation of Ancestors in Madagascar

GILLIAN FEELEY-HARNIK

One of the recurrent debates in African ethnology concerns the definition of ancestors and the nature of their authority. Fortes raised these issues in his ethnographies of the Tallensi (1945, 1949), in his essay on "Oedipus and Job in West African Religion" (1959), and in several articles (e.g., 1961, 1965, 1981), to which Kopytoff (1971, 1981), Brain (1973), Calhoun (1980, 1981), and others have since responded. One of their disagreements has to do with meaning. Do the Tallensi (and some other African peoples) actually distinguish between elders and ancestors, as the English terms imply and as Fortes, Brain, and Calhoun argue? Or, like the Suku in Kopytoff's view, do they include elders, ancestors, and perhaps other persons, animals, and things, in the same category of beings?

Another major question concerns the relevance of ideas to social organization. Fortes argued that Tallensi distinctions supported the projection of authority relations among living members of the same lineage onto the dead. To Kopytoff, the primacy of elders rather than ancestors confirms that "horizontal" boundaries between the living and the dead are secondary to "vertical" boundaries between lineage members and outsiders. Both Brain and Calhoun argue that Kopytoff overlooks aspects of relations between progenitors and their descendants that participants themselves find

73

significant and that vary substantially from one group to another. Other scholars have questioned Fortes's own distinction between descent as a jural principle of group formation and kinship as the product of non-jural interpersonal ties, especially where participants emphasize cognate as well as lineal ties when allocating rights and obligations (e.g., Keesing 1978). Kiernan (1982) has reexamined "the problem of evil" in ancestral intervention among the Zulu of southern Africa. Glazier's (1984) essay on the transformation of Mbeere funeral rites in the context of changing land tenure regulations in east central Kenya focuses on historical and material factors that earlier studies did not consider. I have taken a similar approach in analyzing the labor involved in the reconstruction of Sakalava royal tombs (Feeley-Harnik 1990).

The purpose of this paper is to contribute to the general ethnography on relations between ancestors and their descendants from a Malagasy perspective, and to pursue specific questions concerning the role of cloth and other materials in substantiating ancestral claims to authority. What forms do ancestors take? How are they made? What is the role of acts in articulating ideas where, as in the case that follows, speaking is associated with exchanging and thinking with seeing? As Fortes asked in reviewing the African data, "How does parental and lineage authority, as projected in ancestor worship, link up with political authority and its ritual symbolism and representation as in some forms of African kingship?" (1965:140).

Closer attention to the materials with which people apprehend ancestors and communicate with them may clarify how ancestors achieve authority over kin and non-kin. Cloth is central to the creation of ancestors in Madagascar as in many other parts of the world (see Darish and Weiner in this volume, Schneider 1987). In the Malagasy highlands, for example, indigenous silk textiles, handwoven by Merina and Betsileo women, are the focal point of reburial ceremonies (famadihana), in which kin gather every few years to honor important common ancestors by exhuming them, rewrapping them in new shrouds, and reburying them. Among the Sakalava of western Madagascar, where reburial is not practiced, imported silk textiles are central to spirit possession. People wrap their own relatives and friends in shrouds as they are possessed by the spirits of former kings and queens, a process that recurs throughout the year.

I argue that this possession by royal spirits follows the same pattern as the reburial of commoners' ancestors in the highlands, except that Sakalava exhume the dead by invoking them to speak in the bodies of commoners and rebury them by silencing them. Clothing the spirit is essential to the processes of regenerating it and making it speak, thereby identifying itself. Yet shrouding the spirit is also associated with concealment and eventually silence, even as wrapping a corpse is part of burying it. Cloth epitomizes the ambiguity of speaking through mediums, where it is not always clear whether the medium is acting for its spirit or for itself.

The process of clothing spirits to enable them to speak and to silence them resembles other ways in which Sakalava communicate and exchange with royal ancestors, including annual purification services and generational reconstructions of the royal tomb. In these services, different forms of royalty are unwrapped and rewrapped, regenerated and reburied, using materials like trees and stones in addition to bodies, bones, and cloth. The parallels in these processes by which the living and dead interact appear to rest on fundamental assumptions concerning the complex composition of human beings and the contradictory, often conflict-ridden structure of human relations, requiring various indirect as well as direct forms of expression.

THE SAKALAVA

The term "Sakalava" includes different groups of people along the west coast, who make their living by rice farming, animal husbandry, fishing, trading and wage labor. They are linked by their common and continuing respect for the power of the Maroseraña dynasty that ruled over this area until the French conquest of 1896. The Maroseraña dynasty is still represented in the Analalava region of the northwest coast by a living ruler (*ampanjaka*). She rules together with her ancestral predecessors in office. This is in keeping with Sakalava beliefs that the kin groups of royalty and "simple people" (*olo tsotra*) alike include ancestral dead (*razaña*) as well as living members (*olombelo/ño*). Ancestors are considered to have more power than living people and consequently more voice in domestic and political affairs, owing to their age compounded by their death. Their death is celebrated in spirit possession, where they take the form in which they died (Feeley-Harnik 1978).

Sakalava bury their dead in cemeteries attached to local communities. Burying the body and prohibiting the use of the personal name of the dead person are related acts. As one woman explained in response to my unwitting questions about her family:

I am afraid to say it [her dead father's name], it can't be done. [I would be] ashamed/disgraced [the condition of a person who has not observed the prohibitions entailed by respect]. You cannot utter the names of your parents after they are dead. They would punish you if you did. Your family names are like those of the Hova [Merina] and the Tsimihety, and also the Comorians. All the children get their father's name as well as their own. When Sakalava die, they don't uncover/open (mañokatra) the body like the Hova and the Tsimihety. The Hova dig up the body again, if it died somewhere else, and take it back to its ancestral land (tanindrazaña). The Tsimihety do the same, burying men in rocks in the mountains, in different coffins from women. Sakalava just leave the body in the place where it died, that's it (basy)!

Sakalava observe other prohibitions separating the dead from the living at the burial and afterwards. Nevertheless, ancestors continue to communicate with their living descendants, and thereby influence the changing fortunes of the living. Living people invoke their ancestors by addressing them generically as "Sir" or "Madam" (Tompokolahy/vavy), and presenting them with offerings, the materials for which are kept on a shelf in the northeast corner of the house known as the "ancestors' corner" (zorondrazaña). Sakalava use the phrase "removing the lock" (fangala gadra/hidy) in referring to the opening of a household head's formal speech (kabary) to the ancestors. "He opens the mouth of the speech [like a door], unties the knot constricting formal communication" (mampibihaña ny vavan' ny kabary, mamavatra kabary), exposing what is on his mind in speaking about it.[1]

When a Sakalava ruler dies, his or her personal name is prohibited along with any other words that resemble it. A praise name such as "The Noble One Who Sustained Thousands" (Ndramamahañarivo) is used instead. Teknonyms, like "Soazara's Father" (Baban'Soazara) for Ndramamahañarivo, may be used in referring to or addressing the spirit in less formal circumstances, including spirit-possession ceremonies.

Sakalava royalty are buried with elaborate ceremony that lasted a year in the precolonial period (see Dandouau 1912:165–72, Poirier 1939). Royal regalia, perhaps including relics, are kept at the royal capital (*doany*) on the mainland. The corpse, having been reduced to bone, is buried in a royal tomb (*mahabo*) on an island off the coast. Both of these are elaborately fenced. The "royal ancestors' house" at the capital is enclosed within a palisade of pointed stakes, which is itself enclosed within a second fence made of palm fronds around the royal compound, including the house of the living ruler. The royal tomb is enclosed by an inner palisade of pointed stakes with a place that Sakalava call a "door" in the middle of the west side, where two of the posts are taller than the rest, and an outer hedge with a door in the middle of the west side that opens and closes. The plan of the *mahabo*, surrounded by the houses of ex-slaves and spirit mediums, parallels that of the *doany*, where the royal compound is surrounded by the houses of ex-slaves attached to the living ruler.

The royal ancestors are isolated from the living in various ways, but they continue to interact with the living; their influence is considered to be evident in the overall condition of the region. The living communicate with the royal ancestors in annual purification services that Sakalava compare to domestic offerings. They also speak and exchange with them during other "royal services" (*fanompoaña*), the most important of which is the reconstruction of the fence around the royal tomb that a living ruler is obligated to carry out after burying his or her predecessor. These services focus on the acts of unlocking, opening, closing, and relocking the doors implied in communicating with domestic ancestors. Living people and royal ancestors also communicate through spirit possession, in which the ancestors reappear among the living by "coming to govern on people" (*mianjaka amin'olo*) whom the living clothe in royal form. To explore the processes of wrapping and rewrapping that are common to these interactions between the living and the dead, I begin with a brief account of the role of clothing in making and breaking relationships among the living. Then I discuss spirit possession, the commonest form of relationship between the living and the dead, and conclude with a brief outline of services for the royal ancestors that are more infrequent but are regional in scope.

Figure 4. The Ampanjaka Soazara *as a child, dressed in imported red silks and surrounded by followers (ca. 1936). Photo, Service Photo-Cinéma de la Direction de l'Information, Antananarivo, Madagascar*

CLOTHING, SPEAKING, AND LYING

The rectangular piece of cloth known as the *lamba* is one of the most distinctive features of life throughout Madagascar. Draped differently according to age, sex, and circumstances, it is the common form of dress, a mark of social status, and a valued medium of exchange, sometimes serving as money in the context of highland burial rites (Feeley-Harnik and Mack n.d.). The precolonial cloth trade, especially in indigenous and imported silks, was fundamental to the political economy of several Malagasy monarchies (Figure 4). Cloth remains the greatest household expense after food and shelter, and the most important gift besides hospitality (Feeley-Harnik and Mack n.d.). Sakalava women no longer weave, but sewing is an important form of communal work (Figure 5).

Clothing is the product of reciprocity. Sakalava associate nakedness in daily life with poverty, madness, and other forms of social

Figure 5. Relatives by marriage sewing together; the women are also related through the royal spirits that possess them, but photographing the spirits is prohibited. Photo by Gillian Feeley-Harnik, 1973

isolation. Witches who have deliberately cut themselves off from society are recognized by the fact that they dance "naked on top of [tombs of] dead people." The properly social person is clothed, and the clothing itself conveys the nature of people's affiliations and their quality.

"Malagasy clothing" is wrapped around the body; tailoring implies Muslim or European affiliations. Most women in the Analalava region wear cotton body wraps (salovaña, siki/na): One sewn together at the ends to form a tube that covers the torso, a second worn over the shoulders (kisaly, salampy, lamba) and a third covering the head (foloara, kemba), all of which can be draped and folded in various ways. Men wear hip wraps (lambahoany, kitamby). Men and women combine wraps with tailored tops (a(n)kanjo, kazaka). School children and people in their twenties and thirties usually wear European clothing like T-shirts (tirkô), pants (pantalon), shorts (short), dresses

Figure 6. A Sakalava mother and son, in formal and every-day dress. Photo by Gillian Feeley-Harnik, 1981

(*ankanjo, rôbo, seray*) and outfits (*kombinaison*), and most women prize French underwear, especially bras (*korsaza*).[2] Older men dress up in suit jackets (*kazaka*) together with a shoulder wrap and cane on the most formal occasions. Most kinds of European clothing can be pur-chased from local merchants, but the jackets are usually castoffs, ex-ported from Europe in bulk, distributed through mission churches or the markets of larger cities (Figure 6).

Indians, Chinese, and Malagasy from the highlands distinguish themselves in part by wearing European clothing on most occasions.

Highland Malagasy men no longer combine European suits with Malagasy shoulderwraps, as they did during the nineteenth and early twentieth centuries, but Merina and Betsileo women usually complete their finest outfits by adding shawls distinct from those of coastal people in their white color and in the ways they are draped.

Clothing styles express a broad range of opinions concerning relationships among Malagasy and between Malagasy and Europeans, as illustrated in these comments by a young woman concerning characteristic ways of wearing body wraps:

> Tsimihety [her father's affiliation] wear their body wraps only to just below the knees, Sakalava [her mother's affiliation] to the ankles. Girls really start wearing it when they have breasts, though they start practicing earlier. Sakalava say that Tsimihety are naked (*mijalaña*). If the knees stick out (*miboaka*), Sakalava say they look conspicuous, undressed (*miala lamba*). Tsimihety say that if you wear the body wrap to your ankles you can't be strong, you can't move around. People who wear it to the ankles drag along, weak, lethargic, lazy. You can always tell a Sakalava and a Tsimihety seeing them on the road. The Sakalava walks slowly, in a stately and orderly manner. The Tsimihety—man or woman—trots right along, head forward [demonstration]. If a Tsimihety says something is nearby, a Sakalava knows it's far away. If a Tsimihety says it's far away, a Sakalava knows s/he can't make it there on foot. They need to move along calmly, peacefully, in a stately manner.

When I remarked to some Sakalava women that Tsimihety seem to wear shorter body wraps, they nodded and the older woman said "Yes, they're always running away." Later she added:

> They're always in a hurry, going quickly as if they were running away. They don't know how to move in a calm and orderly manner, they're always [she pulled her *salovaña* to her knees, tied it tightly high up under her armpits, and rushed around with a set expression on her face]. We wear it nicely down [she lowered her *salovaña* to her ankles and wrapped it comfortably around her chest], and when we're working, cooking, whatever, we tie it under the chest or around the waist (*mandreritra ambaniaña*). Those who know how to fix it right can tie their *salovaña* around the waist so neatly that it looks like a dress (*rôbo*).

These conflicting perspectives on energy, order, self-possession and modernity, which are quite widespread, probably originated during the early twentieth century, when French administrators distinguished Malagasy groups according to their capacities for work, and thus "progress" along Western lines. However, the name for the branch of the Sakalava monarchy that settled in northwestern Madagascar is *Bemihisatra*, meaning "The many who move forward so slowly as to stop" or, more broadly, "The many rooted in the land." These meanings date back to the early nineteenth century, according to Sakalava oral tradition in the Analalava region (and see Richardson 1885:266).

Sakalava identify themselves most completely as *Bemihisatra* during services for the royal ancestors, where all forms of European clothing are prohibited, including anything sewn rather than wrapped.[3] Men are prohibited from wearing underwear, trousers, belts, shoes, and brimmed hats (brimless *kofia* worn by Muslims are allowed); they must wear hip wraps (Figure 7). Women are prohibited from wearing underpants (bras are allowed), shoes, or sewn body wraps. They must wear a *sambelatra* or *helaka* (literally, "peeled" "skinned", "flayed"), which Sakalava explain as a body wrap without stitching that opens in the front (*lamba mitatatra*). Women are also prohibited from covering the upper parts of their body with head or shoulder wraps. There are special "dressing places" (*ampisikiña*) outside the royal capital and cemetery where people must change their clothes before entering.[4]

Sewing and tailoring have Muslim or European associations, but any clothing that is knotted or tied shut (*miqadra*) is also prohibited at royal centers. This suggests that besides severing foreign relations, Sakalava are required to be open to involvement with royalty. Covering the body can imply that a person is concealing bad thoughts. Evil characters in Sakalava folktales, usually disguised in the ankle-length robes of a Muslim, are revealed when they lift their clothing crossing a stream or let it fall open while drunk, thereby exposing their tails.[5]

The elaboration of clothing to distinguish people according to age, gender, status, and occupation is matched in most circumstances by its capacity for concealment. For example, babies' heads are covered and their bodies heavily wrapped during the first few months of life, even in the most hot and humid weather. The stated purpose is to keep them warm, but the wrapping is also thought

Figure 7. Sakalava men attending a service at the royal cemetery. Wearing the brimmed hat is prohibited for those actually participating in the service. Photo by Gillian Feeley-Harnik, 1973

to protect them from the harm that might come from others' jealous looks. For the same reason, pregnant women always cover their bellies with their shoulder wraps. Their clothing is governed by prohibitions associated with their patrilineal and matrilateral kin groups. It tends to be untailored because ties and knots could impede the birth.[6]

 Whenever Sakalava feel uncomfortable they tend to cover their heads and shoulders. Conversely, when they feel relaxed, they loosen, open, or remove their head or shoulder wraps. These processes of wrapping and unwrapping the body are directly associated with speech and silence, familiarity and distance. For example, I was sitting in the courtyard of my "mother-in-law" together with her, her oldest son's wife, the wife's older sister ("Big Daughter-in-law"), and our several children, when another of her sons came in wearing a tiny bathing suit. She scolded him for letting his testicles stick out (*miboaka*) like a Frenchman, and he joked, as he could with his sisters-in-law, saying "Balls make money," at which everyone laughed uproariously.[7]

Personal names are equally revealing from a Sakalava point of view. Just as Needham (1954a,b), Fortes (1955), and Beidelman (1974) noted in Southeast Asian and African contexts, names are associated in Sakalava usage with personal attributes and historical experiences, including interactions between the living and the dead. In familiar circumstances, people of the same generation, and usually of the same sex, are permitted to intrude on the distinctiveness (*anjara*) of one another without disrespect by addressing one another by their personal names. Even so, there is a preference for more indirect forms of reference and address like kin terms, and a decided shift, as soon as a person has descendants of his or her own, to teknonyms. When a person is dead, Sakalava prohibit use of the personal name altogether.

Sakalava mourning customs support the inference that wrapping up, social formality, linguistic restraint, and depersonalization are ultimately associated with death, while speaking asserts the renewal of life and naming establishes familiar relations. When a person dies, the body is washed, pieces of kapok soaked in cologne are put in all the orifices and "places between," and incense is burned to cover the smell of the corpse. The clean body is wrapped in cloth and placed in a plain wooden coffin. Sakalava use all the good *lamba* they have stored in trunks, in contrast to Silamo who are prohibited from using anything but a piece of new white cotton cloth (*bafota malandy*). Sakalava may keep the body in the house for a few days, whereas Silamo must bury it before sundown. Whatever the case, the coffin is covered with another piece of white cloth when it is carried to the cemetery to be buried.[8]

Mourning prohibitions impose an analogous kind of wrapping and silence on the spouse as well, once lasting three months, now four to five weeks; women usually observe these prohibitions longer than men. The prohibitions are summarized in the phrase "to keep closed or locked," which may refer especially to the prohibitions against speaking or leaving the house.[9] The widow or widower "must remain in the house, without speaking to people, without going out." She or he may speak to very close kin of the same sex, but then only in a low voice. Very close kin of the opposite sex may enter the house, but they may neither look at nor speak to the mourning spouse, who may remain behind a curtain even inside the house. Greetings from outside must be answered by clapping. In going outside to the *douche*, he or she must cover up completely, leaving only an opening for an eye to find the way. The spouse announces the end of mourning by dressing up in clean clothing, coming out of the house and speaking to people.

Sakalava are not unusual in seeing cloth as an integrative social substance, interpreting the relations of persons to groups and incorporating them into communities, as exemplified in the power of a famous diviner to transform the dust falling from his hands into cloth. These are social facts that find strong support in everyday terminology concerning cloth. The weft of the *lamba* is its *faha/ña*, a term referring to the provision of sustenance, support, or consistency generally, including nourishment to a child, gifts to a stranger, or prosperity to countless royal subjects, as in Soazara's Father's praise name, Ndramamahañarivo, mentioned above.[10] The verb *mamahaña* refers to weaving, feeding, supporting, restoring or revitalizing others. *Manoratra*, to weave patterns into cloth, is also to write, whence "patterned/written cloth" (*lamba soratra*). The little stripes (Malagasy *lamba* are characteristically striped lengthwise) are the "vowels" (*zanatsoratra*), literally "the children of patterns/ writing" (Richardson 1885:224, 589–90).

Sakalava like clothing with writing on it, expressing their views on such subjects as love, wealth, children, and royal service like "Hang on to what's yours, because people won't give you theirs" (*Tahio ny antena, fa nin-olo tsy omeny*) or "I like the one outside, but I wouldn't trade the one inside the house" (*Tiako ny an-tany fa tsy atakaloko ny an-trano*) or "Children with money don't struggle" (*Zanaka misy vola tsy sahira*).[11] The same principle was used to broadcast loyalty to the PSD (Parti Social Democrate), the majority party in Madagascar prior to the revolution of 1972. Red, white, and green colored cloth, printed with then-President Tsiranana's face in black and white and emblazoned with the party motto, *Anio Rahampitso*

Mandrakizay Tsiranana (Today Tomorrow Forever Tsiranana) and the slogan, *Mirehareha izahay manana anao* (We are proud to have you [as our President]), was sold through local merchants prior to the President's inauguration on May 1, 1972. Functionaries and Indian shopkeepers wore shirts and blouses of Tsiranana cloth to party rallies in Analalava. Others, especially the less wealthy, wore clothing in the national colors.[12]

The political rallies in particular evoked comments that people also dress to mislead, even lie about relationships. Politically appropriate clothing may conceal motives that have nothing to do with party loyalty, or it may belie stated intentions. So many people felt they had to wear the cloth, whether or not they could afford it, that merchants selling Tsiranana cloth were accused privately of profiting in a bad way. By the same token, people may profess Islam and so adopt the distinctive skullcap of Muslim men without observing the proper devotions. They are the "skullcap Muslims" or "people who play at being Muslim" (see also Aujas 1927:33 and Mellis 1938:72). One man remarked in this context that male homosexuals may dress like women without really being women, only "images of women" (Figure 8).

Spirit possession turns on precisely these questions of identity and legitimacy, both during the process in which a person comes to be recognized as possessed by a particular spirit, and subsequently as the person maintains his or her relationship with the spirit as genuine. In each case, clothing and speaking together play a central role in the contradictory processes of substantiating identity and concealing falsity. To examine this connection between clothing and speaking in establishing, maintaining, and severing relations between the living and the dead, we now turn to the subject of spirit possession.

SPIRIT POSSESSION

Spirit possession makes people sick.[13] The sick person goes to a diviner who diagnoses the nature and cause of the problem to establish whether, as one woman explained, "it is a royal spirit [*tromba*] that needs to come out, poison, or your own spirits who are bothering you" (*lolo an-teña miqôdaña anao*). Typically, sickness that has resisted all other forms of treatment, including Western medicines, is

Figure 8. This children's dance group, honoring a visiting government official, is led by a man who dresses as a woman and is also well known as a spirit medium. Photo by Gillian Feeley-Harnik, 1971

interpreted as the work of a spirit that wants to "come out" (*miboaka*). Possession is also suspected when the sickness is accompanied by lost clothes and aching teeth. When I asked, what if someone had simply stolen the clothes, I was told that the diviner would explain that a royal spirit possessing the thief had gotten him or her to steal the clothes. Toothaches may result from eating prohibited foods, since spirits have many food prohibitions. Toothaches are also associated with the overall malaise, centered at the "mouth of the heart" (*vava fo*) just above the stomach, that spirits are commonly thought to cause and cure.

A spirit comes out when it speaks through the body of the sick person, openly declaring its reasons for causing the affliction that will result in the victim's death if not cured. The cure consists in fulfilling the spirit's demands, typically demands that involve its reincorporation into the world of the living through the body of its host, as described below. That body then supports not only its own living spirit (*jery*) but, periodically, the spirits of one or more ancestors as well. Despite the intimacy of the relationship between the spirit and its host, often compared to a marriage, Sakalava emphasize that their *jery*, or powers of discernment, are completely different. This general term for thought, intelligence, or reflection applies equally to the acts of seeing or inspecting something.

The diviner's response depends on the kind of spirit involved. The problem of identity involving clothing and speaking in Sakalava spirit possession is not simply a matter of acknowledging ancestral agency in evaluating a person's behavior. Participants must discover which of several kinds of spirits may be involved, and within each category, which specific spirit. The majority of spirits that possess people are called *tromba*, a term that Sakalava contrast with the term for "living persons" (*olombelo/na*). The broadest distinction that Sakalava make within this category is between "good" spirits and "bad" spirits. The former include all the spirits of the royal ancestors (*tromba, tromban-drazaña, zanahary*). The latter include spirits (*lolo*) called *masantoko, njarinintsy, be hondry, be tsioko*, who possess people in order to murder them.

In contrast to good spirits, who are considered to act on their own, bad spirits are thought to carry out the evil intentions of sorcerers. The cure consists of taking medicines that will kill them or hiring a living person who knows how to drive them out, since royal spirits are prohibited from doing so. Bad spirits may torment a person in a characteristic fashion over a long period of time, but the purpose of the cure is to get rid of the spirit altogether. As long as a bad spirit persists in possessing a person, the cure is not complete. Bad spirits never speak. In fact, if it appears right away, and does not speak, "you already know this thing here [*raha 'ty*] is bad, because it's not speaking," as one medium explained. Bad spirits are identified by bodily gestures like violent punching or uncontrollable shivering, not names and clothing. Perhaps this is because they are not considered human or because they are not incorporated into permanent relations with humans, though some people saw them as the necessary precursors of good spirits.

Sakalava acknowledge that a good spirit can look like a bad one when it is "angry" at its host, perhaps for drinking, breaking an ancestral prohibition, or failing to acknowledge a vow. Royal spirits, like living rulers, are thought to be prone to anger, especially if they feel that people "do not recognize [*mijery*] them," in the fullest sense of the term, that is, see them, reflect on them, respect them. Anger is an important cause of sickness. Many royal rituals concerning both living and dead royalty are intended to assuage their anger, "taking care of them by calming them down, cosseting them" (*mitambesatra azy*) by speaking and singing to them and giving them gifts. Nevertheless, the intentions of good spirits, even when they are angry, are entirely different from those of murderously evil spirits. Their actions will, if ignored, result in death. But their ultimate concern is not with killing but with the host's overall well-being— "Good spirits know how to cure; they like people."

Good spirits include all the Sakalava royal ancestors, distinguished as members of the senior or junior branch of the Maroseraña dynasty, that is as "Descendants of the Gold" or "Descendants of the Silver." If they are immediate ancestors of the local ruler or founding ancestors of the dynasty, they are "big" in contrast to the spirits of more distant or more junior royalty who are "little spirits."

As with bad spirits, the cure consists in "calling" the spirit to state its identity and its intentions, which in the case of good spirits will involve some sort of permanent relationship between the spirit and its host. Sakalava speak here too of "making the spirit come out" or "making it come down [onto the head or into the body]," but in practice they must induce it to speak. Royalty cannot be commanded, so people must cajole the spirit into speaking by bringing gifts, burning incense, and clapping and singing praise songs. As one woman explained it, these are all ways of calling the spirit, "Asking, begging, pleading with the spirit to come, come! We are begging you, just come, speak, say your name! When s/he hears this, s/he will arrive." Some spirits are described as easier to bring out than others, but the process of calling a spirit usually requires several meetings held over weeks, months, and sometimes years.[14]

During this time, when the spirit is on the verge of arriving, it may be addressed as "visitor/stranger" (*vahiny, ampenziky*) like a newborn baby, or as "Sir/Madam" (*Tompoko*), and sometimes referred to as the "difficult one" (*sarotro*) or "thing" (*raha*). It may respond to people's pleas to come out by emerging enough to cause the sick person to shake or cry out inarticulately. It may eventually send one of its "royal slaves," male or female followers, to convey its anger at what is preventing it from revealing itself, for example, polluted surroundings, too few royal relatives in attendance, inferior gifts, the wrong kinds of music, or the persistent disbelief of the sick person's kin, often a husband like the one who kept saying, "It's all lies, no royal spirit is involved."

If the spirit greets the crowd, then some aspects of its identity will be revealed in the way it speaks the royal language—as a man, woman, or child from a particular region. Eventually the spirit may answer the basic question: "Are you a senior or junior member of Sakalava royalty?" The lengthy process culminates in the "utterance" (*toñony*) when the spirit identifies the clothing, stick, and silver ornaments that it requires in keeping with its name. Finally the spirit, fully clothed, reveals itself by stating its name, place of origin, and purpose in rejoining the living at the ceremony called "turning the royal compound upside-down" (*vadiky lapa*) to which we will return.

NAMING AND CLOTHING

The processes of naming and clothing are intertwined. The spirit may hint at its identity, but wait until it has received all it requested before revealing itself fully. The sick person, kin, or friends may recognize the spirit by the nature of its requests, especially if it is one of the little spirits that possess a lot of people. It may still be difficult to find or buy all the clothes at once. Even so, Sakalava emphasize that, in one medium's words, "Until the spirit has been fully clothed, it has not been clearly brought out, the process is not yet complete. When it gets the *lamba* it wants, then it will come out. If it has not yet gotten the *lamba*, then its particular requirements have not been fulfilled, and it will not reveal its name."

The spirit's answer to whether it is a member of the senior or junior branch will already be enough to indicate whether it is big or little. Further hints will reveal whether the sick person is possessed by a royal spirit who ruled in some distant place or by one of the local queen's immediate relatives. These distinctions are economic as well as social. Gifts to royalty should be new; second-hand materials are generally prohibited. Old clothing, like an opened package of cigarettes or a half-empty bottle of rum, is classified in the same category as the leftovers from last night's dinner heated up for breakfast the next morning (*ankera*).[15] Furthermore, the materials worn by big spirits are more elaborate and made of more costly materials like silks and precious metals, compared with those presented to lesser royal spirits.[16]

The term for spirits' clothing (*sarandra, lamba tromba, lamban-djanahary*), literally "royal spirits' clothing," refers especially to the mantle.[17] There are no special words in the royal vocabulary for the other garments, which are called by the same terms as their common counterparts. The mantle and the cane are regarded as the most distinctive pieces of clothing and they are typically the most expensive.

The mantle differs in how it is used in the process of possession and how it is worn once the spirit has arrived. When a person starts to shake, and the people around her see that she is becoming possessed, they cover her with a *sarandra* or a large white cloth (*darà*), or a patterned hip wrap (this is not considered proper), as she falls backwards. Holding the four corners, they shake the cloth until the body underneath lies prone on the ground, which indicates that the spirit is there. Then they dress the spirit and uncover it; little spirits usually dress themselves and come out from under the cloth. At the royal cemetery, the host/spirit, still covered by the cloth, may be carried like a corpse into the royal council house just west of the burial compound and dressed there. Once a big spirit is dressed, it is seated upright in its "chair" (*sezy*, from the French word *chaise*), that is, between the legs of a female attendant whose limbs and torso form the arms and back of the chair. The cloth that covered the spirit is not wrapped around its shoulders, but wrapped around the lower part of the body from the waist down and tucked under at the feet, the way a shroud is wrapped around the body of a corpse, except that the upper body and head are left bare.

The red and multicolored silk cloths associated with the senior royal line (*dahalany, sobaiha, tsiampongamena, jakimena*) were once imported along with other silks (*lasoa, hariry, deboan*) by Arab and Comorian merchants from the Arabian peninsula, which Sakalava claim to be the source of most features of the Maroseraña dynasty. Since French colonists curtailed the Arab trade, these cloths have become more rare and expensive than they were reputed to be before.[18]

The stick (*mampingo*) is not sold in stores. It is made from local wood, ideally hard and black like the ebony for which it is named, highly polished and ornamented with silver. The silver differentiates it as a "silver club" (*kobay fanjava*) belonging to a male ruler and often thought of as a weapon, unlike an ordinary man's stick, which is used as a cane. The stick may be purchased, acquired as a gift, or inherited from another person, as long as the person was not a medium. The silver decorations are the work of Indian jewelers, numerous in Analalava during the colonial period, but now found only in the big cities outside the region.

Antique clothing or silver that has been used before must be purified by "washing" it, using mixtures of honey and water to which kaolin and silver have been added. This is how Sakalava purify the royal relics at the capital and the tomb at the royal cemetery every year. One of the several months in which these services are held is devoted to making the liquid. The personal pollution of body and clothing that results from attending a funeral or from breaking a prohibition is cleansed in the same way.[19] Sakalava may also petition royal spirits to relax their clothing requirements, as they do with onerous food prohibitions. A year must pass before appeals concerning food can be made. Such compromises are more difficult to achieve with big spirits than with little ones. Possession is invigorating for the spirit, but still burdensome, sometimes debilitating, for the host even after her or his cure, because of the numerous prohibitions, especially concerning food, and the expenses that are involved in the relationship. The bigger the spirit, the greater the sacrifices are expected to be.

Once these materials have been purchased, or—depending on how difficult it is to find them—*as* they are purchased, they will be presented to the spirit as gifts at the ceremony described as "turning the royal compound upside-down." As one woman, possessed by several spirits, described it:

> The process of urging a spirit to declare itself is called making
> the spirit come out (*mampiboaka tromba*), no matter how many
> times it takes before it finally appears. *Mamadiky lapa* is what it is
> called after a year has passed and it appears (*miboaka*) again and
> reveals all its customary practices (*manambara jiaby ny fomban'azy*).
> *Mamadiky lapa* is when it reveals its prohibitions, to utter its
> name clearly: I am so-and-so, my father is so-and-so, my mother
> is so-and-so, the place where I live is so-and-so.

Another medium explained:

> People who call a royal spirit to turn the royal compound
> upside-down, they are calling [it] again, calling a second time.
> Making a spirit come out (*mampiboaka tromba*) is what [calling the
> spirit] is called when you are first trying to get it out, no matter
> how many times it takes. Turning the royal compound upside-
> down (*mamadiky lapa*) is what [calling the spirit] is called after
> one year has passed. It comes out again and reveals all its cus-
> toms, everything. Until this has happened, you can't heal oth-
> ers. Once that has finished, you can heal or make royal spirits
> come out yourself. [Why is it called *mampiboaka tromba* no matter
> how often or how long it takes?] Because the person is sick! It is
> a sickness after all! You are curing a sickness by making it come
> out!

"To utter the name" (*Manoñono anarany*) is "to raise or reveal the
name" (*manonga anarany*) as Sakalava also express it, using a phrase
that otherwise refers to removing one's clothes. A person's character is expressed not only in his or her name, but in his or her customary ways of acting, especially through clothing. The end of the illness entailed in revealing the name and the character through the
clothing is the beginning of a new relationship between the spirit
and its host, and between the host and his or her kin, to whom the
prohibitions are explained at the same time. A person will still become "sick" in the process of being possessed, but only immediately
prior to the act of possession, not interminably. On the contrary,
provided that the host observes the spirit's prohibitions, the relationship is considered to be a source of good health and fortune,
including the financial benefits of curing others in turn.[20]

The income from such activities, like the clothing and other
things involved in possession—the offering dish, silver coins, ornaments and charms, kaolin, incense and incense burner—are considered to belong to the spirit, not its host. The spirit's clothes,
wrapped in cloth or stored in a plastic bag, are kept with the rest
of its things on a set of shelves hung on the eastern wall of the
house, opposite the ancestor's corner in the southern corner or in
the northeast corner of the southern room. The shelf (*taky*), like the
shelf with the same name and purpose in the ancestors' house at
the royal capital, is covered with a piece of plain white cotton cloth
(*gora, bafota*) called a *lamba* or *darà* in commoners' houses, but a

tsafoday/tafonday in the case of the ancestors' house. The stick and other special possessions, for example, a spirit's folding chair, propped against the wall below the shelf, are likewise covered with white cloths (and they are usually kept covered that way when they are carried to meetings). They must be given to the ancestors' attendants at the royal cemetery when the host dies, although kin may later petition to get them back. These objects, covered in white, serve to bring the spirit not only into the body of its host, but also into its house. Their presence transforms the host's house, like her body, into a shrine honoring the royal ancestors, comparable to the royal capital and royal tomb and requiring many of the same prohibitions, especially concerning pollution.

SUBSTANTIATING IDENTITY AND CONCEALING FALSITY

Clothing, naming, and speaking are the central issues in spirit possession. Specific royal spirits possess people in order to be able to speak out and be spoken to in ways they could not if they remained buried. Frequently they speak to express their anger at something that has happened and their demands for changing it. Their way of speaking is compared to the bellowing of a bull. Their words, uttered in the royal language, are referred to as "ancestors' orders," a phrase that also emphasizes their commanding aspect.[21]

Sakalava acknowledge the role of economic power in political expression when they explain that rulers, not commoners, speak after death because a ruler is buried with coins in his or her mouth, whereas it is prohibited to put money in the mouths of commoners. The money is what gives royal spirits a voice, even as money buys the clothing that creates the forms through which they speak, substantiating their identity.[22] Still, the mouths of royalty are tied shut like those of commoners when they are buried. Royalty speak only when wrapped in the bodies of commoners who are wearing the clothing that identifies them, which includes the shroud that silenced them in the first place. Furthermore, once the intertwined processes of clothing and speaking have revealed the spirit's identity and the host's cure, the relationship between the two is to some extent reversed. People usually refer to their relationships with spirits by saying "Government sits on me" (*Fanjakaña mipetraka aminakahy*) rather than the spirit's praise name or teknonym. Furthermore they emphasize the spirit's autonomy, saying that you can never know when the spirit might possess you "because your minds (*jery*) are not the same."

However, in giving its name, the spirit has relinquished some of its power to its host. Sakalava women converted to Islam regularly prevent their spirits from speaking during Ramadan. They do this by "tying their mouths shut," as one woman put it. They disagree with the orthodox Muslim view that *tromba* are evil spirits (*setoan*), arguing that spirit possession is a serious illness. Yet they are careful to observe the prohibition against possession during the month of Ramadan, dedicated to purification through fasting and prayers. They call the spirit and say, as the same woman continued: "I am tying myself up!" (*Zaho mifehy!*—"I am fasting!" in the context of Ramadan). "Keep silent and don't make me sick!" Once this is done, they can attend spirit-possession meetings during Ramadan, and their spirits will neither speak nor make them sick in their efforts to speak. Sakalava "tie up" (*mifehy*) the mouth of a corpse before it is wrapped and buried. The term also applies to governing, whence the name of the royal district administrators (*mpifehy*, literally, "tiers-up") and the districts over which they have jurisdiction (*fehezina*, "tied bundles") in Sakalava monarchy.

People silence the dead by tying their mouths shut, wrapping them in shrouds and burying them. They make them speak by clothing them in the bodies of commoners, but clothing them in part as if they were unwrapping and rewrapping them again in shrouds. The spirit's clothing is just as articulate as that of any living person. Indeed, people often explain the differences among spirits by comparing them to the living, but periodically the mantle covers it all. The act of wrapping the spirit in its shroud, rewrapping it every time it reappears, seems to be instrumental in bringing it into the living body of the medium and identifying its voice. Spirits are rewrapped *to* reappear, *to* speak. But at the same time, their speech is veiled by having to emerge from the body of another as it is veiled by their death recalled in the mantle that serves first as a shroud.

Irvine's (1982) comparative analysis of spirit mediumship and possession from a sociolinguistic perspective highlights the complexity of the creative process by which spirits are identified. She argues that semantic analysis alone is insufficient because the meaning attributed to behavioral forms, even if generally agreed upon, may vary according to the context in which they occur, the personal interests of participants, and the histories of their relations with one another. Irvine suggests that the attribution or declaration of identity in spirit possession is simply a specific instance of a more general social process, and that comparable factors may be involved in participants' interpretations of identity on a broader scale. The Sakalava data confirm Irvine's observations. Moreover, they suggest that in this case at least, much of the participants' own sense of the complexities involved in substantiating identity lies in their perceptions of the spirit's clothing.

Someone may appear to be possessed, but people will say, "only the clothes possess her" or "the spirit is not doing it, the body is doing it," suggesting, without having to say so directly, that the person is a "lying medium" or even a sorcerer. For example, one woman said about the group of little spirits from Betsioko that possess people the most frequently:

> There are so many of them. All the things about them (*ley raha jiaby amin'azy*) possess everyone, but the real them (*ley teñan'izy*) seldom does. Their things, their handkerchiefs (*mouchoir*), possess people, but only a very few are actually possessed by the real thing. In every village, almost everyone in the place is possessed by one of those royal spirits. A lot of people just get possessed so that people will see. It's appearance (*fizahaña*), few people really have it (*misy azy vantaña*). [How do you know the real thing?] They chronicle (*mitantara*) what happened before they died. The ones that aren't really it can't *say* much about it [her emphasis]. If the real one comes when the others are there, then the others will leave. But there are too many that just appear to have it. [What about the living ruler's ancestors? The Father and Son possess so many mediums.] If a person dares to become possessed at the royal cemetery, it's it (*izy*)! If it doesn't go to the royal cemetery, it's not it. If it comes there, this one's really it (*izy ankitiny 'ty ê*)! They have a trial (*fitsaraña*) for it there. There's questions they ask in case of deception (*mihaboka*). *Mihaboka* concerns possessions (*fañanana*). It means to claim you have things you don't have. The true ones (*ley marigny*) are ordered to go to the royal cemetery, ordered by the royal spirit possessing them. The false ones just need to get possessed. When they get there, people see.[23]

The *vadiky lapa*, when a spirit comes out and declares its name, the names of its parents, its place of origin, its prohibitions, and other customary observances, is compared to the trial at the royal cemetery. It is a validation, but on a lesser scale. As one man explained, speaking about the little spirits associated with the junior branch of Sakalava royalty,

> Little spirits, Kotomena, Fotsy, Ley Sarotro, don't go through a trial. They *mamadiky lapa*. Ampela Be [an elder father's sister in the junior branch]—she might pronounce her name before, but at Andampy [their royal center] she really does it all. They elevate her/reveal her name (*mampanonga azy*). Zafinimena [members of the senior branch] don't go through the *vadiky lapa*, just the trial.

Big spirits must undergo the trial at the royal cemetery before they can live there all year round. The process of legitimation is considered suspect in certain cases. Yet even here, people will explain that "the spirit just hasn't come out clearly yet." Whereas an outsider like a Muslim shopkeeper may say bluntly, "Spirit possession is nothing but deception (*politique*), lies, foolishness," Sakalava rarely challenge false mediums openly; they simply avoid them (see also Ottino 1965:92). Indeed, these suspicions about possession appear to be unresolvable. The alternatives are clear. Everyone is aware of divided loyalties, commonly expressed in terms of insides and outsides. People try to sort them out by distinguishing good from bad spirits, big ones from little ones, and the "real ones" from the "appearances." It is not so much the alternatives as the "turning" (*mivadiky*) from one to the other, the inevitable consequence of conflicting obligations, that preoccupy people when they examine their relationships with one another. As one man said,

> To turn against a blood brother (*mamadiky fatidra*) is very bad. For example, he comes asking for something, and you say you don't have it. You have taken an oath, "If I could help, but don't, may I become air, ashes, dust. May I cease to exist here above," like that. In turning away from a friend, you face scrutiny (*mivadiky amin' ny namana, astrikanao ny zavàna*). Turning against someone is like committing sorcery, murder. God sees it and sends sickness to that person.

Sakalava describe the transformation of a famous spirit/medium into a sorcerer in the same terms: "He was famous, but in the end he turned" [and would be destroyed for it].

"Turning" (*vadiky*), the commonest expression for deceiving or betraying someone, has its counterpart in the Sakalava royal vocabulary, where "to roll or turn over like a canoe" (*mihilaña*) is the term for dying, and "turning" is the root of the Merina term for reburials, *famadihana*.[24] Perhaps the *vadiky lapa* is so named because it begins to turn over the relationship between the spirit and its host. But all social relationships are thought to have the potential to turn, and this enduring indeterminacy in human affairs seems vested in the very materials with which the tromba is clothed. The generative force of the cloth brings the spirit—its voice—to life, but also shrouds its pronouncements with uncertainty, so that it can never be clear whether the spirit speaks for itself or for its medium, for Sakalava as a whole or for some restricted group within it.[25]

In fact, there are no sharp distinctions between host and spirit, living and dead, kin and non-kin (in that one can "get kin" by means like blood brotherhood) to facilitate people's understanding of how relations become transformed. The resolution must be worked out through time and space. There is an historical dimension to the contrast between inside and outside—knowing the genealogical relationships and the events in which people participate—that cannot be separated from the geographical dimensions of the process by which people are drawn into the royal centers, especially the royal cemetery.

I will amplify these points by describing the kinds of Sakalava royal service that I see as variations on the themes of burying, exhuming, rewrapping, and reburying the dead as a means of speaking to them and silencing them. Sakalava do not make the same explicit comparison between clothing and architecture that Murra (1983:1–2) noted among contemporary descendants of the Inkas. Nevertheless, these royal services raise the question of how other combinations of hard and soft materials besides bones and cloth, sticks and mantles, are used to convey the complexity of human beings, their opposed and common interests, and their different ways of talking about the contradictions of politics. This work focuses on the fences enclosing the royal residence and relic house at the capital and the royal tomb at the cemetery, the doors with which they are opened and closed, and the procedures by which these doors and fences are periodically removed and rebuilt.

CLOTHING SPIRITS, PURIFYING RELICS, AND
RECONSTRUCTING TOMBS

Sakalava celebrate the beginning of every lunar new year by opening the doors in the enclosures around the royal ancestors, purifying
the relics and regalia and the tomb within, and then closing the
doors. These procedures, extending over six months of every year,
begin toward the end of the rainy season. Around April, the doors
in the fences separating people from the royal ancestors are opened
and the courtyards surrounding the relic house at the capital and the
inner fence and tomb at the cemetery are cleaned in the "weeding
service."

The weeding service is followed in the next month by the preparation of mead, which is allowed to ferment during an intervening
"dead" month, when the doors are closed and royal ritual is prohibited. Services resume with the first month of the new year, around
July. The doors are reopened, and the weeding service is repeated,
after which the relics and regalia at the capital and the tomb at the
cemetery are cleaned, using the mead. This service concludes with
a formal obeisance to the living ruler and the royal ancestors, attended by people from the surrounding countryside, during which
people drink the mead that remains. The doors are closed for the
following month, considered inauspicious, and reopened in the
next month, when people may again pay their respects, make or
fulfill vows, and listen to royal spirits speak through mediums on
current events. The doors are then closed for the remainder of the
year.

"We beg for a door" (*mangataka varavara*) is one of the songs that
people sing in making offerings to the royal ancestors. When they
"receive a door" (*mahazo varavara*), when the doors are open, communication is open between the living and the dead, whether it
takes place through spirit mediums, now in full residence at the
cemetery, or through the "supplicator" who intercedes for people
at the entrance to the burial compound. "At the door" (*ambaravara*)
or "at the mouth" (*ambava*), the two procedures are considered
equivalent. Sakalava pay their respects to the royal ancestors
(*mikoezy*); they make vows (*mañano vava*); fulfill vows or otherwise explain their actions (*mamantoko*); beg pardon for their wrongs
(*mañanto, mamonjy, malilo*) and entreat the spirits' blessings (*man-*

gataka, mangataka hatsarana, mangataka radỳ, milamalama, mivalovalo).
Here, as with domestic ancestors, these various acts of speaking are
accompanied by many different kinds of giving. People give money,
cloth, and cattle, and they receive the spirits' blessing in the mark
of kaolin that the supplicator puts on their faces. They sing royal
praise songs and present entertainments to assuage the spirits'
anger, and they receive the spirits' commentary through mediums
on current affairs. When the doors are closed, communication
ceases.

The function of opening and closing the doors in this elaborate
manner is to regulate communication with the royal ancestors. By
undoing, cleaning, and refurbishing the materials in which royalty
are reenveloped every year, Sakalava clarify the nature of the relationships that connect people with the monarchy. By opening and
closing the doors, they continue to unwrap and rewrap the dead in
complex materials that articulate their current opinion of the
politico-religious and economic principles embodied in monarchy,
in the context of alternative forms of government.

Periodically, the fences are removed and replaced. The most important of these royal services involves the replacement of the innermost fence around the tomb. The old posts of the inner fence are
taken down, the tomb is cleaned, the area around it is weeded, and
a new fence is put up around it. The service held in the Analalava
region in 1972–76 was carried out by the guardians of the royal cemetery, assisted by the guardians of the royal capital and the populace
as a whole, under the leadership of spirit mediums representing the
royalty buried in the tomb and a young boy representing the living
ruler, who is prohibited from direct association with the dead.

Participants said that the work took a long time, six to eight
years, during the precolonial period, because of the care required
to select and prepare the materials. The actual construction should
take no more than a day (even as the original burial, following the
year required to reduce the corpse to bone, takes no more than a
night). The posts must be made from certain species of hardwood
tress, ideally trees that have caught fire and died while still standing
in the forest. Soft, green, fallen, or rotten woods are prohibited. The
trees are then debarked, so that only the hard cores remain. They
are then implanted in the ground around the tomb.

People are recruited to work as individuals rather than members
of kin groups. They are organized according to spatial, temporal,

and occupational principles and practices associated with the royal capital and cemetery rather than commoners' villages or administrative centers. The reorientation of participants is achieved primarily through indirect, largely nonverbal means; talk about royal corpses or burials is—as always—prohibited.

The reconstruction of the tomb is essentially a reburial. The data show that the transformation of the trees into posts stuck back in the ground around the tomb exactly parallels the transformation of the fleshy corpse into a skeleton, enclosed in a tree trunk and buried in the tomb itself. The difference is that the royal corpse is multiplied several hundred-fold in the course of being reburied in the form of these posts. And in taking this form, it has become embodied in the labor of commoners, stripped of their associations with kin in the process of reorganizing as individual citizens around the body of royalty (Feeley-Harnik 1990).[26]

The reconstruction of the royal tomb is intended to repair the damage done when participants at the original funeral broke through the fence to bury the corpse in the royal tomb. The spirit of the dead ruler is thought to move the pallbearers on that occasion, so they could crash through the fence at any point. Dandouau (1911:171–2) and Poirier (1939:104) report that both the inner and outer fences of the royal tomb are repaired or rebuilt at that time. Mellis, long resident in northwestern Madagascar, says that the break in the innermost fence is first covered with a white cloth. The fence is reconstructed only when the dead ruler reappears in the body of a commoner who is recognized as his or her legitimate medium (1938:61, photographs 62,67). In other words, the reconstruction of the royal tomb coincides with the reemergence of his or her voice in political affairs.

My data on the Analalava region support Mellis's account, suggesting that the logic of "reclothing" the royal tomb through the labor of commoners in the reconstruction service matches the logic of reclothing spirits in the bodies of commoners through spirit possession. Both actions give discreet but persistent voice to Sakalava political opinion. Because the Sakalava were denied that voice throughout the colonial period and early independence, permission to undertake the service following the death of the queen's father in 1925 was consistently refused. Only with the change of government in 1972, when the Sakalava voice counted quite literally in elections, was permission granted by General Gabriel Ramanantsoa, who received the benefit of their voices. Apparent consensus at the national level was achieved by tacitly permitting alternative views to flourish locally.

WRAPPING ANCESTORS AND CLAIMING POWER

Sakalava spirit possession, like the Sakalava royal rituals for celebrating the new year and reconstructing the fence around the royal tomb, are comparable to procedures for stripping and reclothing the dead found throughout Madagascar, the best known being the reburials (*famadihana*) celebrated by the Merina and Betsileo. As Malagasy ethnology indicates, there are many ways of understanding the significance of these rites. The parallels among them suggest that they would benefit from comparative analysis in a regional or national context. To do so would expand Kottak's (1980) argument about the involvement of Betsileo funerals in political-economic relations among the Betsileo and between the Betsileo and the Merina. Such analysis might also modify Bloch's (1971, 1982) arguments about Merina reburial as a refuge from change, affirming an enduring ancestral order associated with men in the face of human mortality associated with women. Bloch generalizes this interpretation to all Madagascar without taking into account the cloth, the ostensible focus of Merina reburials, which is in part the product of women's work and arguably a form of women's wealth.

From a regional perspective, Malagasy reburials are all ways of making ancestors, wrapping them to make them speak, and wrapping them to separate people with ancestors and descendants from those without, people with the history embodied in those generations from people without, and thus people with political power and authority in this life from people without. Malagasy burial ceremonies raise the question of whose *voice* counts in political affairs. In pluralistic societies, the answer is inevitably equivocal.

To rewrap the dead is to speak about the distribution of power and authority among specific contending parties in specific circumstances. The revelation of identity seems to be a crucial issue in the creation of ancestors, but so is the concealment of peoples' affiliations and opinions. Openness and hiddenness operate simultaneously, not because of any mystery or confusion about the nature of the tensions and contradictions in the political process, but because none of the participants exercises full control in all circumstances. The circumstances are always turning. From the Sakalava point of view, however, people who do not continue to recognize their ancestors are "lost to their ancestors" (*very razana*), just as people taken as slaves are "lost" to their communities, and with the same result. They become subject to the domination of others.

People express political loyalty to regional authorities as they conceal their loyalties to domestic groups and vice versa. Among the Merina and Betsileo, they persist in burying their own dead, while honoring royalty. In the very process of cloaking them, hiding them, they single them out and honor them. Men appear to bury their dead oratorically, while women bring them to renewed life in their shrouds.

Among Sakalava in the Analalava region, the ambiguity of political expression is also embodied in the shroud. Rewrapping the royal tomb in the hard cores of trees multiplies royalty, but it also extols the collective power of commoners. It calls into question the single voice of royalty by making it the creation of commoners. In spirit possession, royalty are brought to life in the very bodies of commoners, typically women, aided by men. Enshrouding these mediums makes them speak, but they may speak as much for themselves and their own kin as for others, a potential source of trouble for monarchy in the precolonial period that the Sakalava may have turned to their advantage in protecting monarchical institutions from the French.[27]

The ambiguity, the potential for turning, inherent in all social situations, is embodied in the materials with which spirits are wrapped: Combinations of soft and hard materials like cloth and sticks, trees and stones, cores and bark, trunks and leafy branches, analogs of shrouds and corpses, tombs and bodies, the bones and flesh of human beings, both female and male. The interconnections of these different materials, and their transformations back and forth in time between fragile and more enduring states, is the root of Malagasy burial rites. In their transformations, they are commentaries on the complex composition of human beings and of human relations, especially relations of domination and subordination that call for silence as well as speech, concealment as well as open confrontation. Strategies like these have drawn on both the strengths and the weaknesses attributed to men and women in ever-changing combinations throughout the precolonial, colonial, and postcolonial periods in Madagascar.

Sakalava in the Analalava region now question whether to re-build the royal tomb in perishable tree trunks and branches that will decay like cloth, or whether to switch to harder materials, cement and tin, as Sakalava elsewhere on the west coast have already done. In other words, they question whether to rewrap the ancestors in substances that embody the continuing involvement of local people in principles and practices associated with monarchy or whether to bury them forever, to relinquish these institutions and become sup-porters of national government. Indeed, it is unclear whether these choices are absolutely opposed. Perhaps there is still some value in maintaining political alternatives for parties on both sides, given the currently inadequate capacities of either to achieve more than partial political integration of the region and nation respectively. Covell's recent assessment of patron-client relationships in Malagasy bu-reaucracy concludes bleakly:

> . . . the system persists *because* [my emphasis] the bulk of the
> population is only partially incorporated in it. The general popu-
> lation of a country like Madagascar enjoyed a brief period of po-
> litical relevance at the time of the pre-independence elections
> and before the consolidation of a one-party or military regime.
> Since then the system has shrunk, as has the number of people
> whose opinions must be taken into account by the political elite.
> It is within this group that reliable channels of communication
> are necessary; for the partially integrated, partial channels suffice
> (n.d. [c. 1978]:32).

Covell's data suggest that former President Tsiranana made some effort to organize development schemes along the lines of tradi-tional reburial ceremonies. Nevertheless, tax-collecting has re-mained the dominant model for communication between the na-tional government and the people (Covell n.d.:23–4; see Covell 1974). Without the reembodiment of political ideals in material rela-tions of exchange on a national level, interest in regional alternatives will continue to flourish.

Royal spirits speaking through mediums have consistently re-jected the use of these new materials. Despite their resistance, the materials were bought in the 1950s, but they were never used, and finally they were resold. The outsider who bought them to build a house is said to have died as a consequence. The tomb, when it was finally reconstructed in 1972–76, was wrapped in trees that would eventually rot, requiring the attention of Sakalava again in the future.

DEATH, LIFE, AND POLITICS

I have described the role of cloth in Sakalava spirit possession, arguing that the process of clothing the spirit is essential to creating it, by inducing it to identify itself and state its intentions concerning its host. This is the immediate objective of the procedures surrounding spirit possession. Once the relationship between the spirit and its host is regularized, clothing the body serves, together with calling the spirit, to bring it back into its host to speak on various issues, including current affairs. The processes of clothing, naming, and speaking are associated in the recreation or revival of the dead but also in their reburial, in the revelation of political opinion but also in its concealment.

I have pointed out the parallels in the Analalava area between spirit possession and other forms of royal service, suggesting that they are all variations of practices involving the exhumation and reburial of the dead found in other parts of Madagascar. The way in which these practices are handled and their regional distribution suggest that they make the expression of political opinion possible under pluralistic circumstances on a broader scale.

The many forms of ancestors in Madagascar and the diverse materials with which they are revived and reburied, ranging from cloth to trees to cement, raise questions about the relationship of materials to ideas and behavior that merit further research. How do hand production (women's work) and commercial exchange affect the evaluation and use of different kinds of cloth in Malagasy funeral rituals? What accounts for the analogies between cloth and other materials or, perhaps more accurately, the combination of cloth and other "hard" materials like sticks and bones with other complex combinations of materials like fenced tombs? What is the relationship between these materials of wealth and power and the regionally and historically varied kinds of human bodies they constitute or represent? A closer examination of the relations between the living and the dead helps to elucidate differing conceptions of the very substance and value of human beings in the context of changing political-economic circumstances.

ACKNOWLEDGMENTS

This paper is based on 21 months of ethnographic field research in the Analalava region of northwestern Madagascar, from July, 1971 to November, 1973 and briefly in 1981, funded by a Predoctoral Research Grant from the National Institute of Mental Health and a Grant-in-Aid from the Wenner-Gren Foundation for Anthropological Research. I am grateful to these institutions for their support and to the members of the Wenner-Gren Foundation Symposium on "Cloth and Human Experience" for their comments on an earlier draft of this paper. I especially thank Jane Schneider and Annette B. Weiner, organizers of the conference, and T.O. Beidelman, George Bond, Pamela Feldman, Alan Harnik, Ward Keeler, and Michael Lambek for their helpful comments on later drafts.

NOTES

1. Because of the importance of cloth in exchange relations throughout Madagascar and the possibility of historical connections between trade and the exchange of ideas, I have drawn attention here and in the footnotes below to some comparable data from other Malagasy contexts, past and present, as well as some additional data concerning the Analalava region.

The opening words of a Betsileo funeral oration for a commoner in the late nineteenth century link speaking to weaving: "It is true that to have something to warp is to have something to weave; to have a dead person is to have to speak. When an ox is dead, it is cut up with a knife; when a person is dead, s/he is cut up with the tongue [in detailing his or her life]" (cited in Dubois 1938:684–5). *Mamelon-tenona*, "to stretch out the warp on the loom for weaving" is one of a group of words derived from the root *velatra*, which have to do with exposing the inside of something by spreading it out, including *mivelatra*, which also means "to begin a formal speech" (see Richardson 1885:748–49). The truthfulness and generosity associated with opening to expose the insides of things is directly opposed to the deceit and avarice associated with the actions of closing or covering so that only the outside or back shows.

2. *A(n)kanjo* probably derives from the Swahili *kanjo* (see French *canezou*). Other commonly used French terms include *tricot, pantalon, robe, [serrée], combinaison, corsage, casaque*.

3. This prohibition sometimes includes Merina and European speech and, at the royal cemetery, European objects like iron bedsteads and kerosene lamps. Similar prohibitions were enforced by Merina monarchs. European clothing came into common use among Merina nobility during the reign of Radama I (1792–1828). As on the coasts, it was always combined with Malagasy clothing, especially the mantle (e.g., Ellis 1835, 1867 *passim*, Guillain 1845:191). European clothing was prohibited in the course of reactions to close European involvement in Malagasy affairs, for example, during the reign the Merina queen Rasoherina ("Silkworm Chrysalis") following the assassination of Radama II in 1863 (Ellis 1867:319, 384–5).

Sakalava prohibitions do not include European textiles, though fabrics do have important politico-historical implications. For example, *dongimena, sobahiya* and other silks from "Araby," which are now rare if not impossible to find, are associated with the former resplendence of the precolonial monarchy. *Sotema* (from SOTEMA, the acronym of the French cloth factory in Majunga, nationalized after 1972), seen as wearing poorly and fading quickly, epitomizes the costliness and miseries of daily life. *Tergal*, imported French polyester, seen as attractive and long-lasting, exemplifies modernity.

4. The principal entertainment during services for the royal ancestors is a war dance in which Sakalava dress like former Sakalava rulers and reenact the battles between them that brought the senior "Descendants of the Gold/Red" (*Zafinimena*) to power over the junior "Descendants of the Silver/White" (*Zafinifotsy*). The clothing of the two rulers is identical except in color. They wear red and white versions of an outfit including a tall stiff hat with a train, a bandolier, and a hip wrap made from royal silks, and they carry a weapon, either a wooden rifle or a long stick, sometimes decorated with silver. The dance is not currently considered to be a form of possession. People compete to see who is the best, while spectators throw money to spur them on. Nevertheless, spirit mediums who put on the rulers' clothing inevitably become possessed in the course of dancing (Feeley-Harnik 1988).

5. In other Malagasy contexts, notably the oratory attributed to the Merina king Andriapoinimerina, covering the body is potentially treasonous. Merina subjects were exhorted to be like a cloth that presents the same face inside and out. Otherwise the "good side" (*vadi-tsarany*, from the root *vadiky* discussed below) is distinguished from the other side (Feeley-Harnik and Mack n.d.).

6. Dandouau (1908:163) reports similar prohibitions against tight, tied, and knotted clothing for pregnant women in the Analalava region. At that time, childbirth occurred in a cloth enclosure inside the house.

7. Concerning clothing and speaking on formal occasions, Ellis, a member of the London Missionary Society in Madagascar during the second half of the nineteenth century, describes a Merina oration in which body wrapping and unwrapping played a prominent role. This form of speech (*kabary*), associated with men, relies heavily on indirect means of expression.

> When anyone from the people came forward to speak [at a royal gathering of the people to hear the laws of a new sovereign], he stepped out in front of his party, with the *lamba* over his shoul-

ders gathered together in front by his left hand on his breast, while he used his right arm by stretching it forward when he began to speak, with the folds of his lamba depending from it.

The speaker usually began in a quiet clear voice, and in a short time moved gently backwards and forwards in front of his companions while speaking, his language being correct, and his utterance easy and free. As he went on his voice became louder, his speech more rapid, his step quicker, both his arms moving as he spoke; and then as he still walked to and fro, he took off his *lamba* from his shoulders, wound it round his waist, fastened it with a bow or knot on his hip, allowing the ends to hang down like the ends of a sash reaching to his ankles [sic], and then, both his arms being at liberty, he would continue his speech with increased action until it ended in a climax. This would generally elicit applause from his friends, into the midst of whom he would rush, untie his *lamba* and cover up his person (Ellis 1867:323).

8. Malagasy speakers in Mayotte are descendants of followers of the Maroseraña ruler Andriantsoly who migrated there from northwestern Madagascar toward the mid-nineteenth century. Lambek (1986) notes that although they are Muslim, there are some points of comparison. A cloth screen is usually put up around the bed of a dying person, and sometimes kept there when the corpse is washed. "Extreme care is taken to wash the corpse through a cloth covering and never to expose any of the flesh. I think this must have to do with protecting the integrity of the self, even when deceased; at the same time it obliterates their personal identity. Immediately after a death the face is covered with a cloth."

9. The Malagasy phrase is *mitaña hidy*, "to grasp the lock." *Hidy* refers to anything used to shut or lock something; to the state of being locked or closed "comme les dents d'un mort;" and to anything prohibited. The reduplicative *hidihidy* refers to clenched teeth, obstinate silence, or angry words. The verb *mihidy vava* (literally, "to close/lock the mouth") means to have the mouth clenched shut without being able to open it, or, figuratively, to keep an obstinate silence (Abinal and Malzac 1970:244–45).

10. Although I never heard Sakalava use *faha/ña* in this context, the Bara of highland Madagascar use the term to refer to the vital energy, associated especially with women, that is celebrated in the songs, dances, and cattle-wrestling contests involved in Bara funerals (Huntington and Metcalf 1979:109–16). Bara speak of their participation in the all-night pre-burial vigils in which these events take place as "going to await *faha*." Otherwise they use the term in referring to a thin cow (lacking *faha*) or to curing ceremonies intended to strengthen people (Huntington 1979:111).

11. COTONA and SOTEMA, the two major cloth manufacturers in Madagascar, send representatives throughout the island to find out which patterns and sayings sell best (Rick Huntington, personal communication). The popularity of "I like the one outside but . . . " may relate to the fact that if a man has an "out-

side child" (*zanaka an-tany*), then he should "cloth [his] wife" (*fampisikinambady*), as the compensation is known among Bemihisatra-Sakalava in the Nosy Be region, by giving her money or jewelry (Ottino 1964:243,n.1).

12. Lambek (1986), noting that cloth is the most important gift that a man gives a woman in Mayotte and that a bride's value to her husband is judged by the number of pieces of cloth he brings on their wedding day, says that the inability to wear the latest styles at public gatherings indicates lack of male support. This applies in the Analalava region as well.

The entertainment on the occasion of Tsiranana's visit to Analalava consisted of dancing by a *troupe folklorique* made up of prisoners from the nearby national penitentiary: Men wearing highland-style pants and sashed tunics in the national colors.

13. What follows is an outline of some salient features of the process by which people come to be recognized as possessed by royal spirits. More detailed descriptions of specific cases will be published elsewhere.

14. The process of "making a tromba come out" (*mampiboaka tromba*) is guided by a person known as a *fondy*, a Swahili word also used to refer to teachers of the Koran. Sakalava are aware the Muslims and Christians belittle them because they have no sacred texts. The *fondy* may be assisted by a "supplicator" (*ampangataka*) or "doorkeeper" (*ampitanambaravarana*), the same terms used to refer to the royal officials (ex-royal slaves) who intercede between the living and the royal ancestors at royal rituals such as those described below. The supplicator is often one of the sick person's relatives, but the *fondy* must be a royal spirit. As one medium said, "Anyone can talk to a royal spirit, but only a royal spirit can make a new royal spirit come out."

Sakalava spirit possession strikingly resembles *pepo* (or *sheitani*) spirit possession among Swahili speakers along the East African coast as described by Skene (1917:420–34) and Giles (1987). Here, too, spirit possession causes sickness. A male or female specialist, known as a *fundi* (or *mganga*), is hired to cure the patient by bringing the spirit out. The spirits have personal names characteristic of other members of the different "tribes" to which they are thought to belong. They are recognized by the language they speak through the person they possess. The "first step [in treating possession] . . . is to get the spirit to 'come into the head' and speak to the *fundi*," explaining what it wants in exchange for leaving the patient. Medicines are used together with music, singing, dancing, food, and drink, to induce the spirit to speak. In speaking, the spirit will name itself, but stating its name does not appear to be the main issue. The goal may be exorcism or continued interaction. When the spirit's identity has been determined, new clothes appropriate to its tribal membership must be purchased for the decisive ceremony (Skene 1917:420–23, Giles 1987:240–41).

The Swahili word *pepo* is "the equivalent of the Arab word *jin*, or devil or evil spirit (Skene 1917:420); Silamo in northwestern Madagascar refer to evil spirits, including the spirits that possess people, as *setoan* (viz. *sheitani*). Sakalava use *pepo* (From Swahili *upepo*) to refer to the wind. *Tsiny/tsigny*, referring to usually malevolent non-human spirits may derive from *jin*. *Tsigny* is also the term for the curse of Sakalava royalty; in the highlands, it means "blame, fault."

15. In fact, *ankera* is what most people eat for breakfast, even as the used

clothing sold by the Catholic Church and in the marketplaces of every large town and city is a part of everyday dress.

16. The complete outfit of the living ruler's father, an important spirit in the Analalava region, includes a tan pith helmet, dark glasses, tan sports coat like that of a French colonial functionary (sometimes called a *trois poches* or "three pockets"), white shirt, striped hip wrap, belt, silver chain bracelet, gold rings, a white cloth to wipe the sweat from his face, and a silk *lamba* (Sakalava also say *darà*) known as *sobaiha*, having purple and yellow stripes down the middle, red stripes at the edges, and red fringes. He may also carry a cigarette case and a staff. Estrade (1977:59) describes his clothing when he made a surprise visit as a "new royal spirit" at the Doany Andriamisara, the Sakalava royal center near Majunga, during the new year's service there in July 1972: "colonial pith helmet, khaki Administrator's vest, dark glasses, and cigarettes."

His son, buried in the same royal tomb though he never ruled, wears a felt hat with a brim, white jacket, white nylon shirt open at the neck, vest pocket hankerchief, striped hip wrap, silver link bracelet, gold rings, and a *sobaiha*, and he carries a gold cigarette case. The son's illegitimate half-brother wears clothing very similar to his, except for the jewelry, because the clothing is meant to indicate the kin relationships among the spirits as well as their own identities.

The clothing of the grandfather and great grandfather are less elaborate because they were so weak when they died, and thus when they possess people, it is said to be difficult to get anything on them before they collapse. Nevertheless, they are the only ones allowed to wear the finest silk cloth known as *dalahany*, which is predominantly red with black and yellow stripes and red fringes.

Lesser *trombas* wear correspondingly simpler clothing. A group of young Zafinimena rulers from Betsioko near Majunga who possess people in the Analalava region wear ordinary cotton hip wraps, undershirts or short-sleeved T-shirts, and brimmed straw hats. The spirits are further distinguished by their tastes and prohibitions in food and drink and other characteristic modes of behavior that, including manner of dress, are known collectively as their *fomba* or "customs."

17. Ellis (1835, I:280) provides some historical data on the *sarandra* in one of his many descriptions of Merina courtly dress: "The *serandrana* (sic), or sash, is used by the nobles and others for binding the salaka or other undergarments to the person of the wearer. This article is often of costly materials and rich in its appearances, being frequently of red silk with beautifully variegated borders." Sakalava in the Analalava region currently identify *sarandra* as a large "cloth from the old days (*lamba taloha*) placed on top of a big spirit possessing someone (*saha mianjaka*)."

18. *Sobaiha*, of which there were three pieces in the seven Indian merchants' shops in Analalava in 1972, then cost the equivalent of $10 = $24. At that time, a woman's body wrap, shoulder wrap, and head wrap cost about $7, and the average salary for occasional labor was $0.50 per day. *Dalahany* was no longer available. *Kikoy*, a white cotton and silk cloth with blue and yellow stripes along the edges and white fringes, worn by Zafinifotsy rulers, was also no longer

available, though a *kikoy*-like cloth made from rayon could be bought for $4 a piece. Some of the *sobaiha*, though made of silk, may have been Indian copies. Indians gradually replaced Arabs as traders on the west coast during the late nineteenth century (Rasoamiarimanana 1981:83, 88). They also may have replaced them in the trade involving Sakalava royal silks.

19. Richardson (1885:721) describes "turning clothing inside out" (*mamadilamba*), from the root *vadiky* discussed below, as "an ancient method of purification after being present at a funeral."

20. Naming is also the focus of Dandouau's (1912) description of Sakalava spirit possession in the Analalava region, attributing the appearance of possession to drunkenness. A "bad spirit"(he includes angry "good spirits" in this category) is exorcised by forcing it to say its name: "When a *tromba* has said its name, it is considered as no longer dangerous. One can invoke it personally, give it offerings and sacrifices that it is known to like" (*ibid.*: 11). Rason (1968) paraphrases Dandouau's (1912) account without acknowledging it.

Rusillon's (1912) description of "the four main stages" in which a Sakalava royal spirit appears, based on data from the Majunga region, reflects this same emphasis on speaking. "The *Misafosafo* ['the coaxing']: the *Tromba* is flattered, enticed, urged to come; the *Vakim-bava* ['the breaking into speech']: the *Tromba* gives signs of its presence; l'*Ampitononina* ['the making to speak']: the *Tromba* is made to speak; it is invoked for all possible purposes; finally the *Valy-hataka* ['the response to the request'] or rejoicing with sacrifice in gratitude (1912:117–18). Lambek also draws attention to the climactic moment in spirit possession among Malagasy speakers in Mayotte (Sakalava refugees from the Merina during the nineteenth century) when the spirit first reveals its name in public, which he sees as an act of "investiture," though he does not deal with the spirits' clothing (1981:126–27,140–50). Lambek's analysis, inspired by Geertz and Ricoeur, focuses on possession as "a system of communication."

21. "To speak" (*mikoraña*) in ordinary languages is *misaonty* in the royal vocabulary; royal persons also "roar like bulls" (*mitregny*). Sakalava explain the term *beko* in "ancestors' orders" (*bekondrazana*) as "orders." It also refers to foreign words, especially those used in drilling soldiers (Richardson 1885:77).

22. Dandouau (1911:167) says the mouth is filled with silver coins, then bound with thin strips of royal silk (*dalahany*) instead of raffia, as in the case of commoners. Two gold coins were put into the jaws of Soazara's Father's body after it had been reduced to bone (Poirier 1939:104). *Fehy vava*, the term for the cord used to tie the mouth shut, also means to impose silence on someone (see below and Richardson 1885:176–7). Among Malagasy speakers in Mayotte, "*Tromba* often have a silver coin pressed between their lips in order to get them to speak" (Lambek 1986). The words for "money" (*vola*) and "speech" (*vola/na*) may be cognates in Malagasy.

23. Estrade (1977:307) cites a Sakalava saying applied to government functionaries who act only after being bribed: "Teta's royal spirit: money appears" (*Tromban'i Teta: vola miboaka*). In referring to the money of those whom Teta has duped, the saying also acknowledges the existence of people who fake posses-

sion for financial gain. Among Malagasy speakers in Mayotte, "The ambiguity of spirits' speech . . . lies less with who is speaking—though the contrast between host and spirit always adds a level of meaning—than with whether the spirit can be trusted" (Lambek 1986).

24. Scholars of Merina reburials interpret *famadihana* (turning over) as referring to the process of turning the body over in the course of wrapping it or moving it from one tomb to another, without considering the connection that Malagasy make between inverting or reversing and subverting or betraying. The counterpart of "turning over" (*mihilaña*) for dying in the Sakalava royal vocabulary was "turning one's back" (*misamboho*) in the Merina royal vocabulary.

25. Lambek (1986) comments: "The inside/outside contrast, often expressed as that one can never know how someone 'really' feels 'inside' is also central in Mayotte experience. It's often symbolized by the *añatin trañu/an tany* opposition [inside the house/outside]. I guess the cloth wrapping of the interior of the house of the newly married couple fits this—to create a unified new interior domain. I wonder whether this concern over what you call the 'enduring indeterminancy in human relations' is related to the lack of unilineal descent and prescriptive marriage rules?"

26. Sakalava also wrap trees with cloth directly. On the northwest coast, as elsewhere in Madagascar (Aujas 1927:32; Renel 1920–21:118–27), spirits are associated with trees, especially tamarind (*madiro*) and *Dracaena* species (*hasina*). In the Analalava region, there is usually one such tree dedicated to a particular spirit that may also possess a member of the village. The tree is often surrounded by a fence to keep it from being profaned. Spirits' trees are also located in the countryside, usually near well-traveled roads. Sakalava make vows to the spirits identified with these trees in the same way that they make vows to spirits embodied in mediums or to the spirits at the royal cemetery through the 'supplicator' at the door. The fulfillment of these vows (*tsakafara*) involves wrapping the trunk of the tree in white cloth or tying pieces of white cloth to the branches.

27. The attitudes of the French to Sakalava spirit possession will be described elsewhere. I will simply note here that, confronted by the spirit's cloth and stick, colonial administrators saw only the stick. They could never decide whether it was a cane or a weapon, just as they could never decide whether the phenomenon was ceremonial or political, harmless or threatening. At best, spirit possession exemplified marked differences in linguistic style, or as Mellis put it, explaining the Sakalava preference for speaking through mediums: "the horror of Malagasy for direct discussion, for the brutal response: yes or no" (1938:71). At worst, it epitomized the natives' capacity for concealment, for lying outright. Rusillon is typical in dismissing a pile of tromba cloths as "a whole wardrobe *de demi-sauvage*" (1912:113). I think that it was precisely the "invisibility" of the soft enveloping cloth and the predominance of women involved in possession (albeit as "men") that contributed to the indecision of French officials and thus their inconsistent and ultimately inconsequential efforts at suppression. Sakalava spirit possession spread rather than diminished under colonial rule.

REFERENCES CITED

Abinal, R.P. and R.P. Malzac
    1970   Dictionnaire Malgache-Français. Paris: Editions maritimes et
            d'outre-mer.

Aujas, L.
    1927   Les Rites du Sacrifice à Madagascar. Mémoires de l'Académie
            Malgache II:3–88.

Beidelman, T.O.
    1974   Kaguru Names and Naming. Journal of Anthropological Re-
            search 30:281–93.

Bloch, M.
    1971   Placing the Dead: Tombs, Ancestral Villages, and Kinship Orga-
            nization in Madagascar. London: Seminar Press.
    1982   Death, Women, and Power. *In* Death and the Regeneration of
            Life. M. Bloch and J. Parry, eds. pp.211–30. Cambridge: Cam-
            bridge University Press.

Brain, J.L.
    1973   Ancestors as elders in Africa—further thoughts. Africa 43:122–33.

Calhoun, C.J.
    1980   The Authority of Ancestors: a Sociological Reconsideration of
            Fortes's Tallensi in Response to Fortes's Critiques. Man (n.s.)
            15:304–19.
    1981   Correspondence. Man (n.s.) 16:137–38.

Covell, M.
    1974   Local Politics and National Integration in the Malagasy Republic.
            Ann Arbor: University Microfilms International.
    n.d.   [c. 1978]   Linkage or Line of Defence? Patron-client Relationships
            in the Malagasy Bureaucracy. ms.

Dandouau, A.
    1911   Coutumes Funéraires dans le Nord-ouest de Madagascar. Bulle-
            tin de l'Académie Malgache IX:157–72.
    1912   Le *Tromba*. La Tribune de Madagascar, Octobre, pp. 8,11,15.

Dubois, H.-M.
    1938   Monographie des Betsileo (Madagascar). Paris: Institut
            d'Ethnologie.

Ellis, W.
    1835   History of Madagascar. 2 vol. London: Fisher.
    1867   Madagascar Revisited, Describing the Events of a New Reign,
            and the Revolution Which Followed. London: John Murray.

Estrade, J.-M.
    1977   Un Culte de Possession à Madagascar—le Tromba. Paris: Edi-
            tions Anthropos.

Feeley-Harnik, G.
1978   Divine Kingship and the Meaning of History among the
        Sakalava (Madagascar). Man (n.s.) 13: 402–17.
1988   Dancing Battles: Representations of Conflict in Sakalava Royal
        Work. Anthropos 83:65–85.
1990   A Green Estate: Land, Labor, and Ancestors among the Sakalava
        of Northwestern Madagascar. Washington, D.C.: Smithsonian In-
        stitution Press, forthcoming.

Feeley-Harnik, G. and J. Mack
n.d.   Cloth Production in Madagascar: A Preliminary Inquiry. British
        Museum Occasional Papers. London: British Museum Publica-
        tions.

Fortes, M.
1945   The Dynamics of Clanship among the Tallensi. Oxford: Oxford
        University Press.
1949   The Web of Kinship among the Tallensi. Oxford: Oxford Univer-
        sity Press.
1955   Names among the Tallensi of the Gold Coast. In Afrikanistische
        Studien Diedrich Westermann zum 80. Geburtstag gewidmet. J.
        Lukas, ed. pp.337–49. Institute für Orientforschung
        Veröffentlichung nr. 26. Berlin: Akademie-Verlag.
1959   Oedipus and Job in West African Religion. Cambridge: Cam-
        bridge University Press.
1961   Pietas in Ancestor Worship. Journal of the Royal Anthropologi-
        cal Institute 91:166–91.
1965   Some Reflections on Ancestor Worship in Africa. In African Sys-
        tems of Thought. M. Fortes and G. Dieterlen, eds. pp. 122–44.
        Oxford: Oxford University Press for the International African In-
        stitute.
1981   Correspondence. Man (n.s.) 16:300–02.

Giles, L.L.
1987   Possession Cults on the Swahili Coast: A Reexamination of
        Theories of Marginality. Africa 57:234–58.

Glazier, J.
1984   Mbeere Ancestors and the Domestication of Death. Man (n.s.)
        19:133–48.

Guillain, C.
1845   Documents sur l'Histoire, la Géographie et le Commerce de la
        Partie Occidentale de Madagascar. Paris: Imprimerie Royale.

Irvine, J.
1982   The Creation of Identity in Spirit Mediumship and Possession. In
        Semantic Anthropology. D. Parkin, ed. pp.241–60. New York:
        Academic Press.

Keesing, R.M.
1970   Shrines, Ancestors, and Cognatic Descent: the Kwaio and Tallensi. American Anthropologist 72:755–75.

Kiernan, J.P.
1982   The 'Problem of Evil' in the Context of Ancestral Intervention in the Affairs of the Living in Africa. Man (n.s.) 17:287–301.

Kopytoff, I.
1971   Ancestors as Elders in Africa. Africa 41:129–42.
1981   Correspondence. Man (n.s.) 16:135–7.

Kottak, C.P.
1980   The Past in the Present: History, Ecology and Cultural Variation in Highland Madagascar. Ann Arbor: University of Michigan Press.

Lambek, M.
1981   Human Spirits: A Cultural Account of Trance in Mayotte. Cambridge: Cambridge University Press.
1986   Letter of August 28, 1986.

Mellis, J.V.
1938   Nord et Nord-ouest de Madagascar. Tananarive: Imprimerie Moderne de l'Emyrne.

Murra, J.V.
1983   The Role of Cloth in Andean Civilization. Footnote to the 1962 article: "Cloth and Its Function in the Inca State". Paper contributed to the Wenner-Gren Foundation symposium on "Cloth and the Human Experience," September 28 - October 5, 1983.

Needham, R.
1954a   Reference to the Dead among the Penan. Man 54:10, art. 6.
1954b   The System of Teknonyms and Death-Names among the Penan. Southwestern Journal of Anthropology 10:416–31.

Ottino, P.
1964   La Crise du Système Familial et Matrimonial des Sakalava de Nosy Be. Civilisation Malgache 1:225–48.
1965   Le *Tromba* (Madagascar). L'Homme 5:84–93.

Poirier, C.
1939   Notes d'Ethnographie et d'Histoire Malgaches: Les Royaumes Sakalava Bemihisatra de la Côte Nord-ouest de Madagascar. Mémoires de l'Académie Malgache 28:41–104.

Rasoamiarimanana, M.
1981   Un Grand Port de l'Ouest: Majunga (1862–1881). Recherche, Pédagogie et Culture 9:78–89.

Rason, R.
1968   Le *Tromba* chez les Sakalava. Civilisation Malgache 2:207–14.

Renel, C.
   1920–21   Ancêtres et Dieux. Bulletin de l'Académie Malgache (n.s.)
              5:1–261.

Rusillon, H.
   1912   Un Culte Dynastique avec Evocation des Morts chez les Sakalava
              de Madagascar. Le "Tromba". Paris: A. Picard.

Schneider, J.
   1987   The Anthropology of Cloth. Annual Review of Anthropology
              16:409–48.

Skene, R.
   1917   Arab and Swahili Dances and Ceremonies. Journal of the Royal
              Anthropological Institute 47:413–34.

4. Dressing for the Next Life

Raffia Textile Production and Use among the Kuba of Zaire

PATRICIA DARISH

 Kuba raffia textiles are recognized as one of the great decorative art traditions of Subsaharan Africa. Their combinations of two-dimensional designs and decorative techniques are renowned. Yet discussion of Kuba textiles has centered on their rich surface design, whereas questions concerning the uses and meanings of these textiles for the Kuba have largely been ignored. Beyond aesthetic appreciation, most accounts have stressed the importance of these textiles as emblems of rank or as indicators of social prestige. But the social significance of Kuba textiles is more complex than these analyses conclude. My research among the Kuba suggests that the meaning of these textiles for the Kuba emerges from the dynamics of their production and their use.

Kuba textiles exist not solely as aesthetic objects, but also as products of a sociocultural framework that places a high value on the making of textiles. Kuba textile production is in sharp contrast to other areas of the world, such as the Pacific, where the use of special textiles is relegated to certain social strata and where exchange and recirculation of textiles dominates the social history of cloth. Instead, textile production among the Kuba requires the interdependent contributions of men and women. This complementarity of the sexes is revealed in textile production and ownership and is vis-

ually expressed in the most important context of use: the display of
textiles at funerals and their subsequent use as burial goods. Traditional Kuba textiles persist to the present because textile production
and use patterns are linked to Kuba ideas regarding social responsibility, ethnic identity, and religious belief.[1]

THE KUBA: ETHNIC DIVERSITY

"Kuba" is a name given by neighboring peoples, and later adopted
by Europeans and Americans, to a consolidation of seventeen or
more ethnic groups that organized into a kingdom as early as the
seventeenth century.[2] Collectively, the Kuba are sedentary agricul-
turists who live in the Western Kasai region of south-central Zaire,
approximately seven hundred miles east of the Atlantic Ocean. Fishing competes with agriculture as the primary occupation along the
major tributaries of the region's rivers.

The historical Kuba kingdom corresponds roughly to the
present-day administrative zone of Mweka. Mweka zone is bounded
on the north by the Sankuru River and on the west and southwest
by the Kasai and the Lulua Rivers respectively. To the north live various Mongo groups, among them the Ndengese and Nkucu directly north of the Sankuru River. To the east are the Songo Meno
and the Binji, to the south live other Kete and Lulua groups, and
west of the Kasai River live the Lele.

The Kuba have been subdivided into ethnic groupings according
to shared cultural, linguistic, and historical traits (see Vansina
1964:6–7; 1978:5). The "central Kuba" grouping includes the Bushoong, the Ngeende, the Pyaang and the Bulaang; they constitute
more than 75 percent of the total population of the Kuba kingdom.
All share a single tradition of migration into their present area and
speak a variant of the Bushoong language. The Bushoong, who
dominate the kingdom politically, are the most numerous.[3]

The "peripheral Kuba" grouping includes the Kel, the Shoowa,
and the Ngongo. Although today they share social and cultural institutions with the central Kuba, their languages and traditions of
migration are different. The Northern Kete constitute still another
Kuba grouping. Some of these Northern Kete, along with the Cwa
(pygmies), are the autochthonous inhabitants of the region.[4]

According to the latest evidence, all of the Kuba groups except for some Northern Kete and Cwa migrated to this region from the north (Vansina 1978). Following protracted struggles between these migrating groups, the Bushoong eventually achieved dominance in the area. Beginning in the seventeenth century, the kingdom was ruled from a capital village called Nsheng by a paramount ruler or *nyim*, who is traditionally chosen from one Bushoong clan.[5] While most Kuba-related ethnic groups are organized into independent chiefdoms, to this day they recognize the traditional authority invested in the Kuba paramount ruler.

From the seventeenth century through the nineteenth century the capital village of Nsheng developed into a bureaucratic center as the kingdom was divided into provinces and chiefdoms, each represented at the capital by a titleholder appointed by the *nyim* (Vansina 1964:167). Paralleling elaborate developments at the capital, titleholding evolved in most Kuba villages. A system of titleholding, which continues to the present day, is common throughout the region.

Kuba ethnic groups are organized into chiefdoms consisting of several villages, except for the Northern Kete, for whom each village is an independent chiefdom. Except for the Cwa, Coofa, and Mbeengi, the Kuba are matrilineal (Vansina 1978:6). Most Kuba villages are composed of "clan sections" made up of matrilineages. A clan section is defined as ". . .the localized expression of the lineage. It comprised only a handful of lineage members but many spouses and children, married or not, and its composition fluctuated over time" (Vansina 1978:6). Marriage follows a virilocal pattern of residence. Vansina writes elsewhere that nearly 50 percent of married people did not live in the village where they should live according to the "rules" (Vansina 1964:58–59; 1978:6). An average village contains two to four hundred people in three to six clan sections, although there are some larger villages with upwards of a thousand people.

Although village structure varies somewhat according to ethnic group, the village council (*malaang*) is the local governing body. Vansina describes this council as an outgrowth of clan section organization (Vansina 1978:111). Originally comprised of clan section chiefs, today it is composed of titled individuals. Most titleholders are male. There are two female titleholders who act as representatives for the women of the village, but do not attend council meetings on a regular basis.

Most titles are hereditary, although the means by which one achieves a title varies from ethnic group to ethnic group. In most Bushoong villages the most important title is that of *kubol* or village headman. This title is usually given to the oldest man in the village. Among the Shoowa the village headman is called *itaka* (Shoowa); as in all chiefdoms in the kingdom, he is selected from an aristocratic clan (*mbaangt*, Bushoong). Many other important village titleholders are also selected from these aristocratic clans. Historically it appears that certain titles have been conferred for life (Vansina 1978:135), while others may be vacated by dismissal or elevation to a higher title. The title will then be filled from the ranks below.

A titleholder's rank is given visible form by the right to wear certain insignia of office. For many titleholders, this includes the right to wear specific bird feathers, as certain feathers correspond directly to certain titled positions. For example, the highest ranked titles in the chiefdoms are the "eagle feather chiefs" (*kum apoong*). These chiefs are found among all of the Kuba groupings. Other emblems of regalia, such as special hat forms, belts, or staffs, may correspond directly to specific titles, or may simply indicate that those wearing or carrying such items are prominent titleholders. For example, the hat *ncok* is worn by the titleholder *Mbeem* at his funeral and appears to be worn only by this titleholder, while the belt *mwaandaan* may be worn by a number of titleholders who hold high office.

Research indicates that in the past, certain styles of men's and women's raffia skirts may have been worn only by high-ranking titleholders. Precise information on this is lacking, and although informants from aristocratic clans insist that this was true in the past, it is not current practice. Moreover, I found that patterns and styles of skirts identified by informants as only made or owned by important families were evenly distributed among people of all classes. The only time that textiles per se designate rank or title is when "eagle feather chiefs" (*kum apoong*) add decorative embellishments, such as cowrie shells or brass repoussé, to their costumes.

RAFFIA TEXTILES: COMPLEMENTARITY IN PRODUCTION

Throughout the Kuba area (and indeed throughout Zaire), the cultivation of the raffia palm and the weaving of raffia cloth is exclusively men's activity. Even the onlookers who congregate under the shed while weaving is in process are always boys and men.

Raffia cloth is woven on a single-heddle loom that utilizes untwisted single lengths of raffia fiber for both warp and weft. The size of one woven unit of raffia cloth (*mbala*) varies according to the length of the original raffia leaflet, but a typical piece of woven raffia cloth as it is cut from the loom averages 26 by 28 inches.

Once the warp has been set on the loom, weaving a piece of cloth requires about two and one-half to three hours for an experienced weaver to complete. A man usually completes a piece of cloth in an afternoon (Figure 9).

There are three kinds of woven raffia cloth. A plain woven cloth (*mbala*) is used for most kinds of skirts and is by far the most common variety produced in the region. *Mbala badinga*, woven with an extra design stick, introduces a pattern in the cloth and is used for certain men's and women's skirts. The third kind of cloth is a very coarse weave, employed for utilitarian purposes such as storage sacks or clothing worn exclusively for hunting and other work in the forest.

Woven raffia cloth is part of a labor-intensive continuum that transforms raffia fiber into a medium for the creation of ceremonial skirts. When a piece of raffia cloth is cut from the loom, it is selvageless, stiff, and coarsely textured. If the cloth is used for women's skirts, it undergoes pounding in a mortar and other softening processes before it is hemmed, dyed, and decorated. These treatments change the stiff raffia cloth into a flexible and supple cloth approaching the quality of fine linen.[6] During research in 1981 and 1982, only women were observed treating cloth this way, although in some villages there were mortars similar in style to the one Torday found employed by men. (1910:pl.XXI).

The fabrication of skirts is for the most part gender-specific; only men assemble and decorate men's skirts, and only women assemble and decorate women's skirts. Several kinds of decorative techniques are utilized by both men and women. These include various embroidery stitches, appliqué and reverse appliqué, patchwork, dyeing, stitch-dyeing, and tie-dyeing. Only women, however, practice certain embroidery techniques such as openwork and cut-pile.

It is the length, configuration of skirt panels, and style of the borders that differentiates men's from women's skirts. A woman's

Figure 9. A Northern Kete man cutting a completed unit of raffia cloth (mbala) off the loom. Photo by Patricia Darish, 1981

long ceremonial skirt may be six to nine yards in length and is essentially unbordered. It is worn wrapped around the body three to four times and secured with a belt. Much shorter "overskirts," approximately one and a half yards in length, are worn over the longer skirts. Men's raffia skirts are usually half again to twice as long as women's skirts. Generally, men's skirts are assembled with square central sections, framed by narrower, composite borders completed with a raffia bobble fringe. Men's skirts are worn so that the length is fully gathered around the waist and hips and the top border folds downwards over a belt.

Many younger women presently wear imported cloth for daily wear, in much the same manner as do women in larger African cities. Younger men prefer to wear western-style trousers and shirts. Wearing plain, undecorated raffia cloth skirts is now a habit of the older generation. However, some older Kuba men and women mimic the traditional style of skirts by purchasing imported cotton cloth and machine-hemming it in the same style as raffia skirts. Even though changes in the style and fabric used for everyday attire are apparent in the region, the weaving of raffia cloth and the production of raffia textiles are still important daily activities.

THE DYNAMICS OF TEXTILE FABRICATION

Raffia weaving and skirt fabrication and decoration are not relegated to specialists or restricted to certain clans or lineages. Traditional decorated raffia skirts and cut-pile cloths are considered tangible wealth that everyone wants to accumulate, so the participation of every adult is expected. One Bushoong informant told me that textile fabrication is just as important as hunting.

Many proverbs underline the importance of raffia textile production in everyday life. For example, an older Northern Kete man or woman may say to an unmarried woman, "If you want to marry [well], consult the diviner so that you will find a man who will make you a skirt" (that is, weave raffia cloth). This proverb illustrates that knowledge about textile fabrication is both appropriate and valued in Kuba culture. Other Bushoong proverbs affirm the integrity and importance of traditional work, such as, "A calabash without a purpose is hanging over the hearth," and, "A man without work? We'll give him black mushrooms to eat." Black mushrooms belong to a category of wild foods consumed by women and children; they are not considered "proper" food to serve to men. Both proverbs imply that a person without work to do is considered useless.[7]

For most adults, work on textiles is both a part-time activity and a part of daily routine. Thus, the processes of weaving cloth and decorating textiles typically are relegated to short work periods. Some men prepare the fiber, set the warp, or complete one of the preliminary stages of weaving or dyeing early in the day, before they go to the fields or visit their traps. Many women are able to sit down and relax for a short period after returning from their fields. During this interval, they may embroider or complete another stage of skirt decoration or construction before they prepare the evening meal. Other women only have time during the two days a week (Fridays and Sundays) when they do not usually work in their fields.

Some individuals, by the nature of their talents and preferences, regularly weave raffia cloth or specialize in certain details of fabrication. Other individuals, due to infirmity or old age, are confined to the village and therefore restricted in their activities. These individuals also spend a proportionately larger part of their time in textile production. In one Bushoong village, a woman with an arthritic hip spent most of the day embroidering cloth and caring for small children. The number of hours she spent sewing was many times that of the average woman, as she was not able to work in the fields, draw water, or pound flour.

There are certain occasions when people regularly spend more time working on textiles. During the first half of the dry season, both men and women are able to devote more attention to textile production, because they are not busy clearing fields, planting or harvesting. During periods of mourning, the immediate family of the deceased is confined to the village and the women remain in their houses from dawn to dusk. During this period, which may last anywhere from three to nine months, much time is devoted to sewing and embroidering. This labor is required to replenish the family's supply of textiles, which is depleted at the funeral (Figure 10).

OWNERSHIP OF TEXTILES

During my research, especially among the Bushoong, I found that most decorated raffia skirts are neither fabricated nor owned by a single individual, but result from the cooperative efforts of the men and women of the clan section of a matrilineage. For example, the

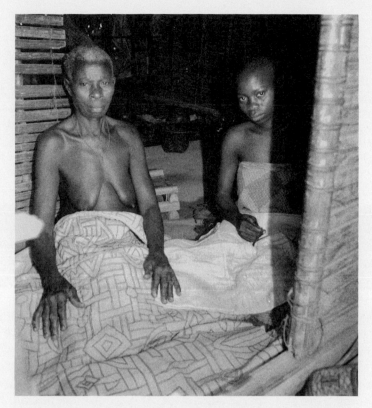

Figure 10. Two Bushoong women, restricted to their home during a mourning period, are embroidering and assembling the panels of a skirt (ncaka nsueha). Photo by Patricia Darish, 1981

construction of a long woman's skirt may be the work of half a dozen women of various ages. This fact alone challenges the Western notion of "artisanship" and "ownership;" a single raffia skirt may be interpreted as a chart of social relations and of communal artistry. While individuals may be singled out for the quality of their work, it is exceptional to find a long, elaborately decorated textile made by only one individual. Even textiles that are obviously the work of only one person are never considered the property of that person.

Several Bushoong proverbs collected by the author illustrate this assumption of group ownership:

One person can weave cloth, many can wear them.

There is no one else who can weave cloth as well as this man,
but when someone in his family died, they buried him nude.
His cloth is only for sale (to someone outside of the clan section).

The weaver is weaving, the blacksmith's helper is working the
bellows, but they are all wearing leaves!

These last two proverbs refer to the individual who does not fulfill
his (and by implication her) social responsibility—that of contributing to the group effort of textile fabrication. Thus, while the role of
individuals in the production of raffia textiles may be important, it
is often disguised and must be discussed in relationship to production within the clan section. This is especially true for women's
skirts, due to the time-consuming fine embroidery and appliqué
technique. For example, a particular Bushoong long woman's skirt
(nsueha) may be composed of more than thirty individually embroidered units, each consisting of black embroidered designs finely
stitched on doubled sections of raffia cloth. It would take one person
several years to complete a long skirt such as this.

The female head of the clan section typically directs the cloth
production of several women in her clan section. First, she chooses
the format and style of the skirt. Then she acquires cloth from her
husband or another male relative, or purchases it outright. After the
cloth has been softened, she determines the dimensions for a section of the skirt desired, doubles over the cloth, and hems it. Any
holes in the cloth resulting from the pounding process are covered
with appliqué. At this point, she may furnish one or more prepared
sections of cloth to other members of her clan to embroider.

If she supplies cloth to a novice or less skilled embroiderer, she
may baste the lines of the design onto the cloth beforehand. She
may also do this for married women living at some distance from
their matriclan. For example, the author observed a Bushoong
woman, living in another Bushoong village two days distance from
her natal home, embroider a section of a skirt her mother had given
to her to complete. In this way, completion of the textile is hastened
as large and small sections of a skirt are simultaneously worked by
several women at the same time.

As each unit of embroidered cloth is completed, it is returned
to the clan section head and sewn to other sections of the skirt al-

ready completed. Thus, the assembly of the skirt proceeds in an organic fashion over a period that may extend for several years. Aesthetically, the finished textile documents the varying skills and the repertoire of traditional designs at the disposal of the women who contributed to its fabrication.

The combination of style and decorative techniques utilized in the assembly and decoration of men's skirts dictates a working sequence different from that for women's skirts. Unlike the latter, in which each section is compositionally different, most men's skirts repeat the same design or designs throughout the entire length of the central panels and the skirt borders. Because of this linear repetition, individuals usually create men's skirts in an assembly-line fashion.

This does not mean that men's skirts require significantly less time to fabricate. Because so many separate units of decorated raffia cloth are needed to complete a man's skirt, it may take several years to acquire sufficient cloth to construct an entire skirt. This procurement is more difficult if the man fabricating the skirt does not weave raffia cloth himself.[8]

RAFFIA TEXTILES AND THEIR USES

For centuries, raffia cloth has been woven across a wide region of Central Africa (see distribution map 1, Loir 1933). In addition to its use as clothing, from the sixteenth century onward the use of raffia cloth as currency has been documented among various societies in Central Africa (Birmingham 1983; Douglas 1963; Martin 1984; Vansina 1962). It appears that in the Kuba area, raffia cloth squares were the principal currency initially and were replaced later by the cowrie imported by the Imbangala and Chokwe groups living to the south and west of the Kuba.[9] During this period, ten raffia squares or the approximate length of a skirt formed a larger unit of value (Vansina 1962:197). That cloth has retained its association with wealth or value in the Kuba area can readily be seen in the several other uses for which it has been employed.

Vansina notes that raffia cloth, among other items (including dried foodstuffs, salt, iron, utilitarian and decorative objects), formed a part of the annual tribute of many villages at the end of the dry season. Exact amounts of cloth given to the *nyim* are unknown but one village is mentioned as paying one raffia cloth for each adult man. In addition, special tribute could also be imposed whenever there was a need for certain items at the capital. Quantities of raffia cloth were also given to the *nyim* by subject chiefdoms at the death and installation of eagle feather chiefs (Vansina 1978:140–42).

Among some Kuba groups in the nineteenth century, raffia cloth and decorated skirts figured in marital contracts. For the Bushoong the bride-price was composed of both material goods and services. These services might include clearing a field, or building a house for the future mother-in-law. The future bridegroom might also weave a skirt, which his mother or sister would embroider, so that he could offer it to his mother-in-law. The actual items of the bride-price, payable at the time of marriage or even later, included cowries in bulk or in the form of *mabiim* (320 cowries sewn to a raffia cloth backing), camwood, raw raffia cloth (*mbala*), or decorated mats.[10] In the case of divorce, the spouse who initiates the divorce is responsible for the repayment of the bride-price to the other family (Vansina 1964:31–34).

Another type of marriage formerly practiced among the Bushoong calls for a bride-price much higher than that of an ordinary marriage. In this marriage the woman (*ngady akan*) was considered a "pawn" of the lineage and any children that resulted from the marriage were negotiated between lineages, according to the contract (Vansina 1978:6) Recorded bride-prices for this form of marriage listed several men's skirts as well as women's skirts, *mabiim*, beaded bracelets, necklaces, and hats. Even though among some Kuba groups, such as the Northern Kete, the payment was less, raffia cloth was always mentioned as a component of the bride-price (Vansina 1964:40–41).

Raffia cloth and skirts have also formed a required part of many legal settlements. One account mentions the loan of raffia cloth by one man to another to repay a debt (Hilton-Simpson 1912:110). In a case of adultery, a man was required to give the village tribunal 300 cowries, a man's skirt (*mapel*), and a ceremonial knife to the injured husband. After a fight that resulted in bodily harm, the guilty party was heavily fined. This fine included iron gongs, spears, swords, and raffia cloth (Vansina 1964:147).

One of the most frequently cited uses for decorated raffia textiles concerns their appearance during public events. A number of festive occasions are mentioned by early visitors to the region, although more often than not, the reason for the event is not given. Hilton-Simpson describes large dances, held frequently at Misumba (an important Ngongo chiefdom), in which women dressed similarly in either red or white skirts (1912:110–11). Hilton-Simpson also describes a dance held at the end of mourning for the *nyim's* sister. He was so fascinated by the visual impact of Kuba dress that he published a color illustration of this event on the cover of his book.

> As the sun was beginning to sink a little and the great heat of
> the afternoon became rather less oppressive, the elders assem-
> bled in the dancing-ground attired in all their ceremonial finery.
> This consisted of voluminous loin-cloths of raphia fibre bordered
> by strips of the same material elaborately embroidered in pat-
> terns, and in some cases ornamented by fringes of innumerable
> small tassels; around their waists they wore belts covered with
> beads or cowrie shells, and upon their heads nodded plumes of
> gaily coloured feathers (Hilton-Simpson 1912:201).

Torday describes the funeral of a high-ranked titleholder at the capital as follows: "A funeral dance took place the same evening, and all the elders turned up to it in their best finery. Their skirts were of rich embroidered cloth, and in their bonnets they wore bunches of gaily colored feathers" (1925:157).

Other important occasions requiring the display of elaborate dress are the *itul* rituals (described by Vansina 1964, Cornet 1980) and the funeral of a paramount ruler and subsequent installation of his successor (Vansina 1964:111–16). But these events occur infrequently and only at the capital.

Today, the most common occasion for the display of Kuba textiles is at funerals. This was true historically throughout the Kuba region, although only royal funerals are mentioned in early accounts. Torday (1925:197) described the funeral of the mother of a titleholder at the capital: "When we arrived it (the coffin) had not yet been closed and we could see the corpse, thickly painted with camwood paste and enveloped in fine cloth." Wharton (1927:128–29) states that the casket of the *nyim* Mbop aMbweeky was lined with embroidered raffia cloth, and that:

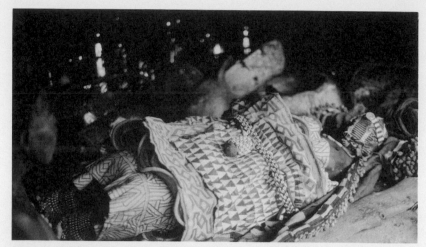

Figure 11. The body of a deceased female Bushoong titleholder, lying in state. Photo by Patricia Darish, 1981

. . . great quantities of cowrie-shell money were placed near the body so that the king might not want for funds on his long journey. Lest he hunger or thirst, meats of every description and many molds of bread, together with gourd on gourd of palm-wine were disposed within the casket. At the king's feet space was reserved for a trunk, in which were laid piece on piece of the rarest examples of the Bakuba art of cloth-weaving and embroidery.

THE CONTEXT OF USE: RAFFIA TEXTILE DISPLAY AT FUNERALS

Today, the display of elaborately decorated raffia textiles most typically occurs at funerals, when the body of the deceased is dressed with a prerequisite number of textiles and related costume accessories, including hats, bracelets, belts, and anklets. In this state the deceased is presented to mourners for several days and then buried with the textiles and other gifts (Figure 11).

The majority of textiles and costume accessories displayed on the corpse belong to the clan section of the deceased. As discussed earlier, most raffia skirts are neither owned nor fabricated by a single individual, but are the result of a cooperative effort by several people. As property of the clan section, textiles are placed on the body following a formal meeting of the section members. During this meeting, decisions are made as to precisely which textiles and other gifts will be placed on the corpse and buried with it. The textiles possessed by the clan section are unwrapped and each piece is closely examined for the quality of its workmanship. Any damage since the last examination is noted and taken into account when making the final selection. At all other times, these textiles are securely wrapped and stored with one or more leaders of the clan section.

While meetings are restricted to members, aspects of the decision-making process were gathered from interviews with numerous clan section heads and from examinations of their textile holdings. These informants often related aspects of the history of specific raffia textiles and of the individuals who created them. For example, in one Bushoong store of textiles, I was shown a short overskirt (*ncaka ishyeen*) which had a border much older than its central panel. The informant explained that the original central panel had been detached from the border and buried with a family member a number of years previously. The older border (which had been made approximately fifty years earlier by her great-grandmother) had been kept because of its age and the quality of its workmanship. She also kept the border because she wanted to show her children and her grandchildren how finely embroidered textiles used to be.

Other informants told the author that they were putting aside very old textiles for their own funerals. For example, one Bushoong woman had an extremely fine and old example of a decorated overskirt made by a relative who lived during the reign of the Kuba paramount ruler Kot aPe (ruled 1902–16). This woman was in her late seventies and could still recall the relative who had sewn the textile.

Textiles placed on the body of the deceased may also come from other sources. The spouse of the deceased (whether male or female) must also contribute one or more textiles of appropriate value to the clan section of the deceased. The type of textile given by the spouse follows the gender of the spouse, not that of the deceased; thus a widow contributes one or more women's skirts while a widower provides one or more men's skirts. These skirts are usually displayed with the corpse and subsequently buried with it.

The value and aesthetic merit of the textile given by the spouse is determined by the clan section of the deceased. Decisions may be reached after much heated discussion. At one meeting held in a Southern Bushoong village in 1982, the widow of the deceased brought a textile which was immediately rejected. The clan argued that the textile was not suitable because it was not long enough and the quality and quantity of embroidery was insufficient. The widow angrily left the meeting but later returned with a longer and more completely embroidered textile, which was accepted, subsequently displayed, and buried with the body of the deceased.

At another funeral in a Northern Kete village, I observed a man offering an incomplete man's skirt (in this case the borders of the skirt were missing) to the head of the deceased's clan section. The man was criticized and rebuffed; he was reminded that one would never wear an unfinished skirt, so why would he offer one as a gift to the deceased?

Friends are also free to contribute textiles or other gifts to the clan section of the deceased. These gifts (labaam) from individuals outside of the clan section of the deceased insure the giver a reciprocal and equivalent exchange between clan sections upon his or her own death. Labaam may consist of textiles as well as contemporary currency (Zaires), cowrie and beaded bracelets or anklets (mabiim), and necklaces or decorated belts. The bracelets, anklets, and necklaces usually adorn the deceased while he or she lies in state. These gifts may be buried with the deceased or stored in the coffers of the clan section until needed at a future occasion. Gifts of money also may be used by the clan section to defray funeral expenditures, such as those incurred for the food and palm wine consumed by relatives and friends while they attend the funeral.

While many of the gifts displayed with the deceased are traditional and customary in nature, other items relate directly to the individual's rank. Certain hat forms and other elements of regalia may also correspond directly to titleholding and therefore will be prominently displayed. As discussed earlier, this includes the types of feathers that indicate the title the deceased held in life. For example, one deceased Bushoong man held the important title of Mbeem in his village. A conical shaped hat (ncok) and guinea fowl feathers are the prerogative of this titleholder, so this special hat and feathers were included in his funeral attire. But a modern symbol of success was also included. This man had been an agricultural purchasing agent, in charge of the collection of corn, manioc, and coffee from local farmers. To represent this aspect of his rank and achieved status, the deceased was displayed and later buried with his attaché case.

PRESENTATION OF THE BODY AT FUNERALS

After the death of an adult, the women of the clan section wash the body of the deceased, then anoint it with red camwood powder.[11] The body is then dressed for display and subsequent burial.

Among all the ethnic groups in the area, a series of textiles varying in size, style, and gender are wrapped around the body in a prescribed order. Generally, the first textile encircling the body is a red-dyed raffia skirt, *mapel nshuip* (for men) or *ncak nkaana* (for women), which is devoid of surface decoration. These skirts are the simplest in design of all long Kuba skirts. Informants likened this textile to an undergarment.

Included with this first skirt is a small packet of cowries tied to a corner, just as Kuba men and women secure money or other small valuables into a knot in the corner of a skirt. Cowries are included because it is believed the deceased will use them to pay for river transport to the next world (*ilueemy*), discussed below.

Several different styles of textile may be placed on the deceased over this first skirt. With a woman, two styles of long, embroidered, and appliquéd skirts (*nsueha* or *mhahla*) are added next. Both are about six yards long. *Nsueha* and *mhahla* are similar in form and design except for two distinctive characteristics. The former is embroidered with black thread on undyed raffia cloth; the latter is first embroidered with undyed raffia thread and when completely assembled, the entire skirt is dyed red.

In Bushoong practice, these two skirts are the minimum requirement. However, the number of skirts on the body increases in proportion to the importance or wealth of the deceased. For this reason, multiples of long, embroidered textiles may also be added. Shorter women's overskirts are also employed as the top layer of the ensemble.

For a deceased man, several different skirt styles may be added over the underskirt. A very popular choice is a red-dyed skirt with a patchwork black-and-white rectangular border and bobble fringe (*kot'a laam'a mbokihey*). It is made and used all over the region. There are other styles of long men's skirts which may also be added (*ndono kwey*, *masheshela*, and *kumishinga*).

Some Kuba-related ethnic groups elect to add additional textiles as the final covering. For example, the Shoowa add sections of cut-pile and embroidered cloth (*winu*) as a final covering over the displayed body. Research indicates that this is the primary, traditional purpose of these cut-pile cloths.

As noted above, in addition to textiles there are many other costume accessories made by the Kuba, consisting of strands of beads or beaded raffia bracelets, belts, and anklets. These are rarely worn except as costume elements at the time of burial. Other items, such as hats, feathers, and belts, differentiate titled men and women from non-titled individuals. The total ensemble, the multiples of textiles and costume accessories, is of overriding importance to the Kuba aesthetic at funerals.

When the body is completely dressed it is displayed, usually sitting upright on a wooden support bier, for several days under an open shed. Three days seems to be the usual number in contemporary practice. Women of both clan section and village maintain a vigil under the shed with the body during the entire time it is displayed. Men gather under a shed some distance away. If the deceased was an initiated man, prescribed rituals, including songs, dances, and possibly masquerade performances, may take place during this time (Binkley 1987a).

Shortly before burial, the men of the clan section oversee construction of a coffin made from large decorated mats secured to a bamboo framework. The coffin may be fabricated in imitation of a pitched-roof house, and is often meticulous in its attention to architectural detail. Other coffins are fashioned in the same manner but with a flat roof. At the time of burial, the corpse is placed in the coffin and taken to the cemetery. Just before it is lowered into the ground, additional items such as currency, drinking cups, or costume elements, may be placed in the coffin. At one Bushoong funeral, a relative lifted the edge of the coffin and placed the tattered everyday hat worn by the deceased inside.

DRESSING FOR THE NEXT LIFE

The dressing of the corpse reflects both individual and group beliefs about proper burial. Although ideas concerning life after death are not systematically codified, there is a general belief in *ilueemy*, the land of the dead. The deceased is thought to travel to this land by crossing a river and to reside there until his or her spirit returns to the land of the living, usually after one or two generations.[12] For this reason coffins are fabricated in imitation of house construction while currency—both modern, in the form of Zaires, and traditional, in the form of cowries—is included with the body. Although Vansina (1978a:199) states that belief in *ilueemy* is archaic, I found it prevalent in the Kuba area in 1981 and 1982. I met individuals in many villages who were believed to be reborn (*nshaang*). One informant commented upon the depth of knowledge and other unusual talents of a young man as proof of his *nshaang* status.

Because of the pervasive belief in *ilueemy*, there is overwhelming concern that the deceased be dressed properly at burial. The Kuba believe that only raffia textiles are an appropriate mode of dress for burial. Several informants noted that they would not be recognized by deceased relatives in *ilueemy* if they were not dressed in traditional textiles. In addition they were concerned with ethnicity; they wished to be recognized by relatives and visitors to the funeral and in the afterlife as being a Bushoong, a Kete, or a Shoowa person, replete with all emblems of attained title or status.

In the Kuba area, to be buried in anything but traditional attire is tantamount to being buried nude. Even individuals who have not worn raffia skirts for twenty years or more have stated that when they die, they will be buried in traditional dress. Another Bushoong proverb expressed this attitude succinctly: "As bamboo does not lack roots, a man cannot dismiss his origins." To Bushoong (or Kete or Shoowa) men and women, it is imperative to express this belief in cultural heritage, especially at funerals and in visual form through the display of traditional attire. This is not an archaism or a revival but rather a conscious preservation of cultural values.

If individuals are concerned with the appropriate self-presentation at their own funerals, the clan section also is concerned about the proper burial of its members for several reasons. It is widely believed that deceased people have a malevolent spirit (*mween*), and that this spirit may become angered if all due respect is not paid to the deceased at the funeral. It is believed that the *mween* is particularly concerned that respect due his or her rank and achieved status be recognized by the clan section at the funeral (Binkley 1987a).

Fear of reprisals from the slighted *mween* acts as a strong motivating force on the clan section. A slighted *mween* may cause problems ranging from unsuccessful hunting or fishing to illness, infertility, or death for members of the clan section. The malevolent spirit of a deceased titleholder is considered far more powerful than that of an untitled individual; if an important titleholder's *mween* is angered, the entire village may be harmed. In order not to offend a powerful *mween*, there may be protracted discussions among clan section members to make certain that burial arrangements have been properly made.

Concern for prestige provides another motive for displaying the appropriate number and quality of textiles on the deceased. If the clan section of the deceased presents the proper textiles in sufficient number and quality, it shows the village that the clan section acknowledges its responsibilities and honors and respects its members at the time of death, and thus allows the clan section to enhance its prestige. Understandably, a public funeral provides an open forum for gossip and unsolicited criticism. At one Bushoong funeral, a woman outside the clan section criticized the textiles displayed on the corpse. She said that the quality of a certain textile was insufficient as it did not have enough embroidery, and that the clan section should have placed a greater quantity of textiles on the body. Another Bushoong informant stated that gossip such as this is the primary activity at funerals.

Following most adult deaths, a crucial ritual is conducted at the grave site before the coffin is fully lowered into the ground and covered with earth. This ritual is performed by the surviving spouse and a member of the opposite sex from the clan section of the deceased. Kneeling on opposite sides of the coffin, each marks the little finger of the other's right hand with white clay or kaolin. This gesture severs the social bonds of marriage and kinship ties between the deceased and the living. If this ritual is not performed, the deceased will appear in dreams (especially to the spouse) and may also be a source of harm to other members of the clan section. For surviving clan-section members, this ritual shows the deceased that the clan section has fulfilled its responsibilities to the deceased and should be left in peace.

WHY THE DEAD WEAR DECORATED RAFFIA TEXTILES

In Kuba villages today, the use of undecorated raffia cloth for everyday clothing has been largely supplanted by western dress such as shirts and trousers for men, and blouses and printed cotton wrappers for women. But despite this adoption of modern dress, the display of decorated raffia textiles continues to be a central element in the ritual surrounding death. Undoubtedly, the aesthetic appeal of these textiles in ceremonial and funeral contexts is strong. But the Kuba have many reasons in addition to aesthetics for giving decorated raffia textiles such a major role at funerals. The persistence of this tradition is fundamentally linked to the burial of textiles at funerals, because the Kuba believe that the process of making textiles is as important as the textiles themselves.

As we have seen, both male and female members of the clan section are essential participants in all of the stages of textile production. Thus, the display of textiles at funerals powerfully reaffirms the enduring social relationships that encompass the complementary and interdependent efforts of the men and women of the clan section. These relationships are acknowledged and reproduced in the social arena of the funeral. Both men's and women's skirts are placed on the body of the deceased when it is displayed in the village. These textiles are made and given by clan section members and others who expect the same tributes in return at their funerals. In this respect, exchange of textiles is a one-way process, moving from the living to the dead as the textiles are buried with the deceased. Yet this very process supports Kuba assertions of ethnic identity and adherence to traditional beliefs in the afterlife.

Even though Kuba textiles do not recirculate, burying them is not seen as a depletion of the system. Members of the clan section are constantly renewing this aesthetic and unifying resource as part of their everyday work. A Bushoong proverb states: "You can take from a raffia palm, but you can never deplete its supply."[13] For the Kuba, both the decorated textiles and the material from which they are made are powerful symbols of abundance and wealth. The raffia palm has been an inexhaustible resource for centuries, exploited not only for decorated and plain clothing, but also for shelter, palm wine, and food. Moreover, raffia cloth squares have been a principal currency and have formed a major portion of the wealth of the Kuba paramount ruler. The burial of these labor-intensive raffia skirts at funerals recalls these ancient ideas of abundance and wealth. Thus the Kuba still choose raffia cloth for funerals because it is a potent symbol of security and continuity, actively linking the living to one another as well as to the community of the recently deceased.

ACKNOWLEDGMENTS

Research among the Bushoong, Shoowa, and several Northern Kete peoples residing in Mweka zone, Republic of Zaire was supported by the Fulbright-Hays Doctoral Dissertation Research Abroad Program through Indiana University for 21 months during 1981 and 1982. This paper is dedicated to Norm Schrag, whose scholarship, friendship, and sense of humor are an enduring memory to his Indiana University colleagues. I would like to thank Mary Jo Arnoldi, David Binkley, Ivan Karp, Doran Ross, Jane Schneider, Jan Vansina, and Annette Weiner for reading previous versions of this paper.

NOTES

1. Except for the Lele (Douglas 1963), we do not have precise ethnographic details of past or current use patterns for raffia textiles among neighboring peoples.

2. See Emil Torday (1910;1925) and especially Jan Vansina (1954;1964;1978a) for detailed accounts of Kuba history, ethnography, and linguistics.

3. The last census taken of all the Kuba people was in 1950, when the population was estimated to be over 70,000 (Vansina 1964:8).

4. These groupings have been outlined by Vansina (1964:6–7;1978:5).

5. All terms are cited in the Bushoong language, unless otherwise noted.

6. Some decorated textiles, such as the cut-pile and embroidered Shoowa *winu*, the Bushoong *ncaka buiin*, and the raffia cloth employed for the borders of men's skirts, do not utlilize softened cloth.

7. These proverbs were collected in Kete and Bushoong villages by the author during 1981–82.

8. I returned to one Bushoong village a year later to find the production of the center sections of a man's skirt at the same stage I had observed a year earlier.

9. According to Jan Vansina, personal communication, 1987.

10. In the late nineteenth century and into the twentieth, bride-prices in cowries and francs rose tremendously, because young men did not want to work for their mothers-in-law and the reduction in services caused the amount to rise (Vansina 1964:31–34). Though I do not have data for contemporary practices, I suspect that even the custom of bride-price has been dropped by many of the Kuba groups.

11. Camwood powder is used as a cosmetic in Central Africa; it is still favored by many older Kuba women today.

12. Vansina (1978:198–99) states that the "proto-Kuba" practiced ancestor worship, but adopted some of the religious beliefs of the Kete, in this case the concepts of *nshaang* and *ilueemy*, when they moved south of the Sankuru River. These concepts are more thoroughly discussed in Vansina 1958.

13. Recorded at a Southern Bushoong funeral in 1981 (Binkley 1987b).

REFERENCES CITED

Adams, Marie Jeanne
    1978   Kuba Embroidered Cloth. African Arts, 12(1):24–39,106–07.

Binkley, David Aaron
    1987a   Avatar of Power: Southern Kuba Masquerade Figures in a Funerary Context. Africa, Journal of the International African Institute, 57(1):75–97.
    1987b   Personal communication.

Birmingham, David
    1983   Society and Economy before A.D. 1400. *In* History of Central Africa, Vol. I. David Birmingham and Phyllis M. Martin, eds. pp. 1–29. London: Longman Group Limited.

Cornet, Joseph
    1980   The Itul Celebration of the Kuba. African Arts, 13(3):28–33,92.

Douglas, Mary
    1963   The Lele of the Kasai. London: Oxford University Press.

Hilton-Simpson, M.N.
    1911   Land and Peoples of the Kasai. London: Constable and Company Ltd.

Loir, Helene
    1935   Le tissage du raphia au Congo belge, Musée Royal de l'Afrique Centrale, Anthropology and Ethnography, Sér.3, Vol. 3, No. 1. Brussels.

Mack, John
    1980   Bakuba Embroidery Patterns: a Commentary on their Social and
            Political Implications. *In* Textiles of Africa, Dale Idiens and K.G.
            Ponting, eds. Bath: The Pasold Research Fund Ltd.

Martin, Phyllis M.
    1984   Power, Cloth and Currency Among the Societies of the Loango
            Coast. Paper presented at the annual meeting of the African
            Studies Association, New Orleans, 1984.

Picton, John and John Mack
    1979   African Textiles, Looms, Weaving and Design. London: British
            Museum Publications Ltd.

Torday, Emil and T.A. Joyce
    1910   Notes ethnographiques sur les peuples communement appelés
            Bakuba, ainsi que sur les peuplades apparentées: les
            Bushongo. Musée Royal de l'Afrique Centrale, Anthropology
            and Ethnography, Sér. 4, No. 2. Tervuren.
    1925   On the Trail of the Bushongo. London: Seeley Service and Co.

Vansina, Jan
    1954   Les tribus Ba-Kuba et les peuplades apparentées. Musée Royal
            de l'Afrique Centrale, Ethnographic Monographs, No. 1,
            Tervuren.
    1954   Les valeurs culturelles des Bushong. *Zaire* 8:899–910.
    1958   Les croyances religeuses des Kuba. *Zaire* 12:725–58.
    1962   Trade and Markets Among the Kuba. *In* Markets in Africa, Paul
            Bohannan and George Dalton, eds. Evanston: Northwestern Uni-
            versity.
    1964   Le Royaume Kuba. Musée Royal de l'Afrique Centrale, Anthro-
            pology and Ethnography, No. 49. Tervuren.
    1978   The Children of Woot, A History of the Kuba Peoples. Madison,
            Wisconsin: University of Wisconsin Press.

Wharton, Conway
    1927   The Leopard Hunts Alone. New York: Fleming H. Revell.

5. Why Do Ladies Sing the Blues?

Indigo Dyeing, Cloth Production, and Gender Symbolism in Kodi

JANET HOSKINS

The unusually large, bold patterns and rich blues and rusts of Sumbanese warp ikat cloth have attracted foreign buyers for over a century, making the textile traditions of this isolated Eastern Indonesian island the focus of an important export trade. To European visitors, the cloths appear as objects of ostentatious display and public presentation. Worn as ceremonial costume by both men and women, they form part of marriage payments from the bride's family, are used as "sails" on the "ships" that drag stones for megalithic graves, and as banners in feasts, processions, and welcoming ceremonies for important officials. Suspended from the walls or ceiling on ceremonial occasions, warp ikats also make sumptuous funeral shrouds, wrapping the corpse in as many as a hundred different layers (Adams 1969, Hoskins 1986).

The exuberant unfolding of several meters of color-saturated textiles, patterned with plant, animal, and human designs, is the public face that Sumbanese cloth producers present to the outside world. In isolated huts secluded in the bush, another face of cloth production is hidden: Here, indigo dyeing is conducted as a cult of female secrets. Hedged by a system of taboos that forbid access to all men, and to women at certain stages in their reproductive cycles, older women practice an occult art that is associated with herbalism,

141

midwifery, tattooing, and (more covertly) witchcraft. Soaking in the indigo bath, threads take on sacred powers that make obligations binding, proffer blessings, and enclose fertility in a sheltered bundle. In the bath, tied clusters of thread define the white outlines of motifs that will appear, like a photographic negative, against the blue background of the finished cloth. The design is created when the dye is applied, etching out shapes reminiscent of the bridewealth objects and animals controlled by men, in a pattern that will assume its final form once the weft threads are interwoven to produce the cloth.

The art of traditional dyeing is merged with the production of herbal medicines, poisons, abortifacients, and fertility potions in a body of occult knowledge known as *moro*, "blueness," which is the exclusive possession of a few female specialists. In its magical aspects, as a series of mysteries that only cult initiates may penetrate, this "blue art" is a ritual as well as a technological process. Associated with myths about a witch ancestress from the neighboring island of Savu, the production of Sumbanese textiles is also linked to theories of human conception and the growth of the fetus within the womb. A metaphoric parallel between the production of children and the production of cloth informs exchange relations established through the transfer of cloth and the transfer of women from one ancestral village to another. Finally, cloth itself becomes the medium for an inarticulate protest against perceived injustices that afflict women and give their sorrow its particularly "blue" coloring.

THE SUMBANESE "BLUES": INDIGO DYEING IN CONTEXT

Sumba is the fourth island east of Bali, lying south of the Lesser Sunda Island chain which stretches out toward Timor and eventually Australia. With an arid climate and an often-precarious agricultural base, the Sumbanese subsist on a mixture of garden-grown rice and corn, pastoralism (raising cattle, buffalo, and small spirited horses for export), and trade. Slaves, livestock, and textiles were the most important items of trade in the nineteenth century, both between traditional domains and to ships from Holland, Makassar, Java, and Sumbawa. Many of the finest cloths from this period ended up in Dutch homes as blankets and wallhangings, because their appealing variety of shapes and representational forms was dramatically different from the stripe patterning of textiles produced on neighboring islands. Export of Sumbanese textiles continued after the Dutch took political control of the island in 1913, and has intensified since independence in 1949.

Warp ikat cloths are produced along the coastal areas, where wild indigo plants grow, and the most famous cloths are those from Kanatang and Kaliurang, in the eastern half of the island. Kodi, at the farthest western tip, produces a distinctive style of ikat-patterned textile, whose more abstract, geometric design shows a greater influence from imported Indian *patola* cloths. Kodi is the major textile-producing area for the western part of the island. During the "hungry season" of October to December, indigo-dyed Kodi textiles are often traded for food from the more fertile interior regions.

Fieldwork in Kodi, undertaken over a period of three years (from 1979 to 1981, with return visits in 1984, 1985, and 1986) revealed a still-lively production of traditional cloths, despite the increased use of commercial threads and dyes, especially for the reddish colors. Indigo-dyed cloths remain the only ones that are acceptable for the most important ritual and ceremonial occasions. Virtually all Kodi women learn to bind the threads into patterns for ikat dyeing, and to weave on a backstrap loom. Only a few, however, become initiated into the mysteries of indigo dyeing, which is part of a complex of magical and technical skills usually passed down the maternal descent lines.

When young, unmarried girls are introduced to the cults, they learn to chew up the herbal preparations used to make the dyes. They are not allowed to bring cloths to be dyed until they have reached sexual maturity—but then they are excluded from the dyeing process for long periods of time, because it is seen as dangerous to menstruating or pregnant women. Regular practitioners of indigo dyeing are all women past menopause, who have already borne children and acquired the tattoos on the forearm and calf that mark female achievement of wifehood and motherhood. Thus, participation in cloth production marks stages in the female life cycle, and creates a "rite of maturity," celebrating the culmination of a woman's career by her acquisition of hidden knowledge and greater control over the processes not only of dyeing, but also of childbirth, menstruation, and menopause.

Indigo dyeing serves to define boundaries: Between men and

women, between those who have learned its mysteries and those who have not, and between degrees of competence and knowledge of the herbal preparations used. It creates a hierarchical order, in that participants in indigo dyeing and the "blue arts" are not only transformed but gain status. Dyeing also involves some degree of danger, suffering and pain. The indigo bath is seen as polluting to women at certain stages in the reproductive cycle, and its unpleasant smell evokes (for the Kodi) the odor of corpses, decay, and putrefaction.

Overcoming such fears and learning the secrets of the indigo dye bath may also qualify a woman to practice as a midwife and healer (*tou tangu moro*, literally a "person who applies blueness"— referring here to herbal medicines). After she has passed the age of childbearing herself, a woman may transform her passive role as a "receptacle" for the growing fetus into the more active one of controlling and regulating the fertility of others. She acquires knowledge which gives her greater control over physiological functions, and wears indigo-colored tattoos on her forearms as a badge of her reproductive success. Differences between men and women are elaborated as a contrast between durable, male objects such as metal and stone, and female vitality and production of semidurables (cloth and children) in a mysterious domain of their own. The very secrecy of these rites is presented to men as part of the "mystery" of the reproductive process, which women are believed to affect through occult techniques.

Kodi belief emphasizes similarities between indigo dyeing and the processes of pregnancy and childbirth. The "binding medicines" used in the dye bath to make colors fast are also administered to women after childbirth to control bleeding. However, the degree of control possible in indigo dyeing is greater than in the dangerous and often-unpredictable practice of midwifery. The transfer of substances from one domain to another reflects a conscious effort to marshal "the blue arts" as a form of control over the body, as well as female ornamentation.

In addition to its association with the production of children, the logic of exchange, and the life cycle, indigo dyeing finds expression in women's most developed form of the verbal arts: The singing of formalized songs of lament (*hoyo*) at funerals and other situations where misfortunes are recalled and shared. The songs use metaphors taken from textile production to reflect on situations of loss—bereavement, serious illness, the departure of a loved one to prison or exile. They are most often performed at mortuary ceremonies, but also treat the painful separation of the bride from her natal home at marriage. The transfer of brides and of corpses, both wrapped in textiles and reduced to a state of passive detachment, is part of a larger pattern in which weddings and funerals are modeled after one another. Feelings of detachment and separation are the focus of the songs, which speak of the heart (*ate dalo*, literally, "liver") as tinged with the blueness of affliction. Like the tradition of "blues" in our own society, they show a kinship of suffering among persons who consider themselves powerless.[1]

Kodi indigo cults are distinct from male cultic preoccupations with ancestors, headhunting, and warfare. They show that female arts and weapons are distinct from those of men, and have a darker and more mysterious coloring, directly grounded in the bodily experience of childbearing. I will explore the meanings of these differences, their implications for an understanding of the female resentment, and the development of alternate arenas of power. My portrait of the "blue arts" has six sections: (1) the place of indigo dyeing in relation to patrilineal ancestral villages and matrilineal clans; (2) the dangers of "blueness"; (3) the metaphoric and metonymic relations between cloth production and the production of children; (4) cloth in mythology and song; (5) the social meanings of the exchange of cloth and the exchange of women; and (6) the tattooing of textile designs on the body, to enclose female reproduction within the partrilineage and celebrate the legitimate sexuality of mature women. Finally, I will consider how these themes relate to differences established between women at varying points in the life cycle, the fragile and ephemeral character of cloth valuables and human children, and the linkages established between women and cloth in this and other societies.

PATRILINEAGES, MATRICLANS, AND THE SECRETS OF INDIGO

About 50,000 Kodi live in scattered hamlets near their gardens, returning to large ancestral villages along the coast for calendrical ceremonies, funerals, and feasts. The prestige economy of feasting, bridewealth payments, and fines is based on the circulation of large numbers of horses and buffalo, although ownership of herds is concentrated in the hands of a few wealthy men. The agricultural work of planting and harvesting garden crops of dry rice, corn, and tubers is shared by both sexes, but men have exclusive control of the public domain of exchange. They negotiate transfers of land and livestock, marriages, mortuary payments, and feasting obligations. The most prominent men may attain the ceremonial title of *rato*, "great feast giver," which assures them of a permanent place in ancestral genealogies. A few women, famous priestesses and singers, were also said to have become *rato* in the past, but none were living at the time of my research.[2]

Alongside the competitive system of prestige feasting which creates "Big Man" leaders, ideas of hierarchy and complementarity are developed through a diarchic division of ceremonial tasks. Notions of rank and precedence define the holders of important priestly offices from among the descendants of particular ancestral villages. Noble families in the past had large numbers of slaves, transferred along with brides at marriage and attached to their houses as dependents, working in the gardens or tending livestock for absent owners. Many of the most sacred heirloom objects are still stored in cult houses inhabited only by slaves, who guard these objects at considerable risk to their lives because of the taboos associated with them. Three-fourths of the population describe themselves to government census takers as followers of the traditional system of spirit worship, called *marapu*, while about 13 percent are Protestant and 9 percent Catholic.

Kodi has long been known for its unusual system of "double descent" (Van Wouden 1956, Needham 1980) where membership in "houses" (*uma*) and villages is established around a core of agnates, and women are recruited into them through the exchange of marriage gifts. Inalienable ties of birth and blood are traced along the matriline (*walla*), establishing strict rules against incest within the female bloodline. Members of a house worship patrilineal ancestors and other guardian deities (*marapu*) dwelling in the house tower and pillar, and also share rights to land, ritual office, livestock, and the heirloom objects making up its sacred patrimony. Even when they live for much of the year in isolated garden hamlets, they return to their ancestral villages for major rituals and funerals.

In contrast to the corporate rights and obligations transmitted along the patriline, members of a matriline share a common bodily substance, and are believed to show similarities of personality and character. They have no collective functions to bring them together, nor are female ancestresses named and propitiated separately from their husbands.

While the name of a given patriclan is often taken from the tree that is planted in the center of the ancestral village and serves as a communal altar, the name of a matriclan is a personal name or the name of a region. The term *walla* means "flower," and refers to the "flowering" of a woman's descendants like blossoms along the boughs of the great trees planted in the village squares. But the seeds and sprouts of future clansmen are identified as male children. (*Ha wu wallada*, literally the "seeds and flowers," is translated as male and female children, while *kahinye mono katulla*, the "sprouts and shoots," are male descendants who will continue the patriline.)

There is no official ritual associated with the matriclans, but secrets such as those used in dyeing thread, preparing certain herbal medicines, and assisting childbirth or abortion may be passed along the female line. Blood ties between members of the same matriclan can surface as important in situations where factions form across clan boundaries, and these ties are often blamed for divisiveness within ancestral groupings. Some specific matriclans are associated with the hereditary transmission of witchcraft and sorcery.

Because of such negative associations, people's matriclans are often kept secret from all but their closest relatives. They may not be openly discussed until marriage negotiations, when rules of matriclan exogamy make it necessary to reveal those bloodlines. Although both matriclans and patriclans are exogamous, incest within the matriclan is much more dangerous. It can result in immediate hemorrhaging, miscarriages, or even death, and cannot be ritually mediated. In contrast, persons from different houses who wish to marry within the patriclan can do so by arranging an adoption and a change in marriage payments.

Women's bodies are seen as vessels for the transmission of immutable substances, whereas men's bodies contribute form, social position, and membership in agnatic groups which must be verified by exchange payments. Kodi theories of conception stress the necessity of both male and female contributions, but acknowledge that women have more control over pregnancy and childbirth, and that the infants born to them remain "of the mother's substance" until adulthood.

Indigo-dyeing secrets are passed on as part of the lore of matriclans, but are seen as having an exogenous origin: The bringer of the art of indigo dyeing was a woman from the neighboring island of Savu (*warico haghu*), who migrated to Sumba at some point in the distant past. Current Savunese inhabitants of Sumba are usually credited with considerable occult knowledge, but are also known as witches and practitioners of a kind of "black magic," locally associated with the color blue.[3] Some accounts say that the ancestress of dyeing was accompanied by her husband (*mone haghu*) who was a metalworker. Metalworking and textile dyeing are associated in a couplet that refers to both of these imported arts (*beti kyamba, buri bahi,* "dipping cloth, pouring iron"), and must be repeated in invocations to their respective ancestral spirits whenever the arts are practiced.

The two arts are also associated in the couplet name for the Creator, a double-gendered deity addressed as the Mother Binder of the Forelock, Father Smelter of the Crown (*Inya wolo lindu, Bapa rawi ura*). The female aspect of creation is presented as a parallel to the female crafts of binding and dyeing thread (here, the hairs at the forelock, seat of the vulnerable life force or *hamaghu*), while the male aspect smelts the harder skull at the crown (seat of destiny, the enduring soul or *ndewa*). Each of these traditional crafts establishes gender boundaries in a rigorous and exclusive fashion: It is forbidden for women to witness the process of metal smelting, just as it is forbidden for men to see the indigo bath for dyeing thread.

Both Sumba and Savu are famous for their elaborately decorated textiles, which have been exported to foreign markets since the nineteenth century. The motifs used on Savunese textiles are primarily floral and ornamental, although traditionally they indicated membership in a matrilineal moiety system called the "greater" or "lesser" blossom (Fox 1977). In East Sumba, representations of horses, deer, crocodiles, roosters, snakes and skulltrees fill the horizontal panels with symbols of wealth and male animals. In West Sumba, and particularly Kodi, more geometric motifs depict animal parts (the "buffalo eye" and "horse's tail") as well as wealth items like the gold omega-shaped ear pendants used in bridewealth payments (*hamoli*).

THE DANGERS OF "BLUENESS"

Textiles are the most important wealth items produced by women, and they are also the best way for modern women to enter the cash economy. Most cloths sold at local markets are of inferior quality and use modern thread and dyes, but valuable pieces are privately bought or exchanged at the price of a large pig, horse, or buffalo. Because of the constant demand for quality indigo-dyed cloth for ritual exchange, the "blue-handed women" (*warico kabahu moro* or *tou betingo*, "indigo dippers") of Kodi are highly respected and enjoy a certain economic independence.[4]

The advantages of acquiring skills in textile dyeing are hedged by the dangers involved in the process, and its associations with witchcraft, death, and the acrid smell of corpses. The term for the color produced by indigo (*moro*) designates a range of colors from blue to green, and is also used to mean raw or uncooked. The darkest shades, a kind of blue-black, are the most valued. Among the mysteries associated with indigo dyers, their secrets for making the dye as dark and heavily saturated as possible receive special attention. Descendants of two specific *walla* (Walla Kyula and Walla Cubbe) are said to have acquired these secrets from the indigenous peoples of the area. Significantly, these *walla* are also the ones most commonly associated with the hereditary transmission of witchcraft.

Witches, who can be either male or female, are believed to have extensive knowledge of local herbs and medicines, and to eat their foods raw, since their ancestors did not know how to make fire, cook food, or plant crops at the time that the Kodi arrived. Folk etymology links their name, *tou hamarango*, to either the "eaters of raw foods" (from *mu moro*) or the "eaters of blue substances," depending on how the term *moro* is used. Witchcraft can be detected through bluish marks at the navel, fingertips, or eye sockets, and victims of witch attacks often complain of seeing a bluish color moving around them, interrupted by flashes of a red light.

A death caused by a violent accident, murder, or drowning is called a "blue death" (*mate moro*), and the soul of the victim is said to fly off into the sky. Relatives cannot bury the body within the stone tombs of the ancestral village until a special ceremony has been performed to "call back" the lost soul. As the corpse waits, rotting, for a temporary earthen burial, its putrefying smell is said to be particularly intense and reminiscent of the indigo dye bath.

The association of death and indigo makes the dye bath dangerous for women who are in the process of creating a new life within their bodies. Pregnant women may not look at the dye pots, because it is believed that the sight of churning, dark liquids within the pot would dissolve the contents of their wombs and cause an immediate abortion. Conversely, menstruating women are barred from the indigo dyeing, since the flow of their blood would make the dyes "run" irregularly. The two-directional magical effect is interesting: Female fertility that is not being used to produce children is dangerous to the indigo bath, but once conception has occurred it is the indigo which has the dangerous power to dissolve the fetus.[5]

I interpret the idea that indigo dyeing threatens normal female fertility as an effort to create a conceptual separation between two forms of creative production: The coagulation of blood within the womb (caused by the father's contribution of sperm) and the coagulation of dyeing agents in the textile bath. A metaphoric parallel is obviously established between womb and dyeing pot, and the use of some of the same herbs and barks reinforces the association metonymically. Kodi theories of human conception refer to the father's sperm as the form-giving agent, comparing the male role to the metalworker who smelts a vat of molten liquids into an enduring shape. The lime that is added to the indigo pot, called the "male ingredient" or the "husband" (*laghi*) of the indigo plant, is the chemically active substance, the mordant, that causes the color to "take."

Kodi theories of sexual reproduction also follow a betel metaphor. As in the quickening process of pregnancy, the lime is added to the betel quid, producing a reddish liquid from the green pulp of the areca nut and betel catkin that gives a caustic "bite." Betel chewing has a clear role in courtship, usually as a preliminary to sexual relations. A girl indicates her willingness to sleep with a suitor by agreeing to chew betel with him, and a neglected wife may complain to her relatives if her husband does not "give her betel" in order to produce a child. The exchange of betel is a public activity initiated by men, whereas in textile dyeing women procure their own lime and combine it themselves in secret. The cloth "child" that they produce is created independently of men, and quickened by their own powers.

Betel and cloth differ in other ways as well, which define male and female domains of creative activity. The betel quid is a blue-green mixture of fresh nuts and leaves or catkin, which is made red by the addition of lime. The indigo bath, in contrast, is an originally muddy reddish-brown mixture of ash, barks, and roots, which is "quickened" into a deep blue by the fermenting action of lime. Betel is the marker of public social interactions and visiting, which may lead to marriage and childbirth. Textile dyeing presents once again an inverse pattern: It is secret, restricted to women, and carried on in the privacy of secluded huts. I propose that indigo dyeing is dangerous to men because it represents an independent female creation, an appropriation of male "quickening" substances without male control, and a process similar to childbirth that is outside of the ancestral value system.

CLOTH PRODUCTION AND THE PRODUCTION OF CHILDREN

The metaphoric parallels Kodi women establish between the dyeing of cloth and the formation of a child in the womb can be discerned in the language used to describe the two processes, and their sharing of certain taboos. First, there is the "quickening" (*pa kati,* "the bite") induced by the male lime when it is added to the mud bath in which stems and leaves of the indigo plant (*rou kanabu*) have been soaking along with various plant nutrients (among them tamarind, ironwood, and rice straw). This is akin to the conception of the child, as it allows for the chemical reduction of fermentation. Second, there is the stage of soaking the thread (bound into bundles with gewang leaf or commercial twine) in the dissolved and fermented indigo (yellow or light green in color) so that the soluble indigo can penetrate the fibers. Only after the pale liquid has saturated the threads evenly can they be taken out of the bath and exposed to the air for oxidation. An insoluble compound is formed on the thread during this period, which eventually defines the shapes and patterns of the motifs bound into the lengths of thread. The Kodi term for this is "dampening" (*mbaha*), also the name of the stage of a fetus in the womb when it is believed to absorb a great amount of the mother's blood, but does not yet have a firm skeleton or shape. Threads removed from the dye bath at this stage are not yet fast in color, just as a fetus born during the first few months of pregnancy is not viable outside the womb.

Considerable skill is needed to determine when the almost colorless soluble indigo has penetrated all of the thread, and it can be taken out and shaken for a few minutes to separate individual strands for oxidation.[6] As the threads hang on the branches of a nearby tree, the pale greenish color oxidizes to a deep blue. The thread is then immersed in the dye bath again, the stages of dye saturation and oxidation being repeated at least four times to get the deepest possible hue. The repeated "dipping" (betingo) uses the same fermented bath, the mixture of alkali, tannin, and nutrients being maintained, but without new additions of lime. The dye bath should not be stirred vigorously or turned even when threads are removed, because stirring would cause a premature oxidation. Women who described the process noted that when a fetus is in the final stages of its development, a husband is also not allowed to disturb the contents of his wife's womb, for fear of stirring up the delicate mixture and causing a miscarriage.

If the chemical interactions within the bath are not properly controlled, or the threads are incompletely penetrated by the indigo solution, then the blue produced may become brownish, greenish, or grayish as it is woven into cloth. In similar fashion, birth defects and breech births are often traced to male violations of the taboo on sex in the last month or two before birth. However, maternal death in childbirth is always explained not by male violations but by incest or adultery on the part of the mother. As in the taboos associated with access to dyeing sites, male transgressions endanger the "product" (the thread being dyed, the fetus), while a woman's immorality is violence inflicted against herself, the container (the indigo dye bath, the female womb).

Once properly saturated, oxidized, and dried, indigo on cotton thread is fast to water and its blue is brightened with each washing. The precise combinations of chalk, ash, herbs, and roots used in preparing dyes are all "secrets of the trade," which cannot be revealed to men or to other women who have not made offerings to the spirit of the Savunese ancestress who first brought these practices to Kodi. Also secret are the locations of the best indigo plants along the sea-

Figure 12. An older Kodi woman shakes out freshly dyed threads from the indigo pot and hangs them up to dry. Photo by Laura Scheerer, 1985

shore, the other roots used to "bind" the color, and the time needed for the mixture to ferment.[7]

Two other expressions used to describe childbirth difficulties draw on the vocabulary of indigo dyeing: An aborted fetus (*manuho*) during the first six months of pregnancy is said to have been expelled when it was "incompletely saturated" (*njaha mbaha ndaha pango*, literally, "not yet fully dampened") with the life-giving substances of its mother's body. If a women dies while pregnant, she is said to "bring along the funeral shroud in her womb" (*ngandi ghabuho ela kambu dalo*)—showing that the placental envelope is associated with the textiles used to wrap corpses. The metaphoric cloth that shields the infant in the womb is also made to serve as the mortuary bundle for its voyage to another world.

The ritual surrounding the preparation of the dye pot is similar in many respects to the rites that a midwife performs at childbirth: A chicken must be sacrificed before each dye pot is prepared, its soul dedicated to the Savunese ancestress who introduced dyeing (the *mori ghuro, mori nggilingo*, "mistress of the dye pot, mistress of the indigo") and its entrails examined to determine whether or not she has given her consent for the secrets to be shared. The same ritual preparations are made for the two women who normally assist in births—the "one who pushes" (*tou pa tunda*) massaging the child out of the womb, and the "one who receives" (*tou pa himbia*) holding the child as it emerges.

Similar offerings are made to the objects that are used to ease both childbirth and dyeing. At birth, the strip of barkcloth that a woman grasps in her labor receives an offering of betel, cooked rice, and cooked meat from the chicken killed for the ritual specialists. In indigo dyeing, this offering is usually set in front of the pot as the dye is prepared. Men cannot be present at either childbirth or dyeing, nor can they hear the chants that are pronounced to ease childbirth or quicken the dyes. The names of the ingredients used in women's herbal medicines and the spirits of the places where they were collected also must remain secret.

The metaphoric association between the process of conception in the womb and the "fixing" of indigo dyes in secret production centers is reinforced by a metonymic one, because some of the same herbal potions are used to control both processes. Such potions can be either drunk by the expectant mother or used in a healing bath after childbirth. They are intended to cleanse the "dirty blood" that may remain after labor and to stop excessive bleeding. Herbalism and massage were used by midwives to detect problems with the fetus before birth. Specific foods might be prescribed to treat "softness" of the spine, or to help "turn around" a breech birth through massage. A root (*amo ghaiyo*) identified to me along the seashore was said to be useful in "closing" both colors and the womb. The running of poorly dyed sarungs when they are washed is also linguistically linked to irregular female bleeding, a symptom of reproductive disorders.

In a broader sense, women are seen as dangerous when they are "open," their reproductive energies not properly channeled and contained, the flow of their blood unregulated by the flow of prestations between patrilineally defined groups. The perforated "openings" in women must be bound, sealed, and controlled, "locking" their blood into their bodies just as indigo dyes are "locked into" threads. These ideas are reflected in the steps taken by the most respected and powerful women to control and contain both colors and reproductive substances. Such women spend a large part of their days binding threads stretched across a wooden frame. Patterns are tied off with *gewang* fibers that protect the threads from successive dye baths. The tighter the leaf fiber is tied, the less likely that the colors will "bleed" into one another, thus allowing white, yellow, and red motifs to be distinguished through different saturations of the reddish *kombu* dye. The final stage is alway the indigo bath that seeps into all of the unbound threads and provides the dark background for the whole cloth. Through these stages, "binding" is equated with sexual restraint and the production of healthy children.

Unmarried women wear their hair loose and unparted, but married women part it in the center and bind it in a bun at the back of the head. Their hair is never publically unbound again until the husband's death, when it is loosened for the period of mourning and keening as the widow guards the corpse inside the house. During mourning, a woman is forbidden to wear the bright patterns of ikat textiles, although she will receive gifts of cloth (contributions to the funeral shroud, *ghabuho*) from each person who attends the funeral. The textiles that a woman produces and wears do not become her "inalienable wealth" (Weiner 1985), until they are bound around her body at her own funeral and transformed into the garments that she will take with her to the afterworld.

CLOTH IN MYTHOLOGY AND SONG

The use of cloth to replace the normal organs of female reproduction is a theme in a number of mythic accounts, which present a model of a knowledgeable older woman who is able to substitute a textile bundle for a uterus. Adams (1970:96) has published a myth from Kapunduk, East Sumba, in which a miscarried fetus, the ancestor of the first royal line, is brought to life by being wrapped in cotton and stored in a sacred gong by an ancient noblewoman.

I collected a similar myth in Kodi. A princess who lives in the upper world first summons her suitor to the heavenly kingdom by sending down her spindle, inviting him to climb up the thread into her bedroom. Her unrestrained sexuality is signaled by the loose, undyed thread which instead of being prepared for the loom, is used to snare a bridegroom from the world below. Once she has conceived, her child falls to the earth as a blood clot, torn out of her body by the thunder of a heavy rainfall. It falls into a stalk of white millet, where it is found by a wise older woman who stores it in fine textiles in the attic of her house, near the family heirlooms, until it grows into a beautiful young man.

Enveloping the fetal blood in cloth creates a false womb, a concentration of fertility for an older woman who would herself be unable to bear a child. In some older versions, she also fetches bananas and papayas for the infant to suckle, since she cannot offer him her breasts. A solution of rice water and cucumber juice is fed to the newborn, who grows as tall and pale as the millet stalk where he was found. Significantly, birth is less miraculous than nurturing the blood clot outside the womb: The child produced is not an artificial child but a real one, endowed with unusual abilities. Similarly, a post-menopausal woman well versed in herbalism and indigo dyeing has the skills and knowledge that allow her to preserve a life under unusual circumstances, even if she cannot bear children herself. Her occult knowledge of plants and cloth is used to bind people to her by these services.

Miscarriages, mourned as reproductive failures, are compared to imperfectly dyed cloths in lament songs, linking indistinct motifs to the child born too soon, before the limbs and organs are fully formed. Here is one woman's lament, addressing the creator deity, which asks that the spirit of the lost child be called back to reenter her womb, so that she can conceive the same child a second time, and carry it to term more successfully:

Here is the child aborted like	*Henya a ana manuhu*
the cucumber flower	*wala karere*
Whose birthday never came	*Na dadi inja dukingo*
Here is the one fallen like	*Henya a ana kanabu*
the gourd flower	*wala karabu*
Whose appearance never arrived	*Na hunga inja tomango*
Let him return to the barkcloth of	*Pa kambala waingo kiyo*
the father's lap	*ela baba bapa*
Let him roll back to	*Pa maliti waingo kinggolo*
the mother's breast	*ela huhu inya*
You who carved the straight limbs	*Yo na hanganto timbu rowa*
Who separated crooked chicken feet	*Yo na katara witti myanu*

So he can return to the mother's	*Tanaka bali kingo ela*
breast of cucumber milk	*huhu inya wei karere*
So he can go back to the father's	*Tanaka bali kingo la*
lap of wide thighs	*baba bapa kalu kenga*
To be poured without spilling	*Buri nja kahagharo*
To be smelted with no faults	*Lala nja ta nibyuro*

The fetus is dispatched to be reimmersed in the creative juices of the mother's dyeing and binding, and reformed by the father's metal working skills.

A kind of reincarnation for the souls of children who die shortly after birth is believed to be possible through eating certain herbs and vegetables, which may store the child's spirit for a short time after its death. Here, once again, the art of herbalism links textile processing to birth and healing. Only certain plants are appropriate, and the woman concerned may consult a midwife for advice in this matter. A song such as the following one can be interpreted as a prayer asking for reincarnation through a vegetable intermediary. It directly addresses the spirit of the dead child, who must have died within four days of birth (that is, before the naming ceremony that would fix his ancestral identity):

Why were you born into the light	*Pangu bu dadi la manggawango*
Why did you appear to our senses	*Pangu bu hunga la mandendo*
When like wilted sirih leaves	*Bu inja kuta mate baka*
You dissolved in the layers of	*La taneikya lipu*
my rotting intestine	*njamu nggu*
When like dried areca nut	*Bu inja winyo mate note baka*
You fell apart like rice in	*La hambule pare*
the stomach cavity	*moyo nggu*
Why once born didn't you	*Pena bu dadi inde*
leap over the danger	*pada tongo nyahi*
Why once evident didn't you	*Pena bu hunga inde*
slip past the abyss	*tombe longo reyeda*
When the rain begins to fall	*Ba na kawunga a ura*
Wait at the bud of	*No kalungguka ela hangula*
red-tailed reeds	*kiku laka*
When the year starts anew	*Ba na kabondi a ndoyo*

Wait at the sprouts of   *No kalungguka ela kapundu*
black-tipped ferns   *mandi myete*

When the child is still unnamed, it has not yet acquired the spirit name (*ngara marapu*) or ancestral destiny (*ndewa*) that secures its fate, and it can still be reformed and reborn. A fetus or unnamed child must be wrapped in a simple cloth and buried underneath the floorboards of the house, so that its spirit will not leave. Relatives are not permitted to express sorrow through a funeral sacrifice or using fine textiles for the shroud, as this would place the child in the category of ancestors rather than incompletely processed raw spirit material.

The textile shroud, finally, evokes regeneration. In the myths reviewed above, we saw how a magical child was gestated in the artificial womb of an old woman's cloth. Similarly, the tying, binding and dressing of a corpse is a preparation for a later rebirth. The textiles that wrap the body will provide a splendid costume for the deceased in a new life in the village of the dead. The soul of a dead person is explicitly compared to a bride, and the rites of marriage and burial are self-consciously modeled after one another. The sorrow that women express in funeral dirges is a reflection on the trauma of detachment which they first experienced as brides, forced to leave their natal homes to marry into another village. They lament this separation as a characteristic of the "female condition" which binds them to passive acquiescence in many endeavors, and defines their mode of action as more constrained than that of men (Hoskins 1987a).

THE EXCHANGE OF CLOTH AND THE EXCHANGE OF WOMEN

The bride who is transferred to another ancestral village is enveloped in many layers of fine *sarungs* and dyed indigo shoulder cloths, contributing to her sexual attractiveness. But the erotic appeal of the cloth also lies in its objectification of the woman: Through motifs that enclose her first on the textile surface and are later (in tattooing) transferred to her skin, she is made into an exchange valuable, representing the wealth that must be given to her patrilineage by her husband's ancestral village. The new daughter-in-law is even described as the *wei haranga*, the "water received for the livestock," whose fertile liquids are acquired in exchange for livestock and used to reproduce the male line.

The motifs on textiles exchanged at weddings are icons of the wealth offered up as the brideprice. Each marriage payment must include a basic "price" of at least ten horses and buffalo, paid by the wife-takers (*nobo vinye*, literally, "sister-takers"). It is reciprocated by an equivalent counterpayment in cloth (equal amounts of male cloths and female *sarungs*) and pigs. Since one large pig and a pair of cloths is given for each ten head of livestock, the wife-giver's payment may seem lighter economically, but in social terms, the gift of a woman is seen as superior and more encompassing, as is evident from an analysis of textile motifs.

In both East and West Sumba, textiles depict symbols of wealth and prestige that are given by the wife-takers. In East Sumba, these include horses, deer, roosters, and dogs. The more geometric designs characteristic of Kodi cloth contain references to body parts of these animals. A common motif on women's *sarungs* is the *mata karimbyoyo* or "buffalo eye," and some also contain "horses' tails" (*kiku ndara*), An undulating zigzag line is identified as the "scales of a python's skin" (*karaha kaboko*), and small white dots refer to decorations on spears (*kambora nambu*) or the crosshatch footprint of a buffalo hoof (*kadanga karimbyoyo*). Significantly, pigs are never depicted on textiles because they are given along with the bride and must come from the wife-giver.

The textile motif could be said to offer a "miniaturization" (Lévi-Strauss 1966:23) of the marriage payments from both sides, since the representation of decomposed animal parts in a geometric pattern provides visual evidence that the obligation to give has been fulfilled. The women's cloths are marked with the buffalo's eye and the horse's tail because in a procession of marriage gifts, the most expensive and prestigious gifts (usually gold and buffalo) are generally presented before the more humble ones (horses). The buffalo's eye marks the beginning of the presentations; the horse's tail their completion. When a new wife first moves into her husband's house, her ceremonial transfer marks a finished exchange transaction, and she must wear the textiles and gold brought from her parent's house. As these contain representations of brideprice cattle, the gifts given for her continue to parade across her hips and thighs, reduced to miniature artistic depictions. Thus, the new daughter-in-law clothes her reproductive organs with textiles given by her family as emblems of her properly legitimated status within her new home.

The names of the geometric motifs are well known to women, but often obscure to men—who do almost none of the work of tying the patterns into thread, and refuse to weave. Moreover, the bride's mother-in-law (*inya yanto*) receives the gift of textiles that accompanies the bride, judging its appropriateness and equivalent value. (If the counterpayment as a whole does not include textiles of fine quality, it can be refused—although this occurs rarely.)

If the new wife seems "objectified" by the representations of exchange gifts on her clothing, the husband dresses in garments that recall marriage prestations as well. The border area of many men's cloths is lined with images of the *hamoli* gold ear pendant, given to the bride's parents "to replace the glimmer of the girl's dark eyes" (*ndali ha mata mete a lakeda minye*). A single gold piece must accompany each ten head of livestock, and here the play of mirrors, reflections and rereflections, becomes even more complex: The form of the pendant is a kind of omega shape with an opening in the middle and two tube-like extensions that curve up on either side. Most observers, including the Kodi, recognize it as a stylized presentation of female genitalia. The bride's father must receive this pendant to console him for the loss of his daughter, substituting a metal emblem of the value of her sexuality for the real person.

The extended tips of the *hamoli* pendant may be elaborated with the heads of animals—horses or pythons being the most common. Thus, in this object, the girl's sexuality is surrounded and contained by male animals. The female wealth object is itself bounded by the male wedding gifts of livestock and authority. (Although pythons are never given as part of the brideprice, they appear as wild spirits who can magically help a young man to acquire such goods.) By these symbols, the opening through which a woman's blood would flow to her descendants is shown as being enclosed and regulated by male control.

The symbolism of marriage gifts in Eastern Indonesia usually opposes the "male goods" (livestock and gold) paid by the wife-takers to the "female goods" (pigs and cloth) with which the wife-givers reciprocate. In Kodi, this association is not made terminologically explicit. However, both pigs and cloth can only be produced by women, and livestock are only tended and traded by men, so the

Figure 13. A young woman weaves a sarung, *which incorporates both the omega-shaped ear-pendant design and the buffalo-eye motif. Photo by Janet Hoskins, 1980*

categories do seem to apply. But the motifs on cloth also encapsulate and depict the pattern of exchanges of which they are a part: Male cloths are covered with emblems of female sexuality, while female *sarungs* are spotted with the male buffalo eye and horse's tail. The two can only exist in tandem, as part of a balanced transaction, so each partial image reminds the owner of its missing counterpart.

Wearing a fine *sarung* can also serve as a visual mnemonic for an unfulfilled obligation. If the groom's parents had promised a brideprice of thirty head, ten delivered at the time of the bride's move to her husband's village and twenty to be delivered over the years, then when the daughter-in-law wears her wedding textiles at a funeral or feast, her husband's family is reminded of their promise to make additional payments. There is no exact correspondence between the number of animal eyes and tails depicted and the brideprice established, but the finer clothes usually contain more densely detailed work. If a schedule of livestock payments cannot be kept, then an extension must be requested from the wife-givers by giving them an additional small textile gift along with an explanation. The textile does not replace the animal owed. It is simply a kind of interest paid on the loan of the daughter's fertility.

FROM CLOTH TO SKIN:
FEMALE TATTOOING AS A RITE OF MATURITY

Tattooing is a female rite restricted to women who have proven their ability to reproduce. A young bride, just conceiving her first child, may have her forearms tattooed, but she cannot have her calves and thighs tattooed until she has produced several healthy children. The tattooing is done by an older woman, often one who is also a midwife and herbalist, rubbing candlenut and ash into a series of tiny puncture wounds made with citrus thorns. Women are tattooed individually, after a small ceremonial offering of a chicken to the spirit of her maternal village (the *lete binye*, or "doorway and steps" that she came out of) to assure the consent of her ancestors.

The motifs tattooed onto the skin are the same as the ones used on textiles. In East Sumba, these are representational–pythons, horses, roosters and dogs. In West Sumba, they are geometric, decomposed representations of the exchange items given in bride-price payments (horse tails, buffalo eyes, omega ear ornaments). Their permanence on the skin reflects the more permanent position of the married woman within her husband's patrilineage. She has already been incorporated with a sacrifice to introduce her to his ancestors. If she has danced at feasts sponsored by her husband's village, she may have already received a special gold payment made for "stepping down onto the dancing ground" (*ndali nataro*), given by her natal house/lineage to the house of her husband. Above all, by bearing children for her husband's line, she acquires an enhanced rank and status, qualifying her to serve as a representative of the house in public settings such as bride-price negotiations.

The process of tattooing is painful. Older women who described it to me stressed how much they had suffered and cried as the thorns dug into their skin, and the bleeding wounds stung with the application of ground candlenut and other herbs. But they felt that the tattoos themselves were badges of accomplishment. One very old woman told me that she had been tattooed just before the Dutch took control of the area in 1911. Her husband's family was afraid that the foreign invaders might rape the younger women, and assumed that tattoo markings showing that they were already wives and mothers would provide some sort of protection.

Although most women over the age of fifty have elaborate tattoos on their forearms, and some all the way up the thigh, the practice has now died out. Older courtship songs reveal that the thigh tattoo had a strong erotic lure: As the upper thighs were always covered by clothing, only a secret lover could know what patterns were represented there. Children still exchange insults by crying out to a friend "Your mother has no tattoos on her thighs!"—implying that intimate knowledge of her body had become common. While the tattoo was designed to be the private secret of the conjugal pair, its existence was also used to provoke the speculation of others. A man told me that his mother was kidnapped by another man, who eventually made her his wife, because he had heard stories of the beauty of her tattooed thighs.

The cessation of tattooing as a marker of female maturity came at about the same time as the cessation of circumcision as a male rite. Circumcision, like tattooing, has been performed in Kodi as a secret, individual operation carried out in seclusion by an older man. Boys were circumcised shortly before marrying, but their sexual initiation was the task of an older woman or a slave attached to the house, because the first semen ejaculated after the operation was dangerous "water from the knife" (*wei kioto*) and could sear a female womb. Tattooing and circumcision are classified together by the Kodi because they are both rites of "sharpness" (*lakiyo*), the key characteristic of a violent and inauspiscious death (*mate pa lakiyo*).

The violence of ritualized sharpness is, however, made auspicious by its intentional infliction. Boys who willingly submit to the circumciser's knife become "clean" enough to marry. Mature women who submit to the lengthier agonies of tattooing establish their public virtue as wives and mothers. Their resistance to pain dignifies them as the survivors of childbirth—although the more intimate tattoos on the upper thighs seem to have been motivated mainly by personal vanity. Hidden by their daily *sarungs*, these designs remained an enticing mystery to the men who could not gaze on them, enhancing a woman's appeal through suggestion.

The dangerous heat of the circumciser's knife suggests that

there may exist a parallel complex of men's crafts, centered on metalwork and similarly marked by dangerous and polluting periods of creative activity. Headhunting is defined as a response to the seething heat of the skull tree, which steams and burns with anger at an unavenged killing.[8] Warfare, feuding, and high murder rates in contemporary Kodi are all attributed to "hot blood," which rises in men at certain times and enflames their passions to violence. The influence of cloth is usually portrayed as cooling and soothing, while metal objects are formed through a hot smelting process and remain charged with ritual heat if they are misused.

All important social events require a conjunction of the sharp heat of metal and the conciliatory softness of textiles. In negotiating a peace in front of the ancestral spirits, the divination spear is first used to "cut through" to the source of ancestral anger, after which the litigating parties exchange cloth to cool their anger and provide the proper atmosphere for peace-making. Yet the complementary balance of male and female elements is also slightly asymmetric in its consequences on the lives of men and women—as the meaning of indigo "blueness" can show us.

"BLUENESS," CLOTH, AND GENDER IDENTITY

Indigo dyeing and the color blue constitute important symbolic associations for women in their reproductive functions, their exchange as wives between partrilineages, and their achievement of maturity and enhanced status in old age. The residual meaning underlying each of these contexts is an emotion of resentment, a sadness and negativity that appears almost antisocial. I argue that when Kodi women "sing the blues," they are expressing an ambivalence towards the process of female creation. This creation is expressed by metaphoric extension in a number of domains—the creation of infants within the body, of cloth within the dye bath, of daughters in the home—but it is always accompanied by knowledge of an incipient loss. Infants will come out of the body, cloth will be exchanged and traded by male intermediaries, daughters will be separated from the house and sent to live in another village at marriage.

Kodi women are symbolically identified with the cloths that they produce. Indigo-dyed textiles are both the evidence of their labors and the envelopes that enclose them and show them to be socially legitimated wives and mothers. Throughout the lifecycle, transitions between stages of female identity are linked to participation in or exclusion from textile production, and the secrets associated with it. Initiation into indigo dyeing is in a sense an initiation into womanhood—but it is not accomplished at or around menarche. Instead, initiation extends throughout the lifespan, to be completed only upon burial in the indigo funeral shroud that most women dye and weave for themselves.

Young girls are taught to bind the threads for textile dyeing, often assisting at the dye bath by chewing the various barks and herbs added to the mixture of chalk and ash to prepare the dye. The rules prescribe that herbal ingredients and copra base be chewed by unmarried girls, who have not yet accepted the betel quid of courtship. Once a girl enters adolescence, she is excluded from the dyeing hut, sent home to practice weaving on the backstrap loom, and encouraged to produce *sarungs* that may be used for her own wedding costume.

At her marriage, a girl's family matches the value of the livestock and gold given for her with a counter-gift of pigs, jewelry, and cloth. The cloth produced in her home village and taken to her husband's village thus epitomizes her own personal history, and is referred to as the "companion" (*ole*) that she brings with her into a strange home. As a new daughter-in-law, she wears textiles that remind her husband's family of their obligation to keep bringing livestock payments to her village of birth. She also produces children—sons who will be descendants or "fruit" of her husband's "house," and daughters who will be exchanged with other villages as "flowers" sent to bloom in other lands. Married women spend four or five hours a day tying thread bundles and weaving textiles for sale or exchange.

When a woman grows past childbearing age, she may begin to practice one of the traditional female arts of midwifery, herbalism, or indigo dyeing. In doing so, she achieves a greater degree of knowledge and control over bodily processes, and learns from other women the secrets of which plants can be used to prevent excessive bleeding at childbirth or leaking in the dye bath. She wears tattoos on her arms and legs that display the motifs that she has already portrayed on a textile surface, and that have now become part of her body.

Cloth is a master symbol for the transitions of a woman's life, wrapping her as an infant, a bride, and a corpse. Men also wear cloths with indigo coloring, but they are never identified with the processes and substances that go into their production. Instead, theirs is the world of public exchange, feasting, and the distribution of raw meat at ceremonies to fulfill past obligations. The world of indigo dyeing is conceptually opposed to that of the male activity of feasting. It is taboo to come close to an indigo pot carrying blood or raw meat, and no woman can cook food for men at the same time that she prepares the ingredients of the dye bath. The male blood of feasting and headhunting can never come in contact with the female blood of reproduction, or the blue substances that magically control and aid this process.

The contrast between metal goods and textiles plays on more pervasive themes in Kodi gender symbolism. It is not simply that women are seen as "things," exchange goods, while men are not. On the contrary, for both sexes, the link between persons and possessions is rather indistinct and hard to define. Men are identified with named gold valuables that are stored in lineage house attics. Like metal objects in general, gold is part of a sacred patrimony which is passed vertically, down through the generations of a single agnatic clan, rather than horizontally, in affinal exchanges that follow the paths of women. The ancestry of men can be traced in the ancestry of swords, spears, and knives, a metaphorical skeleton of metal that symbolizes the indestructible relatedness of the patrilineage.

In contrast, women are linked to the more ephemeral life cycle of cloth, known to tear and disintegrate over time, fragile but often poignantly beautiful. Both cloth and children are only semidurable: They assure their creators of a certain semblance of immortality, but they are ultimately also subject to the processes of aging, fading, and falling apart. It is the difference in durability between metal goods and textiles that defines their symbolic values. When men exchange land or gold in formal transactions, they refer to these forms of indestructible wealth as the "cloth that does not tear, the pig that will not get sick" (*kamba nja madiryako, wawi nja kapore*)— acknowledging only too clearly the contrasts with organic objects, subject to the same frailty as human beings.

Cloth is portrayed in myths and prayers as offering protection and blessings, a shelter from life's dangers. Promises can be made binding by the ceremonial presentation of a textile, said to provide an "umbrella against the sun, a block from the rain" (*kada ngindi lodo, haluri tipu ura*). But it is clear that the shielding, binding power of cloth is not eternal: It offers only the shadow of an obligation, the memory of a convenant. As long as this is honored, the cloth will provide a cooling and refreshing shade to its new owner. But it cannot be allowed to rot before the proper payments are made. Like the mother's womb, it offers a refuge which must be left behind, a mantle of protection which can be pierced by human weakness, illness and mortality.

The vulnerability of cloth represents the vulnerability of women, exchanged along with their textiles. But the secrets of indigo form an occult tradition of resistance to the forcible alienation of women from the products of their labors. Women do not like to lose their daughters, their cloths, their powers to the male world. They also feel the sting of male disdain for their association with the messy business of birth and death—the handling of bloody infants and rotting corpses. What to the male world is a fearful and polluting activity (the dyeing of thread with indigo dyes) becomes for older women a way of regaining control over their own destinies, and also often a source of additional wealth.

Women both subscribe to and resent many of the restrictions placed on them. When indigo dyeing or funeral songs present a note of protest, it is largely inarticulate. The enforced secrecy of female indigo cults is a response to the constraints of the male world and an effort to police their own in reproductive matters. In clandestine meetings, women share knowledge of herbal preparations used not only for successful childbirth recovery, but also for abortion and contraception. They may apply "binding" roots to treat irregular menstrual bleeding or hasten menopause. It was unclear to me, and to most of my male informants, how effective these preparations were. Gheru Wallu, my first Kodi landlady and a skilled herbalist and midwife, told me, "Men will never know women's secrets about these things, and they will always think that we can control even more than we can."

Older women consciously cloak their secret knowledge of reproductive matters in a mystique that not only excludes men but disciplines their sisters: Kodi word play links "loose dyes" and "loose morals" through the image of a "leaking woman" who cannot control her sexuality. Magical herbal preparations can be used by jealous wives or fearful mothers to cause a woman's own body to rebel against her wayward behavior. A fetus will "leak out" of an unfaithful bride before it is brought to term. An adultress who refuses to confess will have the placenta bound inside her, and can die if she does not relent. Incest, as noted, produces a huge gush of maternal blood that must be treated with binding roots. Inappropriate actions create a physical syndrome of "incomplete closure" in the body, and are often life-threatening.

The model of textile production presents a way of understanding Kodi notions about the creation of gender identity through a temporal process: "Womanhood" is not given at birth as a "natural" attribute, nor is it automatically assumed at puberty, with the onset of menses. Instead women, like the textile they produce, must be created through stages such as the one in which their bodies are "opened" in childbirth and then closed again by the application of the proper medicines. Their movement from one patrilineage to another, marked by the exchange of valuables, is represented first on the textiles which they wrap around their bodies and later directly on the skin of their calves and forearms. These valuables are also seen as "enclosing" their sexuality and reproductive potential within the confines of the new descent group. It is the movement from one lineage house to another, the partial severing of ties of birth and their replacement by ties of marriage, that defines the shared attributes of Kodi womanhood.

There is no separate "sisterhood" characterized by female solidarity, and in fact herbalism, midwifery, and indigo dyeing are all arenas for intense female rivalry. The complex of "blue arts" is concerned with reproduction and fertility, but does not promote these arts exclusively, or present any public moral instruction to cult members. These members work at the periphery of the male world, neither opposing it or nor imitating it directly. Although the secrets of the woman's world in Kodi may intimidate or intrigue certain men, they do not threaten the larger social order. Moreover, the policing of sexual behavior lends tacit support to the normative order established by male ancestors. Nonetheless, across the generational and hierarchical divisions of Kodi society, women share a common experience of loss, the painful detachment from loved ones. And these female feelings have a place of refuge. Indigo cults articulate the emotions of displacement and separation experienced as both children and textiles slip away, with parts of the person attached.

Evoking women's painful move to another home at marriage, the secluded cults also help them produce valuables that provide an inalienable link to their place of origin, and to their personal history.

ACKNOWLEDGMENTS

Doctoral research in 1979–81 was supported by the Fulbright Commission, the Social Science Research Council, and the National Science Foundation, under the auspices of the Indonesian Academy of Sciences (LIPI) and Universitas Nusa Cendana of Kupang. Return visits in 1984, 1985, and 1986 were funded by the Research School of Pacific Studies, Australian National University and the Faculty Research and Innovation Fund of the University of Southern California. I would like to thank Marie Jeanne Adams, James J. Fox, Nancy Lutkehaus, Jane Schneider, Annette Weiner, Valerio Valeri, and members of the ASAO panel on "Female Initiation in the Pacific" for their comments on an earlier version of this paper.

NOTES

1. Sources that associate women and the color blue proliferate throughout the Pacific, but I will cite only a few. Uli, the goddess of sorcery and also of the sea water, is an important example from aboriginal Hawaii. Uli is defined in the Pukui and Elbert *Hawaiian Dictionary* as referring to "any dark color, including the deep blue of the sea, the ordinary green of vegetation, and the dark of black clouds; the black and blue of a bruise" (1971:340). It is also the name of the goddess of sorcery, said to come from Kahiki, the land of origins, and can refer to an early stage in the development of a fetus, as the body begins to form.

In other parts of Polynesia, its cognates refer to darkness and dampness. In Samoa, *uri* means the darkness of clouds and the deep blue sea, and also malevolent feelings and emotions (Tregear 1969:578). In Tahitian, it suggests that which is "deep, unfathomable, as in the sea," and also obscure. In Tongan, the associations are most negative; *uli* is "filth, contamination, nastiness, dirty, polluted" and terrifying (Tregear 1967:578). Firth (1970:103) speaks of a "Dark God called Atua Pouri" who receives the victims of sorcery and is in contact with the spirits of miscarried foetuses. In some areas, specific goddesses are associated with the magical powers of blueness; in others, the color is more generally associated with stories of sorceresses and witches.

Lila Abu-Lughod's *Veiled Sentiments* discusses another tradition of women's laments, also with certain similarities to the American blues, among the Awlad

'Ali Bedouins of Egypt. Messick's (1987) analysis of women's weaving in North Africa also suggests that it is a "subordinate discourse" which embeds a distinctively female worldview.

2. The disappearance of female priestesses seems related to historical reinterpretations of the diarchic division of power between ancestral villages and lineages which came after the imposition of Dutch colonial control. These reinterpretations are discussed in Hoskins (1987b, 1988a).

3. On the island of Roti, the origin of weaving and metalworking is also traced to a neighboring island, that of Ndao (Fox 1980). It is possible that Sumbanese theories of "Savunese" dyers and metalworkers also refer to Ndao (Hoskins 1988b). Neighboring Indonesian societies make similar links between indigo dyeing and spiritual malevolence, as the cloths are almost universally used as funeral shrouds (Schulte-Nordholt 1971, Traube 1983, Fox 1973). On Roti, a folk etymology associates the local name for indigo (*tau*) with the words for "fear" or "frighten," and the terrifying spirits of the outside are conceived of as "darkening" or "blueing" their victims (Fox 1973:350). Wild indigo plants, called the "indigo of the spirits" (Fox 1973:351), are thought to be used by spirits for nefarious purposes. But such powers can also be used to ward off dangerous spirits. After someone dies a "bad death," an entire pot of indigo dye must be poured on his grave before the funeral is finished (Fox 1973:360). The dark dye serves to "fix" him in the grave and keep his soul from wandering. A similar ambivalence is reflected in the description of sorcerers as having the power to poison or to cure through the use of "blue powers" (*mana-momodo*).

4. Dyeing is the most remunerative of the stages of textile production, particularly in relation to the time invested. In 1980, I collected the following fee scale for tasks involved in the production of a *sarung* commissioned by an outsider: Tying the threads to create the ikat pattern (*wolo*) cost Rp. 2000 and took about a week; dyeing the threads in the indigo bath (*betingo*) cost Rp. 3000 and took four or five days once the bath was prepared; weaving the thread on a backstrap loom (*tanungo*) cost Rp. 1500 and took from two weeks to a month of labor. Weaving is a tiring process, but it involves little specialized knowledge or creativity in design, so it is often delegated to younger, less skilled women.

5. The dangerous effects of contact with the dye bath on a pregnant woman can be reversed if the mistress of the dyeing shack (*mori kareke nggilingo*) calls out a warning to her visitor. In so doing, she sacrifices the contents of the dye pot, which are ruined, but saves the life of the fetus. A pregnant woman who unexpectedly finds herself near a secret dyeing site may also recite the following prayer addressed to the female spirit of indigo, hoping to placate her anger and save the contents of her womb:

From your throat and	*Wali kyoko*
from your liver	*wali ate kinyani*
Mistress of the pot,	*Mori ghuro,*
mistress of indigo	*mori nggilingo*
Foreign woman,	*Minye dawa,*
Savunese woman	*minye haghu*

Surely you know yourself	*Angga peghe do kinyaka*
I did not mean to obscure the liquid	*Nja ku kabaro tonoma*
Surely you saw yourself	*Angga ice do kiyaka*
I did not want to soil the cloth	*Nja ku pyunakao taloki*
Clouding the swampy source	*Myata rende kabaro*
Polluting the head of the river	*Kataku loko mbunako*
So turn friendly eyes toward me	*Maka marere mata nuri*
As we chew betel together	*Moka la hamama*
So open your mouth in laughter	*Maka wiala ghoaba ndeha*
As we eat tobacco	*Moka la mu mbaku*

Her prayer must be accompanied by an offering of betel and areca nut, and a promise to later sacrifice a chicken and a pig to atone for the violation.

If a man should happen by, such procedures are not necessary: It will be the dye pot that is ruined, because he does not have the same "reproductive vulnerability" as women. However, the textile-dyeing women would certainly retaliate by sending him the "blue sickness" of witchcraft. Each sex has its own weaknesses, and its own weapons.

6. Proper indigo dyeing involves a combination of chemistry and technology, acquired through long practical experience. Dyers monitor the timing of chemical interactions through smelling, feeling, tasting, and examining their materials at every stage of the process. As Kajitani (1980:307) notes: "Each dye compound with its impurities is unique in its ability to bond or react with fibers . . . . So the good traditional dyer, like the medieval alchemist, develops his or her own preferred materials and techniques, which become guarded secrets that often disappear upon the dyer's death."

7. Taboos regulated by the Kodi traditional calendar restrict the gathering of wild indigo plants to the time when the quality of indican in the leaves of these plants reaches it maximum level, shortly after the rainy season begins. It is forbidden to pick wild indigo or prepare the dye bath during the "bitter months" (*wulla padu*), which usually fall in October and November on the lunar system. Technical processes (all of them usually carried out by women) that involve white substances—dyeing thread, baking lime, and boiling sea salt—are said to be particularly dangerous because their light color attracts the lightning bolts and strong winds of the beginning of the rains. After a ceremony in January to "make the tips of the young plants bland" (*kaba wei kapoke*), women are permitted to begin dyeing thread in preparation for the large-scale festivals that greet the swarming of the sea worms (*nale*) in February.

8. Headhunting is often paired with textile production and childbearing in other areas of Indonesia. Among the Iban, the same taboos apply to the preparation of thread for dyeing and to childbirth within the longhouse (Freeman 1970:125), and the laying out of the thread is called "the warpath of the women" (Gittinger 1979:219). Among the Belu of Timor, a new mother coming out of seclusion after childbirth is ceremonially dressed in the textiles and head decora-

tions of a headhunter (Gittinger 1979:33). In Kodi, both freshly taken heads and freshly dyed threads are hung on trees to dry, but these associations are not made as explicitly as the links to metalworking (See Hoskins 1987b). The skull tree is often depicted on East Sumbanese textiles, but there is no special use of textiles in headhunting ritual. Rogers (1985) notes that the opposition of textile production to metal work (associated with the opposition of female to male) is important among the Batak of Sumatra, the Ngaju of Borneo, the Lamaholot peoples of Flores, and the Tanimbarese of the Moluccas.

REFERENCES

Abu-Lughod, Lila
    1986   Veiled Sentiments. Berkeley: University of California Press.

Adams, Marie Jeanne
    1969   System and Meaning in East Sumba Textile Design: A Study in Traditional Indonesian Art. Southeast Asia Studies Cultural Report Series No. 16. New Haven: Yale University.
    1970   Myth and Self Image among the Kapunduku People of Sumba. Indonesia 10:81–106.

Fox, James J.
    1973   On Bad Death and the Left Hand: A Study of Rotinese Symbolic Inversions. In Right and Left: Essays on Dual Symbolic Classification. Rodney Needham, ed. Chicago: University of Chicago Press.
    1977   Roti, Ndau and Savu. In Textile Traditions of Indonesia. Mary Hunt Kahlenberg, ed. Los Angeles: County Museum of Art.
    1980   Figure Shark and Pattern Crocodile: The Foundations of the Textile Traditions of Roti and Ndao. In Indonesian Textiles. Mattiebelle Gittinger, ed. Washington D.C.: The Textile Museum.

Firth, Raymond
    1970   Rank and Religion in Tikopia. London: George Allen Unwin.

Freeman, Derek
    1970   Report on the Iban. New York: Humanities Press.

Gittinger, Mattiebelle
    1979   Splendid Symbols: Textile and Tradition in Indonesia. Washington D.C.: The Textile Museum.

Hoskins, Janet
    1986   So My Name Shall Live: Stone Dragging and Grave-Building in Kodi, West Sumba. Bijdragen tot de Taal-, Land en Volkenkunde 142:31–51.
    1987a   Complementarity in this World and the Next: Gender and Agency in Kodi Mortuary Ceremonies. In Dealing with Inequality: Analyzing Gender Relations in Melanesia and Beyond. Marilyn Strathern, ed. Cambridge: Cambridge University Press.

1987b   The Headhunter as Hero: Local Traditions and Their Reinterpretation as Natural History. American Ethnologist 14(4).
1988a   Matriarchy and Diarchy: Indonesian Variations on the Domestication of the Savage Woman *In* Myths of Matriarchy Reconsidered. Deborah Gewertz, ed. Sydney, Australia: Oceania Monographs, University of Sydney Press.
1988b   Arts and Cultures of Sumba. *In* Islands and Ancestors: Indigenous Styles of Southeast Asia. Jean Paul Barbier and Douglas Newton, eds. Catalog for an exhibit at the Metropolitan Museum in New York. Geneva: Barbier-Muller Museum.

Kajitani, Noboko
1980   Traditional Dyes in Indonesia. *In* Indonesian Textiles. Mattiebelle Gittinger, ed. Washington, D.C.: Textile Museum.

Lévi-Strauss, Claude
1966   The Savage Mind. Chicago: University of Chicago Press.

Messick, Brinkley
1987   Subordinate Discourse: Women, Weaving and Gender Relations in North Africa. American Ethnologist 14(2):210–26.

Needham, Rodney
1980   Principles and Variations in the Structure of Sumbanese Society. *In* The Flow of Life. James J. Fox, ed. Cambridge: Harvard University Press.

Pukui, Mark K., and Samuel Elbert
1971   Hawaiian Dictionary. Honolulu: University of Hawaii Press.

Rogers, Susan
1985   Power and Gold: Jewelry from Indonesia, Malaysia and the Phillipines. Geneva: Barbier-Muller Museum.

Schulte-Nordholte, H.G.
1971   The Political System of the Atoni of Timor. The Hague: Martinus Nijhoff.

Traube, Elizabeth G.
1980   Affines and the Dead: Mambai Rituals of Alliance. Bijdragen tot de Taal-,Land- en Volkekunde 136(1):90–115.

Treager, Edgar
1969   The Maori-Polynesian Comparative Dictionary. Oosterhout: Netherlands Anthropological Publications.

Van Wouden, F.A.E.
1956   Locale groepen en dubbel afstamming in Kodi, West Sumba. Bijdragen tot de Taal-, Land- en Volkenkunde. 11:204–46.

Weiner, Annette
1985   Inalienable Wealth. American Ethnologist 12(2):210–27.

PART II.

Capitalism and the Meanings of Cloth

6. *Rumpelstiltskin's Bargain:*

Folklore and the Merchant Capitalist Intensification of Linen Manufacture in Early Modern Europe

JANE SCHNEIDER

 According to the folklorist Ruth Bottigheimer, many of the European folktales collected in the late eighteenth and early nineteenth centuries portray spinning as "highly undesirable despite the surface message that it will lead to riches" (1982:142,150). These tales present spinning as a form of subjugation or punishment for women, whose occupational hazards include "hips . . . too wide to pass through a doorway, lips licked away from . . . moistening the thread," noses engorged from lint dust, a thumb grown to grotesque proportions (Bottigheimer 146). Moreover, "although many tales declare that spinning mediates wealth in the form of gold, it is primarily associated with poverty . . . above all it is the archetypical employment of domesticated, poverty-stricken womanhood" (Bottigheimer 150; also Ferguson 1979:83).

The tales also suggest that malevolent spirits can heighten the perils of spinning. For example, in the Briar Rose and Sleeping Beauty stories, spinning implements or rough flax fibers are the instruments of a curse: A mere scratch puts whole kingdoms to sleep for a hundred years. Even more to the point is the tale of Rumpelstiltskin, in which a poor miller tells the king that his daughter can spin straw into gold, whereupon the king invites her to his castle, a veritable warehouse of fiber. As she despairs over her impossible situation, a dwarfed and crippled poltergeist appears and, in exchange for gifts of a necklace, a bracelet, and the promise of her firstborn child, does the spinning for her, ensuring her marriage to the king. In some versions of the story, she is ultimately spared from handing over her child by a messenger who, at "a high mountain near the edge of the forest, where foxes and hares say good night to each other," overhears the little demon say the name (Rumpelstiltskin) that, if she can guess it, will release her from the bargain. In other versions, the child cannot be saved. Similar is the story of the Three Crones, or the Three Old Women, in which a poor mother slaps her daughter for her lazy neglect of spinning. The mother then explains the girl's tears to the passing queen as the consequence of the family's inability to supply her with sufficient flax, so much does she love to spin. The queen, delighted, announces that the castle is full of flax; once the girl spins it, she is welcome to marry the prince. Three old women magically appear to assist the terrified maiden, in exchange demanding to be presented as aunts at her wedding.

In Rumpelstiltskin-like tales, achieving status through marriage carries a negative evaluation. These girls achieve status not from their own industriousness, but from their willingness to risk their lives in a devilish pact with spirit helpers, often at the instigation of desperate or ambitious parents. Curiously, this negative evaluation is linked to a demonized view of spirits who, in other contexts of European folklore, appear benign. In many stories, for example, fairies do housework or thresh grain out of a desire to create a trusting relationship with humans, and disappear if humans attempt to repay them with clothes or food. If such helpers exact a price, it is explicitly to give reproductive potential to the spirit world, for in folk belief, fairies cannot reproduce without human wombs to carry their offspring and human midwives to deliver them. In contrast to such generous spirits, and to spirits whose requests are well justified, the assistance of a Rumpelstiltskin entails dangerous bargains. Fear of such danger found daily expression in spinning communities, where it was the custom to place carded flax under a weight and remove the belt from the spinning wheel before retiring for the night, to discourage unsolicited spirit help (Evans 1957:305).

Bottigheimer contrasts the infanticidal Rumpelstiltskin with elves and dwarfs who, like the generous Frau Holle, assisted spinners in their tasks without extorting a reward in return. She suggests that elves and dwarfs underwent a transformation from benign to demonic in the period preceding the late eighteenth century, when collectors like the Grimms began recording folktales (1982). When they identify a fiber, the spinning tales generally refer to flax (or hemp, which is closely related). This suggests that these stories, with their demonization of spirit helpers and their painful marriage bargains, bore some relation to the intensification of linen manufacture in the seventeenth and eighteenth centuries. Spurred by the opening of the New World economy and the related explosion of fashion-driven consumption in Europe, this intensified activity engaged rural communities in a merchant-organized putting-out system of linen cloth production. In this paper, I consider the possible connections between this system and the Rumpelstiltskin story, looking first at the entrepreneurial promotion of linen manufacture, then at how the linen promoters mobilized labor, and finally at the environmental impact of the industry as a whole—an impact of special relevance for spirit beings.

If the Rumpelstiltskin tale mirrored the experience of linen producers in Early Modern Europe, it did so as a sociological and moral reflection on the ambivalence of spinners and flax growers, as they weighed the contradictory implications of a new mode of production. As Rebel (1988:5) shows for a group of Hessian tales of the same period, the peasant voice was one of uncertain accommodations, "a disturbing and open-ended meditation on the desperate choices of the poor, on the temptation to advance socially by serving the rich. . . ." Far from offering "banal and homiletic conclusions," Rebel argues, the tales confront us "with paradoxes that demand reflection . . . ." A ubiquitous example is the dilemma of superfluous children, often expressed in the motif of parents misrepresenting their daughters to get them married off. As we shall see, marriage was precisely the institution on which the intensification of linen manufacturing turned.

LINEN IN EUROPEAN HISTORY

In the history of European textiles, cotton and linen played interchangeable roles. Unlike silk and the finer wools, both were relatively inexpensive to produce, and unlike coarser wool fabrics, they were comfortable to handle and wear. Both are composed of cellulose fibers, making them amenable to bleaching rather than the more involved and costly process of dyeing. Until their latter-day experiments with imitation chintz and calicos, Europeans rarely elaborated either cottons or linens through the complex resist-dye techniques of Islamic and Asian civilizations. As Mazzaoui has suggested, they concentrated instead on a "diverse line of serviceable, attractive and low priced products," mostly "light-to-medium weight cloth suitable for undergarments, bedding and summer clothing" (Mazzaoui 1981:89–90). Included in this diverse line was a mixed cloth, called fustian, with a linen warp and a cotton weft. Linens, cottons, and fustians enhanced the living standards of the urban middle and lower classes, and displaced coarse homespuns in peasant households as well.

Although similar in terms of appearance and markets, cotton and linen followed substantially different production paths. Cotton, a tropical plant, could not be cultivated in temperate Europe, where the cultivation of flax was widespread. This distinction underlay the far greater role of accumulated capital in the organization of cotton manufacture when compared with linen, and its closer association with urban craft guilds. Most of the linen industries were less capital-intensive and more rural. Cotton production was also the first to undergo technological innovation. The shift from distaff and spindle to the Indian-invented, foot-pedaled spinning wheel, and from the vertical to the horizontal loom, transformed this industry in the twelfth century. In the eighteenth century, cotton manufacture ushered in the industrial revolution. Linen entrepreneurs, by contrast, did not promote wheel spinning, with its threefold increase in capacity, until the early modern period, and even then the changeover was never quite complete (Endrei 1968:85–91; Grant 1961:220–27).

Maureen Mazzaoui's (1981) book on the medieval Italian cotton industry divides Europe's involvement with cotton into three great periods. The first, from the twelfth through the fifteenth centuries, was a period of substantial growth when Italian merchants, assisted by advances in shipping and navigation, imported cotton from the Eastern Mediterranean, Sicily, and Spain, putting the fiber out to thousands of producers in the Po Valley and Tuscany. The second was a period of uncertainty, from the sixteenth to the eighteenth centuries, during which Italian cotton entered a steep decline. In part its undoing was at the hands of transalpine cotton manufacturers, who had gotten their start importing cotton or cotton yarn from Italy, and then imitated Italian wares. The Fugger-financed South German fustian industry, which flourished in the sixteenth century, represents the most powerful instance of such competition. Equally damaging was the rising cost of imported raw cotton, as the Ottoman Empire consolidated its hold over primary products on behalf of Ottoman industries, spurring in Europe a search for new sources of supply. The third great phase of European cotton history, in the eighteenth century, was marked by slavery in the New World plantation zones of cotton production, ever-cheaper transport costs for moving the raw material, and a staggering technological breakthrough in manufacture.

Linen history complemented the history of cotton. During the first phase, it was produced on two levels: in peasant households as a homespun, and in urban workshops as a luxury. The former was widely diffused, the latter quite concentrated, above all in Northern France and Flanders where towns like Ypres, Cambrai, and Laon gave names to such well-known fabrics as Diaper, Cambric, and Lawn. Here, hand spinning with saliva-moistened fingers and weaving in damp, stone vaults, enhanced the value of the precisely cultivated and carefully tended local flax crop (Endrei 1968:85–91; Horner 1920:317–28). Neither this industry nor the peasant household industry kept up with cotton in the already expanding market for "decent cloth"—the cloth that provided a comfortable, inexpensive, and hygenic material for underwear, tablewear, and bed clothes. Starting in the late eighteenth century, cotton once again outdistanced linen in the competition for this mass market.

What about the middle period, between the two cotton booms? I have noted these booms precisely to highlight the dynamism of linen in these intervening centuries when the spinning tales were told. For, despite the decline in cotton manufacture in this period, the market for decent cloth had not contracted. On the contrary, a growing population and the hegemony of a fashion-conscious Renaissance culture guaranteed its continued expansion. Especially important was the growth in demand that followed the opening of the Atlantic economy (Kriedte 1983:32). As early as 1594, Brittany sent nearly a million linen cloths to the West Indies, while in 1601 it was confessed in Rouen that "linen cloths are the true gold and silver mines of this kingdom, because they are developed only to be trans-

Figure 14. Linen served as a comfortable, inexpensive, and hygienic material for underwear, tablewear, and bedclothes. Painting, "Le Lever de Fanchon," by Nicolas-Bernard Lépicié; Musée Hotel Sandelin: Pas-de-Calais, France

ported to countries where gold and silver are obtained" (quoted in Kriedte 1981a:35). Echoed in the Hessian declaration that linen exports were the "main channel through which Spanish gold and silver flows into our coffers" (quoted in Kreidte 1981a:36), this pronouncement underscores the importance of linen manufacture from 1600 until the cotton revolution.

MERCANTILIST DOCTRINE AND THE LINEN PROMOTERS

The intermediate centuries saw more linen intensification in some European regions than in others. Generally, peasants made the greatest commitment to flax and linen manufacture in areas that had not been dominated by the manorial system, with its emphasis on cereals and mixed husbandry. Most favorable to linen production were the Celtic western edge of feudal development and the Germanic and Slavic frontiers, where subsistence strategies focused on dairy cattle or other livestock. The pattern conforms to Joan Thirsk's analysis of industrial location, according to which the most welcoming environments were those where the predominance of pastoral pursuits ensured a surplus of labor, especially in the winter season (Thirsk 1961; but see Spencely 1973). Within these broad zones of linen manufacture there was considerable variation, dedication to linen being more pronounced in some localities than in others (see Mendels 1981; Tilly 1964; Kriedte 1981:17–20; Kisch 1981:179–81).

By the seventeenth century, a few places—above all Haarlem—had emerged as specialized centers of cloth export without a supporting base of flax cultivation and yarn production. That is, they concentrated on the more lucrative end of the trade—the weaving, bleaching, and finishing of cloth—while importing the fiber, usually in its spun form, from Celtic or Baltic Europe, where regional weavers lamented the competition for yarn. For Haarlem, the special water of the town's lake provided such a strategic advantage for bleaching that the Dutch exported as "Hollands" a linen cloth that was spun, and often woven, outside of Holland (Horner 1920:350–65). Manchester and Nuremberg also exported cloths that underwent the initial stages of the manufacturing process elsewhere. Nevertheless, because flax cultivation was widely diffused in Europe, commerce in flax and linen yarn was less developed than in other textiles. A common pattern was for each linen district to organize its own manufacturing, from planting the (possibly imported) flax seed to bleaching and finishing the cloth. It is these specialized regions of "proto-industrial" linen manufacture that concern us here.

I have attempted to reconstruct the process of intensification in these regions, using both secondary sources and a series of letters, pamphlets, and broadsides written in the seventeenth and eighteenth centuries by men who called themselves "promoters" or "undertakers" of linen manufacture. Although most of my primary source material is from the British Isles, its themes are consistent with documents quoted in secondary sources that trace the development of linen on the continent. Most of the authors of the primary sources were merchants and landlords who stood to accumulate either profit or rent from cloth production schemes. In the Scottish lowlands, Silesia, and the non-black-earth areas of Russia, rent was often at stake, taking one of two forms: in kind (as yarn or cloth) or in cash (e.g. Horner 1920:472–77; Kisch 1981:179–81; Smout 1969:127–28).

Regardless of the type of exaction, rent and profit were not the linen promoters' sole objectives. On the contrary, some claimed to be unfairly victimized by the rancor of others who, out of envy, failed to see how their innovations and initiatives served the public good (Haines 1677:4,14–15; Hill 1817:Preface). Linen manufacture, they all seemed to feel, could solve the most pressing problems of the mercantile state.

First among these problems was the foreign exchange of the nation, earned through manufactured exports, lost through importing the manufactures of others. The promoters argued that if indigenous producers could supply indigenous markets as well as penetrate colonial and foreign markets, they would alleviate the "exhaustion of the treasury," reversing the drain of bullion to purchase linens abroad.

A second mercantilist problem amenable to solution through the intensification of linen manufacture was the alarming impoverishment of rural populations, due to a convergence of demographic growth, staggering price inflation, and the incipient commoditization of land resources (Kriedte 1983:52–54). The specter of a falling standard of living for much of the peasantry loomed large in the promotion literature which, in virtually every case I reviewed, mentioned beggars and vagrants, children whose parents could not afford to keep them, and the "idle" poor. Unable to pay their rents without selling the family cow, tenants and cottagers were slipping precariously toward dependence on public or religious charity.

Linen promoters took a dim view of charity, which they thought of as "pernicious" (one of their favorite words)—a parasitic burden on those who worked. Gifts to the poor, they argued, would encourage nonchalance and reinforce habits of mendacity and sloth. This vocabulary is reminiscent of Protestant culture, which many of the promoters embraced. Guignet's detailed account of linen manufacture in Valenciennes in northern France, however, quotes Catholics voicing similar concerns (1976:407–53). Whatever their religion, the promoters advocated an expansion of flax cultivation and linen manufacture as an alternative to charity for poorer peasants. They anticipated that such developments would sort out the "worthy and industrious" poor, who were victims of genuine adversity in their own or their parents' lives, from those who lazily abused the guilt of others. Such an expectation came across clearly in the sermon which an English vicar delivered to his "lambs" in 1715, commemorating a merchant's gift of a linen workhouse to the community. Unlike distributions of money, he preached, the workhouse had transformed a "barren wilderness" into a "well-watered green" (Acres 1715).

The promotion of linen manufacture as an alternative to charity spoke to the quality and quantity of population—cornerstones of the mercantile state. An eighteenth-century Scottish merchant provided a representative view of quality when he wrote that the discontented and turbulent idle poor made bad soldiers. Seditious or mutinous in wartime, impossible to disarm in peace, they contrasted markedly with the "working poor" who, even though they had no property, "cheerfully [risked] their lives in war." This was in itself a reason to invest in linen (Lindesay 1736:6–9). As Guignet suggests, the promoters believed that work, no less than property, was morally redemptive and that the working poor could be saved (1976:30–52,420–34).

In addition to quality of population, mercantilist doctrine also emphasized numbers. The strength of a nation derived not from its silver and gold mines, but from the density of its active population. Given that for many of the promoters, a root cause of pauperism was an excess of population manifest in over-large families, a populationist argument on behalf of linen seems contradictory. An Irish landlord-undertaker acknowledged as much when he described as his country's "fatal problem" that "we want people, and yet we have more than we know how to Employ" (Anon 1729:10). Flax cultivation and linen manufacture were his proposed solution. He shared with other promoters the conviction that these activities would not only occupy the vagrant and dispossessed, but also increase the rate of population growth. So prevalent was this idea that promoters aware of military planning proposed linen schemes for coastal areas in need of better defenses (Haines 1677:9).

There were three ways in which linen manufacturing was expected to enhance population. By providing employment, it would stem the migration of the poor and indigent to the colonies. Industrial areas could also be expected to attract immigrants, particularly skilled craftsmen. Most important, employment opportunities would encourage fertility through an increase in mating and marriage. As one promoter put it, when the "multitudes of poor are starving, they are frightened from marriage;" by contrast their "natural inclinations, which are heightened by Plenty and Satisfaction, prompt them to marry and beget Children." Their happiness, moreover, also "prompts foreigners to come" (Anon 1738:52). When, in 1677, A. Haines proposed that linen workhouses be established in every county of England, his rationale was that then there would no longer "be need of so great caution to prevent the Marriages of the meaner sort, since now the Parishes need not so much fear a Charge, knowing a means how to employ all their Children. . . " Far from "causing any depopulation," the scheme, he said, "may increase our Inhabitants; and the more the better, since we know how to dispose of them in such laudable Employment" (Haines 1677:10–11).

Hindsight suggests that the linen promoters were correct. Several well-known studies not only have shown an association between rural "proto-industry" and rising population, but also have identified the principal mechanism of this demographic increase as a shift to younger and more universal marriage (Braun 1978; Crawford 1968:32; Guignet 1976:335–55,622–23; Medick 1981; C. Tilly 1978; L. Tilly 1984:307–10). In Franklin Mendel's somewhat over-determined characterization of the linen districts of interior Flanders, "an improvement in the relative price of linen produced surges in the number of marriages" (1981:176).

The populationism implicit in the linen promotion schemes takes us part way toward understanding the moral and sociological issues raised by the spinning tales. In both the tales and the schemes, marriage was portrayed as a pivotal institution of rural life. Both also identified poverty and unemployment as the primary obstacles to marriage, while presenting the manufacture of linen as the main way out. The equation does not, however, tell us why the spinning tales present such ambivalent messages about this solution. Why did the inventors and transmitters of this folklore not declare a wholehearted enthusiasm for the industry that would save women from spinsterhood? To better grasp this ambivalence, two more steps are necessary: a closer look at the promotion schemes to discover how capital mobilized labor, and a look at the ecology of the manufacture within its agricultural setting. In the first instance, we will learn how the linen promoters played upon the motivations of producers, including their motivation to marry. In the second, the task is to uncover something intelligible to our modern secular consciousness about the dwarf demon, Rumpelstiltskin.

LINEN PROMOTION AND THE MOBILIZATION OF LABOR

There were two basic modes of textile production in Early Modern Europe. In the first, which German scholars call the *kauf* system, households organized the production of handicrafts. Although pressed to manufacture a surplus to meet their need for cash, they controlled and integrated the production process from the raw material to the finished cloth, which they then sold to merchants or used to pay their rent. The second, *verlag* system, based on putting-out, opened the door to a division of labor among the various stages of production, and to merchant ownership of the raw materials and semifinished goods as they moved from stage to stage.

Because flax cultivation was widespread among Europe's peasant households, the linen industry naturally gravitated toward the *kauf* pattern—much as peasant households in the cotton-growing areas of China organized production, from planting the fiber to the finished textile (Chao 1977). The German historian Jürgen Schlumbohm attributes the marked seasonal variation in the marketing of cloth in Osnabruck, Hanover, to the *kauf* system. Cloth came to market mainly in the summer months because, as contemporaries observed, it took nearly a year to cultivate and harvest the flax, and to process, spin, weave, bleach, and finish it. Because all of these steps occurred within individual households, they had to be sequential, so the time of planting the fiber determined the time of eventually selling the cloth (Schlumbohm 1983).

In describing the *kauf* system of Osnabruck, Schlumbohm emphasizes that it was not a retrograde movement. Like its Chinese cotton counterpart, it generated a substantial export trade, evident in the large number of "Osnabrucks" that clothed New World slaves. Yet, except for the fact that adult women managed most of the weaving, the system discouraged a division of labor, whether between agriculture and industry, or, within households, between men and women, adults and children, all of whom labored on the crops, and all of whom spun (Schlumbohm:104–08; also see Guignet 1976:204–14; L. Tilly 1984:303–07).

Some observers praised the system for its close articulation of activities, such that "the disadvantages of bad spinning soon became apparent in the weaving" and could be corrected. Others, however, blamed the decline of Osnabruck linens on the seasonal, part-time commitment of the rural population and their inefficiency in the assignment of tasks. Most important, Osnabruck was but an island in a larger sea of linen production that struck a balance between household manufacture and putting-out. In nearby Bielefeld, in Prussia, for example, spinning, weaving, bleaching, and finishing developed as separate industries, integrated by merchants. The result was not fully a putting-out system, because flax was locally produced and the spinners, if they did not cultivate it themselves, could purchase the processed fiber from local farmers and brokers, selling the yarn "in small quantities to the weavers or the yarn dealer . . . " (Schlumbohm 1983:107–15). Nevertheless it bore the stamp of the linen promotion schemes.

Several features were common to these schemes. The promoters generally had capital which they invested in one or more of the following ways: To advance credit for flax seed, sowers, spinning wheels, reels, or looms to producers; to construct or rehabilitate buildings for processing the fiber and for spinning, weaving, and bleaching the cloth; and to purchase housing and other amenities that would attract skilled textile craftsmen. The diasporas of religious persecution, of which the Huguenots were a particularly relevant example, provided many of these craftsmen.

Most of the promotion literature also marshaled arguments in favor of government intervention in linen development, whether through tariff legislation against competitive imports, through capital investment, or through the maintenance of a regulatory apparatus to control quality without stifling the production schemes. The pamphlets and broadsides that the promoters wrote were, in fact, often addressed to government bodies.

Of all the plans for investment capital, whether public or private, the most interesting were proposals for prizes and bounties to reward initiative and industriousness among the producers. These rewards and punishments reflect a view of the rural population as so many actors "naturally" distinguishable by their "unequal skills" and "differential capacities." The promoters' rewards were designed to play upon these distinctions in order to increase productivity (e.g., Guignet 1976:562–81). Credit was an important tool of social engineering. Advances against flax, yarn, or cloth expanded or contracted in relation to personal assessments of a debtor's honesty, cheerfulness, reliability, zeal, sobriety, or dedication to work. Additional loans helped favored clients pay their rent and purchase such household and personal "decencies" as silver plate, drapes, utensils, furnishings, ornaments, and apparel. Under special circumstances, credit made possible the repurchase of items that had earlier been pawned (Guignet 1976:585–91; Anon 1729).

Premiums and bounties augmented credit in the structuring of rewards and punishments. For example, the Irish landlord Sir Richard Cox in 1749 advertised as a "sure method to Establish the Linen Manufacture" his annual distribution of a dozen monetary prizes to those tenants who raised and dressed the most flax, spun the most and the best yarn, spun diligently for two years in a row, wove the most and the best cloth, and kept the most looms in operation. In addition, he boasted of setting aside an equal number of premiums for immigrant Protestant weavers who agreed to settle in his town, which between 1735 and 1749 had grown from 87 to 117 households, with 226 flax wheels. "I am persuaded," Cox wrote of the gold-lettered plaque that he had hung on the master weaver's house in honor of his "superior industry," that "the Invention has forwarded the Work, more than all the Money I have expended. It is a Natural Vanity to desire to be distinguished . . . And surely ought to be indulged, since it is productive to much Good" (Cox 1749:23–26). Elsewhere (1749:21) Cox described himself as "stirring up"—his French counterparts used the word "animating"—a "generous and useful Emulation between the new comers, which of them shall first become rich," and recommended this strategy for creating "in a short time different Classes of Rivals," until all become rich. "I forsaw," he wrote "that these good effects . . . would make others ashamed of their indolence, and stir up a Spirit of Industry" (1749:23).

Cox's promotion scheme included an overhaul of the ritual calendar; he discouraged his tenants from celebrating their traditional feast days and transformed May Day into "the joyous season of Determining the Premiums" (1749:32). Then, a full assembly gathered for the applauses and demerits that each deserved. In determining who got what, firsthand "Acquaintenance" and "Observation" were essential, for it was Cox's view that the "Undertaker must attend personally the growth of the Undertaking" (1749:48). He should not "receive Reports from others; For those will often be partial, through Love, Malice, or Envy; and then his Favours will be refused to the Deserving, and unprofitably conferred on those who will not deserve them. He must himself be the Witness and the Judge of Merit as well as the Distributor of Rewards" (1749: 29–30). Acknowledging that competition among producers could be in itself a source of envy, Cox also recommended that the Undertaker keep his inhabitants from "litigiousness and contention," using "a strong hand, watchful eye and resolute heart" against those who "grow rich under the Pretense of procuring Right, but are indeed even doing Wrong." Allowing free rein to their machinations would be as if a Cheesemonger were "rearing and cherishing Rats in his Shop" (1749:35).

Cox described his promotion scheme in a letter to a fellow undertaker, whom he thought could use it in the publication of how-to-do-it manuals. Other schemes, while less detailed, reveal the same understanding of promotion: One had to "stir-up" or "animate" the producers' ambitions and vanity; hold out to them examples of a better standard of living that they would want to emulate; attend to the talent, "capacities, genius and inclinations" of individuals (Lindesay 1736:52); encourage the right attitude with bounties and premiums while punishing obstinacy, carelessness and sloth. Having set the producers in competition with one another, each one "striving to excell the rest" (Haines 1677:6–7), a good undertaker had then to calm disputes (Bailey 1758). At cross-purposes with such peace-making was the system of remuneration for piecework, whose rates varied according to producers' "unequal skills" and "differential capabilities." As Guignet shows for lace makers, the "rapidity of work and quality of execution" were "naturally factors of social differentiation" and affected the price that was paid (1976:571–56).

From the accounts I have seen, it is fair to say that the promoters who energized flax cultivation and linen manufacture in seventeenth- and eighteenth-century Europe thought that spinning was the "bottleneck" of textile production, yarn the "strategic material," and spinners the "infantry"—it took up to eight spinners to keep a weaver in work (Guignet 1976:42,126–38,392; Deman 1852:90–91). In a *kauf* system of household manufacturing, everyone spun while the women wove. But in their schemes, the linen promoters singled out children and young women as the most promising candidates for the spinning task. Many of them justified this emphasis with the mercantilist arguments that female spinners "conserved the sinews" of the adult male for war, or tapped the greatest reservoir of rural idleness (Anon 1735:23; Bailey 1758:47). They also feminized the production of thread and yarn through the claim that small and delicate hands did it better. An English promoter on a visit to Ireland felt enthused by his discovery that "no women are apter to spin [flax] well than the Irish, who, labouring little in any kind with their hands, have fingers more supple and soft than other women of the poorer condition amongst us" (quoted in Horner 1920:21–21; Warner 1864:390). To a Scottish promoter, it was in the interest of all governments "to teach tender fingers as soon as tongues" (Anon 1715:1–8).

Schemes that feminized spinning did not necessarily envision mobilizing the spinners through the authority structure of the peasant household. On the contrary, many promoters advocated the organization of autonomous spinning institutions, free of parental control. Their argument included the observation that youthful women, when at home, were unruly. Unless sent out to be servants or chambermaids, their idleness led to "tearing hedges, robbing orchards, beggaring their fathers" (Anon 1715:14–19). If gathered to spin away from home, they might be more productive, for "when so many are employed in sight of each other" and with proper encouragement, "small and great" will strive to excel (Haines 1677:14). Of course, the fathers would also benefit. Without linen manufacturing, a man with many children was desperate; with it, he who had the most children lived the best (Acres 1715:14–19). Indeed, the daughter who spun was a "treasure," the more so because she could also spin her own clothes (Anon 1735:23).

Orphanages and workhouses that taught spinning represented the greatest separation of work from family and the most rigorous application of work discipline. Somewhat more relaxed were the spinning schools that the promoters organized and staffed with skilled instructors. An English traveler of the late seventeenth century recorded an example from Silesia. The mistress, holding a wand, stood at a pulpit in the center of the room, around which some 200 boys and girls, aged eight and older, sat spinning with distaff and spindle (the wheel was yet to arrive). The children produced yarn from flax supplied by their parents, graduating to higher benches, and eventually from the school, according to their proficiency. When one of them had spun all the flax on a distaff, the mistress rang a bell, and an assistant appeared to store the bobbin and deliver another distaff. The spinning mistress also summoned this assistant to mete out humiliations and floggings for idleness and sloth (Horner 1920:402–03; Warden 1864:365).

In addition to the spinning schools, the linen promoters encouraged the formation of a vast network of spinning mistresses, "fanning out" from a few source points to teach wheel spinning and improved techniques to the "most docile," who would in turn teach others. As with linen promotion generally, premiums "animated" this network. Another source of animation was the conscious recruitment of elite women to participate in spinning demonstrations because "Examples of this kind would stir up the lower Sort of People to practice and delight in an Employment so beneficial to themselves and the Public" (Bailey 1758:66). Seeing women of the "best Distinction" at the wheel, they would understand that "to spin is looked upon to be the greatest Honour and Perfection of the female sex" (quoted in Horner 1920:83). Other promoters characterized spinning as "the most genteel [occupation] for the delicate sex," and as "delightful and intellectual" (e.g. Deman 1852:90–91). One could, thought a Scottish merchant, solve the yarn problem by "prevailing on a Wise Woman in each parish to set an example." He also argued for a continuation of spinning premiums "which have already had so good effect that most of them are won by Ladies, whose Bread does not depend upon their Labour" (Anon 1734:20).

To some of the linen promoters (e.g., Acres 1715; Cox 1749), female spinners were like the enterprising woman in Proverbs Chapter 31, who chose flax, toiled at her work, and "like a ship laden with merchandise . . . [brought] home food from far off." Working through the night, never allowing her candle to expire, this "capable wife" even purchased land and planted a vineyard. Other promoters, however, wrote disparagingly of spinners who had become too enterprising. Valenciennes merchants, for example, claimed that the spinners of their district "perniciously" bypassed the local weavers, selling their yarn to itinerate bandits and interlopers, from whence it entered an international trade (Guignet 1976:42). Obsessed with the shortage of yarn, and with foreign (especially Dutch) competition for it, many promoters argued for the creation of a yarn market to reduce the spinners' options and control what they called the "hemorrhage" of yarn (1976:130–31). Some, however, attributed the young spinners' participation in contraband to their position at the bottom of the textile hierarchy, where remuneration was pitiful and the risk of indebtedness through advances dangerously high (1976:133).

Whether their remarks were couched in a language of sympathy, admiration, or mistrust, it is clear that the linen promoters considered the female spinners to be self-motivated persons, capable of diligent work if only their ambitions could be "kindled." And what were these ambitions if not marriage? The Scottish minister who preached the commemorative sermon for the merchant-donated workhouse in his parish alerted the "virgins" of his congregation that "the wheel and the distaff are an human nuptial wagon" (Acres 1715:14). His words were strongly echoed in the spinning bees, the nodule that formed throughout the vast network of "fanned-out" spinning instruction and that, even more than the schools and orphanages, structured the intensification of yarn production in the linen districts. For descriptions of this institution, we have Hans Medick's synthesis and interpretation of German language sources on the *Spinnstube* (1984).

Spinning technology, whether with distaff and spindle or with the pedal-operated wheel, was portable. Thus, when the work was a by-occupation of the long winter evenings, it made sense for neighbors to assemble in one place, save on light and fuel, and spin together. As we have seen, the promoters favored such collective spinning, claiming—contrary to the opinion of some—that when young women worked away from their families, their productivity improved (e.g., Acres 1715:13–18). However, the spinning bees, or *spinnstuben*, were controversial, because the assembled company lightened the burden of a tedious and repetitive activity with frivolity and entertainment. According to Medick, this fact did not deter the enthusiasm of the "defenders of mercantile performance" who, unlike contemporary religious and moral reformers, emphasized,". . . the economic usefulness and productivity of the specific forms of sociability and 'merriment' of the *Spinnstube*. The special connection between work and free time appeared to offer advantages as over against the tiring work inside household and family." Noting that "there was a clear connection of *Spinnstuben* work and sociability with the intensification of rural commodity production in textiles since the seventeenth century," Medick quotes an observer of the time who claimed that the "merriments" of the bees were "originally connected by our wise forefathers with this kind

*Figure 15. Painting, "Removing Flax from the Lint Hole, County Antrim";
Ulster Folk and Transport Museum, Holywood, County Down, Ireland*

of spinning, and that it chiefly caused the spinning of thread to become the most widespread and continuous manufacture, indeed a
real national industry"(Medick 1984:326–29).

   Spinnstube entertainment typically involved courtship play for,
as Medick shows, the institution was closely tied to "youth sexual
culture" and rural mating (1984:318). In the course of a typical evening, young men dropped by to flirt. Although they also devoted
much of their leisure to card-playing and smoking tobacco, they ate,
drank, and danced with the girls and, carrying their wheels, es-
corted them home. Flandrin, describing how French rural spinners
gathered in barns where the body heat of the cows kept their fingers
moving, quotes a contemporary to the effect that "a great many
striplings and lovers" regularly attended (quoted in 1976:109). So
much did the spinning bees nurture courtship that religious reformers, both Protestant and Catholic, attacked them as dens of vice, se-

duction, and immodesty where youths enjoyed too much autonomy from parental chaperoning (Medick 1984).

Some accounts of the spinning bees suggest an atmosphere of antagonism between the sexes that ranged from play to violence. For example, in the linen district of the Scottish lowlands, coy young women were reported to have used the rocks that weighted their spindles to batter unworthy suitors and escorts, as matrons sometimes battered their husbands, and the spinning assemblies in barns or houses were called "rockins" (Warden 1864:246). Similarly, Medick reports the mid-eighteenth-century severe beating of a weaver-journeyman with a distaff by the female company of a *spinnstube*, because he "visited unwanted attentions" on one of them (Medick 1984:331). Yet to characterize the work culture of spinning in terms of female solidarity is to miss the competitive relationships that flourished among young girls as they entered the mating game.

Redfern Mason describes the typical Irish spinning song as "an impromptu dialogue on the love affairs of the young people present," with nonsense verses inserted to punctuate the repartee of matching names (Mason 1911:118–24). A singer's keen wits and sharp tongue entertained the group as she dangerously skirted the edge of malicious ridicule and "saucy gossip." A line such as "you mannerless girl, he's your match," could make its subject feel "struck in the face" should the beau named be taken by another. "If the man is worth it, don't let her take him," was a possible retort—or, "There is no tree in the wood that I could not find its equal" (Mason 1911).

When a young girl's name became coupled with the name of an acceptable man, the sharp-witted dialogue shifted to the household furnishings that the newlyweds would try to acquire: "A twelve hundred tick with white feathers filled; white linen sheets and white baskets abundant; a quilt of fine silk, the dearest in Limerick; candlesticks of gold upon tables-a-glistening; Good gold and silver in their pockets-a-jingling . . . " (Mason 1911). Lists of this sort, as well as the taunting dialogue over names, suggest a double association between the spinning circles and courtship. The circles encouraged encounters between youths outside of parental sponsorship, and they drew attention to girls' chances for status mobility through marriage. Indeed, men hung around the gatherings not only to flirt, but also to evaluate the industriousness and skill of the women. According to numerous contemporaries, spinning skills contributed to marriageability and the better the spinner, the better the mate she might catch.

According to Medick, the mercantile defenders of the spinning bees were explicit on the link between marriage chances and spinning output. Finding value in what the moralists berated, they praised "the gatherings of both sexes in the *Spinnstube* and the competition of the women in terms of the village marriage market as a motive which could be used for the national economy." In the words of a contemporary, this arrangement "encourages work in a large society of compeers, especially when many young males are there to cast a watchful eye on the industry and quickness of the girls who would be their future wives. This is much better than when a girl spins alone with her mother or sister" (quoted in 1984:329). Medick concludes that neither the market nor the rulers gave "form or impetus to the rhythm of production of linen thread"; rather "the village marriage market" organized the "necessary coercion" (1984:332).

Should we wonder then, that competition in love and status mobility through marriage were central themes in the spinning tales? As Bottigheimer notes, it was in spinning bees that countless of these tales were invented, rearranged, and retold (1982:143).

We have seen that the linen promotion schemes typically had a populationist bent. Their authors claimed that the expansion of this industry would increase the rate of marriage in the countryside, multiplying the citizenry of their nation. Now it is apparent that this emphasis on marriage fit into their strategy for intensifying production—the strategy that deployed capital to animate labor through a system of punishments and rewards. Among the promised rewards for good spinning were prizes, decencies, and a decent husband.

The spinning tales, I think, commented with ambivalence on this structure of "capital penetration," expressing neither unqualified support nor clear opposition. In their juxtaposition of fabulous marriage opportunities with impossible spinning tasks, they warned of risk to the daughters of the poor who overcommitted their labor to marry up, or had it overcommitted by their parents. This ambivalence, it seems, reveals a sociological understanding of the manipulative aspects of the promotion schemes which, as Guignet suggests, created a pattern of subordination that was simultaneously "cordial" and "conflictual." Contacts between spinners or their parents and the agents of these schemes were, as we have seen, solicitous yet potentially dangerous. Even as the puppeteers of promotion dangled the hope that "superfluous children" could marry and even climb, they initiated debts, obligations, and potential legal entanglements that engulfed the spinners, to use Guignet's expression, "in quicksand" (1976:577–81). The Rumpelstiltkskin-type tale underscores this contradiction by weighing a strategy for marriage and mobility through rural textile manufacture against the costs to a future generation.

FLAX, FAIRIES, AND THE DEMONIZATION OF SPIRITS

According to the spinning tales, it was, despite appearances, spirits rather than the spirit of industry that animated spinners. Nor were spirits far removed from the spinners' world. Writing of the silk-reeling equivalent of the linen *spinnstube* in Lyons, Natalie Davis re-creates an atmosphere that in rural settings could only have been more enchanted: "a broken thread meant a quarrel; a man crossing a thread stretched at the doorsill . . . bore the same name as one's future husband." The water for washing threads "laughed" instead of boiled. And there were night visitors who came to finish the spinning or steal the spindles (Davis 1982:61). In the linen areas, spirit helpers participated in all the stages of production. Dwarfs and fairies could weave and bleach; from a single hank of yarn they could make the sails for an entire ship. Similarly, they were known to tailor shirts from miniscule fabrics, three inches square. Most impressive was their ability to spin, converting mountains of flax into yarn or gold at night. But fairies could also wreak mischief. For example, they fashioned horses and boats for the fairy kingdom from stalks of hemp or flax that they stole from mortal's fields. A flax crop with stunted plants was understood to have provided a means of fairy transportation.

On the whole, European peasants portrayed fairies, dwarfs, and trolls as "little people," no less worthy of the good things of life than humans. Indeed, it was common for folk tales to describe agreements between these spirits and humans, and to justify fairy pique when humans failed to live up to their part of the bargain. The animistic belief system underlying this perspective included the idea that the little people had inhabited the land first, but had yielded it, however unwillingly, to settle in rocks and caves, woods and streams, as human populations and agricultural activities expanded. Thus deprived of space, the fairy societies came to depend upon human contributions to ensure their perpetuation. It was widely held that fairy children could not be born except with the assistance of human midwives, and that, to maintain their numbers, fairies would at times kidnap a mortal woman of childbearing age, or rob a human cradle, leaving behind a changeling. In exchange, however, they offered the powers of magic on behalf of human goals, often without thought of repayment. If they occasionally stole from the flax field, perhaps it was because they had once lived under its soil.

Beliefs about fairies, trolls, and dwarfs shaded subtly into a set of ideas about evil spirits and witches, yet these concepts were not the same. Evil or witchlike spirits were thought to be motivated by envy and spite, and therefore quick to distort their side of the relationship with humans. Fairy tricks and shakedowns could ultimately find justification in an overall balance of give and take, particularly in the context of the fairies' prior claim to the land. But the very same acts when attributed to witches violated the model of reciprocity. Witches would stunt your flax crop, not to acquire the raw materials for a boat that they needed, but because they hated you and relished seeing you ruined.

Apparently, witches were after flax in the linen districts of the Celtic fringe, the Germanies, Switzerland, and Eastern Europe. Frazer collected for *The Golden Bough* (1890) many stories linking this crop to the ritual fires that peasants lit, whether to give light to reciprocating spirits or to destroy witches and vampires. On the eve of May Day, in conjunction with the midsummer solstice, and again on All Hallow's eve, peasants typically celebrated the transitions in the agricultural cycle with great bonfires (originally bone fires). Young people, impersonating spirits or magically transformed through spiritual intervention, mummed and begged for pieces of wood and brush to use as fuel. It was risky not to contribute, for a good fire was the best defense against personal and household misfortune in the form of hailstorms, crop failures, and the wasting diseases so prevalent among the peasants' livestock and their children. The idea that fire could destroy malevolent spirits led neighboring villages to vie for the largest conflagration, and to burn their most hated enemies in effigy. The fires were also believed to promote fertility. Young unmarried couples—perhaps the same couples who flirted in the *spinnstuben*—leapt over the glowing embers, celebrating the pending marriages and procreative yearnings of sexually maturing youth.

Flax figured importantly in bonfire rituals, especially the midsummer fires of June 24, which the Church assimilated to the feast of Saint John the Baptist. One belief focused on height through imitative magic; the height of the flames foretold how tall the crop would grow. More commonly, it was held that the higher a young couple jumped in the air when leaping over the still-burning embers, the taller their eventual flax stalks. Parents of the youth who leapt the highest could count on the tallest crop, unless they had failed to contribute fuel to the fire. In some apparently more Christianized villages, nubile girls climbed the bell tower to ward off witches through bell-ringing, and it was said that the girl who swung highest on the bell rope would have the tallest crop (Frazer 1980:247–48).

In addition to staging fertility campaigns based on imitative magic, peasants attempted to harness energy from the spirits they were destroying and channel it into fecundity and renewal. In Bavaria, for example, they slew a dragon-monster during the Midsummer ritual, spreading the blood-soaked (linen) cloths on their flax fields. Almost everywhere, the charred sticks from the bonfires were considered prophylactic for witchcraft; people took them home, fashioned cattle prods from them, and planted them along with their flax. The flames, too, were protective; in planting decisions one took account of the direction in which the wind blew them.

The idea that witches threatened the flax crop is closely related to the idea that the spirits who showed up to help spin it were dangerous to human reproduction. The Rumpelstiltskins, intensely interested in the offspring of those they helped, were also witch-like. By what process did the "little people" become so demonized? How were the rocky or forested peripheries of settled areas transformed into redoubts of spiritual danger? Part of the answer undoubtably lies in the witch-hunt that tore up rural Europe in the sixteenth and seventeenth centuries.

Subjecting peasants to an elite demonology that assimilated all earth spirits and spirits of the dead to the Christian devil, both Catholic and Protestant reformers spread witch-hunt propaganda with the newly available printing press and a state-supported apparatus of courts and itinerant prosecutors. Yet peasants must also have contributed to the transformation, their vision of the demonic becoming more elaborate as linen production intensified. According to peasant belief, the dairy cattle that provided the food staple in so many of the linen districts had already displaced the spirit dwellers of fields and meadows, and thus were constant targets of witchcraft and vindictive spirit tricks. People not only prodded their cattle with charred sticks snatched from the midsummer fires, but drove them through these fires for greater protection. Where flax cultivation and linen manufacture overlaid subsistence agriculture, the environmental impact was many times greater than that of cattle alone. Keeping in mind the "little people"—the prior inhabitants of the landscape—let us see how dramatic, and unwelcome, the linen intrusion was.

THE ENVIRONMENTAL IMPACT OF FLAX PRODUCTION

The climate range that flax can endure is broad; the best-known fields were as far apart as the Nile valley and the deltas of northern Russia. Yet since the industrial revolution unleashed the unrelenting competition of cotton, 96 percent of the world's flax supply has come to be grown between 49 and 53 degrees latitude, with more than 82 percent of the acreage now in the Soviet Union (Dempsey 1975:3,6–7). The reason is that flax is a "long day" crop which benefits from northern light. In addition, it thrives in moderate temperatures, evenly distributed rainfall, and moist winds. Most important is the quality of nutrition it receives, with both the yield and fineness of the crop enhanced by well-drained alluvial or loam soils, located in river deltas or near the shores of lakes, where the water table is high (Dempsey 1975:7–10). The plant sinks deep roots, so these soils must be pulverized through several plowings. They should also be weeded, because flax competes poorly with weeds and is exceptionally vulnerable to fungal diseases introduced through spores. Finally, flax is sown broadcast so that weeding is a hands-and-knees operation, conducted when the flax plants are still young enough to be crushed and stand up again (Dempsey 1975:14–26; Warden 1864:4–17,33–34). According to estimates from Flanders, to harvest an acre of flax took twelve to fifteen adult workers while eighty-two "woman" days were necessary to weed it (Mendels 1981:175–76).

Like cotton, flax exhausts the soil. In virtually all rotation systems, cultivators allow five to ten years between flax crops (Dempsey 1975:14; Horner 1920:449–50). According to Slicher van Bath, it had already become apparent to north Italians by the late Middle Ages that too much flax was a threat to their grain crops, which also taxed the soil. Their solution, adopted as well by south German manufacturers of fustian, was in some ways a harbinger of eighteenth- and nineteenth-century British imperialism: Import cotton from the tropics and conserve temperate soils for food (Slicher van Bath 1963).

In addition to causing soil exhaustion, flax requires a heavy burden of labor to prepare it for textile manufacture. A ton of dried flax straw yields no more than 400 pounds of long linen fibers and another hundred pounds of short fibers or "tow." The crop must be pulled, not cut; left in place, its roots would injure successive cultigens (Horner 1920:450). Having dried out for two to three days, it must then be steeped or retted—arranged in one layer and anchored with stones just below the surface of a slowly flowing stream or pond. This process, which takes from ten days to two weeks, loosens the cellulose fibers from the plant's woody core and surrounding bark. The water ferments the resins and gums that hold these parts together, yielding as its byproduct a fetid, pungent-smelling scum and sediment that is capable of killing fish. This explains the many laws that governed the disposal of retting water, as well as the places where retting could take place (Warden 1864:36–40).

Once retted, the flax crop is carefully lifted from the water, using hands rather than rakes, which would injure the fibers, and laid out on a meadow to be "grassed." The more thinly it is spread, the less the need to turn it during the week or more that it spends distended and exposed to air. An exposure of three weeks to a month can substitute for submerged retting in some moister climates, the fermentation taking place from the action of dew (Kirby 1963:25).

Grassing is followed by breaking and scutching, operations that today take place in mills, but before the late eighteenth century were performed with a simple wooden press that fragmented the bark and core. This was followed by several twists with the hands to dislodge the fragments, and finally, by shaking and beating with a wooden knife. One last step before spinning was to "hackle" or "heckle" the fibers, removing all remnants of gum and resin as well as the short fibers or tow, with combs of several grades made by the village blacksmith. To remove impurities without shredding the long fibers took considerable skill, and in many flax-growing regions, itinerant combers did the job. Elsewhere, it was thought to be women's work and men had to learn an "artificial weakness" to do it (Horner 1920:379). In such areas, women owned hatchels and combs as well as spinning wheels, reels, and yarns.

Once spun and woven into cloth, linen was usually bleached, both to remove residual impurities and because, as a cellulose vegetable fiber, it was hard to dye. Degrees of whiteness, rather than hues of color, were (in addition to fineness) the index of a linen cloth's reputation. The bleaching process did not become efficient until after 1760, when Irish bleachers developed a chloride of lime, or slaked lime, powder that allowed them to eliminate steps without jeopardizing the fibers. Before then, the multiple steps could take up to seven months. The cloth was first washed in soap and water, then rinsed and steeped or boiled in a cauldron with lye, potash, bone ash, or cow dung. After a 48-hour soak came more washing and beating, followed by two days of "grassing." Then the fabric was laid on a "bleach green" to air, being watered periodically. These operations were repeated several times before souring, usually in a vat of buttermilk, for up to three weeks. After souring came more washing, beating, and grassing. The souring and grassing series, like the preceding series of alternate lye steeps and airings, was repeated five or six times, until the desired whiteness was obtained. Attempts to shorten this process through the use of pure lime or acids ran the risk of over-oxidizing the delicate fibers (Coons and Koob 1980:62; Horner 1920:40–41; Trotman and Trotman 1948:124–25).

Clearly, a linen industry brought many sources of irritation to other users of the land. Its impact can be heard in the strident voices

Figure 16. Before Irish bleachers developed slaked lime in 1760, fabrics were spread out on "bleaching greens." Painting, "Bleaching Ground," by David Teniers; Semper Galerie: Dresden

of the agricultural improvers (another kind of promoter in the eighteenth century), and seen in the dilemmas faced by peasants who worried about their cows.

The improvers could rightly be concerned about soil exhaustion, the pollution of ponds and streams, the absorption of rural labor for harvesting, processing, and spinning, and the tendency of both flax and cloth to overrun good meadows. Fields for grassing and bleaching, abundant in regions of linen manufacture, were often as large as seven acres. Dew retting, common east of the Elbe, took up especially large areas "which [could] not be used for any other purpose" while the fermentation took place (Kirby 1963:25). Hence the argument that perservering with flax would "prove destructive both to the tenant and to the soil." Note the contempt of the late eighteenth-century agricultural reformer, Arthur Young:

> View the north of Ireland and you behold a whole province
> peopled by weavers; it is they who cultivate, or rather beggar,

the soil, as well as work the looms. Agriculture is there in ruins;
it is cut up by the roots, extirpated, annihilated. The whole region is the disgrace of the kingdom. All the crops you can see
are contemptible, are nothing but filth and weeds; no other part
of Ireland can exhibit the soil in such a state of poverty and des-
olation. But the cause of all those evils, which are absolute ex-
ceptions to everything else on the face of the globe, is easily
found. A most prosperous manufacture, so contrived as to be
the destruction of agriculture, is certainly a spectacle for which
we must go to Ireland. It is owing to the fabric spreading all
over the country, instead of being confined to towns. There, literally speaking, is not a farmer in a hundred miles of the linen
country of Ireland. The lands are infinitely subdivided (and the)
weaver . . . has always a piece of potatoes, a piece of oats, a
patch of flax, and grass for a cow . . . If I had an estate in the
south of Ireland, I would as soon introduce pestilence and famine upon it as the linen-manufacture . . . (quoted in Horner
1920:52).

The voices of tenants and cottagers came through less clearly than
the voices of improvers like Arthur Young, not only because they
were illiterate, but also because their relationship to linen was more
complicated. After all, the manufacture began as their by-
occupation, a welcome source of income to make ends meet. Moreover, up to a certain point, linen was compatible with—even complementary to—the cattle husbandry that ensured subsistence in
many of the linen districts. Did not cloth makers sour this textile
in several successive buttermilk baths (sometimes also in cattle
dung), while linseed (flax seed) and linseed cake made excellent cattle fodder? Did not the body heat of cows keep the fingers of the
spinners warm? In 1736, Stephen Bennet, an English promoter visiting Sweden, argued for raising more cattle in a linen district "for
without milk whey for the perfection of the bleaching, all labour is
in vain . . . " (Geijer 1979:175). Buttermilk, however, was also an
ideal substance on which to wean calves, whose removal from their
mothers was essential to milk production for the farm. And linseed
was not known as cattle feed until a Norfolk farmer of the mid-
nineteenth century discovered this possibility. Furthermore, to raise
flax as a fodder required a different technique than to raise it as a
fiber. One had to sow the crop widely to encourage branching and

leave it in the field until the seeds had thoroughly ripened, by which time the stalks were tough. When intended as a fiber, flax plants were sown thickly and pulled green, just after they had flowered. One could still remove their seeds, through a process called rippling, and allow them to ripen thereafter, but they would not then excel as feed. Moreover, some producers claimed that if flax were retted with the seeds still attached, it would come out finer (Warden 1864:17ff).

Surely, the greatest losses to cattle from having linen in their midst came from "grassing." The very word suggests competition for grazing areas, above all the bottomland meadows enriched from the overflow of rivers and streams. As one promoter put it in describing the proper conditions for bleaching greens and airing the retted plants, it was important to select "short, thick pasture ground . . . clean and free from cattle" (Warden 1864:36,47), that is, level ground, safe from wind and floods, and "not in danger of being disordered by Cattle, Fowl or Vermin" (Bailey 1758:51–64). Finally, in the complex rotation cycles developed to incorporate flax, it often replaced clover or hay or shared a divided field with them. (Warden 1864:33). It is no accident, therefore, that in the tiny area of Flanders, famous for early improvements in *both* dairying and flax cultivation, there developed an internal division between maritime agricultural and internal textile zones (Mendels 1981). Such a division was paralleled in the Vendée where, as Tilly has shown, the plains and valleys became devoted to commercial farming, while subsistence farming coupled with rural textile industries characterized much of the Bocage (Tilly 1964:33–35). Similar descriptions exist for the Scottish lowlands (Smout 1969:127–28), and for the micro-environments of Silesia (Kisch 1981).

At the same time that linen manufacture undermined local agricultural resources, posing a particular challenge to cattle, it contributed to population pressure on the land. This in turn caused many of the linen districts to import food, rendering their inhabitants more vulnerable than before to price inflation and periodic shortages (Schlumbohm 1981:117–25). The resulting subsistence crises reinforced the perception that what linen added by way of additional income could quickly disappear because of the new dependencies it created. Particularly destabilizing were the crises in which food shortages and sagging textile markets coincided, threatening the return of pauperism (e.g., Kisch 1981). Yet, despite the dangerous implications of linen intensification for subsistence farming (and over the objections of the agricultural improvers), the linen promoters held firm.

It was not a problem, they argued, that the land became fragmented and more densely populated, for this increased its value to the lords who collected the rents (Cox 1749:40). Besides, an expanding population could clear or drain the forest and bog, creating enclosures on these once communal resources (1749:41–43). Of course, critics would label flax as "pernicious," but the retting water killed beasts and fish only if it were left to stagnate. Allowed to evaporate on the fields, it provided a fertilizer (Crommelin 1705:11; Hyndman 1774:26). Most important, the "great aversion" to flax could be explained away. Perhaps it grew out of the pastoral bias of the ancestors, who wanted the land for grazing and clothed themselves in wool. Perhaps it was merely the propaganda of the already successful flax farmers who sought to monopolize this most valuable source of "wealth and grandeur" (Bailey 1758:51; Hyndman 1774:33). For some promoters, the aversion was attributable to the "venom and rancour" of landlords who made their living by "settling the land with dairies and poor cottagers," and to whom "able tenants" and industrious immigrants were a threat. Anticipating the "eternal objections" of those who forever "discouraged any new venture," the linen promoters felt confident of the contribution their projects would make to the cottagers' standard of living and the "publick Good" (Cox 1749:46–48). Needless to say, they proferred numerous prizes and premiums to "induce individuals" to expand their flax fields and bleaching greens, and advocated considering only the dryness of the ground, not the position of the moon and other superstitious indications, when planting the crop (Hill 1817:20; Hyndman 1774:8).

It seems to me that the fairies and trolls, dwarfs and green men of the linen districts became demonic to the degree that linen production intruded on their living space, over and above the prior intrusion of subsistence crops and livestock. For, while promising love and money, the linen promotion schemes undermined not only an earlier autonomy and earlier social ties, but also earlier uses and users of the land. It matters little that some of the prior users were ancestors (dressed in wool, perhaps), and some were earth spirits;

these two categories of spirit often merged. What does seem significant was their resentment of the new activity and their motivation to sabotage those who benefited from it.

PROMOTERS, PEASANTS, AND RUMPELSTILTSKINS

I have attempted to show that the intensification of the rural linen industry in Early Modern Europe met neither unmitigated opposition nor unbounded support from the peasant producers of yarn and flax. During times of high food prices and rising unemployment, riots sometimes broke out. But as recent scholarship demonstrates, the food riot was a long way from expressing the solidarity and consciousness of a "producing class" (Reddy 1984). More revealing of the ambivalent positions of the flax growers and spinners was their folk ideology as encoded in customs, tales, and songs. The linen-related motifs of this folklore offer clues to the producers' moral and sociological assessment of merchant capitalism as it organized linen manufacture. I have emphasized that their assessment raised, without ever being able to resolve, a series of troubling contradictions in the intensification process. The process brought improved marriage chances and jeopardy to one's offspring; money or "riches" and the shift from trusting to litigious social relations; material rewards in the form of "decent" apparel and furnishings and vulnerability to periodic crises in which these items were pawned. It is no wonder that the intensified uses of the landscape would also transform fairies into devil-like Rumpelstiltskins.

Note that the demonized spirits of the spinning tales did not seek to eliminate linen manufacture. On the contrary, Rumpelstiltskin and the witch-like crones contributed to its development, magically producing yarn and facilitating the status mobility through marriage that the linen schemes promised as the reward for diligent spinning. The spirits did, however, claim a piece of the action through their malicious sabotage of human reproduction. As such they splendidly dramatized the core dilemma of the linen "proto-industry." Inextricably mixing opportunity with danger, it rescued poor women from celibacy, shame, or migration only to jeopardize their and their children's social support and health. Caught in this dilemma, the producers crystallized their ambivalence toward the promotion of linen in tales of misfits like Rumpelstiltskin, who were nasty and yet helpful at the same time.

REFERENCES CITED

Bottigheimer, Ruth B.
1981   Tale Spinners: Submerged Voices in Grimms' Fairy Tales. New German Critique 27:141–50.

Chao, Kang
1977   The Development of Cotton Textile Production in China. Cambridge, Mass. and London: Harvard University Press.

Coleman, D.C.
1969   An Innovation and its Diffusion: the "New Draperies." Economic History Review (Second Series) 22:417–29.

Coons, Martha and Katherine Koob
1980   All Sorts of Good and Sufficient Cloth. Linen Making in New England 1640–1860. North Andover, Mass.: Merrimack Valley Textile Museum.

Crawford, W.H.
1968   The Rise of the Linen Industry. In L.M. Cullen, ed. The Formation of the Irish Economy. Cork: The Mercier Press.

Cullen, L.M. and T.C. Smout
n.d.   Comparative Aspects of Scottish and Irish Economic and Social History, 1600–1900. Edinburgh: John Donald Publishers.

Davis, Natalie Zemon
1982   Women in the Crafts in Sixteenth-Century Lyon. Feminist Studies 1:47–80.

Dempsey, James M.
1975   Fiber Crops. Gainsville: University of Florida Press.

Endrei, Walter
1968   L'évolution des techniques du filage et du tissage du moyen age à la révolution industrielle. Paris and Le Haye: Mouton.
1971   Changements dans la productivité de l'industrie lainière au moyen age. Annales E.S.C. 26:1291–99.

Evans, E. Estyn
1957   Irish Folk Ways. New York: Devin-Adair.

Flandrin, Jean-Louis
1980   Families in Former Times: Kinship, Household and Sexuality. Cambridge and New York: Cambridge University Press.

Frazer, Sir James George
    1890   The Golden Bough. New York: Macmillan.

Geijer, Agnes
    1979   A History of Textile Art. London: Philip Wilson.

Grant, I.F.
    1961   Highland Folk Ways. London: Routledge and Kegan Paul.

Guignet, Philippe
    1976   Mines, Manufactures et Ouvriers du Valenciennois au XVIIIe Siècle. Contribution à l'histoire du Travail dans l'ancienne France. 2 Vol. 1977 edition, New York: Arno Press, Dissertations in European Economic History.

Horner, John
    1920   The Linen Trade of Europe During the Spinning-Wheel Period. Belfast: M'Caw, Stevenson and Orr.

Kellenbenz, Hermann
    1976   The Rise of the European Economy: An Economic History of the Continent of Europe, 1500–1700. New York: Holmes and Meier.

Kirby, Richard Henry
    1963   Vegetable Fibers: Botany, Cultivation and Utilization. London: Leonard Hill Books.

Kisch, Herbert
    1981   The Textile Industries in Silesia and the Rhineland: A Comparative Study in Industrialization (with a postscriptum). *In* Peter Kriedte, Hans Medick, and Jürgen Schlumbohm, eds. Industrialization before Industrialization. Cambridge and New York: Cambridge University Press.

Kriedte, Peter
    1981a   The Origins, the Agrarian Context, and the Conditions in the World Market. *In* Peter Krietde, Hans Medick, and Jürgen Schlumbohm, eds. Industrialization before Industrialization. Cambridge and New York: Cambridge University Press. pp.12–38.
    1981b   Proto-industrialization between Industrialization and De-industrialization. *In* Ibid. pp.135–61.
    1983   Peasants, Landlords and Merchant Capitalists: Europe and the World Economy, 1500–1800. Cambridge: Cambridge University Press.

Leggett, William F.
    1945   The Story of Linen. Brooklyn, New York: The Chemical Publishing Company.

Lythe, S.G.E.
    1960   The Economy of Scotland in its European Setting, 1550–1625. Edinburgh and London: Oliver and Boyd.

Mazzaoui, Maureen Fennell
1981   The Italian Cotton Industry in the Later Middle Ages, 1100–1600. Cambridge: Cambridge University Press.

Medick, Hans
1981   The Proto-industrial Family Economy. *In* Peter Kriedte, Hans Medick, and Jürgen Schlumbohm, eds. Industrialization before Industrialization. Cambridge and New York: Cambridge University Press. pp.38–74.
1984   Village Spinning Bees: Sexual Culture and Free Time among Rural Youth in Early Modern Germany. *In* H. Medick and D. Sabean, eds. Interest and Emotion; Essays on the Study of Family and Kinship. Cambridge: Cambridge University Press.

Mendels, Franklin F.
1981   Agriculture and Peasant Industry in Eighteenth Century Flanders. *In* Peter Kriedte, Hans Medick, and Jürgen Schlumbohm, eds. Industrialization before Industrialization. Cambridge: Cambridge University Press.

Nicholas, David
1976   Economic Reorientation and Social Change in Fourteenth Century Flanders. Past and Present 70:3–29.

Rae, Gordon and Charles E. Brown
1968   Geography of Scotland, General and Regional. London: G. Bell and Sons.

Rebel, Hermann
1988   Why Not "Old Marie"—Or Someone Very Much Like Her? A Reassessment of the Question about the Grimm's Contributors from a Social Historical Perspective. Social History 13:1–24.

Reddy, William M.
1984   The Rise of Market Culture: The Textile Trade and French Society, 1750–1900. Cambridge: Cambridge University Press.

Sabean, David
1975   German Agrarian Institutions at the Beginning of the Sixteenth Century. Upper Swabia as an Example. The Journal of Peasant Studies 3:76–89.

Schlumbohm, Jürgen
1981   Relations of Production—Productive Forces—Crises in Proto-industrialization. *In* Peter Kriedte, Hans Medick, and Jürgen Schlumbohm, eds. Industrialization before Industrialization. Cambridge and New York: Cambridge University Press. pp.94–126.
1983   Seasonal fluctuations and social division of labour: rural linen production in the Osnabrück and Bielefeld regions and the urban woollen industry in the Niederlausitz (c. 1770–c. 1850). *In*

Maxine Berg, et al, eds. Manufacture in town and country before the factory. Cambridge: Cambridge University Press.

Sharp, Buchanan
1980   In Contempt of all Authority. Rural Artisans and Riot in the West of England, 1586–1660. Berkeley and Los Angeles: University of California Press.

Slicher van Bath, B.H.
1963   The Agrarian History of Western Europe A.D. 500–1850. London: Edward Arnold.

Smout, T.C.
1969   A History of the Scottish People, 1560–1830. New York: Charles Scribner's Sons.

Spenceley, G.F.R.
1973   The Origins of the English Pillow Lace Industry. Agriculture History Review 21:81–94.

Taylor, Peter and Hermann Rebel
1981   Hessian Peasant Women, their Families and the Draft: A Social Historical Interpretation of Four Tales from the Grimm Collection. Journal of Family History 6.

Thirsk, Joan
1961   Industries in the Countryside. In F.J. Fisher, ed., Essays in the Economic and Social History of Tudor and Stuart England. pp.70–88. Cambridge: Cambridge University Press

Tilly, Charles
1964   The Vendée; a Sociological Analysis of the Counterrevolution of 1793. New York: John Wiley and Sons.
1978   The Historical Study of Vital Processes. In C. Tilly, ed. Historical Studies of Changing Fertility. Princeton: Princeton University Press.

Tilly, Louise
1984   Linen was their life: family survival strategies and parent-child relations in nineteenth-century France. In H. Medick and D.W. Sabean, eds. Interest and Emotion: Essays on the Study of Family and Kinship. Cambridge: Cambridge University Press.

Tits-Dieuaide, M.J.
1980   L'évolution des techniques agricoles en Flandre et en Brabant du XIVe au XVIe siècle. Annales E.S.C. 35:362–81.

Trotman, S.R. and E.R. Trotman
1948   The Bleaching, Dyeing, and Chemical Technology of Textile Fibers. London: Charles Griffin.

Warden, Alex J.
    1864   The Linen Trade, Ancient and Modern. London: Longman, Roberts and Green.

Primary Documents from the Seligman Collection, Columbia University Libraries

Anon. 1700. A Letter from a Merchant in Scotland to his Correspondent in London Relating to the Duty upon Scotch-Linnen. Printer unnamed. (L569)

Anon. 1729. A Scheme for Supplying Industrious Men with Money to Carry on their Trades, and for better Providing for the Poor of Ireland. 2nd edition. Dublin: Printed by Thomas Hume, opposite Essex Bridge. (B513)

Anon. 1734. A Letter to the Author of the Interest of Scotland Considered; Containing some Hints about the Linnen Manufactures. Edinburgh: Printed for Gavin Hamilton by R. Flemming. (L564)

Anon. 1735. Some Considerations on the Improvement of the Linen Manufacture in Ireland, particularly with Relation to the Raising and Dressing of Flax and Flax-Seed. Dublin: Printed by R. Reilly on Cork Hill. (R73)

Anon. 1739. Some Thoughts on the Importance of the Linnen-Manufacture to Ireland and How to Lessen the Expense of it. Dublin: Printed by and for George Faulkner. (S052)

Anon. 1740. The Rules to be Observed by the Flax-Raisers appointed by the Trustees for the Manufactures, and by all others who Apply to Them for a Premium for Raising Lint, etc. No publisher. (R86)

Anon. 1753 (orig. 1738). A Letter from a Merchant Who has left the Trade, to a Member of Parliament, in which The Case of the British and Irish Manufacture of Linen, Thread, and Tapes is fairly stated; and all the Objections against the Encouragement proposed to be given to that Manufacture fully answered. London. (B512)

Anon. 1762. A Review of the Evils that have Prevailed in the Linen Manufacture of Ireland. Dublin: Printed for Peter Wilson.

Anon. 1778. A Linen Draper's Letter to the Friends of Ireland. Dublin: no printer named. (L64)

Acres, Joseph, 1715. The Linen Manufacture. A Sermon Preach'd at Blewbury Sept. 19, 1715. Being the Day appointed for an Anniversary Sermon, upon the Account of the Large Charity given to the Poor of that Village, by William Malthus, late Citizen and Merchant of London. London: Printed for J. Baker in Pater-Noster-Row. (AC76)

Bailey, William. 1758. A Treatise on the Better Employment and More Comfortable Support of the Poor in Workhouses, Together with some Observations on the Growth and Culture of Flax with diverse new Inventions, neatly engraved on copper, for the Improvement of the Linen Manufacture of which the Importance and Advantages are Considered and Evinced. London: Printed for and Sold by the Author at the Corner of Castle Cort in the Strand. (B15)

Cox, Sir Richard. Bart., 1749. A Letter to Thomas Prior, Esq. Shewing, from Experience, a Sure Method to Establish the Linen-Manufacture, and the Beneficial Effects, it will immediately produce. Dublin: Printed for Peter Wilson. (C839)

Crommelin, Louis, Overseer of the Royal Linnen-Manufacture. 1734 (Orig. 1705). An Essay Towards the Improving of the Hempen and Flaxen Manufactures in the Kingdom of Ireland. Dublin: Reprinted for R. Owen, Bookseller in Skinner Row. (C88)

Distaff, Jenny. 1720. The Linen Spinster, in defense of the Linen Manufactures No. One. London: Printed for F. Roberts at the Oxford Arms in Warrwick Lane.

Haines, R. 1677. Proposals for Building in every County a Working-Alms-House or Hospital; as the Best Expedient to perfect the Trade and Manufactory of Linnen Cloth. London: Printed by W.G. for R. Harford. (H127)

Hill, Samuel Esq. 1817. A Plan for Reducing the Poor's Rate by Giving Permanent Employment to the Labouring Classes with Some Observations on the Cultivation of Flax and Hemp and an Account of a new process for dressing and preparing flax and Hemp without water-steeping and dew-retting. London: printed for J. Harding, St. James Street. (H55)

Hyndman, C. 1774. A new method of Raising Flax; by which it is Proved that Ireland may raise annually many Thousand Pounds Worth more Flax than the usual Quantity of Land, and from one Fourth less seed than by the Common Method. With Tables, Shewing what Quantity of Seed will sow any Lot of Ground. The whole Containing Many useful and Curious Remarks on that Valuable Plant, never before made Publick. Belfast: Printed by James Magee for the Author. (H99)

Laing, Alexander. 1872. Lecture on the History of the Linen Manufacture in Newburgh (Fife). Newburgh on Tay: James Wood.

Lindesay, Patrick. 1735. Reasons for Encouraging the Linnen Manufacture of Scotland and other parts of Great Britain. Humbly submitted to Parliament. London: Printed for John Peele. (L64)

Lindesay, Patrick 1736. The Interest of Scotland Considered with Regard to its Policy in Employing of the Poor, its Agriculture, its Trade, its Manufactures, and Fisheries. London: Printed for T. Woodward and J. Peele. (L645)

Merchant, C.S. 1760. Information to the People of Ireland Concerning the Linen Trade of Spain, Portugal and the Spanish West Indies. Dublin: Printed for Richard Watts. (In3)

7. Spun Virtue, the Lacework of Folly, and the World Wound Upside-Down

Seventeenth-Century Dutch Depictions of Female Handwork

LINDA STONE-FERRIER

 Pictures of everyday scenes from seventeenth-century Holland—the Golden Age of Dutch art—have often been interpreted as superficial reflections of daily life. In actuality, such scenes were not just casual depictions; they embodied traditional attitudes towards societal roles. Moreover, popular attitudes towards certain important roles were not reflected in artistic imagery because no appropriate pictorial conventions existed. Brewers, for example, were highly admired in the seventeenth century, particularly in Haarlem, where brewing represented the most important industry and was praised in city histories. The success of brewing, however, did not inspire images of the brewer at work because there was no pictorial precedent for such a depiction. Conversely, certain earlier conventions, such as depictions of religious figures, were untapped by most Dutch seventeenth-century artists because of the contemporary prohibition against iconic religious imagery.

The numerous seventeenth-century Dutch paintings and prints

of spinners and winders differ from other scenes of daily life. They represent one popular subject in the history of art that not only retained its favor in Holland, but also appeared in newly conceived pictorial contexts. As in earlier imagery, the traditionally female occupations of spinning and winding were shown in many paintings and prints of domestic interiors, exemplifying the roles for ladies that were recommended in contemporary treatises and handbooks. When these traditionally female activities were shown performed by men, spinning and winding represented a symptom of the world-turned-upside-down—the folly resulting from women gaining the upper hand in their domestic domain.

These time-honored scenes of virtuous females and foolish males, spinning in domestic interiors, expanded in the mid-seventeenth century to include unprecedented paintings by Haarlem artists of female winders in the traditionally male milieu of professional weavers. The depictions of female and male spinners and winders in domestic interiors had their roots in literary sources—either moralizing or satirical. But the paintings of female winders in weavers' workshops reflected the extraordinary economic success and international fame enjoyed by seventeenth-century linen producers in Haarlem. The traditionally popular image of the virtuous female spinner or winder in a domestic interior provided the pictorial vocabulary for a new context; the positive associations of this female activity were transferred to the male professional arena.

EXEMPLARY FEMALE SPINNERS AND WINDERS

The view of spinning and winding as appropriate women's work had been accepted in many cultures for countless generations. The terms "distaff side," meaning the female side of a family, "spinster" and *Spindelseite* all derive from the traditionally female occupation of spinning (Ciba Review 28:983).

Sixteenth- and seventeenth-century Dutch paintings of female spinners and winders showed them consistently in their traditionally virtuous roles. Innumerable examples abound, both in portraits and in images of anonymous women in domestic interiors. To show a woman spinning in a portrait was to illustrate her moral character rather than her profession (Bruyn 1955:31). Maerten van Heemskerck's portrait of Anna Codde from 1529 is only one example of many (Amsterdam, Rijksmuseum). The spinning performed by the sitter does not allude to her family's profession, wine marketing, nor to her husband's profession, brewing (Bruyn 1955:27). Instead, the spinning image gives the viewer vital information regarding Anna Codde's character.[1]

Paintings and prints of anonymous spinners in domestic settings outnumber even the spinners in portraits. The sheer numbers testify to the popularity of the image. The depicted spinners were young and old, rich and poor, and rendered in both paint and prints throughout the seventeenth century by many Dutch artists. Quirijn Brekelenkam's "The Bible Lecture" (Private Collection) and Esaias Bourse's "Woman at a Spinning Wheel" (Amsterdam, Rijksmuseum:1661) capture the warmth of the Dutch home in two paintings of the female spinner. Other examples focus on the spinner or winder, using various pictorial devices: Brekelenkam framed a winder in a niche in one painting (Private Collection, Frederik Muller), and spotlit her with streaming light beside an open door in another (London, Alfred Brod Gallery). In two paintings of old women spinning (Amsterdam, Rijksmuseum), Nicholas Maes combined deep shadows with an unidentifiable light source, which embraced the spinners and imparted a warm, homey ambience to the images. Gerard Ter Borch painted his sister as a well-to-do spinner elegantly dressed in a fur-trimmed satin jacket (Rotterdam, Museum Boymans-van Beuningen) (Figure 17). In an early seventeenth-century pen drawing, Jacob de Gheyn captured the old spinner carefully adjusting the thread on the wheel's spindle (Private Collection, G. Bainbridge). In a 1667 painting by J. Toorenvliet, the elderly spinner studiously examines the flax being spun (Karlsruhe, Gemäldegalerie). Still another celebration of the spinner appears in a mid-seventeenth century print series of female virtues by Geertruydt Roghman (Atlas van Stolk #1031).

What these images of spinning women have in common is a decisively domestic level of production. There is no suggestion that the spinners are part of a textile production team; that would have been indicated by several accompanying weavers or spinners. The spinners' production is actually limited by their status as housewives. Such assumptions concerning their behavior and activities were voiced in sixteenth- and seventeenth-century books written for women by men. Several different treatises existed, but invariably

Figure 17. "Spinner," painted by Gerard Ter Borch, shows the artist's sister performing what was considered to be a virtuous woman's work. Museum Boymans-van Beuningen, Stichting Willem van der Worm: Rotterdam

four topics were discussed: the war of the sexes; the training and duties of a wife; love and beauty; and the court (Kelso 1956:2). The advice applied to all women, regardless of rank.

In these treatises, the only occupation recommended to the female readers was that of housewifery (Kelso 1956:4), and their appropriate tasks or arts were needlework, spinning, and weaving (Kelso 1956:46).[2] The purpose of such tasks was to fill a lady's leisure hours in order to preserve her virtue (Kelso 1956:45). Needlework, spinning, and weaving were appropriate ways in which women could "reveal their own sharp and pregnant wit" which required "great knowledge, pains and skill," a sixteenth-century Englishman wrote, whereas men showed their wit by strenuous toil.[3]

In a similar book by Vives, the author defended sewing, cooking, weaving, and spinning from attacks by those who regarded them as base exercises performed only because of poverty. To Vives, those with the latter opinion were merely ignorant. Noble and rich women had to busy themselves in this way so as to fill their hours profitably (Kelso 1956:46).

In still another book on the subject, Torquato Tasso added that a highborn lady should occasionally perform domestic tasks, although not in the kitchen, where she might soil her clothes. The spinning wheel and loom were the appropriate tools of the noble matron (Kelso 1956:112). Such industriousness was, according to one Englishman, a source of national pride:

> The labours that be both decent and profitable for gentlewomen
> are these, most meete in my minde, and also in daylye use with
> many, as spinning of Wooll on the greate compasse Wheele, and
> on the rocke or distaffe, wherewith I would not that any should
> be so daintee, as to be offended thereat but rather commende
> and use them as an ornament, and benefit of god bestowed
> upon oure flourishing countrey, surpassing all our princely
> neyghbours.[4]

The popular association between spinning and women had ancient roots. The most renowned female spinners included Lachesis, one of the Three Fates who spun the thread of life, subsequently cut by another Fate (Hall 1974:288); the Virgin, spinner of the thread of life; and the mythological Minerva and Arachne.[5] Numerous images of these famous spinners preceded the seventeenth-century Dutch paintings. Sixteenth-century prints of the Three Fates, such as Hans Baldung's 1513 engraving (Hollstein 1954,II:138) and Joris Hoefnagel's 1589 engraving (Vignau-Schuurmän 1969,II:Fig.128), exemplify the popularity of the mythological imagery, which came to symbolize *memento mori*, the fleeting quality of life. An emblem from Jani Jacobi Boissardi's 1593 *Emblemata, Auss dem Latein verteutscht* (Frankfurt) shows four women, one of whom spins while another cuts the thread. A grinning skeleton carrying an hourglass watches a third woman as she inscribes on a slab, "*sola virtus est funeris expers*" (Valor alone is spared the grave). The image clearly stems from the story of Lachesis and the Fates (Boissardi 1593:95).

Seventeenth-century emblematic images that symbolize *memento mori* demonstrate the enduring strength of the original associations with Lachesis and the Three Fates.[6] An emblem in Andreas Friedrichen's 1617 *Emblemata Nova* (Frankfurt) shows a woman spinning with an hourglass resting on her head. A skeleton, also holding an hourglass, advances toward her in what appears to be an attempt to cut the spun thread. Above them is written, *"Das Leben hangt an ein Faden"* (Life hangs on a thread) (Friedrichen 1617:165). On the title page of Hieremias Drexelius' *Nuntius Mortus, Aeternitatis Prodromus Mortis Nuntius Quem Sanis Aegrotis Moribundus*, 1629, a woman spins on the left, facing a skeleton on the right. A large hourglass separates them.

The specific association between spinning and *virtuous* women, seen in seventeenth-century Dutch paintings and recommended in contemporary handbooks, stemmed originally from the image of the Virgin as the spinner of the thread of life.[7] As the model of female virtue, the spinning Virgin traditionally represented the paradigm for the religious woman's emulation, as in Jacob de Gheyn's 1593 engraving (Amsterdam, Prentenkabinet, Holls. 32g II/Pass. 200:II). St. Elisabeth was similarly depicted spinning by Hans Baldung in the sixteenth century (Hollstein 1954,II:125). Spinning as a metaphor for domestic industriousness was also explicitly set forth in the Bible; Proverbs 31:10–13, 19, and 24:

> Who can find a capable wife?
> Her worth is far beyond coral.
> Her husband's whole trust is in her,
> and children are not lacking.
> She repays him with food, not evil,
> all her life long.
> She chooses wool and flax
> and toils at her work . . . .
> She holds the distaff in her hand,
> and her fingers grasp the spindle . . . .
> She weaves linen and sells it,
> and supplies merchants with their sashes.
> (*New English Bible 1971*).

In the seventeenth century, the biblical image of the virtuous female spinner was adopted in Johannes de Brune's 1624 *Emblemata of Zinnewerck, voorghestelt in Beelden, ghedicten* (Amsterdam) in which a woman spins while her husband carves by their hearth. The association with the Virgin's traditional role is reinforced here by the fact that Joseph was a carpenter. An inscription accompanies the image:

> What rest and profit give little loss. How exquisite is it for God, how sweet for us to behold it! That man and woman together maintain themselves from her handwork, and by watching over by the Lord. Now what the world gives, much unrest, good and honor, but with a cheerful heart, based on rocky ground from God's truth and oath, and on her duty bound. Of the heavens rest and desire, trusting that the man, who seeks God's kingdom, never can be lacking (De Brune 1624:318).[8]

An emblem in *Emblemata Selectiora* (Amsterdam 1704) continues the visual tradition of the virtuous female spinner who follows the Virgin's example. A well-dressed young woman spins on a wheel before a hearth, with a dog and a cat resting at her feet. Beneath is written: "Domesticity is women's crown jewel, such a crown to ornament a woman as dutifully running the peaceful house" (Anonymous 1704:4).[9]

On the evidence presented so far, the image of the clearly virtuous female spinner or winder in seventeenth-century Dutch paintings appears to reflect both the contemporary treatises and handbooks for women, and the pictorial precedents in which the female spinner represented the Virgin's virtue. Although there were negative literary and pictorial contexts associated with the spinner, apparently these did not affect the seventeenth-century *painted* view of her. The negative views of women spinning and winding appeared only in prints. In contrast, both prints and paintings showed both virtuous and lascivious embroiderers and lacemakers, despite their literary and pictorial associations with spinners and winders.

FEMALE HANDWORK AS AN EROTIC METAPHOR

What negative didactic contexts were associated with traditionally female tasks in the production of textiles? Seventeenth-century

Dutch emblems of spinning, embroidering, and lacemaking presented erotic visual plays, based on popular Dutch metaphors for copulation derived from the motion of the textile professions' tools.[10] Such erotic images clashed with the ideal of the sober industriousness of Dutch society. In the emblem book *Nova Poemata ante hac nunquam* (Leiden 1624), a young woman is shown spinning while she gazes out a window. The accompanying inscription presents a licentious double meaning for the woman's relationship to the spindle:

> I am stretched long, white—so you see—and fragile. At the uppermost am I the head, slightly big. My mistress wishes me steady, often has me in her lap; or instead, she lays me nearby her side. She holds me many times—yes, daily, may I say, with her hands. She pulls her knees up, and in a rough place, now she sticks my top. Now she pulls it out again. Now she goes to place it again (Anonymous 1972 (1624):71).[11]

In another emblem book, *Nederduytsche Poemata* (Leiden 1621), under the section *Het Ambacht van Cupido* (The Occupation of Cupid), a cupid spins before an elegantly dressed young woman (Heinsius 1621:3). Therefore, spinning could be one of love's occupations.

Similarly, three other emblems depict the correspondence between lovemaking and needlework and embroidery. An example by Jacob Cats in *Sinn-en-Minne-Beelden en Emblemata Amores Morelqüe Spectantia* (Amsterdam 1622) presents an explicit reference to lovemaking. A young, well-dressed woman sews in the company of her well-dressed suitor. The inscription beneath the image reads, "I spoke last with my love, while she sat and sewed. I placed her before my grief; hear, yet, how she captured me. Watch what I am doing, she spoke, notice how it all goes. First, the needle makes a hole that is filled with the thread . . ." (Cats 1622:171).[12]

Another emblem by Jacob Cats from the same emblem book depicts a fashionably dressed young woman embroidering while a cupid sits watching her. Again the inscription presents an explicit lovemaking analogy: ". . . Your needle bores a hole; your thread makes the stitch. Love, treat me in the same way; keep all the same strokes. You know I am wounded by your sweet mouth. Go on, heal the pain there where you gave me the wound" (Cats 1622:54–55).[13] The association was still strong by the end of the seventeenth century, as reflected in an emblem from Willem den Elger's *Zinne-*

Beelden der Liefde (Elger 1703:149). Here a cupid actually assists the young woman in her embroidering.

The erotic associations of the female spinner in prints, as well as the virtuous image of her in paintings, were shared by embroiderers and lacemakers, although the latter two were depicted positively and negatively in both media. Mid-seventeenth-century paintings of lacemakers and embroiderers by Jan Vermeer (Paris, Louvre), Nicolaes Maes (Vienna, Liechtensteingalerie; London, National Gallery of Art) and Gabriel Metsu (Vienna, Gemäldegalerie) picture the female worker as a figure of domestic industriousness, similar to the spinner in paintings. Nothing intrudes on the virtuous ambience in these examples.

Just as common, however, were painted images of embroiderers and lacemakers that reflect the erotic love play seen in emblematic prints. Seated working women are interrupted by courting men, who woo them with varying degrees of explicit behavior. In a mid-seventeenth-century painting by Jan Steen, a young, cloaked suitor bows slightly and doffs his hat to a woman who sews in her bedroom (Private collection, Stephenson Clark). In a painting by Quirijn Brekelenkam, the young caller advances towards the embroiderer, his cloak over one arm, and he gestures with the other (Hamburg, Kunsthalle). In a second example by Brekelenkam, the cloaked and hatted suitor reads to the young lacemaker, possibly from a love-song book (Amsterdam, Rijksmuseum). A lacemaker depicted by Gabriel Metsu is closely watched by her suitor who leans over her table, a wine glass in his hand (Dresden, Gemäldegalerie). In another painting by Jan Steen, a cocky caller is seated with a woman sewing (Private English collection). His legs are flung apart; one fist is planted on his knee and there is a leer on his face. In two of these paintings, the figures are drinking—an activity less conducive to lace production than to lovemaking. In three of these paintings, the young woman has discarded one of her shoes, which sits prominently in the foreground. Clearly this is an allusion to her abandonment and vulnerability in her suitor's presence. [14]

The consistent portrayal of virtuous women spinning and winding stands in contrast to the ambivalent portrayals of female embroiderers and lacemakers. The female spinner or winder may have been consistently depicted as virtuous in paintings—a medium more expensive and more seriously regarded than prints—because spinning and winding constituted the vital steps of clothmaking.

Embroiderers and lacemakers, who were depicted in both virtuous and lascivious contexts, produced ornamentation that was valued by many but was considered a superfluous and condemnable luxury by others.

Various moralizing sermons, tracts, and emblems from the seventeenth century express the criticism that such ornamentation and fancy apparel often received. Such elegantly made clothing was associated with prodigality, lasciviousness, vanity, foolishness, and *memento mori*. In Johannes Stalpaert's *Vrouwelick cieraet van Sint Agnes versmaedt* of 1622, and J. de Decker's *Lof der Geldsucht*, c. 1640, all female ornamentation was condemned. In the former tract, St. Agnes was held to be a model of sober dress (Van der Heijden 1966:9). An emblem in Iohannem à Nyenborg's 1660 emblem book, *Variarum Lectionum Selecta Figuris aeneis applicata* (Groningen), shows female clothing piled atop a pedestal in a niche decorated with garlands, heraldry, accouterments of civilization, and a mirror. Beneath the image is inscribed, *"de usu & abusu vestium, & de superbia"* (The use and abuse of clothing, and vanity) (Nyenborg 1660:79). The layering of this pile of clothing clearly recreates its relationship with the wearer. The skirt on the bottom spills over the pedestal's edge; the bodice with its stiff sleeves extends outward; the wide ruff and the lacy, spiked cap are perched upright. The assembled clothing symbolizes the superficiality of such fashion in the way the outfit has collapsed. Finally, the noticeably faceless cap further underlines both a literal and figurative lack of character in the potential wearer.

The specific relationship between fine apparel, ornamentation such as lace or embroidery, and lasciviousness was also recognized and proclaimed by sixteenth- and seventeenth-century moralists. Vives, in his advice to ladies, insisted the clothes should be woven of clean, coarse wool or linen, unadorned with jewels. They should be worn without perfume in order to maintain one's humility. Rich dress served only to attract men, which endangered a lady's chastity (Kelso 1956:47).

The earliest pictorial association between elegant dress and love play occurred in moralizing satirical prints, and also in various engraved and painted five-part series on the senses. In a sixteenth-century Dutch print satirizing fashionable attire, a lady hides her lover under her skirt, while two other women and a man hit her skirts in an attempt to reveal the lover.[15] Thus, the indulgence associated with fashionable dress encompasses lovemaking literally and metaphorically. Similarly, moralizing pictorial series of the senses often showed elegantly dressed young couples in various amorous occupations. The popularity of such associations between dress and lovemaking in seventeenth-century paintings became widespread. Thus, the popular metaphors comparing the movement of tools used in lacemaking and embroidery to copulation were joined by similar associations between lace or embroidery and their alluring appeal to the opposite sex.

THE MALE SPINNER AND WINDER: THE TOPSY-TURVY WORLD

The consistently positive *painted* image of the female spinner or winder, which contrasts with the painted image of the embroiderer and lacemaker, can be regarded in yet another context. Whereas there were not depictions of male lacemakers or embroiderers, male spinners and winders represented the predominant negative image of those activities. Foisting men into the female role of spinning or winding was a function of *omnia vincit amor* (love conquers all), or a reversal of roles referred to as "women-on-top."[16]

Seventeenth-century emblems show that such role reversals were the ancient fate of Hercules and Sardanapalus. In the 1601 *Emblemata Moralia* (Horozcii 1601:Plate 43), the 1612 *Minerva Britanna*, and the 1653 *Devises et Emblesmes d'Amour Moralisez* (Flamen 1653:37). Hercules spins in response to the whims of his love, Omphale. The inscription beneath the 1612 emblem informs the reader of Hercules' folly:

> Alicides heere, hath thrown his Clubbe away,
> And weares a Mantle, for his Lions skinne
> Thus better liking for to passe the day,
> With *Omphale*, and with her maids to spinne,
> To card, to reele, and doe such daily taske
> What ere it pleased, *Omphale* to aske.
>
> That all his conquests woune him not such Fame,
> For which as God, the world did him adore,

As loves affection, did disgrace and shame,
His virtues partes. How many are there more,
Who having Honor, and a worthy name,
By actions base, and lewdness loose the fame.
(Peacham 1973 (1612):95).

Similarly, King Sardanapalus was undone by love. His spinning tes-
tifies to his weakness in the face of womanly wiles, as depicted in
emblems by Ian Moerman in *De Cleyn Werelt: Daer in claerlijcken door
seer schoone Poetische, Moralische en Historische exempelen betoont wort*
(Amsterdam 1608), L. Haechtanus in *Paruus Mundus* (Frankfurt
1618), and Henricum Oraem Assenheim in *Viridarium Hieroglyphico-
Morale* (Frankfurt 1619). The inscription beneath the 1608 emblem
reads, "Here sits the king of the Assyrians, whom he has forsaken
by spinning out of love" (Moerman 1608:27).[17]

This demeaning image of the spinning leader doubtless inspired the early seventeenth-century German and Netherlandish
political broadsheets that satirized the Spanish invading general,
Ambrosio Spínola, during the Eighty Years' War. The first depiction
of Spínola in a political broadsheet was, in fact, praiseworthy, as the
accompanying text makes clear. A 1607 German sheet celebrated his
victories against the Dutch by depicting him spinning the weapons
from his distaff. The image of spinning was a visual pun on his
name, Spínola. His assistant to the right grabs Time or Fortune by
the hair. The political uneasiness of the Dutch leader, Maurice of
Nassau, is represented by the thorns piercing his soles (Coupe
1966–67:156).

By 1620, the spinning Spínola had acquired pejorative connotations. In the German political print entitled *"Spanische Spinnstuben
oder Rockenfahrt,"* the Pope blesses the Jesuits as they card flax from
which Spínola spins weapons. Three *"dapffer Deutsche Knecht"* (brave
German youths) on the left gather the spun swords and arrows in
order to tangle Spínola's murderous thread (Coupe 1966–67:156).

The German engraving was apparently influenced by a similar
1617 Dutch broadsheet satirizing spinning Jesuits, *"Een arge verward
Maienschel ende quaet Gespin der Iesuwijt"* (A very confused man and
evil spinning Jesuit) (Coupe 1966–67:156) (Figure 18). Good Intention, seated on the left, spins from a distaff with flax prepared by

Figure 18. This 1617 Dutch political broadsheet, "Spinning Jesuits," satirizes Jesuits by showing them in the negative, reversed role of male spinners. Stichting Atlas van Stolk: Rotterdam, no. 1325

a devil on the far right. Another small devil tangles the yarn spun by Good Intention. Lady Discord oversees the sabotage. Across the bottom of the image a spider creeps, wearing a cardinal's hat which is connected by the spider's spun thread to the pile of twisted yarn. Against the back wall, a caricature of Spínola is stuffed into a hunting horn (a member of the Stichting Atlas van Stolk staff in Rotterdam pointed this out to me). Fighting troops can be seen through the open window.

The depiction of a common man spinning also represented a slanderous image of male subservience to women. In P. Adrianus Poirters' emblem book, *Het Masker Van de Wereldt* (Antwerp 1588), a woman beats a man above an image (by Pieter Quast) of a woman spinning and a man winding, with a devil between them. Beneath the image is an inscription that reads, *"Quaet Huysgesin, Duyvels gespin"* (Devils spin in an evil household) (Poirters 1588: 333).[18]

A later version of the same threesome appears in a copy by Salomon Savery (1594–1664?), part of a series entitled *Siet 't verwarde gaernes* (This is how things turn out when the threads of life are tangled). The seated woman now has snakes in her hair as she spins, beneath the label "*Bedroch*" (Deceit). A devil, labelled "*Quaet Ingeven*" (Suggest Evil), holds the spun thread to her left. To the devil's left, a man with a codpiece winds the yarn. Above him is written, "*Geveldt d' uijt wercker*" (Overpower the one who does the work). The winder has been undone by his own folly, presumably love.

Significantly, such demonic imagery associated with spinning or winding commented on a social order rather than on the real Dutch textile industry. Jane Schneider has shown (Chapter 6, this volume) that elsewhere in early modern Europe, competition and tension between the rural textile industry and the agricultural sector contributed to the demonization of folkloric figures. Two pieces of evidence suggest that similar tensions did not exist in seventeenth-century Holland. First, the linen industry—specifically, bleaching outside Haarlem—depended on the dairy industry for buttermilk, a discard product, that was the secret of the *Haarlemmer bleek* (Haarlem bleach) (Van Ysselsteyn 1946:27), introduced to the Dutch by the Flemish émigrés in the late sixteenth century (Horner 1920:348–50; Van Ysselsteyn 1946:327). Most of the polder lands served for dairy-cattle grazing beyond the Haarlem dunes where the linen was bleached. The great satisfaction and pride taken in both the bleaching and the dairying industries are manifested in two groups of paintings that enjoyed great popularity at mid-century: The landscape views of the linen-bleaching fields outside of Haarlem and neighboring communities by Jacob van Ruisdael and his followers,[19] and the monumental paintings of cows, most notably by Paulus Potter and Aelbert Cuyp.

The second piece of evidence that the textile industry and the agricultural sector were in harmony in Holland, even though they were a threat to each other elsewhere in Europe, is the notable absence of witch hunts and trials in the seventeenth-century Netherlands. Among the European nations, the Dutch were the first to ban the execution of witches. The last witch burning occurred in 1595 in Utrecht. In 1610, the last recorded witch trial in the United Provinces took place; it ended in acquittal (Huizinga 1941:59). This is precisely when an enormous influx of Flemish émigrés to Haarlem brought with them the secrets of the full-milk or buttermilk bleaching, which led to the subsequent success and fame of the linen-production industry.

SPINNING ROOMS AND "WOMEN-ON-TOP"

In addition to the pictures of spinning or winding men surrounded by demonic figures, the common male winder was depicted in the specific context of the spinning room. The *Rockenstube* or spinning room, was an important center for yarn production in German villages from the late fifteenth through the seventeenth centuries. It was economically advantageous for women to spin in one room because it saved on light and heat (Coupe 1966–67:155). Although the spinning room was intended to be a working place for women only, it evolved into a center for village social life when men began to join the women after working hours (*Ciba Review* 28:1012–13). The festive racousness and sexual promiscuity that often ensued cast the spinning rooms into ill repute. In the seventeenth century, such spinning rooms did not play the same role in the production of textiles in the Netherlands as they did in Germany. The production of linen in Haarlem, for example, depended upon the import of spun flax from Silesia (Horner 1920:353). Thus, depictions of spinning rooms by Dutch artists may have been based more on German pictorial precedents than on real Dutch spinning rooms.

Sixteenth- and seventeenth-century Dutch artists gave spinning-room festivities a particular emphasis. The raucousness of the revelry and sexual promiscuity were well presented; the artists captured the turbulence of a world-turned-upside-down. The women clearly held the upper hand—after all, the spinning room was their domain—and the men were kept winding or spinning.

When discussing such images, art historians have traditionally focused on the disorder of this world in which women dominate. It has been shown that such domestic chaos was a popular comic mode in the Netherlands and the rest of Europe, in literary farces, poems, proverbs, and prints. Besides spinning, a submissive man was also forced to kiss his mistress' thumb and kneel before her; he had furniture thrown at him, and faced the ignominy of the woman literally donning the trousers (Gibson 1978:677–78). Almost invaria-

Figure 19. In Barthel Beham's 1524 woodcut "The Spinning Room," sexual promiscuity and disorder are rampant in the topsy-turvy world where women have the upper hand. Graphischen Sammlung "Albertina": Vienna

bly, these diverse humiliations and comic variations of the "women-on-top" took place in spinning rooms, those female strongholds that were alien territory to men.

Various examples suggest this theme's popularity. Barthel Beham's woodcut of a spinning room (1542) highlights the sexual promiscuity (Figure 19). The scene is littered with spinning paraphernalia, and couples cavort in various sexual positions (Hollstein 1954:2,245).[20]

In the later sixteenth-century anonymous engraving of a spinning room printed by Boscher, the emphasis shifts to the power of women in their own domain.[21] A female spinner in the left background waves a banner embellished with the picture of a hand and the words, *D'Overhant* (the upper hand), while her sister spinners lambaste the male intruders into submission. In the foreground two men beg for mercy, while another male resentfully winds thread in the left background. Tools of the spinning trade are strewn over the floor.

The early-seventeenth-century painting of the spinning room by Pieter de Bloot (RKD) follows in the tradition of the Boscher engraving. A female spinner carries a banner decorated with pictures of a hand, a winder, a spindle, and the words, *Voer 'Hant* (the upper hand). Spinners on the left thrash a male intruder's bottom. In the middle a male holding a winder is beaten, while on the right a female offers a kneeling, supplicant male something to eat, as though giving communion to a repentant sinner.

In a mid-seventeenth-century painting by Jacob van Loo, the imagery of the spinning room assumed a morally tempered ambiguity (Leningrad: Hermitage). In the background, two couples engage in the traditional spinning-room love play. Musical instruments and a wine glass are near at hand. In the foreground, an elderly spinner at her spinning wheel offers a contrast to the frivolity. Bent forward, her hand held at her lips and her brow furrowed, she looks directly at the viewer, obviously concerned about the activity behind her. The virtuous image of the female spinner, as found in portraiture and genre scenes, is contrasted with the promiscuity of the two background couples. Because of this juxtaposition, the subdued love play in the background appears more erotically provocative than the comic spinning room scenes with their explicit and unrestrained display of sexual escapades.

In J. Toorenvliet's painting of a spinning room from the mid-seventeenth century, the tradition of sexual promiscuity and female dominance is expressed less forcefully (RKD). In the background, a female spinner bends over a male who looks up at her fondly. In the foreground, a second female spinner stands beside a seated, pipe-smoking male visitor who has laid his satchel at his feet. Smiling, the foreground female spinner holds a distaff in one hand while offering the spindle to the man with her other hand. He leans on the table top, clearly less interested in the spindle than in what the offering of the spindle suggests. The love play of this spinning-room scene is mild in comparison with our previous examples, and it lacks the titillation seen in the Jacob van Loo painting.

Perhaps the image of "women-on-top" lacks force in the Toorenvliet painting because mid-seventeenth-century Dutch spinning rooms were not meeting places of the sexes. By that time they had become houses of correction for female harlots, drunks, and other offenders of social propriety (Amsterdam, Amsterdams Historisch Museum 1972:20; Haley 1972:159).[22] The degree to which the Dutch spinning house came to be regarded as a center for exemplary behavior and productivity by the end of the seventeenth century is demonstrated by prints of working women in C. Arnold's *Waare Afbeelding der Eerste Christenen* (Amsterdam 1701); by P. Fouquet, Jr.'s, "*Het vrouwen Tuchthuys of Spinhuys van Binne, tot Amsterdam*" (Amsterdam Atlas); and by Feullantines' "*t' Spinn-huis, La Maison des Feullantines.*"[23] A portrait by Bartholomeus van der Helst of the Amsterdam Spinhuis regentesses (Amsterdams Historisch Museum) includes elegant, engraved, ceremonial glassware— evidence of the institutional respectability the Dutch spinning house had acquired by the end of the century.

A NEW PICTORIAL CONTEXT FOR THE FEMALE WINDER

When women who wound entered the textile domain that was traditionally male—the weaving workshop—they were not depicted as fools, unlike the men who entered the traditional domain of the woman, the spinning room. Women remained respectable because winding and spinning were traditionally female tasks, regardless of the milieu.

In an unprecedented group of paintings, produced around the mid-seventeenth century only by Haarlem artists, women are depicted winding in the company of male weavers who work at large looms. Twenty-five examples of these paintings are represented by photographs in the Rijksbureau voor Kunsthistorische Documentatie in the Hague, which suggests that a much larger number of such paintings were on the market in the seventeenth century.[24]

These Haarlem scenes depict a weaver's cottage. The walls of the workplace are wood-beamed; the floor is strewn with straw, tools of the weaving profession, and household utensils: a broom, a pump, a bucket, a basket, a barrel. Light entering from a window illuminates the weaver's prominent loom. Paintings by J.D. Oudenrooge (RKD) and Cornelis Beelt (The Hague, Haags Gemeentemuseum) show the weaver at his loom in the company of female workers. A 1653 example from a group of paintings by Cornelis Decker depicts a male weaver who is working at his loom accompanied by a woman who sews in front of her winder (The Hague, Dienst Verspreide Rijkscollecties).

These mid-century paintings of female winders and male weavers in a workshop have no pictorial precedents. A market for these paintings appears to have been inspired by the extraordinary success of the Haarlem linen industry, a success which was celebrated in seventeenth-century poems and histories of the city. To satisfy the market's demand for visual celebrations of the linen industry's success, the traditional view of the domestic spinner or winder was transformed into a new pictorial context, in which the female artisan retained her traditional virtuous associations.

The public's high regard for both the Haarlem linen workers and the product of their labors is reflected as early as 1588 in Hadrianus Junius' *Batavia*. Junius praised the whiteness and fineness of Haarlem linen (Six 1913:87).[25] In 1596, Karel van Mander celebrated '*t Hollants lijnwaet de werelt door bekent* (Holland's world-famous linen goods) (Van der Loeff 1911). In *Des Crizione de Tutti i Paesi Bassi* 1567 (published in 1612 as *Beschrijvinge van alle de Nederlanden*, that is, Description of all the Netherlands), Guicciardini described Haarlem linen as ". . . having been woven very well for a long time . . . so that the city appears to have returned to its former bloom" (Guicciardini 1612 (orginally 1567):201).[26]

By 1621, the praise of Haarlem's linen production had escalated to a new level. In Samuel Ampzing's *Het Lof der Stadt Haerlem in Hollandt* (In praise of the city of Haarlem in Holland) (Haarlem 1621), we find the following passage:

> Due to our citizens' art and spirit, she (Haarlem) holds up her
> head, and with her name and fame bursts through the heavens,
> by which our city and citizen are known, as far on the globe as
> he has sent his arts. Has he no good things? So good is he in
> this art, excellently skilled! It is a wonder what amount and variety of very artful works he prepares on his loom. His linen reflects a lot of light even as it competes in its perfection with
> silk's delicacy. The rest is so artistically colored with patterns it
> is unpredictable what his spool is able to create. So
> Tradesmanship, here, was also pursued with fervor, and most of
> them there have weaving as their main concern; from thread,
> and from flax, and all linen goods, by which the trade of our city
> exists (Cited in Van Ysselsteyn 1946:31).[27]

In a second version from 1628, *Beschrijvinge ende lof der Stad Haerlem in Holland* (Description and praise of the city of Haarlem in Holland), Ampzing praised Haarlem's linen by comparing it with Italy's production:

> The Italian has indeed invented silk-damask, and because of it, fame has sent her name everywhere. But Haarlem has reflected that even further in linen, even the Italian thought it better than his own. Here is the correct school to learn the art well. And respect is not a little, but hold it, indeed, in honor (Heppner 1938:9).[28]

It is no accident that Italy's silk-damask and linen production was Ampzing's poetic foil. Dutch painting and craftsmanship stood in the shadow of Italian artistic renown. Thus, Ampzing could not have made his point more emphatically.

Praise of Haarlem's linen came from foreign countries as well. In *Des wereldts proef-steen, ofte de Ydelheydt door de Waerheyd* (The world's touchstone, or vanity through truth) (Antwerp 1643), A. à Burgundia wrote:

> Holland sends us very fine yarn, and the finest linen wares. Kamerijk and Kortrai show us also the same, and we make great pleasures with that nicely woven cloth, because through the firm thread it is comfortable to wear and to sew, so that often someone wished that the finest spider webs hanging there in the corner were better than Holland's cloth (Burgundia 1643:3–4).[29]

These seventeenth-century statements about Haarlem linen and damask weaving have a decidedly chauvinistic tone. It is Haarlem linen and Haarlem linen workers that are being extolled. The literary statements reflect societal pride in the linen professions, a pride that fostered a market for the paintings of weavers and winders by Haarlem artists. Although linen was produced elsewhere in seventeenth-century Europe, paintings of weavers and winders appeared only in Haarlem, where the most famous and desirable linen was woven and bleached.

This unique group of Haarlem paintings depicts the production of linen in Haarlem with some inaccuracies. Much of Haarlem's linen was woven in large, rented rooms, which contained several looms owned by wealthy entrepreneurs. With the exception of one painting by J.D. Oudenrogge, in which two looms are depicted

(RKD), the Haarlem paintings of weavers' workshops showed only one loom. They are images of peaceful domesticity and suggest only limited production for personal use, rather than large-scale commercial output. In reality, weaving was a commercial venture, and cloth was not woven at home for personal use. Seventeenth-century rural Dutch inventories of domestic possessions, written at the time of a death, never include a loom, although they often include a spinning wheel (De Vries 1974:224). However, the artists depicted the weavers and winders in a domestic context in order to exploit the positive associations of the milieu.

The depiction of winders rather than spinners in the painted weaving scenes does represent accurately one aspect of linen production. Only for a short time after the advent of the Flemish émigrés at the end of the sixteenth century was high-quality yarn spun in Holland (Horner 1920:353). The coarse yarns used for the bulk of Dutch linen came mostly from Silesia where they had been spun. The flax was then wound by Haarlem workers. Evidence of the importation of spun flax to Haarlem was mentioned as early as 1567 in Guicciardini's account of Haarlem's linen production in *Des Crizione de Tutti i Paesi-Bassi* (published in 1612 as *Beschrijvinge van alle de Neder-landen*): ". . . trading various handcrafts especially all kinds of woven works as linen cloths, dyes, silks, and cloth mixtures; through which the shipping and the merchant trade of the long yarn from Silesia, exported to here, have been woven well for a long time" (Guicciardini 1612 [1567]:201).[30] Such facts alone do not explain the depiction of winding as a respectable, seemingly domestic task. Winders could be presented in this way because the positive connotations of the industrious spinner also were suggested by depictions of the winder. Thus, the exemplary painted image of the winder in the mid-seventeenth century Haarlem weaving scenes continues the traditionally respectful depiction of female spinners and winders in earlier sixteenth- and seventeenth-century paintings.

NOTES

1. Heemskerck painted other portraits of women spinning (Bruyn 1955:27–35).

2. Such advice was given as early as in Jerome's writing, (Kelso 1956:274).

3. A Booke of Curious and Strange Inventions, 1596 (cited in Kelso 1956:46).

4. John Jones, The Arte and Science of Preserving Bodie and Soule, 1579:20 (cited in Kelso 1956:2). The writers of these treatises ignored national distinctions in this womanly advice. All the authors apparently drew on the same original sources: Aristotle, Plato, Cicero, Jerome, and Paul (Kelso 1956:267).

5. For a fuller account, see Duke University Museum of Art 1972 and Ciba Review 1939,28:986.

6. Emblem books contained proverbs, aphorisms, and biblical quotations juxtaposed with pictorial images. The inscriptions in combination with the pictures presented intellectual puzzles which, when solved, revealed a moralizing meaning. Emblem books were extremely popular throughout Europe in the seventeenth century, in various languages (See Praz 1939–47).

7. In the sixteenth-century theater, the spinner's distaff also was used as an attribute of virtue, which was personified by a woman. (De Jongh 1967:65).

8. (Wat rust en ghewin gheeft luttel onderwin./ Hoe kost'lick is't, voor God, hoe zoet, voor ons, t'aen -schouwen!/ Dat man en vrouw to zaem haer zelven onderhouwen,/ Van haerer handen werck, en wachten, van de Heer,/ Niet wat de weereld geeft, veel onrust, goed en eer,/ maer met een vrolick hert, gevest op rotsche gronden/ Van Godes trouw en eed, en aen haer plicht verbonden,/ Des hemels rust en lust; vertrouwend' dat de man,/ Die Godes rijcke zoeckt, noyt yet ontbreken kan.)

9. (Huislykheid is't vrouwen kroon cieraad/ Wat kroon zoo em een vrouw te cieren/ Als 't neerstig vreedzaam huis bestieren!) Virtually the same message was dictated in the early seventeenth century by Jacob Cats, although without an accompanying image (Cats 1776, I:370). For a discussion of the housewife's pictorial role in the Netherlands since the seventeenth century, see Boot 1978:168ff.

10. The metaphors for copulation included the needle piercing a hole in cloth and the loom's shuttle driving the woof threads through the warp.

11. (Ick been een spanne lang/ wit/ so ghy siet/ en teeder/ Aen't upterste ben ick het hooft een weynich groot/ Of anders leyt sy my by hare zijde neder. Sy grijpt my menichmael ja dag'lijer mach ick segghen/ Met hare handen aen/ sy doet haer knein op/ En in ruyge plaets steeckt sy nu mijnen top/ Nu trecktser hem weer uyt/ nu gaetser hem weer leeghen.)

12. (Ick sprack lest met mijn Lief, terwijl sy sat en naeyde,/ Ick steld' haer voor mijn smert, hoort doch, hoe sy my paeyde,/ Let eens, op't geen ick doe, (sprack sy)/ merckt hoe't al gaet,/ Eerst maeckt de naeld' een gat, dat stopt/ daer na den draet.)

13. (. . . U naelde boort een gat, u draet vervult de steke:/ Lief, handelt soomet my, hoet al de selve streke;/ Ghy weet, ick ben gequetst door uwen soetten mont;/ Wel aen, gheneest de smert daer me ghy gaeft de wont.)

14. The image of the barefoot young woman suggests a movement towards undress. The erotic implications of this image are corroborated by more explicit seventeenth-century paintings in which a young woman's shoes lie prominently

in the foreground. E. de Jongh has shown in his analyses of Jan Steen's painting "Morning Toilet", ca 1663 (Amsterdam, Rijksmuseum and London, Buckingham Palace) and Adriaen van de Venne's *"Geckie met de kous"* (Warsaw, Museum Narodowe) that the image of a young woman pulling her stocking on or off plays on the meaning of that stocking as a metaphor for an immoral woman or a woman's genitals, and of the foot as a phallic symbol. (Amsterdam, Rijksmuseum 1976:245,259–61). Shoes flung off obviously may anticipate both real and metaphorical love play.

15. *Spotprent* on fashionable clothing, sixteenth-century Dutch. *In* Veth n.d.:Fig.16.

16. "In hierarchical and conflictful societies that loved to reflect on the world-turned-upside-down, the *topos* of the woman-on-top was one of the most enjoyed. Indeed, sexual inversion—that is, switches in sex roles—was a widespread form of cultural play in literature, in art, and in festivity . . . . Erhard Schoen's woodcuts (early sixteenth century) portray huge women distributing fools' caps to men. This is what happens when women are given the upper hand; and yet in some sense the men deserve it" (Davis 1975:129,136).

17. (*Hier sit den Coninck der Assyriers verheven, Die hem ovt liefden tot spinnen heeft begheven.*)

18. E. de Jongh states that the author of the emblem book was as well known in the northern Netherlands as was Jacob Cats (Brussels, Koninklijk Museum voor Schone Kunsten 1971:145).

19. The paintings of Haarlem's linen-bleaching fields are discussed in chapter 4 of my revised Ph. D. dissertation, published in 1985 by UMI Research Press as Images of Textiles: The Weave of Seventeenth-Century Dutch Art and Society, and in my article, Views of Haarlem: a Reconsideration of Ruisdael and Rembrandt, Art Bulletin 67 (3): 418–36.

20. Earlier pictures of humiliated spinning men include a late Gothic engraving by Israhel van Mechenem, and an early sixteenth-century Netherlandish sculpture for a choir stall (Hollstein 1954:II:678,No.27).

21. For a discussion of the engraving's attribution and the identity of the publisher, Boscher, see Gibson 1978:679.

22. The *Rasphuis* was the corresponding house of correction for male petty thieves, cheats, tricksters, and perpetrators of minor violent crimes. There the men were forced to rasp a weekly quota of brazilwood, which was used in dyeing (Haley 1972:159).

23. See: C. Arnold, engraving in: *Waare Afbeelding der Eerste Christenen*, 1701; P. Fouquet, Jr., *"Het Vrouwen Tuchthuys of Spinhuys van Binne, tot Amsterdam,"* Amsterdam Atlas, engraving, n.d., Atlas van Stolk #3853; Feullantines, *"t'Spinn-huis, La Maison des Feullantines,"* engraving, n.d., Atlas van Stolk #3852.

24. These paintings are discussed in chapter 2 of my book *Images of Textiles: The Weave of Seventeenth-Century Dutch Art and Society*, UMI Research Press, 1985.

25. Damask is not mentioned because it had yet to be introduced into Haarlem (Six 1913:87).

26. (. . . *lange tijdt seer goet is gheweeft . . . Soo dat de stadt scheen weder in den ouden fleur to gheraken . . . .*)

27. *(Ons' Burg'ren konst, en geest, waer door sy't hooft opsteken,/ En met haer naem en faem den Sterren-tent verbreken,/ Waer door dat onse Stadt en Burger is bekent/ So wijdt op d'Aerden-kloot als hy zun konsten sendt./ Heeft hy geen goedt verstandt van alderley te* Weven?*/ Wel is hy in dees' konst uyt nemend wel bedreven!/ 't Is wonder wat hy al, en wat verscheydenheydt/ Van wercken op zijn boom seer konstlich toebereydt./ Syn lijwaet sal veel-licht self Indien wel lyden/ In fijnheydt met haer syd' en sachticheydt te strijden:/ De rest is konsten-rijck met verwen so doorschaekt,/ Dat niet om seggen is wat voorts sijn spoel al maeckt./ So werdt oock hier met macht de* Koopmanschap *gedreven,/ En meest wel die daer heeft haer opsicht op het Weven,/ Van Garen, en van Vlas, en allen Linne-waedt:/ Waer by de nering meest van onse Stadt bestaet.)*

28. *(Italian heeft wel het* Sij-damast *gevonden/ En over-al hierdoor den roem haers naems gesonden:/ Maer Haerlem heeft dat voords in 't lywaet nagedacht,/ Dat selfs Italien meer dan 't haere acht./ Hier is de rechte school die konste wel te leeren:/ En achtze ook niet kleijn, maer houdze wel in eren.)*

29. *(Hollandt seyndt ons heel fijn gaeren./ En de fijnste lijnwaet-waeren/ Camerijck en Corterijck/ Toonen ons oock desghelijck/ En wy scheppen groot vermaecken/ In dat net-gheweefde laecken,/ Want het door den vasten draet/ Is bequaem tot dracht en naet./ Maer oft iemandt wilde hebben/ Dat de fijnste Spinnewebben/ Die daer hanghen in den hoeck/ Beter zijn als Hollandts doeck?)*

30. (. . . *handelende verscheyden handtwercken/ besonder alderley gheweven wercken/ soo van Lynen lacekenen Coleuren/ Smallekens ende Noppen: waer door de reedinge ende den koophandel van het lanck garen/ uyt* Silesien *herwaerts over ghevoert/ langhe tijdt seer goet is gheweeft.)*

REFERENCES CITED

Ampzing, Samuel
  1628   Beschryvinge ende Lof der Stad Haerlem in Holland. Haerlem: Adriean Rooman.

Ampzing, Samuel
  1621   Het Lof der Stadt Haerlem in Hollandt. Haerlem: Adriean Rooman.

Amsterdam, Amsterdams Historisch Museum
  1972   Regenten en Regentessen Overlieden en Chirurguijns, Amsterdamse groepportretten van 1600 tot 1835 (exhibition catalog).

Amsterdam, Rijksmuseum
  1976   Tot Lering en Vermaak (exhibition catalog).

Anonymous
1704   Emblemata Selectiora. Amsterdam: Apud Franciscum van der
        Plaats.

Anonymous
1972   Nova Poemata ante hac nunquam edita, Nieuwe Nederduytsche,
        Gedichten ende Raedtselen. Soest, Holland: Davaco Publishers.
        (Original text, 1624).

Assenheim, Henricum Oraem
1619   Viridarium Hieroglyphico-Morale. Frankfurt: Lucam Iennis.

Boissardi, Jani Jacobi
1593   Emblemata, Auss dem Latein verteutscht. Frankfurt: Dieterich
        Brn von Lüttich.

Boot, Marjan
1978   'Huislykheid is 't Vrouwen Kroon Cieraad. Openbaar Kunstbezit
        Kunst Schrift 22(4):168ff.

Brussels, Koninklijk Museum voor Schone Kunsten
1971   Rembrandt en zijn tijd (exhibition catalog).

Bruyn, J.
1955   Vroege portretten van Maerten van Heemskerck. Bulletin van het
        Rijksmuseum, 27–35.

Burgundia, A. à.
1643   Des wereldt proef-steen, ofte de ydele-heydt door waerheyd.
        Antwerp: Petrus Gheschier.

Cats, Jacob
1622   Sinn-en-Minne-Beelden & Emblemata Amores Morelqüe
        spectantia. Amsterdam: Willem Iansz Blaeuw.
1776   Alle de wercken van den Heere Jacob Cats. Amster-
        dam: J. Ratelband.

Ciba Review
1–141   1961–69,Basel, Gesellshaft für Chemische Industrie.

Coupe, W.A.
1966–67 The German Illustrated Broadsheet in the Seventeenth Century,
        Historical and Iconographical Studies. Bibliotheca Bibliographica
        Aureliana Series, 20, Baden-Baden: Heitz.

Davis, Natalie
1975   Society and Culture in Early Modern France: Eight Essays. Stan-
        ford; Stanford University Press.

De Brune, Johannis
1624   Emblemata of Zinnewerck. Amsterdam: J.E. Kloppenburch.

De Jongh, Eddy
1967   Zinne-en minnebeelden in de schilderkunst van de zeventiende
        eeuw. Nederlandse Stichting Openbaar Kunstbezit en Openbaar
        Kunstbezit in Vlaanderen in samenwerking met het Prins
        Bernhard Fonds.

De Vries, Jan
1974   The Dutch Rural Economy in the Golden Age, 1500–1700. New
        Haven and London: Yale University Press.

Drexelius, Hieremias
1629   Nuntius Mortus; Aeternitatis Prodromus Mortis Nuntius Quem
        Sanis Aegrotis Moribundis. Baltalaris Belleri.

Duke University Museum of Art, comp.
1972   Recent Tapestries (exhibition catalog). Durham, North Carolina.

Elger, Willem den
1703   Zinne-Beelden der Liefde. Leyden.

Flamen
1653   Devises et Emblesmes d'Amour Moralisez. Paris: Chez Louis
        Boissevin.

Friedrichen, Andreas
1617   Emblemata Nova. Frankfurt: Lucam Iennis.

Gibson, Walter S.
1978   Some Flemish Popular Prints from Hieronymus Cock and His
        Contemporaries. Art Bulletin 60 (4):673–81.

Guicciardini, Lodovico
1567   Des Crizione de Tutti i Paesi-Bassi. Dutch 1612 translation:
        Beschrijvinge van alle de Nederlanden. Amsterdam.

Haechtanus, L.
1618   Paruus Mundus. Frankfurt: Apud Lucam Iennis.

Haley, K.H.D.
1972   The Dutch in the Seventeenth Century. New York: Harcourt,
        Brace, Jovanovich.

Hall, James
1974   Dictionary of Subjects and Symbols in Art. Introduction by
        Kenneth Clark. Great Britain: J. Murray.

Heinsius, Daniel
1621   Nederduytsche Poemata. Leyden: Hernien van Westerhuisen.

Heppner, A.
1938   Wevers Werkplaatsen Geschilderd door Haarlemsche Meesters
        der 17 eeuw, A. van Ostade, C. Decker, G. Rombouts, C. Beelt,
        J. Oudenrogge, Th. Wijck. Haarlem: De Erven F. Bohn N.V.

Hollstein, F.W.H.
1949   Dutch and Flemish Etchings, Engravings, and Woodcuts. 20 Vols. Amsterdam: Menno Hertsberger.
1954   German Engravings, Etchings, and Woodcuts, ca. 1400–1700. 22 Vols. Amsterdam: Menno Hertsberger.

Horner, John
1920   The Linen Trade of Europe during the Spinning Wheel Period. Belfast: M'Caw, Stevenson & Orr, Limited.

Horozcii, D.D.IO.
1601   Emblemata Moralia. Agrigenti.

Huizinga, J.H.
1941   Dutch Civilization in the Seventeenth Century and Other Essays. Arnold J. Pomerans. Collins, Transl. London.

Kelso, Ruth
1956   Doctrine for the Lady of the Renaissance. Illinois: University of Illinois Press.

Moerman, Ian
1608   De Cleyn Werelt: Daer in claerlijcken door seer schoone Poetische, Moralische en Historische exempelen betoont wort. Amsterdam: Dirck Pietersz.

The New English Bible with the Apocrypha
1971   New York: Oxford University Press.

Nyenborg, Iohannem à.
1660   Variarum Lectionum Selecta Figuris aeneis applicata. Groningen: Jacobum Sipkes.

Peacham, Henry
1973   Minerva Britanna, English Emblem Books. No 5. John Horden, Ed. London: Scholar Press. (Original text, 1612).

Poirters, P. Adrianus
1588   Het Masker van de Wereldt, afgetrocken door . . . Antwerp: Johannes Stichter in den Bergh Calvarien.

Praz, Mario
1939–47 Studies in Seventeenth Century Imagery. Two Vols. London: The Warburg Institute.

RKD   (Rijksbureau voor Kunsthistorische Documentatie): The Hague.

Six, Jhr. J.
1913   Paschier Lamertijn. Oud Holland 31:85–109.

Van der Heijden, M.C.A.
1966   Johannes Stalpaert van der Wiele, Bloemlezing met inleiding en aantekening. Zutphen: N.V.W.J. Thieme & Cie.

Van der Loeff, J.D. Rutgers, Ed.
  1911   Drie Lofdichten op Haarlem, Het Middelnederlandsch Gedicht
         van Dirk Mathijszen en Karel van Mander's Twee Beelden van
         Haarlem voor Vereeniging "Haerlem." Haarlem.

Van Ysselsteyn, G.T.
  1946   Van Linnen en Linnenkasten. Amsterdam: P.N. van Kampen &
         Zoon N.V.

Veth, Cornelis
  n.d.   De Mode in de Caricature. Amsterdam: van Munster's Uitgevers-
         Maatschappij.

Vignau-Schuurmän, Th. A.G. Wilberg
  1969   Die Emblematischen elemente im werke Joris Hoefnagels. 2 Vols.
         Leiden: U. pers Leiden.

8. *Embroidery for Tourists*

A Contemporary Putting-Out System in Oaxaca, Mexico

RONALD WATERBURY

 If you wander through the bustling Friday market-place of Ocotlán in Mexico's Valley of Oaxaca, you will see many women vendors seated on the ground next to their produce, occupying the time between clients by embroidering multicolored pansies, roses, and birds entwined in leafy branches onto finger-smudged swatches of cloth. If you go farther afield, into any of the many villages of the district, you will encounter other women, sitting in doorways or under a mesquite tree in their patios, busily embroidering. Back in the marketplace again, you may notice a number of women—some at produce stands, others sitting under the portals of the buildings that surround the central square—receiving pieces of embroidered cloth from peasant women. After examining the embroiderer's work, these women hand back a small roll of money, another cut of cotton cloth, and several skeins of thread.

What you have witnessed is but a small part of the extensive putting-out system that has grown up spontaneously over the last two decades in the Valley of Oaxaca, especially in the Ocotlán branch of the valley. The end-products of the process are the color-fully embroidered blouses or dresses of the type most people call Mexican wedding dresses. To those who know Mexican needlework, they are "San Antonino" dresses, after the community in which this particular style originated and in which the putting-out system is organized.[1]

Most San Antonino dresses end up in the wardrobes of North American or European women, who purchase them for reasons that include nostalgia for handicrafts. In the real world of Oaxaca, however, the economics of their production is far from romantic. In 1978, a common-quality dress sold for $50 in the import boutiques of North America, but the peasant woman who embroidered it earned less than 10 cents an hour for her labor. The goal of this paper is to describe the development and organization of this less-than-romantic production system, and to analyze its social and economic significance for San Antonino and the region as a whole.

In a putting-out system, merchant-entrepreneurs mobilize labor to produce commodities without incurring much risk, and with a minimal investment in fixed capital. Such systems represent an intermediate stage between precapitalist and capitalist forms of production. Putting-out entrepreneurs exercise only partial domination over labor by controlling the supply of raw or semiprocessed materials, and by controlling the marketing of the completed product. Historically, putting-out systems functioned to augment production under preindustrial technological conditions. In Europe, they expanded significantly in rural areas during the seventeenth and eighteenth centuries, creating what some authorities call the "proto-industrialization" stage in the evolution of industrial capitalism (Kriedte and Schlumbohm 1977; Mendels 1972).

Putting-out systems were eventually replaced by full-fledged industrialism for the production of most commodities. But under certain conditions they have survived: or, as the example presented here will illustrate, they can be spontaneously reborn. (For some contemporary cases in Mexico and elsewhere see Brown 1983; Charlton 1988; de Mauro 1983; Cook 1982b,1984; Ferretti 1983; Hopkins 1978; Lamphere 1979; Littlefield 1978,1979; Swallow 1982.) One necessary condition for their survival or rebirth is sufficient consumer demand for handmade or quasi-handmade goods. Another is the presence of a population compelled by economic circumstances to sell its labor cheaply.

Despite the hegemony of industrial production, demand for handcrafted artifacts endures. Garcia Canclini (1981:72–75) attributes this to "nostalgic fascination for the rustic or the natural." There is also the aesthetic judgment of some consumers that industrial goods are without personality. Being the product of anonymous labor, they are mere commodities that lack individuality, artistic merit, or cultural meaning. By comparison, a handcrafted object evokes the aura of human tradition, the sweat and skill of its individual maker, and—since craftsmanship avoids the repetitive precision of a stamping machine—uniqueness and originality.

One of the most effective ways to project a distinctly personal image is to wear clothes that are not mass-produced. In industrial society, members of the artistic or Bohemian subculture have long worn "folk" or "ethnic" clothing as a way of rejecting factory standardization. This interest in handmade ethnic clothing diffused more widely following World War II, influenced by the expanding number of tourists who traveled to remote and exotic places and brought back pieces of folk art and craft, among them handmade or hand-adorned clothes. The greatest demand for "ethnic" garb, however, grew out of the American counterculture movement of the 1960s and early 1970s. Among other things, its ideology rejected narrow patriotism in favor of cultural pluralism, and forswore mainstream materialist values. One symbol of this ideology was the wearing of peasant dress. Since then, many elements of counterculture dress style have become incorporated into Euro-American mass popular culture. The style has also diffused into the upper-middle class.

In addition to the new demand for "ethnic" dress in the postwar United States, many Third World governments have grown to appreciate the multiple uses to which folk artisanry can be put. (See García Canclini 1977, 1981; Graburn 1976; and Smith 1977.) Among the most active countries in this regard is Mexico, whose past and present Indian cultures are officially venerated as a critical component of the nation's cultural patrimony and as a unique symbol of national identity. Several Mexican government agencies, the most important of which is FONART (the National Fund for Artisanry), actively stimulate the production and distribution of traditional and quasi-traditional arts and crafts. These agencies hold that folk arts bring a multiplicity of economic benefits, as advertisements to attract tourism, as a major source of foreign currency from direct sales to tourists and from exports, and as a way of lifting the standard of living of the rural producers, thereby presumably diminishing the tide of urban immigration. Substantial returns flow to the public treasury through taxes, to store operators and exporters through profits, and to the eventual consumers through the availability of moderately priced handmade goods. The actual producers, however, benefit hardly at all (Cook 1982a, 1982b; Garcia Canclini 1981; Littlefield 1979; Novelo 1976).

In addition to demand, a putting-out system requires a population compelled by poverty to sell its labor cheaply. In preindustrial Europe, the principal font of outworkers was rural households for whom piecework, often performed by women, provided a welcome supplement to inadequate agricultural incomes (Goody 1982; Hobsbawn 1965; Jones 1968; Klima 1974; Klima and Macurek 1960; Mendels 1975; Scott and Tilly 1975; Thirsk 1961). Similar conditions prevail in the contemporary Third World. Exploitation of this labor force, as this study demonstrates, need not always be carried out directly by urban merchants, although they take the largest cut of the surplus value by the time the product reaches its eventual consumers. Rather, when the outworkers are rural peasants, the product of local peasant origin, and the capital requirements low, a putting-out system lends itself well to peasant entrepreneurship—the direct exploitation of peasants by peasants.[2]

THE ORIGINS OF EMBROIDERING IN SAN ANTONINO

The state of Oaxaca is touted in political speeches, in the press, and by the tourist industry as a wellspring of the nation's indigenous cultural patrimony. Among Mexico's states it has the largest variety of indigenous ethnic communities, and is perhaps the richest in traditional and quasi-traditional crafts. The state's annual government-sponsored folkdance festival, *Lunes del Cerro*, is shown on national television, several of its master artisans are periodically featured in the media, and photographs of its monumental precolombian ruins and picturesque peasant marketplaces decorate travel posters and tourist advertising. Paradoxically, Oaxaca's Indian peasants, the source of all this national pride, are among the poorest people in the nation (See also Cook 1982a, 1982b).

The central Valley of Oaxaca, in which San Antonino lies, is dotted by over 250 peasant communities, many of which specialize in specific crops, crafts, or trade. The bulk of the region's peasant products are exchanged in the centuries-old and still vigorous system of periodic marketplaces (Beals 1975; Cook and Diskin 1975; Malinowski and de la Fuente 1982).

San Antonino is adjacent to Ocotlán, the district headtown,

some 30 kilometers south of Oaxaca City, to which it is linked by a paved road. The community is relatively large (population c. 4000) and, by local standards, relatively prosperous. Its inhabitants are of Zapotec descent, and most adults speak both Spanish and the indigenous tongue. Most of the community's residents are farmers, involved in intensive cash-crop horticulture on small plots, and most of these households supplement their agricultural income with earnings from other activities such as butchering, baking, and petty marketplace trading. Thus, the ways of the market, at least on a regional basis, are not new to *Tonineros*, as the people from San Antonino often call themselves (Waterbury and Turkenik 1975).

Exactly when the craft of embroidery began in San Antonino is not known, although it probably was introduced by Dominican friars during the colonial period. Certainly, the cut of the blouse, with its yoke and sewn-in sleeves, is post-conquest. According to elderly informants, embroidering has long been a common female pastime, devoted predominantly to the decoration of women's clothing. Traditional dress customs mandated the use of embroidered blouses, simple ones for daily wear and ornate ones for fiestas. Most women embroidered only for their own families, but a few especially skillful needleworkers occasionally made blouses for others as a part-time, income-producing activity. Their most frequent customers were the parents of young husbands-to-be, who were expected to present the bride with a complete fiesta outfit including an elaborately embroidered blouse.

Although the wearing and making of embroidered blouses began to decline in the late 1930s as part of the general shift from Indian to *mestizo* peasant dress style, the craft did not die out completely. It was preserved by a handful of women who continued to make traditional blouses on special order and who occasionally sold blouses to the two or three tourist shops in Oaxaca City.

The revival of embroidery in San Antonino began in the 1950s, sparked by the growth of post–World War II tourism to Oaxaca which increased the market for all of the region's crafts. This augmented demand was communicated to the village by city tourist shop operators, who began coming to San Antonino in search of merchandise. Some of the village women who had continued to make and sell blouses on a small scale stepped up their production. The women who still remembered how to embroider began teaching young girls, and a few *Tonineras* established themselves as interme-

Figure 20. A modern-style blouse worn with traditional fiesta-style garb by the late Doña Sabina Sánchez, one of the women responsible for adapting the blouse for the tourist market. Photo by Ronald Waterbury

diary traders by purchasing completed garments from other *Tonineras* and reselling them to tourist shops in the city. By the mid-1960s, embroidering had again become a common female activity in San Antonino.

Throughout this period demand increased steadily, but the actual production process remained traditional. Factory-made cloth and thread were used, as they had been for many years, and the tasks of cutting, embroidering, and assembling of blouses were not yet differentiated; each woman made the entire garment herself. Then in the late 1960s tourism to Oaxaca increased dramatically and, more importantly, the demand for peasant and ethnic clothing spread beyond tourists into the general international market. Not only did purchases by the growing number of Oaxaca City tourist shops increase, but buyers from Mexico City and abroad also began to come directly to San Antonino in search of embroidered dresses. The traditional organization of production could no longer keep pace and several village women initiated putting-out operations.

THE RISE OF PUTTING-OUT OPERATIONS

Putting-out arrangements were not unknown to San Antonino, as a few men already sewed trousers as piece-rate outworkers for Oaxaca City clothing merchants. In fact, the wives of two of these men were among the first putters-out of embroidered dresses. For labor, the new putting-out merchants recruited young, predominantly unmarried girls in San Antonino, particularly those from poorer families. The money derived from piecework provided these girls with a small supplement to household income or, in some cases, savings for the cash portion of the girl's dowry.

Beginning about 1970, the pool of outworkers in San Antonino became insufficient. To meet ever-rising demand and to keep costs down, the putting-out merchants—who were also growing in number—sought pieceworkers beyond their own community. The greatest need was for embroiderers, that being the most time-consuming of the steps in making a dress and thus the one requiring the greatest number of workers. The putting-out merchants were obliged to search for embroiderers outside of San Antonino, not only because the number of *Tonineras* able to embroider was insufficient to meet production needs, but also because the *Tonineras* were reluctant to accept the low fees they were offering. The long tradition of marketplace trading in San Antonino's women made alternative occupations available to them—and in this relatively prosperous community, many households did not need to engage in the self-exploitation that piecework embroidery entails.

In their quest for outworkers, San Antonino dress merchants first looked to nearby villages in which some women already knew how to embroider. Based on his independent survey of the economics of craft production in the region, conducted between 1978 and 1980, Scott Cook states (1982a:64,fn.11) that of Ocotlán district's twenty municipalities:

only three or four . . . have little or no embroidery; 11 of the 12
communities surveyed . . . had a significant incidence of families
engaged in this work—ranging from 100% of the households
censused in one community to a low of 16% in another, with the
average incidence being 56% of the 467 households censused in
the eleven communities.

By then the network of outworkers had already spread to other districts, mostly to the south of Ocotlán, and included communities
more than 40 kilometers away. Most of the more distant communities were agricultural villages that produced no crafts and in which
the women had never embroidered. This expansion was technically
possible because embroidering, at the level of expertise necessary
to satisfy mass wholesale standards, demands the least skill of all the
steps and is relatively easy to learn. It was economically possible because most of these villages are located in marginal agricultural
zones where the soil is too poor to sustain an acceptable living. Indeed, permanent emigration is common from these villages, and
among the remaining households most of the adult males migrated
seasonally in search of work. For households that comprised mainly
women and children with few alternative sources of income, self-
exploitation through embroidery was almost welcome. In fact, even
at the risk of appearing effeminate, a few men in the outlying villages became embroiderers too.

Most embroidery on commercial-grade dresses is now performed by women in communities other than San Antonino. However, those phases of the production process such as crocheting or
pattern-drawing, which require greater skill and are somewhat better paid, are still largely performed by *Toninera* outworkers or in the
merchants' own households.

THE ORGANIZATION OF THE WORK

Although the putting-out system has fundamentally changed the
organization of production, the product itself has changed only su-
perficially. The traditional garment was a short-sleeved white blouse
embroidered in white. Presently most garments are dress length
and are embroidered with colored thread, sometimes on colored
cloth. A band of embroidery down the front has been added and

some models now have long sleeves with embroidered cuffs. The basic construction of the garment has remained the same, as have the embroidery designs.

The tasks required to produce an embroidered dress are identical, whether made by a single artisan or through the putting-out system. There are seven steps: (1) cutting the cloth to form the parts of the dress (yoke, sleeves, and body); (2) drawing the embroidery design on the cloth; (3) embroidering the parts; (4) smocking a narrow strip across the top of the body in a pattern of *monitos* (small figures); (5) crocheting the edge of the neck and sleeves; (6) sewing the parts together into a dress; and (7) washing and ironing the completed garment.

The tools used by outworkers, which they supply themselves, are simple and inexpensive: a ballpoint pen for drawing the embroidery pattern, sewing needles and a hoop (which not all embroiderers use), and crochet hooks. The putting-out household needs a sewing machine to assemble the dresses, and a washtub and iron to prepare them for final sale. Sewing machines are common possessions in San Antonino because they have long been given as wedding presents to brides by their parents. A new electric Singer (with zigzag capability) cost P/7,270 ($320) in 1978 and could be purchased on credit.[3] Many women continued to use their old treadle machines, more often due to preference rather than price. An electric iron cost about P/250 ($11).

Under the putting-out system, the merchant assigns each task to a different outworker, who usually specializes in only one step of the process. All San Antonino merchants provide the cloth, pay their outworkers, collect the completed pieces, and sell the finished product. Early in the development of the system, piecework embroiderers were required to provide their own thread. However, as many of them—particularly those from outside San Antonino—skimped on the amount of thread used or chose color combinations considered inappropriate by buyers, the dress merchants soon undertook to supply the thread.

The major variation in the work process is the number of steps carried out in the merchant's own household. Small-scale merchants usually perform many of the tasks themselves, thereby compensating for limited volume by investing more of their own labor. One informant, for example, put out only the drawing and embroidering; she and her 13-year-old daughter did all the rest. Large-scale producers, in contrast, put out everything except cutting and final assembly, and a portion of the latter was often put out too, if the volume of work surpassed the household's own sewing capacity. In 1978, all but one of the merchants distributed and collected all the parts themselves at each phase of the process. The notable exception was the largest merchant who, because of the volume of his business and the size of his network of outworkers, subcontracted out some of the embroidery distribution to agents in two different towns.

COSTS AND RETURNS

Production costs to San Antonino putting-out merchants for a commercial-quality dress in 1978 are itemized in Table 1. Since assembling, washing, and ironing of dresses are usually performed in the merchant's own household, figures for those phases are not included in the table. When those tasks were also put out, additional costs of P/8 and P/5 respectively were incurred, raising the total to approximately P/245 (U.S. $10.92).

Fees paid to pieceworkers are quite standardized because the number of actual and potential outworkers is vast compared to the limited number of merchants, most of whom are from a single community. Among San Antonino's dress merchants, however, formal collusion to control wages is definitely not practiced. Unlike the butchers, bakers, and petty marketplace traders, who are organized, no formal association of dress merchants exists. Nonetheless, information derived from outworkers and buyers and from the village's universal espionage corps—the children—makes costs and prices common knowledge.

Wages earned by outworkers differ according to the level of skill associated with the task and the time required to complete it. Our calculations reveal that on an hourly basis, embroidery paid the least of all: approximately P/2 per hour (U.S. $0.09).[4] Crocheting yielded P/3 to P/6 per hour ($0.13 to $0.27); smocking (making the *monitos*) earned P/6 to P/8 per hour ($0.27 to $0.35); drawing the embroidery design returned the most, at least P/8 per hour (U.S. $.35).[5] In mid-1978, wholesale buyers were paying an average of P/300 ($13.25) per dress, which provided a 30 percent markup for the San Antonino merchants. By the time the garments reached retail shops in the United States they had increased in price a minimum of 400 per-

TABLE 1
Dress Production Costs to San Antonino
Putting-Out Merchants in 1978

Item	Cost	
	Pesos	Dollars
Materials		
Cloth (approx. 3.5 m. at 20)	70.00	3.10
Thread (10 skeins at 2.50)	25.00	1.11
Labor		
Design drawing	10.00	.44
Embroidery	100.00	4.42
Smocking and *monitos*	12.00	.53
Crochet	12.00	.53
Miscellaneous (soap, electricity, travel, etc.)	2.50	.11
Total	230.00	10.25

Note: *Pesos are converted to U.S. dollars at the rate of 22.60 to 1, which was in effect in mid-1978. The totals have been rounded to the nearest 5 pesos and 5 U.S. cents.*

cent, selling there for at least $50 each.[6]

Since most garments are exported or purchased by foreign tourists, devaluation of the peso and subsequent price inflation also affected the embroidered dress trade. As is evident from Table 2, between 1970 and 1978 the already miserably paid outworkers absorbed a disproportionate share of the effects of the devalued peso, while all others—must notably the cloth manufacturers—managed to keep their selling prices ahead of the rising value of the dollar.

The size of putting-out networks varies considerably. The smallest merchants in 1978 employed no more than 10, whereas the largest operator in San Antonino estimated that he put out to about 900 workers in 15 different communities. But as the scale increases, so do organizational problems. Accounting becomes increasingly onerous (especially for those merchants who are functionally illiterate), quality less controllable, and distributing and collecting the parts less manageable, more time-consuming, and more costly. Fur-

TABLE 2
Inflation 1970–78
In Pesos

Item	1970	1978	Percentage Rise
Cost of factory-made cloth (per sq. meter)	5	21	300
Selling price of quality dress	250	900	260
Selling price of commercial-grade dress	150	300	100
Value of U.S. dollar	12.50	22.60	81
Wages paid by putting-out merchants per dress for:			
Embroidering	60	100	67
Design drawing	7	10	43
Smocking and *monitos*	10	12	20
Crocheting	10	12	20

thermore, the expansion of the system to distant villages engendered some theft. The utilization of subcontractors in other communities by San Antonino's largest trader was an attempt to minimize this problem.

PRODUCT QUALITY

Despite the dress merchants' attempts at quality control, modifications in the production process brought about by the putting-out system were accompanied by a perceptible deterioration in the quality of the garments. The newer pieceworkers tended not only to be less skilled but also less aesthetically motivated, as they never saw nor had any relationship to the completed garment. But as the market became more generalized, wholesale buyers became more interested in low price than high quality and what might be called a "commercial-grade" garment evolved.

Nonetheless, high quality embroidery is still appreciated by discriminating individual purchasers as well as by museum and exhibition buyers. In fact, demand for quality dresses has also risen, although to a much more modest degree than for the commercial-grade dresses. As might be expected, given their greater labor input, better materials, and short supply, quality dresses fetch much higher prices. In fact, from 1970 to 1978 they ran well ahead of the inflating value of the dollar (Table 2).

A few San Antonino women have continued to specialize in making and/or trading of the finer garments. One such woman, Doña Sabina Sanchez, was among those craftspersons elevated by the Mexican press and government agencies (such as the Tourism Ministry and FONART) to the status of national "artisan celebrity" (Cook 1982a:60). Prior to her untimely death in an automobile accident in 1981, she was wooed by exhibitors, featured on national television, and honored with diplomas and awards. She was also the subject of a documentary by a North American filmmaker and was taken to California to demonstrate her craft at a showing of the film at a Los Angeles museum.

MARKETING

Most commercial-grade dresses are marketed through wholesale buyers who purchase directly in the village. A modest proportion of garments, perhaps 10 percent, is taken by San Antonino dress merchants to tourist shops in Oaxaca City, and an even smaller amount to shops in Mexico City. Agents from FONART also occasionally buy, but the volume is insignificant compared to that handled by private intermediaries. Least important of all are direct sales to consumers. San Antonino, lacking exotic attractions, is not on the tourist circuit; anyone who ventures into the village in quest of embroidery must search to find it as there are no retail shops, and putting-out merchants do not put out signs.

The most important marketing agents, the traveling wholesale buyers, are of two types: professionals who come regularly, and amateurs or quasi-professionals who come sporadically. The professionals can be divided into large-volume buyers, nearly all of whom are North Americans or Europeans, and moderate- to small-volume buyers, some of whom are Mexicans. The amateurs and quasi-professionals, mostly foreigners, make purchases in the moderate to small range.

San Antonino putting-out merchants and their customers dis-

TABLE 3
*Sales Volume and Net Income per Month of San Antonino
Putting-Out Merchants in 1978*

Scale	Households (n=40) No. %		Volume of Dresses Sold	Net Income[1] in Pesos	Equivalent[2] in Dollars
1	1	2.5	300-400	18,000-24,000	800-1,060
2	5	12.5	150-250	10,500-17,500	465- 775
3	15	37.5	25-149	1,750-10,430	75- 460
4	19	47.5	5- 24	350- 1,680	15- 75

1. Net income is calculated by assuming a profit of 70 pesos per garment for all but the largest operation. For that case, because of somewhat higher costs (subcontractor's commissions, some putting-out of final assembly, and greater transport costs), I estimate 60 pesos per dress. (See the discussion and Table 1 of the previous section.)
2. Pesos converted to dollars at the prevalent exchange rate at that time of 22.60 to 1, rounded to nearest $5.

play a certain affinity of scale. The large-volume professional buyers, who purchase hundreds of dresses per trip, prefer the efficiency and convenience of dealing with the largest San Antonino merchants (principally those in Scales I and II of Table 3). Conversely, the top San Antonino merchants were able to establish and maintain favored client relations with large buyers by proving themselves to be reliable volume suppliers. Therefore they sell to smaller buyers only if they have stock in excess of that committed to their preferred customers, or if immediate cash is needed. Hence the smaller buyers, even the professional ones, are usually required to make the rounds of the smaller putting-out merchants.

Although most transactions are on a cash basis, the large professional buyers sometimes leave sizable deposits with trusted San Antonino suppliers, to provide them with some of the capital necessary to complete the order. The history of the top putting-out business in 1978 is a case in point. According to the husband's account, several years before a European buyer, to whom they had been periodically supplying a moderate number of dresses, offered a substantial cash advance if they could complete an exceptionally large order within six months. The wife, who until that time had managed the putting-out network while the husband sewed dresses, hesitated for fear of being unable to fulfill the commitment. The husband, however, accepted the challenge, took over and expanded the network of outworkers, and successfully completed the order. The gains from that achievement permitted them to purchase an automobile which, along with referrals to other volume buyers, facilitated further expansion of the business.

GOVERNMENT INVOLVEMENT

In all of these developments, the government's role has been minimal. FONART's purchases are of little importance. The advertising effect of the publicity accorded Doña Sabina and the government-sponsored artisanry exhibitions primarily affects Mexican nationals, whereas the vast majority of San Antonino dresses are sold to foreign tourists or are exported. A representative of the national bank for the development of cooperatives once initiated conversations with a few San Antonino dress merchants, but none expressed interest in organizing because they saw no advantage in doing so. No effort has ever been made to organize pieceworkers.

EMBROIDERY IN SAN ANTONINO'S SOCIOECONOMIC STRUCTURE

The commercialization of embroidery has made an important addition to San Antonino's already complex occupational mix and has substantially improved the standard of living of some but not all of the 40 putting-out households. For the multitude of outworkers in and out of San Antonino, its economic contribution has been minimal, though considered worthwhile given the poverty of pieceworking households. Its effect on gender roles has been nil, despite the fact that all but one of the putting-out businesses are managed by women. Nor has the political status of the putting-out households reflected their rising economic fortunes.

As I noted earlier, for decades most of San Antonino's households have combined agriculture with one or more other occupations. In 1978, the most numerous non-agricultural activities, excluding embroidery, were petty marketplace trading (380 households), making tortillas (75 households), baking bread (25 households), and butchering beef (15 households). Although insignificant in 1965, by 1978 embroidery involved 40 households as putting-out merchants and many more as pieceworkers, and thus formed a major addition to the occupational matrix. Nonetheless, it was still just one occupation of many. Indeed, only two of the putting-out households relied solely upon the dress business for subsistence.

The contribution the putting-out system has made to household incomes is shown in Table 3, which places dress-merchant households in four categories according to their monthly sales volumes and net incomes. As this table demonstrates, the income range among the 40 putting-out operations was great. And as Table 4 shows, there was a wide range in the number of dresses sold by different households. The six households operating at Scales 1 and 2 (Table 4) represented 15 percent of the merchants but nearly half (46.2 percent) of the sales. By village standards, they were growing rich. In fact, their putting-out operations allowed them to enjoy a standard of living comparable to that of Oaxaca City's middle class. That is, most of them had built or were building multi-roomed brick and cement houses, complete with tile floors and indoor plumbing (two eschewed ostentatious displays for reasons that will be made apparent shortly). Furthermore, their homes were furnished and equipped with most of the material conveniences and symbols of the modern lifestyle: plastic-covered upholstered couches and chairs, beds with box springs and mattresses, gas stoves, electric refrigerators, television sets, and radio-phonograph consoles. They also possessed ample wardrobes and an array of personal gadgets such as cameras, pocket calculators, and cassette tape recorders, and spent large amounts on public and private fiestas.

The single Scale 1 dress merchant, who himself represented only 2.5 percent of all the merchants but sold 12 percent of the dresses (Table 5), earned over P/18,000 per month in 1978, which matched the income of most urban professionals. That permitted his family to enjoy not only all the modern amenities listed above but also one of the community's three private cars and the luxury of sending their only child, a son, to the university. Moreover, one of the households that operated at Scale 2 in 1978 had by 1982 risen to even greater heights. In the summer of that year, they inaugurated a brand new Chevrolet Citation with festivities that included live music, fireworks, and a priest to bestow blessings and sprinkle holy water on the car. That vehicle was an addition to the full inventory

TABLE 4
Distribution of Estimated Monthly Sales of San Antonino
Putting-Out Merchants in 1978

| Scale | Merchants | | | Dresses Sold | |
	No.	%		No.	%
1	1	2.5		350	12.0
2	5	12.5		1000	34.2
3	15	37.5		1300	44.4
4	19	47.5		275	9.4
	40	100.0		2925	100.0

of domestic appliances and consumer goods they had already accumulated and to the pickup truck they had purchased two years before.

The lifestyle of most of the pieceworkers, especially those from outside San Antonino, is worlds apart. They travel on foot, donkey, or second-class bus; live in dirt-floored, one-room, adobe houses or mud-daubed cane huts; sleep on mats on the floor; own a few pieces of crude wood furniture and no modern appliances; rarely possess more than one change of clothing; bathe outdoors by ladling water over themselves from a bucket; and relieve themselves on the ground.

San Antonino's fifteen Scale 3 putting-out operations, representing 37.5 percent of the merchants producing 44.4 percent of the dresses, earned returns that were much more modest than those of the top six. Though considerable by village standards, this income alone would not permit anything approximating a middle-class lifestyle. Where dress income was combined with substantial earnings from agriculture and other occupations, however, it did permit a few Scale 3 households—especially those at the upper end of the scale—to approach that level, albeit minus the motor vehicles and university education.

The combined average monthly sales of all nineteen Scale 4 putting-out businesses (comprising nearly half the total) was less than 10 percent of the combined sales of all dress merchants, and even less than the production of the one household in Scale 1. The incomes derived were meager. As an extreme example, in 1978 the smallest putting-out merchant sold but five dresses per month, netting her only P/350, about one quarter of the earnings of the average female petty marketplace trader. As one might expect, turnover is high among Scale 4 dress merchants because insufficient capital and the competition from larger more established businesses for outworkers and especially for buyers makes their chances of expansion slim.

Nonetheless, women continue in the activity for several reasons. First, as a supplemental source of income, it is less onerous and requires less time out of the house than does marketplace trading, the principal alternative occupation for women. For the few Scale 4 households that enjoy substantial incomes from other sources, it provides women with an independent source of petty cash. But for most Scale 4 putters-out, the principal reason is that the earnings, although miniscule, are important because these households are very poor, sometimes as poor as their pieceworkers. In fact, many Scale 4 dress merchants are pieceworkers just trying to break into the putting-out business.

THE WEALTH RANKING OF PUTTING-OUT HOUSEHOLDS

The economic significance of the dress trade can also be appreciated by comparing the wealth ranking of putting-out households to that of the general population.[7] Discarding the single putting-out household in Wealth Rank I (the case is anomalous and the numbers are not statistically reliable),[8] Table 5 shows a significantly greater representation of putting-out households in the community's upper wealth ranks (II and III), and a lesser representation in the lower ranks (IV and V). Because only two putting-out households rely on the dress business as their sole income source, it is not possible to specify what proportion of a household's economic standing is directly attributable to its putting-out activities. Nonetheless, the information in Table 5 is highly suggestive.

These inferences from Table 5 can be corroborated by including landholding data in the matrix, as agriculture is the one income source common to virtually the entire community and land ownership was given the greatest weight in wealth ranking by all informants. Again disregarding the one putting-out household in Wealth

TABLE 5

*Wealth Rank of Putting-Out Households Compared to
the General Population of San Antonino in 1978*

Wealth Rank	Putting-Out Households		General Population	
	No.	%	No.	%
I (VERY RICH)	1	2.5	5	8.5
II (RICH)	7	17.5	39	4.1
III (ORDINARY)	16	40.0	184	19.3
IV (POOR)	13	32.5	554	58.1
V (VERY POOR)	3	7.5	173	18.0
	40	100.0	955	100.0

Rank I, Table 6 indicates that putting-out households were not pulled up in the ranking by land ownership since their mean land holding was either equal to (Rank IV) or less than (Ranks II, III, and V) that of the general population in the same wealth ranks.

In sum, although the size of the operations varies widely, the embroidery trade has been economically important to all of the 40 households with putting-out businesses. In qualitative terms and by village standards, for a few it has meant riches (Scales 1 and 2 of Table 3); for others (Scale 3) it has made a substantial contribution towards attainment of a comfortable standard of living. Even for the many who earn minimal or at best modest returns (Scale 4), it has provided welcome supplemental income.

GENDER RELATIONS AND THE PUTTING-OUT BUSINESS

Because putting-out has become such an important addition to the community's occupational repertory, and because all but one of these businesses are managed by women, we must ask the obvious question: Why have these changes had no effect on the position of women in the community?

A cardinal precept in San Antonino's gender ideology holds that male and female roles should be complementary and based upon the "natural" propensities of each sex.[9] In this scheme of

TABLE 6

Landholdings in Hectares of Putting-Out Households by Wealth Rank Compared to General Population of San Antonino in 1978

Wealth Rank	Putting-Out Households		General Population	
	No.	Mean Landholding	No.	Mean Landholding
I	1	16.7	5	7.9
II	7	2.0	39	3.8
III	16	1.3	184	1.6
IV	13	0.5	554	0.5
V	3	0.0	173	0.06

things, embroidering has long been associated with females, not only because it is allegedly suited to their more delicate hands, but also because it can be performed in the spare time between other naturally appropriate female tasks such as cooking, washing, child-rearing, or selling in the marketplace—and, of course, because the finished garment itself is an item of female attire.[10] Therefore, being simply an entrepreneurial extension of embroidery, the management of putting-out systems was classified as appropriate women's work. This permitted a significant number of households to take advantage of a new economic niche without contravening the "natural" complementarity of male and female work tasks.

However, the strong representation of women in the putting-out business limited their capacity to expand, because the development of large-scale operations infringed upon the time women had to devote to their domestic duties. Only where surrogates, in the form of daughters or servants, were pressed into domestic service did a few large-scale putting-out businesses headed by women emerge. In such cases, the affected households could not conceal the fact that their major source of income was female-generated—a mark of shame in San Antonino, which ridicules a subordinate husband.

Ideally, the Oaxacan family balances women with men. The

wife-mother role in the domestic domain is recognized as indispensable, and accorded full respect. In the many households for which we have intimate information, women participate in virtually all decisions regarding household economic strategies. (Indeed, children's views are considered as well, depending on their age and economic importance.) In fact, it is not uncommon that the wife's is the dominant voice. Yet, however forceful her role, it should not spill over into the public sphere, lest her husband's image as a man, and his legitimate jural authority over the family, be compromised. In public, even the most dominant wife will show deference to her husband; otherwise, they will both become targets of gossip and ridicule, because the public arena is considered the "natural" location of male dominance.

Three of the top six putting-out businesses in 1978 (Scales 1 and 2) posed no problems for men because the largest operation was managed by the husband, and the other two were operated by spinsters residing with a single elderly parent. Two other households in the top group, which were potential targets of gossip, deflected serious criticism in two ways. First, they followed the age-old method of maintaining a relatively humble lifestyle in order to hide some of their material success. Second, the husbands distanced themselves from the putting-out operations by referring to them as "my wife's *negocito*" (little business), thus deemphasizing the economic importance of the new source of income. They also conspicuously pursued manly agricultural pursuits, leaving all aspects of the putting-out management to their wives.

The household that had risen to first place among the putting-out businesses by 1982 became the butt of numerous jokes, because the husband had become "nothing but a *costurera* (seamstress) and errand boy" for his wife's business, which—judging from the family's ostentatious displays of wealth—was obviously successful. During expansion of the business, the husband all but abandoned his agricultural pursuits. He learned how to sew and dedicated himself to assisting his wife, who clearly remained in charge. An additional humiliation was that he did not know how to drive; the couple's sons chauffeured the wife around.

If the gender ideology of separate domains for women and men constrained the development of putting-out businesses within San Antonino, it also limited the expansion of these businesses at the regional level. It is not considered proper for women to travel unaccompanied beyond the marketplaces of the valley, and even there, they are generally accompanied by children, their husbands, or other San Antonino vendors. The few women who do make frequent unaccompanied trips outside those boundaries, regardless of how legitimate their reasons (legitimate reasons include commercial activity and schooling), are gossiped about as loose women and probable prostitutes. This restriction does not hinder the marketing of garments because they can be delivered to shops in Oaxaca City or sold to the buyers who come directly to the village. Furthermore, a substantial network of outworkers can be managed from the local marketplaces that are within the respectable female traveling range. The very largest operations, however, entail traveling farther afield, which for women means delegating the traveling to men, or mobilizing male family members as escorts. Reinforcing this pattern is the fact that women do not drive. Given that buses run infrequently, are often unreliable, and serve only some of the communities, men with motor vehicles have an edge over women in the efficient management of a large network of pieceworkers.

It follows then, that the largest dress business in 1978 was managed by a husband using an automobile. In the household that had gained the top spot by 1982, the wife was driven around in a pickup truck by her sons. In contrast, the only woman dress merchant who regularly traveled alone to Mexico City to sell garments to tourist shops was subjected to malicious gossip concerning her sexual morality. When her teenage daughter began to accompany her because she had no sons, it was rumored that they were both prostitutes.

It also follows that the rising economic position of putting-out households has not seen a parallel rise in their political status. Since at least the late 1930s, the office of municipal president has been held by men whose households were relatively wealthy, although not always the wealthiest, and whose incomes usually derived from non-agricultural sources such as milling, butchering, baking, and wholesale marketing of produce. Even though putting-out has become one of the most important non-agricultural sources of income and has bestowed on several families more than enough wealth to make their heads eligible for the presidency, not a single male from those households has been mentioned as having presidential caliber. The male managers of putting-out businesses would be considered fully eligible, but in 1982 there was only one male manager and he was a foreigner. In San Antonino foreigners, like women, are considered unfit for public trust.

CONSEQUENCES OF THE PUTTING-OUT SYSTEM

In San Antonino, the "tourist" demand for hand-embroidered "peasant" garments outstripped the capacity of a traditional, undifferentiated organization of production to make them. In response, a number of peasant women became entrepreneurs, initiating a putting-out system. This system expanded output through an increased division of labor, but with little reliance on mechanization and capital investment. Notwithstanding these limitations, putting-out has had impressive effects on the local population. The product has been commoditized (Cook 1982a; Greenwood 1977; Hart 1982), the labor that produces it is alienated, and social inequality is more pervasive now than in the past.

Even in San Antonino, the embroidered blouse that goes by this name has lost its use value, both in the practical and in the symbolic sense. In practical terms, almost nobody wears it. In fact, only a few elderly women still wore the simpler version of the blouse by the time the putting-out system was organized. Similarly, the practice of giving elaborately embroidered blouses as wedding presents has ended, terminating their use to symbolize the alliance between intermarrying families.

Perhaps the only remaining symbolic use for embroidered blouses is as part of the costume worn by San Antonino's delegation to the annual state-sponsored folkdance extravaganza, *Lunes del Cerro*. During the performance, the blouses serve to identify the community. As this elaborate event is staged largely for tourists and national television, the spectacle takes on aspects of a commercial advertisement. In short, even this vestige of use value is overshadowed by the value of exchange. The San Antonino embroidered blouse is today more a trademark than an authentic cultural form.[11]

For the vast majority of consumers, the ethnic association of the San Antonino blouse with the community of this name is irrelevant, having been obliterated by what Garcia Canclini (1981:94–99) calls "commodity unification." As circulation and consumption remove products farther from their point of origin, their specific ethnic identities become homogenized as simply "typical." Thus, only some of the Oaxaca City tourist shops label San Antonino dresses correctly; everywhere else, wholesalers, retailers, and consumers refer to them as "Mexican wedding dresses." Even the large Mexico City FONART outlet dedicated to Oaxaca artisanry homogenizes its merchandise in this way. On several visits to the store, I observed the San Antonino garments labeled as "Ocotlán," after the district in which San Antonino is located.

Along with the loss of symbolic and ethnic identity, the putting-out system has been accompanied by labor alienation. Previously the San Antonino dress was made by a San Antonino craftswoman who purchased the materials, performed all the steps at her own pace and with her own tools, and sold or presented the finished garment herself. Now, even though most putting-out merchants perform the final assembly phase in their own households, on their own sewing machines, using the labor of their own families, the phase of the process that gives the garment its distinction and marketability, the embroidery phase, is performed by alienated piece-workers. Although they work in their own homes, at their own pace, and use their own tools, they have no control over the raw materials, the design and colors of the embroidery, the shape of the final dress, or its ultimate disposition. Residing for the most part in the outlying villages, rather than in San Antonino, the outworkers also lack a communal basis for identifying with what they make.

As we have seen, financial remuneration to outworkers is miniscule, and has reinforced the direction of change in the community and regional class structures of the Ocotlán district. To San Antonino, putting-out has meant the formation of a new cash-producing economic sector consisting of the putting-out households. The households involved now constitute an important element in the subclass of peasant-merchants, whose wealthiest and most successful members are politically influential. Because embroidery is associated with women, however, and because the community discriminates against women in politics, the putting-out households have yet to gain political prominence commensurate with their entrepreneurial standing, or on a level with the butchers, bakers, and produce wholesalers.

From the wider perspective of the region, wealth differentials between central and peripheral villages are not new. But the putting-out merchants of San Antonino have exploited this differential, taking advantage of cheap labor in the poorer rural communities and enhancing the favorable economic position of their own village in the process.

Finally, the most far-reaching consequence of the putting-out system has been its effects on social relationships in the work process itself. Most other peasant merchants and processor-vendors in San Antonino, as well as in other rural communities of the region, still rely exclusively on in-house family labor for the tasks that must be performed. Only a minority resorts to the hiring of wage labor, and then seldom more than one or two persons who are employed episodically. Moreover, the relationship between these peasant merchants and their employees is still basically familial. Although the workers are paid, they always take their meals with the family and often live with the family as well. By contrast, the relationship between the putting-out dress merchants and their non-San Antonino outworkers is strictly business—and indeed it is only slightly less businesslike between these merchants and the outworkers who are their fellow villagers.

The new relationship of social inequality in the Ocotlán district, together with the changed meanings of the wedding dress and the increasing alienation of labor, mean that the richly embroidered San Antonino garments of today bear no real relationship to the cloth that circulated in the Oaxacan marriage exchange system of the past. Ironically, the embroidered blouse is still linked to marriage and the embroidery motifs, although dictated by the putters-out, are anchored in tradition. The putting-out structure, however, has transformed what the embroiderers do, both materially and symbolically, substituting for the earlier intimacy between production and use a pyramid of market relations. One wonders if the consumers of "ethnic" clothing understand this transformation any better than the pieceworking embroiderers comprehend all of the steps that intervene between their hands and the final disposition of what these hands create.

ACKNOWLEDGMENTS

This paper is one result of a long-term research project in San Antonino that began in 1965 and, through the summer of 1988, had accumulated over 54 months in the field. I appreciate the direct and indirect support the project has received over the years from the National Science Foundation, the Social Science Research Council, and the PSC/CUNY Faculty Award Program of the City University of New York. I would especially like to thank my wife and research associate, Carole Turkenik, who collected much of the data on which this paper is based, and who provided invaluable editorial criticism. The paper also benefited from comments on earlier drafts by Edward Hansen, Jane Schneider, and Eric Wolf.

NOTES

1. Although the style originated in San Antonino, the dresses are no longer exclusively embroidered there, nor are all putting-out merchants who deal in the dresses from this community. It is still, however, the principal center of operations.

2. Peasant putting-out merchants or agents also existed in historical Europe; e.g., see Klima 1974.

3. The symbol "P/" will be used for Mexican pesos.

4. In the independent survey mentioned previously, Scott Cook arrived at the identical hourly wage for embroidering (Cook 1982a:64,fn.11). This not only corroborates our wage figure but also supports our statement that fees paid by merchants tend to be standardized.

5. For comparison, the wage paid to male agricultural day-laborers in San Antonino at that time, including the value of meals provided, was about P/7.50 per hour ($0.33). Most field hands employed in San Antonino come from other communities, which is further evidence of San Antonino's relative economic prosperity.

6. The U.S. prices derive from our own informal survey of several stores in New York City and Los Angeles, from a knowledgeable Oaxaca City artisanry wholesaler, and from a North American wholesale buyer.

7. The wealth rankings were constructed by utilizing a modification of Silverman's (1966) card-sort technique. A number of key informants, known to be reliable and perceptive, were asked to rate all households according to wealth. A point system was then devised by which we ranked the households. We settled on five categories because that best represented the consensus of our informants and our own observations.

8. The case is anomalous because, although the wife operates a putting-out system at the lower end of Scale 3, the household would occupy Wealth Rank I without her activities. The bulk of their wealth derives from their bakery and the 17 hectares of land they work, one of the two largest holdings in the community.

9. I purposely use the term sex rather than gender here because it is widely believed in San Antonino—by both women and men—that the behavioral differences most social scientists would attribute to socialization are in fact genetically determined.

10. The for-cash production of all clothing in San Antonino is traditionally gender-specific: *costureras* (seamstresses) of women's garments are always women, and *sastres* (tailors) of men's clothing are always men. For home use, however, it is acceptable for women to sew men's pants and shirts.

11. The young San Antonino girls who dance at *Lunes del Cerro* nearly always borrow the blouses they perform in, and would never wear one at any other time.

REFERENCES CITED

Beals, R.
  1975   The Peasant Marketing System of Oaxaca, Mexico. Berkeley: University of California Press.

Brown, E.
  1983   Shetlands to Protect Knitting Tradition. The New York Times, Feb. 25.

Charlton, L.
  1980   Gloveresses Still Stitch in the Cotswolds. The New York Times, April 30.

Cook, S.
  1982a   Crafts, Capitalist Development, and Cultural Property in Oaxaca, Mexico. Inter-American Economic Affairs 353(3):53–68.
  1982b   Craft production in Oaxaca, Mexico, Cultural Survival Quarterly 6(4):18–20.
  1984   The "Managerial" vs. the "Labor" Function, Capital Accumulation, and the Dynamics of Simple Commodity Production in Rural Oaxaca, Mexico. *In* Entrepreneurship and Social Change. Sidney Greenfield and Arnold Strickon, eds. pp. 45–95. Lanham: University Press of America.

Cook, S and M. Diskin, eds.
  1975   Markets in Oaxaca. Austin: University of Texas Press.

De Mauro, L.
  1983   Irish Sweaters to Last Forever, The New York Times, Aug. 28.

Ferretti, F.
  1983   Mystery: the Night Knitters. The New York Times, Aug. 14.

Garcia Canclini, N.
  1977   Arte Popular y Sociedad en America Latina. Mexico: Grijalbo.

1981   Las Culturas Populares en el Capitalismo. Havana: Casa de Las
          Americas.

Goody, E.
1982   Introduction. *In* From Craft to Industry: the Ethnography of
          Proto-Industrial Cloth Production. E. Goody, ed. pp 1–37. Lon-
          don: Cambridge University Press.

Graburn, N. ed.
1976   Ethnic and Tourist Arts: Cultural Expression from the Fourth
          World. Berkeley: University of California Press.

Greenwood, D.
1977   Culture by the Pound: an Anthropological Perspective on Tour-
          ism as Cultural Commoditization. *In* Smith 1977, pp. 129–38.

Gullickson, G.
1982   Proto-Industrialization, Demographic Behavior and the Sexual
          Divisions of Labor in Auffay, France, 1750-1850. Peasant Studies
          9(2):106–118.

Hart, K.
1982   Commoditization. *In* From Craft to Industry: the Ethnography of
          Proto-Industrial Cloth Production. E. Goody, ed. pp. 38–49. Lon-
          don: Cambridge University Press.

Hobsbawm, E.
1965   The Crisis of the 17th Century. *In* Crisis in Europe 1560-1660.
          Trevor Aston, ed. pp. 5–58. London: Routledge & Kegan Paul.

Hopkins, N.
1978   The Articulation of the Modes of Production: Tailoring in Tuni-
          sia. American Ethnologist 5(3):468–83.

Jones, E.
1968   Agricultural Origins of Industry. Past and Present 40:58–71.

Klima, A.
1974   The Role of Rural Domestic Industries in Bohemia in the 18th
          Century. Economic Historical Review 27:48–56.

Klima, A. and J. Macurek
1960   La Question de la Transition du Féodalisme au Capitalisme en
          Europe Centrale (16e-18e siècles). International Congress of His-
          torical Sciences, Stockholm.

Kriedte, P. and J. Schlumbohm
1977   Industrialisierung vor der Industrialisierung. Gottingen:
          VandenHoeck & Ruprecht.

Lamphere, L.
1979   Fighting the Piece-rate System: New Dimensions of an old Strug-

gle in the Apparel Industry. *In* Case Studies on the Labor Process. New York: Monthly Review Press.

Littlefield, A.
1978   Exploitation and the Expansion of Capitalism: the Case of the Hammock Industry of Yucatan. American Ethnologist 5:495–508.
1979   The Expansion of Capitalist Relations of Production in Mexican Crafts. Journal of Peasant Studies 6:471–88.

Malinowski, B. and J. de la Fuente
1982   The Economics of a Mexican Market System. London: Routledge & Kegan Paul.

Mendels, F.F.
1972   Proto-Industrialization: the First Stage of the Industrialization Process. Journal of Economic History 32(1):241–61.
1975   Agriculture and Peasant Industry in 18th Century Flanders. *In* European Peasants and their Markets: Essays in Agrarian Economic History. W.N. Parker and E.L. Jones, eds. pp. 179–204. Princeton: Princeton University Press.

Novelo, V.
1976   Artesania y Capitalismo en México. Mexico: SEP/INAH.

Scott, J. and L. Tilly
1975   Women's Work and the Family in Nineteenth Century Europe. Comparative Studies in Society and History 17(1):36–64.

Silverman, S.
1977   An Ethnographic Approach to Social Stratification: Prestige in a Central Italian Community. American Anthropologist 68:899–921.

Smith, V.
1977   Hosts and Guests: the Anthropology of Tourism. University of Pennsylvania Press.

Swallow, D.
1982   Production and Control in the Indian Garment Export Industry. *In* From Craft to Industry: the Ethnography of Proto-Industrial Cloth Production. E. Goody, ed. pp. 133–65. London: Cambridge University Press.

Thirsk, J.
1961   Industries in the Countryside. *In* Essays in the Economic and Social History of Tudor and Stuart England. F.J. Fisher, ed. pp. 70–88. Cambridge: Cambridge University Press.

Waterbury, R. and C. Turkenik
1975   The Marketplace Traders of San Antonino: a Quantitative Analysis. *In* Markets in Oaxaca. S. Cook and M. Diskin, eds. Austin: University of Texas Press. pp. 209–29.

PART III. *Cloth in Large-Scale Societies*

9. *Cloth and Its Function in the Inka State*[1]

JOHN V. MURRA

Inka rulers used cloth in dealing with defeated ethnic lords but also with peasants and soldiers throughout their realm. Intensive cloth production went on at both levels—state workshops, even manufactures, were kept weaving full time while peasant textiles were hoarded in ethnic treasuries. Cloth from both state and peasant looms was frequently offered, expected, confiscated or sacrificed; the study of textile circulation helps archaeologists, historians and ethnologists to understand how Andean societies functioned in pre-European times.

ANDEAN TEXTILES: AN INTRODUCTION

Years of full-time devotion have been lavished by some students on the description and analysis of the variety and technical excellence of Andean textiles. As Junius Bird, the leading modern student of the craft, has indicated, some of these fabrics "rank high among the finest ever produced."[2] Andean interest in cloth can be documented archaeologically to have endured for millennia, long before the coming of the Inka. Recent ethnohistoric studies show that the extraordinary imagination in creating a multiplicity of fabrics was functionally matched by the many unexpected political and religious contexts in which cloth was used.

The major fibers spun and woven in the ancient Andes were cotton in the lowlands and deserts and the wool of camelids in the highlands. Cotton is found in some of the earliest strata (pre-2000 B.C.), long before the appearance of maize on the Coast. Its twining and later weaving reached excellence very early,[3] and throughout coastal history it remained the important fiber; Bird goes so far as to say that the whole "Peruvian textile craft is based on the use of cotton and not on wool or any other fiber."[4] It is unfortunate that our sixteenth-century historical sources said so little about cotton cultivation, and it is curious that coastal ceramics, which so frequently illustrate cultivated plants and fruits, rarely if ever show cotton.[5]

In the highlands, archaeology tells us little, since textiles do not keep well in Andean conditions; this fact sometimes leads to neglect of the cultural significance and technical quality of highland fabrics, so evident from the early European sources. Although the excavations of Augusto Cardich[6] show that camelids had been hunted for many thousands of years, it has been impossible so far to date the beginning of llama domestication. Judging by camelids as represented on pottery and by sacrificed llama burials found on the Coast as early as Cupisnique times, we can assume that these animals were already domesticated by 1000 B.C. Bird suggests that a growing interest in wool by coastal weavers was possibly the major incentive for the domestication of camelids,[7] but at the present stage of highland studies, the taming of the guanaco and vicuña by those who had hunted them for 5,000 years and who first cultivated the potato is a more likely possibility.

In time, the use of wool increased even on the Coast and it became widespread with Inka expansion,[8] but apparently it had not penetrated everywhere, even in the highlands. Santillán reported in the 1570s that some highlanders carried burdens on their backs as they had no llamas, and even in very cold country their clothes were woven "like a net" from maguey fibers.[9] Garcilaso de la Vega also points to regions where maguey thread was woven into cloth, as wool and cotton were lacking.[10] Although neither source localizes these regions, tradition recorded by modern folkloric research describes some of the early inhabitants of the Callejón de Huaylas as

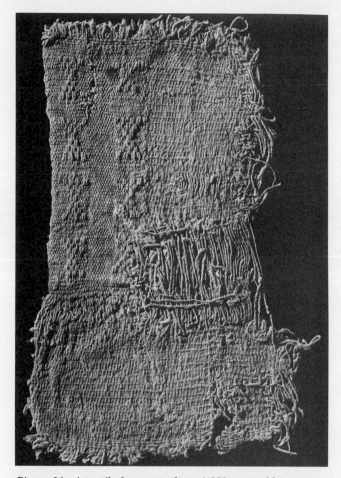

*Figure 21. A textile fragment about 4,000 years old, exca-
vated at Huaca Prieta on the north coast of Peru by Junius
Bird; it is unique in the way in which it combines the techniques of twining and weaving. Photo by Junius Bird,
American Museum of Natural History*

karapishtu, maguey leaf wearers.[11] Felipe Waman Puma, an early
seventeenth-century petitioner to the king of Spain, who reports
and illustrates an ingenious four-stage evolutionary sequence for
highland cultures, claimed that before people learned to weave they
went through a period when they were dressed in "leaves" and

later, through another wrapped in furs.[12] While the wool of vicuñas and alpacas may have been used even before domestication, it was in Inka times that llama-herding expanded as a state policy, much as it encouraged the cultivation of maize and coca-leaf,[13] through the use of *mitmaq* colonists.

The most systematic historical description of Inka looms and classification of fabrics has been recorded by the Jesuit Bernabé Cobo.[14] Although each fabric and weaving or ornamenting technique must have had its own name, European chroniclers were content with a dual classification: (1) *awasqa*, the cloth produced for domestic purposes, which was rather rough, indifferently colored and thick,[15] and (2) *kumpi*, a finer fabric, woven on a different loom. All early observers agreed the *kumpi* blankets and clothes were wonderfully soft, "like silk," frequently dyed in gay colors or ornamented with feathers or shell beads. The weave was smooth and continuous; "no thread could be seen."[16] Comparisons in those early days of the invasion were all unfavorable to European manufactures; only eighteen years later Cieza speaks of it as a lost treasure.[17]

Even today the peasant inhabitants of the Andean *altiplano* recognize ancestral textiles as the standard for beauty and high value. The authorities of Coroma, in the state of Potosí, were until recently the custodians of ten bundles (*q'epi*) of ancient and colonial weavings, one for each lineage. The local middle classes became aware of the high value of these hereditary bundles when some United States pirates took advantage of the 1982–83 drought and "bought" sixteen out of fifty-two garments. The price of each weaving on the illegal market is now in the thousands of dollars.

The Peruvian architect Héctor Velarde suggested once that the startling masonry at Machu Picchu or Huánuco Pampa reminded him of rows of stone that had been woven together. Years later, Bolivia's senior archaeologist, Maks Portugal Zamora, noted that the "peasants at Ojje (near the shrine of Copacabana) call this place *chchuku perqa* or 'sewn wall,' the . . . aboriginal vision building the wall of stones 'united as if sewn together' . . ." (p. 296).[18]

In pre-European times clothing was not tailored but left the looms virtually fully fashioned. The most detailed ethnohistoric description of peasant clothing will be found in Cobo.[19] According to Cieza there were no status differences in the tailoring of garments but only in the cloth and ornamentation used.[20] This is easily noted in the quality of archaeological textiles, since some graves display elegant, new, unused garments which must have required considerable expenditure of time and effort, while others contain ordinary clothes. Ethnic and regional differences in clothing are predictable but cannot yet be mapped beyond the varieties of *llawtu* headdresses, the hairdo, and frequently the type of cranial deformation.[21]

PEASANT USES OF CLOTH

The uses to which textiles were put by the Andean peasant should not be taken for granted. People do have to keep warm when living at 10,000 or 13,000 feet, and clothes are always important psychologically, but in the Andes the functions of cloth went far beyond such universals. Cloth emerges as the main ceremonial good and, on the personal level, the preferred gift, highlighting all crisis points in the life cycle and providing otherwise unavailable insights into the reciprocal relations of kinfolk.

Shortly after a child was weaned, he or she was given a new name at a feast to which many relatives, lineal and affinal, were invited. An "uncle" acted as sponsor and cut the first lock from the child's hair. The kinfolk followed: all who sheared hair were expected to offer gifts. Polo de Ondegardo enumerates silver, cloth, wool, cotton, and "other things." Garcilaso states that some brought clothes while others gave weapons.[22]

Initiation came at puberty for girls and at age fourteen or fifteen for boys. The boys were issued a *wara*, a loincloth woven for the occasion by their mothers. Receiving new clothes woven with magic precautions and wearing them ceremonially was an important part of change in status but details of it for the peasantry have been neglected by the European observers who have concentrated on the initiation of the young from the royal lineages. An inkling into the kind of detail we are missing comes from modern ethnology: as late as the 1920s at Quiquijana, in the Cusco area, pairs of youths would race ceremonially, their clothing fancy and new from head to foot.[23] Special clothes were still woven and all garments ceremonially washed for the young men assuming religious office thirty years ago on the island of Taquile, in Lake Titicaca.[24]

While some chroniclers and modern commentators have accepted some version of the account that marriage in the Andes depended on royal sanction, late sixteenth-century sources like Román, Murúa, and Waman Puma indicated that at the peasant household level, marriage took place on local initiative with textile gifts presented by the groom and his kin. Román, who had never been in the Andes but was widely read, mentioned llamas, but Murúa argued that only *señores*, the lords, could offer these beasts; peasant marriages were preceded by gifts of food, guinea pigs, and cloth.[25] One of the qualifications of a desirable wife was her ability to weave, and we are told that the several wives of a prominent man would compete as to who could "embroider a better blanket."[26]

Of all life's crises and their association with cloth, death is the best documented in archaeology, the early chronicles, and in ethnology. Polo, one of the best of the early observers, points out that the dead were dressed in new clothes, with additional garments placed in the grave along with sandals, bags, and headdresses.[27] This was not only an Inka custom but a pan-Andean preference, going back thousands of years. Coastal archaeology, which has at its disposal a fuller statement of the culture owing to the marvelous preservation of all remains in the desert, reveals that the dead were wrapped in numerous layers of cloth. Confirming Polo's observation, many mummies enclosed scores of garments, some of them diminutive in size and woven especially as mortuary offerings.[28] Yacovleff and his associates have tried to calculate the amount of cotton needed to make a single mummy's shroud from Paracas: it measured about 300 square yards and we are told that this size was not unique; it required the product of more than two irrigated acres planted to cotton. How many woman-hours of spinning and weaving time were involved Yacovleff thought was uncalculable.[29]

Recent ethnological work by Núñez del Prado and Morote Best clarifies the identification of persons with clothing while confirming the utility of checking colonial accounts against modern ethnology: within eight days after death, the relatives of the deceased accompanied by their friends, amidst drinking and singing, should wash every piece of the dead man's clothing, since the soul would return and complain if one garment remained unwashed. If an item be carried away by the water during the ceremonial washing, the soul would sorrow at the place where the garment gets caught in the river; to find and release it, the crowd follows the weeping sounds until the garment is located.[30]

Peasant and ethnic community worship in the Inka state has never been adequately studied since no European bothered to describe it in the early decades after the invasion. Only at the beginning of the seventeenth century when idol-burners like Avila, Arriaga, Teruel, and Albornóz reported on their vandalism do we get a hint of what local, ethnic religion may have been like, as contrasted with the activities of the state church. Arriaga, for example, was proud of having brought back to Lima and burned six hundred "idols, many of them with their clothes and ornaments and very curious *kumpi* blankets." They also burned the *mallki*, bones of "ancestors who were sons of the local shrines . . . dressed in costly feather or *kumpi* shirts."[31] If the ancestor was a woman, her shrine included her spindle and a handful of cotton. These tools had to be protected in case of an eclipse when a comet was believed to threaten the moon (another woman). The spindles were in danger of turning into vipers, the looms into bears and tigers.[32]

Sacrifices are another measure of a culture's values. Santillán tells us that the main offerings of the Inka were cloth and llamas, both of which were burned. The Jesuit Cobo claimed that the offering of fine cloth "was no less common and esteemed (than the llamas), as there was hardly any important sacrifice in which it did not enter." Some of these garments were male, others female; some were life-size, others miniature. Cobo, who frequently copied Polo's now-lost memoranda, reproduces the information that at Mantocalla, near Cusco, wooden reproductions of corncobs, dressed as if men and women, were fed to the sacrificial pyre at maize-shucking time.[33]

CLAIMS ON PEASANT AND ETHNIC CLOTH

There is a standard, much-quoted portrait of the never idle Andean peasant woman spinning endlessly as she stood, sat, or even walked.[34] She spun the thread and made most of the clothes in which she dressed herself and her family; she took the spindle into her grave as a symbol of womanly activity.

In practice, the sexual division of labor was less rigidly defined. Spinning and weaving skills were learned in childhood by both girls and boys. While wives and mothers were expected to tend to their families' clothing needs, all those "exempted from *mit'a* labor services"—old men and cripples and children—helped out by spinning and making rope, weaving sacks and "rough stuff" according to strength and ability.[35] Modern ethnographic research confirms this impression: both sexes weave but different fabrics.[36]

In the Andes, all households had claims to community fibers, from which the women wove cloth: "this wool was distributed from the community; to everyone whatever he needed for his clothes and those of his wives and children . . . ."[37] However, not all villages or ethnic groups had their own alpacas or cotton fields. In that case, housewives got their fibers through barter and other forms of exchange. Iñigo Ortiz's wonderfully detailed description of Huánuco village life in 1562 records various transactions: potatoes and *ch'arki* meat for cotton, peppers for wool.[38]

Still, to say that claims could be made on community resources is a formal statement masking a shortage of useful data on the provenience of the lowland woman's raw materials for weaving. Although coastal archaeology seems to tell us so much about textiles, we know almost nothing about cotton-growing practices and the economics of cotton. For example, it would be interesting to know where coastal households and villages harvested the fibers for their own use. Perhaps each village had its own cotton patch, corresponding to the highland local herd; this seems to be suggested by Ortiz's material from Huánuco. At Machque he found a cotton field "which was of all these Indians" and at Huanacaura there was a hamlet settled "communally to cultivate the cottonfields nearby."[39] But Ortiz was talking of a rather low-lying, dry highland on the eastern slopes of the Andes. On the Coast, our studies of land tenures [40] would suggest that irrigated acreage (and thus cotton fields) were subject to a variety of rights and claims that may not have operated for food crops and pastures in the highlands.

Recent research has stressed not only the contrast between the peasant community and the Inka state, but also the intermediate role of the ethnic lord, the *kuraka*.[41] He was, at the lower echelons, so frequently a member of the community, his authority and expectations reinforced by so many kin ties and obligations, that the weaving contributions of the *kuraka* partake of the reciprocal arrangements prevailing at all levels of village economic life.

The weaving claims of a minor lord like those of Huánuco included automatic access to community wool and cotton. The inspection of 1562 emphasized their claims to labor by enumerating the shirts and sandals the lord "received," the headdresses and carrying bags woven for him by "his Indians." Some of the garments were made by men, others by women, and they did it, according to a formula quoted by the inspector, "when he begged them." We still do not know if these were ordinary villagers whose ties to the *kuraka* were "reciprocal," or if they devoted full time to his service, like one Liquira, a retainer of the Yacha lord. They may have been his several wives, whom the Europeans, ignoring polygyny, called women "de servicio."[42]

Some clarification can be gained from the testimony of lawyers like Polo and Falcón: it is true, claimed the first, that the lords "received" much cloth but the weavers were their own wives.[43] Falcón recorded independently two contradictory versions: the lords insisted that before 1532 they had "received" cloth, which the peasants interviewed by the lawyer denied. Falcón thought that both told the truth: cloth, which was needed by the lord for a multitude of purposes, was mostly woven for him by his many wives but since the invaders had prohibited polygyny, there was by the 1560s a shortage of weaving hands.[44] All sources agreed that all weaving was done with the lord's fibers.

Further understanding comes when we gain access to a description of the arrangements existing in the Lupaqa kingdom, a major polity near Lake Titicaca, with some 20,000 households distributed over a wide territory that spilled west as far as the Pacific shore and to the coca-leaf gardens in the lowlands to the east.[45] In 1567, the European inspector recorded weaving and cloth-gifting obligations, always in a context of rights in land and in human energy. Qhari, lord of the polity's whole upper moiety, testified that in his home province,

> each year they weave for him five garments for which he provides the wool, while in the other six provinces they give him one garment each and some (give) two and sometimes even six or seven as each province decides of its own free will . . . all these are of *auasca* (ordinary cloth) . . . and when this witness

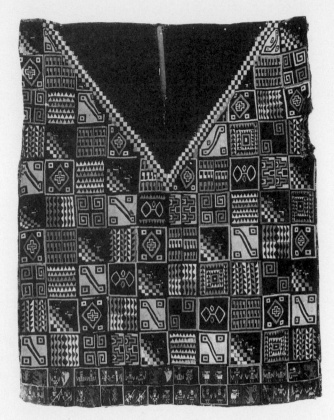

Figure 22. This complex Inka tunic from the Lake Titicaca area may have been created early in the Spanish Colonial period. Photo, American Museum of Natural History

needs a garment of good *cumpi* for personal use, he requests it from the lords of the said towns and they weave it. . . .

The European inspector checked such statements by the lords against the testimony of their subjects. Those of the lower moiety declared that they "gave" their lord, Kusi,

thirty service Indians to herd his cattle (camelids) . . . and to plant for him 20 *tupu* of land which are 60 (European) *hanegas* of potatoes and quinoa and cañagua while he provides the seed . . . and some years they weave him two garments and in

others three and these are of *cumpi* and the said lord gives them
the wool for it . . . and also each year they weave 8 ordinary
garments and sometimes 9 so that he will be able to give them
away according to his wishes to Indians or persons (*sic*) who
come through this town. . . .[46]

Even these very brief quotations convey the significant features of
cloth production and use: the beneficiary of weaving prestations always provided the fibers, much as he issued the seed to those planting his acreage. The primary purpose of most weaving duties, be
they of elegant or ordinary clothing, was their being "offered" or
"given away."

TEXTILES AT COURT AND IN THE ARMY

The perception above is reinforced when we come to peasant-state
relations as expressed in cloth. In Inka thinking there were two main
economic obligations the citizen had toward the state, and to each
of them corresponded an enduring pre-Inka right guaranteeing subsistence and traditional self-sufficiency to the peasant community,
a right that the Inka found it convenient to respect:

Obligation to work the crown and church lands	Right to continue to plant and harvest one's own crops on *ayllu* lands
Obligation to weave cloth for crown and church needs	Right to wool or cotton from community stocks for the making of one's own clothes

This Andean definition of equivalence between weaving and food
production as the peasantry's main obligations to the crown is confirmed by two independent but contemporaneous statements about
tasks considered important enough by the state to give the "Indians
time off." Lawyer Polo argued that such time off was granted only
to work the peasant lands and to weave the family's clothes; otherwise they were always kept busy "with one task or another."[47]
Sarmiento de Gamboa was even more rigid and specific: only three
months were "granted to the Indians"; the rest of the time was spent
toiling for the Sun, the shrines, and the king. The actual work sched-
ules need not be considered accurate; what matters are the implicit
priorities. These are confirmed by the few Andean writers: Garcilaso

is categorical. The "compulsory tribute" consisted only in the delivery of food produced on state lands and of cloth made of Inka wool.[48] Salcamayhua described one of the kings as "a friend of cultivated fields and of cloth making."[49]

Much as the ethnic lords had to provide the fibers that were worked up for them into cloth, the Inka state did not expect the peasantry to use its own raw materials for the weaving *mit'a*. As Polo recorded it elsewhere, "no Indian contributed (to the state) the cloth he had woven from the community's wool for his own garments."[50]

In some ways, lawyer Polo de Ondegardo was the European most knowledgeable about Inka statecraft. However, in one of his statements involving textiles he claimed that "they were inspected to see if they had made it into cloth and they punished the careless; thus all went around clothed . . . . "[51]

Why would inspection be necessary to enforce the making of *one's own* clothing? Polo argued: to insure that people went around dressed. But I feel that this was a manifestation of the perennial preoccupation with the nakedness of "savages." All Andean peoples wore clothes for the simple reason that it was cold; archaeology tells us they did so long before Inka times. Also, the setting up of a bureaucratic system capable of as much "inspection and punishment" as claimed by the European chroniclers is unlikely. Given the compulsory nature of the allotment ("they never took into account if the person receiving wool already had some from their own llamas"),[52] Polo's threat of "inspection" most likely refers to issues of state fibers made routinely to the housewife to be woven into garments for state purposes.

However, such distribution of state fibers to the citizenry does contribute to a misunderstanding of the Inka economy that has haunted Andean studies since the 1570s. Andean writers like Blas Valera, in their nostalgia for ancient rights that contrasted so visibly with European exactions, interpret such compulsory issues of state wool and cotton as welfare features by a diligent paterfamilias.[53] There were "welfare" measures in the Inka state, but they consisted of the enduring pre-Inka reciprocal duties and privileges incumbent on local kin and ethnic units.

The amount to be woven by each household is a matter of some controversy. Cieza claimed that each household owed a blanket per year and each person, one shirt.[54] Three other sources insist that there was no limit or accounting: "they simply wove what they were ordered and were always at it."[55] Interestingly enough, two of the three insist elsewhere, somewhat like Cieza, that each household owed only one garment per year.[56] They may be confusing different sets of obligations—one garment to the state, a uniform, verifiable, quantity, but also an unspecified amount to the ethnic lords, since this obligation was governed by tradition and local reciprocities.[57]

At the state level, some quantitative impressions are available. At the time of the European invasion, state warehouses were located throughout the kingdom, and virtually every eyewitness has indicated his amazement at their number and size.[58] Some contained food, others weapons and ornaments or tools, but the startling and peculiarly Andean aspect was the large number holding wool and cotton, cloth and garments.

Among the participants in the invasion, Xérez reported that at Caxamarca there were houses filled to the ceiling with clothes tied into bundles. Even after the "Christians took all they wanted," no dent was made in the pile.[59] "There was so much clothing of wool and cotton that it seemed to me that many ships could have been filled with them."[60] As Pizarro's cavalry proceeded across the Inka realm, similar stores were found at Xauxa and in Cusco. In the capital, we are told, it was "incredible" to see the number of separate warehouses filled with rope, wool, cloth both fine and rough, garments of many kinds, feathers, and sandals. Pedro Pizarro, musing some forty years later about what he had witnessed as a youth observes, "I cannot say about the storehouses I saw, of cloth and all kinds of garments which were made and used in this kingdom, as there was no time to see it, nor sense to understand so many things."[61]

Later observers added some information on the bookkeeping procedures by which the Inka state administration kept track of all the textiles that had been "tributed" by the people or woven by the state's own craftsmen. Cieza de León reports that in each provincial capital there were *khipu kamayuq* who took care of all accounts, including textile matters. At Maracavilca, near the provincial center at Xauxa, Cieza interviewed one "gentleman," Guacaropora by name, who had kept full records of everything looted from the storehouses in his charge, including cloth, during the eighteen years that had elapsed since the invasion.[62]

One gathers from the eyewitness accounts that warfare and the army were major consumers of fabrics. The military on the move expected to find blankets, clothes, and tent-making equipment on their route. Waman Puma heard in his youth that young men, aged eighteen to twenty, who acted as the army's carriers and messengers, would be issued some hominy and thick clothes as "a great gift."[63] Soldiers who had distinguished themselves in battle were given cloth, and Estete was told that the vast storehouses of "new clothing" found at the king's encampment at Caxamarca were to be issued to his troops on his formal accession to the throne.[64]

Even the royal kin were susceptible to offers of textiles. During the reconquest of Ecuador by Wayna Qhapaq, the king was confronted with a rebellion of his relatives who resented the unprecedented gifts and privileges granted to the Kañari, a local ethnic group promoted to act as an incipient standing army. Sarmiento reports that the king soothed his rebel relatives with clothes and food, in that order.[65] In Salcamayhua's independent report of the same incident, the king had to offer "for grabs" much cloth and food and other, unnamed, valuable things.[66] The much-debated historical sequence of Montesinos may be imaginary but his account that during the reign of one Titu Yupanqui, the soldiers rebelled because they were hungry and had not received the two suits of clothing owed them annually, has a culturally authentic ring. "The king ordered the granaries repaired and the clothing *mit'a* revived; only then were the troops satisfied.[67]

There were other ways of indicating the extraordinary attachment displayed by the army toward textiles. In describing the occupation of Xauxa by the Europeans, P. Sancho says that general Quizquiz's retreating army burned at least one and maybe several warehouses full of "many clothes and maize," in that order.[68] In describing the same events, Zárate tells us that when Quizquiz had to withdraw suddenly, he left behind 15,000 llamas and 4,000 prisoners but burned all the cloth which he could not carry.[69] The enemy was not deprived of the men (who, according to Garcilaso, joined the European army), but of cloth. To the north, in Ecuador, Rumiñ awi, retreating before Sebastián de Benalcazar's invasion, burned down a room full of fine garments kept there since Wayna Qhapaq's time.[70]

None of these attitudes can be understood in terms of matter-of-fact clothing or ornamental needs. Here archaeology is more helpful than alien observers: we find evidence of the magicomilitary importance of cloth back in Mochica times, two thousand years ago. Battle scenes painted on North Coast pottery show prisoners being undressed and their clothes carried off by the victor.[71] These attitudes endured beyond the fall of the Inka state: during the civil wars among the Europeans, their Andean troops believed that the enemy could be harmed or killed by getting hold of his clothes and using them to dress an effigy which was hanged and spat upon.[72] When the Almagristas lost the battle of Salinas, the Indians who accompanied both armies proceeded to undress the dead and even the wounded.[73] One eyewitness claims that during Manco Inka's withdrawal to resistance headquarters in the forest, in the 1540s, a skirmish took place in the highlands; even if details of the encounter were distorted, his statement that the victorious Indians took all the Europeans' clothes [74] is likely to reflect cultural norms. More than two centuries later, in 1781, the European dead were undressed during the Andean rebellions which culminated in the sieges of Cusco and La Paz.[75]

Feather-ornamented cloth seems to have a special association with soldiers and war. The feathers collected by children while herding were used in *kumpi* and "other military and imperial needs."[76] In describing the military warehouses he saw in the fortress near Cusco, Sancho reports one containing 100,000 dried birds whose feathers were used for uniforms.[77]

Since our written accounts are post-European, it is difficult to find accounts of productive processes involved in state weaving as distinct from peasant weaving. Among the few suggestive reports is one from the Bolivian National Archives, recording the presence in Inka times of a manufacture employing "a thousand" full-time male weavers of fine, feathered cloth. The lords of Huancané, near the shores of Lake Titicaca, petitioned the colonial court to help them evict these resettled "aliens." One Martin Chuca testified that "his father was an accountant for the Inka and sometimes (the witness) had accompanied his father to the said town of Milliraya and had seen the thousand *cumbi* weavers . . . and his father counted all the people, who had been resettled there."[78]

While we need not take such decimal accounts literally, a manufacturing center of several hundred craftsmen resettled away from their homes requires organizational and supply arrangements which imply macro-organizational structures archaeology should help us unravel in the future.

Figure 23. Aqlla *state weavers, "selected" from their ethnic communities, are shown in this drawing from about 1614 which appears in Felipe Guaman Pomo de Ayala's book,* El primer nueva corónica y buen gobierno, *written in the early seventeenth century*

A parallel feature of state weaving were the *aqlla* women found at many Inka administrative centers and also at the capital. According to sketchy sixteenth-century accounts, the *aqlla* spent their lives weaving for the state,[79] after having been "selected" out of their ethnic and lineage homes. The Andean writer Waman Puma mentions that there were six kinds of *aqlla*, from princesses of the blood to peasant women. Beyond their weaving duties, what they all had in common was that they were lost to their lineages of origin, a burden the conquered Lupaqa lords, for example, found very taxing. The sketchy accounts left us by the European eyewitnesses stress the analogy to nuns, since they are said to have been selected and guarded by old ex-soldiers. Archaeology has helped: in his study of a major administrative center at Huánuco Pampa, Craig Morris has located and studied an *aqlla wasi*, the house of the chosen. The uniformity of the buildings within the walled enclosure, the tiny gate, the many looms and spindle whorls excellently preserved, have been described and illustrated.[80] Morris thinks the *aqlla* performed other duties beyond weaving, like cooking for the troops coming through the administrative center. We know from the inspection of 1549, conducted only seven years after the European intrusion into Huánuco, that forty men were annually assigned "to guard the women of the Inka."[81]

THE POWER OF CLOTH IN EXCHANGE

The extraordinary value placed on textiles in the Andes cultures and the existence of class differences allowed the manipulative use of this commodity in a variety of political and social contexts. We have seen the compulsory nature of peasant weaving for the lords and for the state. The *kuraka*, in turn, provided "gifts" for the Cusco representatives, including clothes, from the populations to be enumerated and administered.[82] When Wayna Qhapaq passed through Xauxa and organized one of the many wakes for his mother, he was showered with gifts of fine cloth so well worked "the king himself dressed in it."[83]

Since traditional reciprocity was the model of Inka state revenues, an ideologic attempt was made to complement such massive textile exactions through a redistributive policy that exalted the institutionalized generosity of the crown. The simple fact that a fine cloth like *tokapu* or *kumpi* had come to be defined as a royal privilege meant that grants of it were highly valued by the recipient, to the point that unauthorized wear of vicuña cloth is reported to have been a capital offence.[84] On important occasions, such as accession to the throne or at the death of a king, when large crowds gathered at Cusco, the crown distributed among those attending as many as a thousand llamas, women, the right to be borne in litters—and, inevitably, cloth.[85]

Everybody from a humble peasant working for his *kuraka* to a lofty royal who was being removed from the succession race "considered themselves well rewarded" by a grant of garments, particularly if these had belonged to the lord or the king.[86] Anyone who had carried "tribute" or an idol or had come to Cusco on an official errand was given something "in return," depending on status, but always including cloth.[87] Sons of the *kuraka*, who were hostages in Cusco, had their exile sweetened by grants of clothes from the royal wardrobe which they sent home, a sign of royal pleasure.[88]

When an area was incorporated into the kingdom, the new citizens were granted "clothes to wear . . . which among them is highly valued," according to Blas Valera.[89] Recently, we gained additional insights into Inka political grants: soon after the European invasion, one Alonso de Montemayor received in *encomienda* one of the major Aymara polities, the Charka.[90] A record of what Montemayor "received" has been located in the Archive of the Indies in Sevilla: vast quantities of marketable coca-leaf, llamas, cloth, and timber.

Litigation over this early pillaging of Charka resources reveals that their knot-record keepers recorded everything extorted. Among the treasures in custody of lord Ayawiri was one he was reluctant to turn over but after having been threatened with hanging, "having nothing else to give him and to save himself, gave him 35 garments of very fine *cumbi* . . . which the Inka had given to his predecessors . . .."[91] Such a hoard of dynastic cloth, accumulated over four or five generations is one side of the exchanges between the ethnic lords and their Cusco kings. There is no hope of locating archaeologically hoards that would have survived the exactions of the Europeans (Montemayor sold the thirty-five garments at the Potosí fair) given the rainy climate in the highlands. But on the desert coast, where other Aymara polities had their outliers, we may well want to look for them, once the archaeological study of particular ethnic groups becomes the norm.

Understanding the functions of cloth in such political and military contexts may lead to major new insights into Inka economic and state organization. The sources quoted hint strongly at the compulsory nature of these "gifts" of cloth. Several chroniclers, particularly

Garcilaso, have been greatly impressed with what they see as campaigns of peaceful penetration, the paradox of the gift-laden conqueror. They see in this a further example of the "generosity" of the Inka state.

There is another way of viewing such ceremonial grants to the vanquished, at the moment of their defeat: the compulsory issue of culturally valued commodities, in a society without money and only marginal markets, can be viewed as the initial pump-priming step in a dependent relationship. The "generosity" of the conqueror obligated one to reciprocate, to deliver on a regular, periodic basis, the results of one's workmanship to the Cusco warehouses.

To the Andean peasant, the Inka "gift" could be stated as doubly valuable: as cloth and as a crown grant. The state was doubly served: the supply of cloth was ensured and the onerous nature of the weaving *mit'a* could be phased in terms of culturally sanctioned reciprocity. But one can also see in this textile "gift" the issuing of Inka citizenship papers, a coercive and yet symbolic reiteration of the peasant's obligations to the state, of his or her conquered status.

A primary source of state revenues, an annual chore among peasant obligations, a common sacrificial offering, cloth could also serve at different times and occasions as a status symbol or a token of enforced citizenship, as burial furniture, bride-wealth, or armistice sealer. No political, military, social, or religious event was complete without textiles volunteered or bestowed, burned, exchanged, or sacrificed. In time, weaving became a growing state burden on the peasant household, a major occupational specialty, and eventually a factor in the emergence of retainer craft groups like the *aqlla*, the weaving women, a social category inconsistent with the prevailing Cusco claim that services to the state were no more than peasant reciprocity writ large.[92]

NOTES

The dates in square brackets following the names of sixteenth- and seventeenth-century authors refer to the year of first publication or writing; the second, modern date indicates the edition used by the writer for this chapter.

1. Earlier versions of this paper were read at the Boston meeting of the Ameri-

can Anthropological Association in 1955 and the Second Congress of Peruvian History in Lima in 1958. The research was aided by a faculty fellowship from Vassar College and a grant-in-aid from the Social Science Research Council. A first published version of it appeared in Murra 1962.

2. Bennett and Bird 1949:256. See also O'Neale (1949:105), who felt that "on their primitive looms they produced extraordinarily fine textiles [textures?], and in addition they had imagination, ingenuity and the technical proficiency to develop unknown numbers of simple and complex weave variants. Design and color harmonies exhibit a confident sense of proportion which never fails to arouse admiration." See also A.P. Rowe 1986.

3. Carrión 1931. Also Bennett 1946:29.

4. Bennett and Bird 1949:258. Also Bird 1952; Bird and Bellinger 1954. There is an excellent summary of technical information on Andean textiles in Bird 1949:256–93. This discussion, based on archaeological data, dealt mostly with coastal fabrics; my own, relying heavily on ethno-historical material, is primarily about highland woolens.

5. Yacovleff and Herrera 1934:257.

6. Cardich 1958.

7. Bennett and Bird 1949:260; Bird and Bellinger 1954:3.

8. An example: at Pachacamac where cotton was six to eight times more abundant than wool and the latter was found concentrated in the strata with Inka pottery (Bennett and Bird 1949:21).

9. Santillan [1563–64] 1968:99–149.

10. Garcilaso de la Vega [1609] 1960. See Bk. 14, ch. 13, pp. 309-310.

11. Angeles Caballero 1955.

12. Waman Puma de Ayala [1615] 1980:48–56.

13. Murra 1960:400.

14. Cobo [1653] 1956:258–59. Another early reference guide to Quechua phrases on weaving and weavers is the dictionary of Gonzalez Holguin ([1608] 1952).

15. However, from Gonzalez's dictionary ([1608] 1952:17-18) we learn that *ahua* was the weave of the cloth, *ahuani*, to weave, and *ahuac*, the weaver, without any implication about quality. In modern Cusco Quechua, cloth is *away* (Morote Best 1951).

16. Pizarro [1572] 1965:195.

17. Cieza de León [1553] Bk. I, chs. xliv, xciv; 1984:64, 119.

18. O'Neale 1949:106; Bird and Bellinger 1954:15.

19. Cobo [1653] Bk. XIV, ch. ii; 1956:192–93. See also the systematic, modern discussion of Inka clothing by J.H. Rowe 1946:233-35.

20. Cieza de León [1553] Bk. II, ch. xix; 1967:64.

21. Pizarro [1572] 1965:192–93; Murúa [1590] Bk. III, chs. xi, xxxiii; 1946:187, 242; Salcamayhua [1613] 1927:144.

22. Polo [1561] 1940:181; Polo [1571] 1916c:200-201; Garcilaso [1609] Bk. IV, ch. xi; 1960:130-31; Gonzalez [1608] 1952:323.

23. Muñiz 1926.

24. Matos Mar 1958.

25. Romàn y Zamora [1575] Bk. II, ch. x; 1879:287, 290; Waman Puma [1615] 1980:87; Murúa [1590] Bk. III, ch. xxxiii; 1946:240.

26. Ibidem.

27. Polo [1559] 1916a:8; [1567] 1916b:194.

28. O'Neale 1935.

29. Yacovleff and Muelle 1932; Yacovleff and Muelle 1934.

30. Nuñez del Prado 1952; Morote Best 1951:151.

31. Arriaga [1621] chs. 1, 2, 9; 1920:5, 25, 98.

32. Montesinos [1644] Bk. II, chs. xiv, xxii; 1882:48–49.

33. Cobo [1653] Bk. XIII, chs. xiv, xxii; 1956:176, 203.

34. Murúa [1590] Bk. III, ch. xxix; 1946:233; Garcilaso [1609] Bk. IV, ch. xiii; 1960:133–34; Cobo [1653] Bk. XIV, ch. vii; 1956:22.

35. Xerex [1534] 1947:327, 330; Polo de Ondegardo [1571] 1916c:131; Waman Puma [1615] 1980:201–224; Cobo [1653] Bk. XI, ch. vii; 1956:22.

36. Morote Best 1951:15; Franquemont 1986:309-330.

37. Polo [1571] 1916c:66.

38. Ortiz de Zúñiga [1562] 1967:f. 17v.

39. Ortiz de Zúñiga [1562] 1967:f. 144r.

40. Murra 1980.

41. J. H. Rowe 1955; J. H. Rowe 1957; Núñez Anavitarte 1955; Moore 1958.

42. Ortiz de Zúñiga [1562] 1967:f. 128v.

43. Polo [1561] 1940:141.

44. Falcón [1565?] 1916:154.

45. Diez de San Miguel [1567] 1964:f. 94.

46. Ibidem.

47. Polo [1561] 1940:140–41; [1571] 1916c:131.

48. Sarmiento de Gamboa [1572] 1943;117–18.

49. Garcilaso [1609] Bk. V, ch. vi; 1960:155–56.

50. Salcamayhua [1613] 1927:147

51. Polo [1571] 1916c:127. See also [1561] 1940:136, 178. Thirty years after the invasion, the peasants of the Huánuco area still remembered that the Inka crown had issued them wool to be woven for the state warehouses and contrasted with the European exactions in kind.

52. Polo [1571] 1916c:65–66.

53. Ibidem.

54. Cieza [1553] Bk. II, ch. xviii; 1967:59–61.

55. Castro and Ortega [1558] 1974:91–104; Polo [1561] 1940:165; Polo [1571] 1916c:66, 127; Santillán [1563] ch. xli; 1968:115.

56. Castro and Ortega [1558] 1974:102; compare with Santillán [1563] ch. xliii; 1968:115 with ch. lxviii; 1968:126.

57. See also the indignant protests of Waman Puma [1615] 1980:499, 501, 530, 910, and drawings, 578, 668.

58. Morris 1967. See also Morris 1981:327–75.

59. Xerez [1534] 1947:334.

60. Estete [1535] 1918.

61. Pizarro [1572] 1965:195.

62. Cieza [1553] Bk. II, ch. xii; 1967:36–37; see also Espinoza Soriano 1971. Also Murra 1975.

63. Waman Puma [1615] 1980:499.

64. Estete [1535] 1918:f. 8v.

65. Sarmiento de Gamboa [1572] 1943:126.

66. Salcamayhua [1613] 1927:213–14. See also Cabello Valboa [1586] Bk. III, ch. xxi; 1951:375–76.

67. Montesinos [1644] Bk. II, ch. x; 1882:58.

68. Sancho de la Hoz [1535] 1927?:141. See also letter to the king from the cabildo of Xauxa, the first European capital (Porras Barrenechea 1959:124–31).

69. Zárate [1555] Bk. II, ch. xii; 1947:491.

70. Zárate [1555] Bk. II, ch. ix; 1947:481.

71. Muelle 1936.

72. Murua [1590] Bk. III, ch. lviii; 1946:306.

73. Zárate [1555] Bk. II, ch. xi; 1947:491.

74. Cusi Yupanqui [1565?] 1916:83.

75. Villanueva 1948.

76. Waman Puma [1615] 1980:209.

77. Sancho [1535] ch. xvii; 1917:194.

78. Murra 1978:415–23.

79. Murra 1980:chs. IV, VIII.

80. Murra and Morris 1976.

81. See the inspection of 1549, included in Ortiz de Zúñiga ([1562] 1967:289–310.

82. Sarmiento de Gamboa [1572] 1943:88.

83. Cobo [1653] Bk. XII, ch. xvi; 1956:89.

84. Garcilaso [1609] Bk. VI, ch. vi; 1960:201.

85. Cabello Valboa [1586] Bk. III, ch. xx; 1951:359; Murúa [1590] Bk. III, ch. xliv; 1946:266; Cobo [1653] Bk. XII, ch. vi; 1956:69.

86. Cabello Valboa [1586] Bk. II, ch. xx; 1951:197.

87. Falcón [1565?] 1918:153-54; see also the excellent description in Cobo [1653] Bk. XII, ch. xxx; 1956:125.

88. Garcilaso [1609] Bk. VII, ch. ii; 1960:248.

89. Ibidem.

90. Archivo General de Indias, Sevilla: Justicia section, 653.

91. Ibidem.

92. Murra 1980, ch. VIII.

REFERENCES CITED

The dates in square brackets following the names of sixteenth- and seventeenth-century authors refer to the year of first publication or writing; the second, modern date indicates the edition used by the writer for this chapter.

Arriaga, Pablo José de
    [1621]   Extirpacion de la idolatria en el Peru. *In* Colección de
    1920   libros y documentos referentes a la historia del Perú, Serie
        II, Vol. 1. Lima.

Angeles Caballero, César A.
1955   Archivos Peruanos de Folklore 1 (1). Lima.

Bennett, Wendell C., and Junius Bird
1946   The Archaeology of the Central Andes. *In* Handbook of South American Indians. J. Steward, ed. 2:61–147. Smithsonian Institution, Bureau of American Ethnology, Bulletin 143. Washington D.C.: U.S. Government Printing Office.
1949   Andean Culture History. Handbook No. 5. New York: American Museum of Natural History.

Betanzos, Juan de
[1551]   Suma y narracion de los incas. Biblioteca de Autores
1968   Españoles, Vol. 209. Madrid: Ediciones Atlas.

Bird, Junius B
1952   Fechas de radiocarbono para Sud América. Revista del Museo Nacional, 21:8–34. Lima.

Bird, Junius B., and Louisa Bellinger
1954   Paracas Fabrics and Nasca Needlework, 3rd century B.C.—3rd century A.D. The Textile Museum, Catalogue Raisonné. Washington, D.C.: The Textile Museum.

Cabello Valboa, Miguel
[1586]   Miscelanea antartica. Lima: Universidad Nacional Mayor
1951   de San Marcos.

Cardich, Augusto
1958   Los yacimientos de Lauricocha. Buenos Aires: Centro Argentino de Estudios Prehistóricos.

Carrión Cachot, Rebeca
1931   La indumentaria en la antigua cultura de Paracas. Wira Kocha: Revista Peruana de Estudios Antropológicos, 1 (1):37–86.

Castro, Cristobal de, and Diego Ortega Morejon
[1558]   Relacion y declaracion del modo que en este valle de
1974   Chincha . . . .Historia y Cultura, (8):91–104. Lima.

Cieza de León, Pedro
[1553]   La crónica del Peru. *In* Obras Completas, Book 1. Madrid:
1984   Monumento Hispano-Indiana.
[1553]   El señorio de los Incas, Book II. Lima: Instituto de Estu-
1967   dios Peruanos.

Cobo, Bernabé
[1653]   Historia del Nuevo Mundo. Biblioteca de Auto res
1964   Españoles, Vols. 91–92. Madrid: Ediciones Atlas.

Cusi, Yupanqui, Titu
[1565?]   Relacion de la conquista del Peru. *In* Colección de libros
1916   y documentos referentes a la historia del Perú, Serie I, Vol. 2. Lima.

Diez de San Miguel, Garci
  [1567]   Visita hecha a la provincia de Chucuito. Lima: Casa de la
  1964   Cultura del Perú.

Espinoza Soriano, Waldemar
  1971   Los Huancas, aliados en la conquista. Huancayo.

Estete, Miguel de
  [1535]   Noticia del Peru, Boletín 1 (3):300–50, f. 1–12. (Facsimile
  1918   ed.) Quito: Sociedad Ecuatoriana de Estudios Históricos
           Americanos.

Falcón, Francisco
  [1565?] Representacion hecha en Concilio Provincia . . . . *In* Co-
  1918   lección de libros y documentos referentes a la historia del
           Perú, Serie I, Vol. 11. Lima.

Franquemont, Edward M.
  1986   Cloth Production Rates in Chinchero, Perú. *In* Junius B. Bird
           Conference on Andean Textiles. A. Rowe, ed. pp. 309–29. Wash-
           ington, D.C.: The Textile Museum.

Garcilaso de la Vega
  [1609]   Comentarios reales de los Incas. Biblioteca de Autores
  1960   Españoles, Vol. 133. Madrid: Ediciones Atlas.

Gonzalez Holguin, Diego
  [1608]   Vocabulario de la lengua general de todo el Peru. Edición
  1952   del Instituto de Historia de la Facultad de Letras. Lima:
           Universidad Nacional Mayor de San Marcos.

Jesuita Anónimo [Garcia de Toledo?]
  [1575]   Relacion de las costumbres antiguas. *In* Los Pequeños
  1945   Grandes Libros de la Historia Americana. Lima.

Matos Mar, José
  1958   La Estructura Económica de una Comunidad Andina. Ph.D. dis-
           sertation. Universidad Nacional Mayor de San Marcos.

Molina "del Cuzco," Cristobal de
  [1575]   Relacion de las fabulas y ritos de los incas. *In* Los
  1943   Pequeños Grandes Libros de la Historia Americana. Lima.

Montesinos, Fernando de
  [1644]   Memorias antiguas historiales y politicas del Peru. *In*
  1882   Colección de libros españoles raros y curiosos. Madrid.

Moore, Sally Falk
  1958   Power and Property in Inca Peru. New York: Columbia Univer-
           sity Press.

Morote Best, Efraín
  1951   La vivienda campesina en Sallaq. Tradición (7–10). Cusco.

Morris, Craig
    1967   Storage in Tawantinsuyu. Ph.D. dissertation. University of Chicago.
    1981   Tecnología y organización Inca del almacenamiento de víveres en la sierra. *In* Runakunap Kawsayninkupaq Rurasqankunaqa: La tecnología en el mundo andino. H. Lechtman and A. M. Soldi, eds., pp. 327–75. México, D.F.: Universidad Nacional Autónoma.

Muelle, Jorge C.
    1936   Chalchalcha—un análisis de los dibujos Muchik. Revista del Museo Nacional 4:65–88.

Muñiz, César A.
    1926   Del folklore indígena. Revista Universitaria 16(52). Cusco.

Murra, John V.
    1962   Cloth and its functions in the Inca State. American Anthropologist, 64(4):710–28.
    1960   Rite and Crop in the Inca State. *In* Culture in History: Essays in Honor of Paul Radin. S. Diamond, ed., pp.393–407. New York: Columbia University Press.
    1975   Las etnocategorías de un *khipu* estatal. *In* Formaciones económicas y políticas del mundo andino. J. V. Murra, ed., pp. 243–54. Lima: Instituto de Estudios Peruanos.
    1978   Los olleros del Inka: hacia una historia y arqueología del Qollasuyu. *In* Historia, promesa y problema: Homenaje a Jorge Basadre. 1:415–23. Lima.
    1980   The Economic Organization of the Inka State. Greenwich, Conn: JAI Press.

Murra, John V., and Craig Morris
    1976   Dynastic oral tradition, administrative records and archaeology in the Andes. World Archaeology 7(3):270–79.

Murúa, Martin de
    [1590]   Historia y genealogia real de los reyes Incas del Perú. C.
    1946   Bayle, ed. Book III. Madrid: Biblioteca Missionalia Hispanica.

Núñez Anavitarte, Carlos
    1955   El cacicazgo como supervivencia 'esclavista-patriarcal' en el seno de la sociedad colonial. Cusco.

Núñez del Prado, Oscar
    1952   La vida i muerte en Chinchero. Cusco.

O'Neale, Lila M.
    1949   Weaving. *In* Handbook of South American Indians. J. Steward, ed. Vol 6:97–148. Smithsonian Instituion, Bureau of American Ethnology, Bulletin 143. Washington, D.C.: U.S. Government Printing Office.

Pequeñas prendas ceremoniales de Paracas. Revista del Museo Nacional 4(2):245–66. Lima.

Ortiz de Zúñiga, Iñigo
[1562]   Visita de la provincia de León de Huánuco. Huánuco:
1968   Universidad Nacional Hermilio Valdizán.

Pizarro, Pedro
[1572]   Relacion del descubrimiento y conquista de los reynos del
1965   Peru. Biblioteca de Autores Españoles, Vol. 168. Madrid:
      Ediciones Atlas.

Polo de Ondegardo, Juan
[1559]   Instruccion contra las ceremonias y ritos. *In* Colección de
1916a   libros y documentos referentes a la historia del Perú,
      Serie I, Vol. 3. Lima.
[1567]   De los errores y supersticiones de los Indios, sacadas del
1916b   tratado y averiguacion que hizo el Licenciado Polo. *In*
      Colección de libros y documentos referents a la historia
      del Perú, Serie I, Vol. 3. Lima
[1571]   Relacion de los fundamentos acerca del notable daño que
1916c   resulta de no guardar a los indios sus fuero . . . . *In* Co-
      lección de libros y documentos referentes a la historia del
      Perú, Serie I, Vol. 3. Lima
[1561]   Informe al licenciado Briviesca de Muñatones. Revista His-
1940   tórica 13:128–96. Lima.

Porras Barrenechea, Raúl, ed.,
[1534] 1959   Cartas del Perú. Lima.

Portugal Zamora, Maks
1980   Estudio arqueológico de Copacabana. Mesa redonda de arqueo-
      logía boliviana y surperuana 2:285–323.

Roman y Zamora, Jeronimo
[1575]   Republica de Indias. *In* Colección de libros raros y curio-
1879   sos que tratan de América, Vols. 13–14. Madrid.

Rowe, Ann Pollard, ed.
1986   The Junius B. Bird Conference on Andean Textiles. Washington,
      D.C.: The Textile Museum.

Rowe, John H.
1946   Inca Culture at the Time of the Spanish Conquest. *In* Handbook
      of South American Indians. J. Steward, ed. 2:183–330. Smithson-
      ian Institution, Bureau of American Ethnology, Bulletin 143.
      Washington, D.C.: U.S. Government Printing Office.
1955   Movimiento nacional Inca del siglo XVIII. Revista Universitaria
      (107). Cusco.
1957   The Incas under Spanish colonial institutions. Hispanic Ameri-
      can Historical Review 37 (2).

Salcamayhua, Juan de Santa Cruz Pachacuti Yamqui
    [1613]   Relacion de antiguedades deste reyno del Piru. *In*
    1927   Colección de libros y documentos referentes a la historia
              del Perú, Serie II, Vol. 9. Lima.

Sancho de la Hoz, Pedro
    [1535]   Relacion para Su Majestad de lo sucedido en la conquis-
    1927?   to . . . de la Nueva Castilla. *In* Colección de libros y do-
              cumentos referentes a la historia del Perú, Serie II, Vol. 9.
              Lima.

Santillan, Hernando de
    [1563-64] Relación de origen, descendencia política y gobierno de
    1968   los Incas. Biblioteca de Autores Españoles, Vol. 209. Ma-
               drid: Ediciones Atlas.

Sarmiento de Gamboa, Pedro
    [1572] 1943   Historia Indica. Buenos Aires: Biblioteca Emece.

Waman Puma de Ayala, Felipe
    [1615]   El primer nueva corónica y buen gobierno. J.V. Murra and
    1980   R. Adorno, eds. México, D.F.:Siglo XXI.

Villanueva, Horacio
    1948   Los padres betlemitas del Cuzco y la rebelión de Tupaj Amaru.
              Revista del instituto y Museo Arqueológico (12):73–84. Cusco.

Xerex, Francisco de
    [1534]   Verdadera relacion de la conquista del Peru. Biblioteca de
    1947   Autores Españoles. Vol. 26. Madrid: Ediciones Atlas.

Yacovleff, Eugenio and Fortunato Herrera
    1934   El mundo vegetal de los antiguos peruanos. Revista del Museo
              Nacional 3(3):241–332 and 4(1):29–102. Lima.

Yacovleff, Eugenio and Jorge C. Muelle
    1932   Una exploración en Cerro Colorado. Revista del Museo Nacional
              1(2):31–59. Lima.
    1934   Un fardo funerario de Paracas. Revista del Museo Nacional·
              3(1–2):63–153.

Zarate, Agustin de
    [1555]   Historia del descubrimiento y conquista del Peru. Biblio-
    1947   teca de Autores Españoles, Vol. 26. Madrid: Ediciones Atlas.

10. Cloth, Clothes, and Colonialism

India in the Nineteenth Century

BERNARD S. COHN

 In 1959, Mr. G.S. Sagar, a Sikh, applied for a position as a bus conductor with Manchester Transport. His application was rejected because he insisted that he wanted to wear his turban rather than the uniform cap prescribed by the municipality for all its transport workers. Sagar argued that the wearing of the turban "was an essential part of his religious beliefs" (Beetham 1970:20). He didn't understand why, if thousands of Sikhs who had fought and died for the empire in the two World Wars could wear their turbans, he couldn't do so. The transport authorities argued that "if an exception to the rules of wearing the proper uniform were allowed there was no telling where the process would end. The uniform could only be maintained if there were no exceptions" (Beetham 1970:19).

At its most obvious level, this was a dispute about an employer's power to impose rules concerning employee's dress and appearance, and the employee's right to follow the injunctions of his religion. Early in the dispute, which was to last seven years, a distinction was made between such items of attire, as the kilt of a Scotsman, which were expressions of national identities—a "national costume" that could be legally prescribed for workers—and those items of dress that were worn as the result of a religious injunction. The advocates of allowing the Sikhs to wear their turbans on the job said that to prevent them from doing so was an act of religious discrimination. The Transport worker's union supported management in the dispute, on the grounds that an individual worker could not set the terms of his own employment, which they saw as a matter of union-management negotiation.

At another level the dispute was about working-class whites' resentment of dark-skinned, exotically dressed strangers, whom they saw as "cheap" labor allowed into their country, to drive down wages and take pay packets out of the hands of honest English workingmen. The fact that many of these British workers preferred easier, cleaner, or higher-paying jobs did not lessen their xenophobic reactions. Similarly, some of the middle class saw the immigrants from the "new" commonwealth as a threat to an assumed homogeneity of British culture. The turban, the dark skin, and the sari of Indian and Pakistani women were simply outward manifestations of this threat.

In short, the dispute over the Sikh's turban can be seen as a symbolic displacement of economic, political, and cultural issues, rooted in two hundred years of tangled relationships between Indians and their British conquerors. In order to understand this conflict, I will explore the meaning of clothes for Indians and British in the nineteenth century; the establishment of the categorical separation between dark subjects and fair-skinned rulers; the search for representations of the inherent and necessary differences between rulers and ruled as constructed by the British; and the creation of a uniform of rebellion by the Indians in the twentieth century.

TURBANS OF IDENTITY

The dispute over Mr. Sagar's turban also echoed the growing sense of loss of power being felt by the British as they rapidly divested themselves of the Empire in Asia and Africa, and heard their former subjects demanding their independence and some form of equity with their former rulers. The whole social order at home also appeared to the middle and upper classes to be changing, with the revolution being acted out in terms of clothes. The youth of the under class was setting the styles for their elders and betters, and mocking many former emblems of high status by turning them into kitsch and fads for an increasingly assertive new generation.

There is an irony that a Sikh's turban should be involved in the final act of a long-playing drama in which the costumes of the British rulers and their Indian subjects played a crucial role. For the British in nineteenth-century India had played a major part in making the turban into a salient feature of Sikh self-identity.

Sikhism was a religious movement that grew out of syncretic tendencies in theology and worship among Hindus and Muslims in North India in the fifteenth century. Guru Nanak, its founder, whose writings and sayings were codified in a holy book called the *Granth Sahib*, established a line of successors as leaders and interpreters of his creed. Through much of the sixteenth and seventeenth centuries, the Sikhs faced increasing persecution from their political overlords, the Mughals, as much for their strategic location across the traditional invasion route of India in the Punjab as for their growing religious militancy.

This militancy was codified and restructured by the tenth and last in succession of the Gurus, Gobind Singh. He created a series of distinctive emblems for those Sikhs who rallied into a reformed community of the pure, the *Khalsa*, from among the wider population, which continued to follow many Hindu and Muslim customs. In a dramatic series of events in 1699, Guru Gobind Singh chose five of his followers as founding members of this new brotherhood. Those selected had shown their willingness to have their heads cut off as an act of devotion to their guru.

Guru Gobind Singh issued a call for large-scale participation in the celebration of the New Year in 1699. Those Sikh males attending were enjoined to appear with their hair and beards uncut. As the festivities developed, there was no sign of the Guru, who was waiting in a tent, until he suddenly appeared brandishing a sword, and called upon the assembled Sikhs to volunteer to have their heads cut off as a sign of their devotion. One volunteered and accompanied his Guru back to the tent. A thud was heard and the Guru reappeared with a bloody sword. The apparent sacrifice was repeated with four other volunteers, and then the side of the tent was folded back to reveal the five still alive and the severed heads of goats on the ground.

These five were declared the nucleus of the *Khalsa*. They went through an initiation ritual in which they all drank from the same bowl, symbolizing their equality, and then the chosen five initiated the Guru. Next, they promulgated rules: Sikh males would wear

306   BERNARD S. COHN

their hair unshorn; they would abstain from using alcohol and tobacco, eating meat butchered in the Muslim fashion, and having
sexual intercourse with Muslim women. Henceforth they would all
bear the surname Singh. In addition to unshorn hair (kes), they
would wear a comb in their hair (kangha), knee-length breeches
(kach), and a steel bracelet on their right wrist (kara), and they would
carry a sword (kirpan) (MacLeod 1976:14–15; K. Singh 1963:83–84).

J.P. Oberoi has analyzed these symbols as well as an unex-
pressed sixth one, the injuction against circumcision, as establishing
the total separation of the Sikhs from Hindus and Muslims. In addition he sees them as two opposed triple sets: The unshorn hair,
sword, and uncircumcised penis representing "amoral", even dangerous power; the comb, breeches, and bracelet expressing constraint. In the totality of the two sets, he sees an affirmation of the
power and constraint inherent in humanness (Oberoi 1967:97).

Note that this excursus on the formation of the Sikhs and their
symbology does not mention the turban as part of their distinctive
costume and appearance. Most scholars who have written about the
history of the Sikhs and their religion are silent on the question of
when and how the turban became part of the representational canon
of the community. M.A. Macauliffe, translator of and commentator
on the sacred writings of the Gurus, noted in a footnote, "Although
the Guru [Gobind Singh] allowed his Sikhs to adopt the dress of
every country they inhabited, yet they must not wear hats but turbans to confine their long hair which they are strictly enjoined to
preserve" (1909,V:215). W.H. MacLeod notes that the turban is the
one post-eighteenth-century symbol added to the "Khalsa code of
discipline" (1976:53). The wearing of turbans, though lacking "formal sanction . . . during the nineteenth and twentieth centuries has
been accorded an increasing importance in the endless quest for self
identification" (1976:53).

Early nineteenth-century representations by European and Indian artists of the "distinctive" headdress of the Sikhs showed two
different types. One was a tightly wrapped turban of plain cloth,
which was either thin enough or loose enough on the crown to accommodate the topknot of the Sikh's hair. The second type of turban worn by the Sikhs in the early nineteenth century was associated with rulership. This turban was elaborately wrapped and had
a jigha, a plume with a jewel attached, and a sairpaich, a cluster of
jewels in a gold or silver setting. As will be discussed below, these

ornamental devices were symbols of royalty, popularized in India by the Mughals.

In the eighteenth century, Mughal political and military power declined. The Punjab went through a period of invasions and the emergence of contending Sikh polities, which were combined under the leadership of Ranjit Singh by the early nineteenth century into a powerful state. With the death of Ranjit Singh in 1839, the state came under increasing pressure from the East India Company, which in a series of wars finally conquered and annexed the former Sikh state in 1849.

Although the Sikh state was fragmenting, the Sikh armies proved formidable; despite their defeat by the East India Company, Sikhs were treated more as worthy adversaries than as a defeated nation. Those British who fought against the Sikhs were highly impressed by their martial qualities. Unlike many of their conquered subjects, who struck the British as superstitious and effeminate, the Sikhs were considered manly and brave. Their religion prohibited "idolatry, hypocrisy, caste exclusiveness . . . the immurement of women" and immolation of widows, and infanticide (Macauliffe 1909, I:xxiii). Captain R.W. Falcon, author of a handbook for British officers in the Indian army, described the Sikh as "manly in his warlike creed, in his love of sports and in being a true son of the soil; a buffalo, not quick in understanding, but brave, strong and true" (1896:Preface). In short the Sikhs, like a few other groups in South Asia (the Hill peoples of Nepal, the Gurkhas, and the Pathans of the Northwest Frontier) who came close to defeating the British, were to become perfect recruits for the Indian army.

Within a year of their defeat, Sikhs were being actively recruited for the East India Company's army, and the officers who had just fought the Sikhs "insisted on the Sikh recruits being *"Kesadhari,"* from among the *Khalsa* Sikhs who were unshorn (Singh 1953:83). Only those Sikhs who looked like Sikhs—wearing those badges of wildness, the beard and unshorn hair—were to be enrolled. It was also official policy to provide every means for the Sikhs to keep their "freedom from the bigoted prejudices of caste . . . and to preserve intact the distinctive characteristics of their race and peculiar conventions and social customs" (Singh 1953:83 and 1966, II:111–15).

The effectiveness of the British decision, made in 1850, to raise Sikh units for their army was borne out in 1857–58. The bulk of their native army in North India rebelled. The Sikhs enthusiastically and effectively participated in the defeat of their hated enemies, the remnants of the Mughals and their despised Hindu neighbors of the Ganges Valley.

With the reorganization of the British Army in India after 1860, the British came to rely increasingly on the Punjabis in general and Sikhs in particular to man their army. The Punjab, with 8 percent of the population of India, provided half of their army in 1911. The Sikhs, who were 1 percent of the Indian population, accounted for 20 percent of the total number of Indians in the military service (GOI The Army in India Committee, 1913 IA:156).

By the late nineteenth century a standardized Sikh turban, as distinct from the turban of the Punjabi Muslims and Hindu Dogras, had emerged and had become the hallmark of the Sikhs in the army. This turban, large and neatly wrapped to cover the whole head and ears, became the visible badge of those the British had recruited. The Sikh turban and neatly trimmed beard were to stand until 1947 as the outward sign of those qualities for which they were recruited and trained: Their wildness, controlled by the turban, and their fierceness, translated into dogged courage and stolid "buffalo"-like willingness to obey and follow their British officers.

During World War I, the British army replaced the great variety of headgear of both their own troops and their colonials with steel helmets, but by now "the Sikhs had come to associate their uniform *pagri* (turban) with their religion," and the argument that the turban as such was not prescribed by their religious code was to no avail (T.A. Heathcote 1974:103).

Thus, the current significance of the distinctive turban of the Sikhs was constructed out of the colonial context, in which British rulers sought to objectify qualities they thought appropriate to roles that various groups in India were to play. The British sought to maintain the conditions that, they believed, produced the warrior qualities of the Sikhs' religion. In any post-eighteenth-century European army a uniform, in which each individual is dressed like every other one of the same rank and unit, symbolizes the discipline and obedience required for that unit to act on command. A distinctive style of turban, worn only by Sikhs and serving in companies made up of Sikhs, was the crucial item of their uniform, which represented and helped constitute the obedience that the British expected of their loyal Indian followers.

Over time the military-style turban became general, although far from universal, among the Sikhs. The Sikh has now come "home" to the British Isles, but the turban no longer symbolizes loyalty to an old military code identified with their former rulers. Instead, the turban now plays a part in the Sikhs' effort to maintain their unique identity in the face of hostility and pressure to conform to "normal" or expected dress in mass society.

The struggle to maintain the very difference that had been encouraged by their past rulers now is seen as a form of obstinacy. The pressure to conform to the rules of dress for bus conductors has been followed by a long legal struggle over whether Sikhs could ignore the law in England that motorcycle drivers and passengers had to wear crash helmets. The battleground has more recently shifted to the question of whether a Sikh boy could be barred from a private school because he and his father "insisted on his wearing uncut hair and a turban above his blazer" (Wallman 1982:4). This case was settled in 1983, when the House of Lords reversed a lower court, which had found the the Headmaster had "unlawfully discriminated against the Sikh . . . by requiring him to remove his turban and cut his hair" (*RAIN* 1983:16).

THE BRITISH AS THEY WISHED TO BE SEEN

While the British established themselves as the new rulers of India, they constructed a system of codes of conduct which constantly distanced them—physically, socially, and culturally—from their Indian subjects. From the founding of their first trading station in Surat in the early seventeenth century, the employees of the East India Company lived a quasi-cloistered life. Although dependent on the Mughal and his local official for protection, on the knowledge and skills of Indian merchants for their profits, and on Indian servants for their health and well being, they lived as a society of sojourners. In their dress and demeanor they constantly symbolized their separateness from their Indian superiors, equals, and inferiors. Paintings by Indians of Europeans in the seventeenth and eighteenth centuries emphasized the differences in costume, which apparently made little concession to the Indian environment culturally or physically. At home, in the office, in the field hunting, or when representing the majesty and authority of the Company, the British dressed in their own fashions.

The one exception to the cultural imperative of wearing European dress was among those whose careers were spent up-country as British representatives in Muslim royal courts, where it was usual for some of them to live openly with Indian mistresses and to acknowledge their Indian children. These semi-Mughalized Europeans, although wearing European clothes in their public functions, affected Muslim dress in the privacy of their homes. The wearing of Indian dress in public functions by employees of the Company was officially banned in 1830. The Regulation was directed against Frederick John Shore, a judge in Upper India who wore Indian clothes while sitting in his court. Shore was a persistent critic of the systematic degradation of Indians, particularly local notables, intelligentsia, and Indians employed in responsible jobs in the revenue and judicial services. He argued strenuously not just for better understanding of the natives, but also for their full employment in the governance of their own country (Shore 1837).

The practice of maintaining their Englishness in dealing with Indians goes back to the royal embassy sent by King James the First to negotiate a treaty to "procure commodities of saftie and profit" in the Mughal's realm in 1615. The English ambassador, Sir Thomas Roe, was instructed by his ruler: "To be careful of the preservation of our honor and dignity, both as wee are soverign prince, and a professed Christian, as well in your speeches and presentation of our letters as in all other circumstances as far as it standeth with the customs of these Countries" (Foster 1899,I:552). Roe was not comfortable in conforming to the proper behavior expected of an Ambassador at an Indian court. The Mughal, Jahangir, despised merchants as inferior to warriors and rulers. Although amused by Roe, and personally polite and accommodating to his peculiarities, he was sceptical about an ambassador representing a powerful European who seemed so interested in trade. Roe's explicit concern with establishing the means to increase "the utility and profits" of the subjects of King James was not shared by Jahangir.

The English effort to obtain a trade treaty was based on their own ideas about trade, which involved defining certain cultural objects as commodities. Increasingly in the seventeenth and eighteenth centuries, the commodities they sought in India were a wide variety of textiles, to be shipped to England or traded in Southeast Asia for spices and other valued objects to be sent to England. A major problem arose because the Indians were not much interested in the manufactured goods that the British had available—woolens, metal goods, and various "curiosities." What the Indians wanted was silver, copper, and gold. Another problem arose because the British persisted in viewing textiles as practical or utilitarian objects, suitable for providing profit for the shareholders and officials of the Company. The textiles and clothes made by Indians did indeed have a market and a practical value, but there were many other significations involved in the production and use of these objects, which the British defined as commodities.

Roe and his small party, which included the Reverend Terry as his chaplin, began to realize that the clothes worn—and particularly the use of cloth and clothes as prestations in the Mughal's court—had meaning far beyond any "practical use." Jahangir did allow Roe to follow his own customs of bowing and removing his hat, rather than using the various forms of prostration that were the usual means of offering respect to the Mughal. Through the three years that he traveled with Jahangir, Roe and his followers always wore English dress, "made light and cool as possibly we could have them; his waiters in Red Taffata cloakes" Terry, the chaplin, always wore "a long black cassock" (Foster 1899:I:106)

Roe had brought with him to the Mughal Court a considerable number of gifts, among which was a bolt of scarlet cloth that was perhaps more appropriate for the natives of North America than a sophisticated Indian ruler. Roe substituted for the cloth his own sword and sash. This gift was greatly appreciated by Jahangir, who asked Roe to send his servant to tie it on properly and then began to stride up and down, drawing the sword and waving it about. Roe reported that on a number of occasions Jahangir and some of his nobles, wishing to honor Roe, wanted to present him with clothes, jewels, and turbans. Although Roe, in his account, does not explain why he tried to avoid receiving these gifts, I can infer that he probably understood their significance. This kind of gift was the means by which authoritative relations were established and would, in the eyes of the Indians, make Roe into a subordinate or companion of the Mughals. In order to understand why Jahangir was pleased with Roe's sword and sash and why Roe was leery of accepting clothes and jewels, I will now explore the constitution of authority in Mughal India.

CLOTHES AND THE CONSTITUTION OF AUTHORITY

By the fifteenth century, the idea that the King was the maintainer of a temporal as well as a sacred order was shared by Muslims and Hindus in India (Hasan 1937:55–57). Royal functions were centered on the idea of protection and the increase of the prosperity of the ruled. "If royalty did not exist," wrote Abu al Fazl, the chronicler of Akbar's greatness, "the storm of strife would never subside, nor selfish ambition disappear. Mankind being under the burden of lawlessness and lust would sink into the pit of destruction, the world, this great market place would lose its prosperity and the whole earth become a barren waste" (1927,I:2).

The Mughals, who had established suzerainty over northern India in the early sixteenth century, were a Turkic-speaking people from Central Asia who traced their descent to Ghengiz Khan and Tammerlane. They based their authority on a divine relationship with God. The *Padshah* (Emperor), wrote Abu al Fazl, was "a light emanating from God" (I:2). In constituting their authority, the Mughals also drew upon their descent from Ghengiz Khan as a world conqueror. Under the Mongols, the Mughals were a ruling family that was part of a particular clan (*ulus*), which produced the legitimate ruler or Khan. Therefore, the Mughals claimed authority on a historical basis as descendents of the Ghengiz Khan (Khan 1972:11–12 and Tripathi 1959:105–06).

Under Ghengiz Khan and his immediate successors, "the power of the tribe over its members . . . was apparently transferred bodily to the Khan" (I.A. Khan 1972:12). Some of this sense of the embodiment of authority in the person of the ruler, not just of the tribe but of the state, was built upon by Akbar and his successors. In this they were expressing a widespread and older theory of kingship, found in Central Asia, Persia, and India, in which "the king stands for a system of rule of which he is the incarnation, incorporating into his own body by means of symbolic acts, the person of those who share his rule. They are regarded as being parts of his body, and in their district or their sphere of activity they are the King himself" (Buckler 1927/28:239).

This substantial nature of authority in the Indic World is crucial for any understanding of the widespread significance of cloth and clothes, as they are a medium through which substances can be transferred. Clothes are not just body coverings and adornments, nor can they be understood only as metaphors of power and authority, nor as symbols; in many contexts, clothes literally *are* authority. The constitution of authoritative relationships, of rulership, of hierarchy in India cannot be reduced to the sociological construction of leaders and followers, patrons and clients, subordination and superordination alone. Authority is literally part of the body of those who possess it. It can be transferred from person to person through acts of incorporation, which not only create followers or subordinates, but a body of companions of the ruler who have shared some of his substance.

The most literal representation of the act of incorporation into the body of the Mughal *Padshah* was through the offering of *nazr* (gold coins) by a subordinate of the ruler and the ruler's presentation of a *khilat* (clothes, weapons, horses, and elephants). Philologically, *khilat* can be traced in both Persian and Arabic to an Aramaic and Hebrew root *halaf*, "to be passed on," which is central to the Arabic idea *Khilafat*, the succesor to the title of the head of the Muslim community. Narrowly, in Arabic, *khilat* derives from the word for "a garment cast off." By the sixteenth century in India, the term *khilat* came to involve the idea that a king, as a special honor, would take off his robe and put it on a subject. F.W. Buckler suggests that there is a special significance involved in this act, as robes worn by the King could transmit his authority (Buckler 1922:197;1927: 240). Buckler goes on to state: "Robes of Honour are symbols of some idea of continuity or succession," which "rests on a physical basis, depending on the contact of the body of the recipient with the body of the donor through the medium of the clothing. Or to put it rather differently, the donor includes the recipient within his own person through the medium of the wardrobe" (Buckler 1927/28:24).

The sets of clothes through which the substance of authority was transmitted became known as *khilats*, glossed in English as "robes of honor," in French *cap à pied*, "head to feet." In Mughal India the *khilats* were divided into classes consisting of three, five, or seven pieces. A seven-piece *khilat* might include, among other things, a turban, a long coat with full skirt (*jamah,*) a long gown (*ka'bah*), a close-fitting coat (*alkhaliq*), one or more *kamrbands*, trousers, a shirt, and a scarf. Along with the actual clothes, other articles were included.

The most powerful *khilat* was a robe or garment that the Mughal himself had worn, and on occasion he would literally take off a robe and place it on one of his subjects, as a particular honor. Next to such a robe, the garment of most significance was a turban and its associated ornaments.

All forms of salutations in Indian society relate to the head, hands, and feet. In Akbar's court there were three major forms of salutation which entailed manifest acts of obeisance; these were termed the *kornish, taslim,* and *sijda.* Abu'l Fazl states: "Kings in their wisdom have made regulations for the manner in which people are to show their obedience . . . His Majesty (Akbar) has commanded the palm of the right hand to be placed on the forehead and the head to be bent downwards . . . . This is called the *kornish,* and signified that the saluter has placed his head (which is the seat of the senses and mind) into the hand of humility, giving it to the royal assembly as a present and has made himself in obedience ready for any service that may be required of him" (Fazl:166–67).

The *taslim* "consists in placing the back of the right hand on the ground, and then raising it gently till the person stands erect, when he puts the palm of his hand upon the crown of his head, which pleasing manner of saluting signifies that he is ready to give himself as an offering" (Fazl 166–67).

The *sijda,* or complete prostration, was objected to by the orthodox Muslims in Akbar's court as it is one of the positions of prayer. Akbar therefore ordered that it be done only in private, but it appears to have been used in subsequent rulers' courts (Islam 1970:321–2).

Abu'l Fazl makes it clear that in the context of the court, the person offering the salute is offering himself as a sacrifice; his head is being offered to the Mughal. In warfare, this sacrifice was literal. In a famous painting, The Emperor Akbar (1542–1605) is shown receiving the heads of his enemies, some being held by his warriors or piled up at the feet of his elephant. His defeated foe wears neither a helmet nor a turban as, head lowered, he is brought before the victor. (Gascoigne 1971:71–72).

In the eighteenth and nineteenth centuries, an Indian would place his turban at the feet of his conqueror as a sign of complete surrender. This was also used in a metaphoric sense to ask a great favor of someone, indicating a willingness to become their slave. Nineteenth-century guide books written for Englishmen traveling to India warned their readers never to touch a Hindu's or a Muslim's turban, as this was considered a grave insult.

The Sind in Western India, conquered by the British in the 1840s, was a region of Muslim chieftains among whom the turban meant sovereignty. E.B. Eastwick, a company official with an excellent knowledge of Persian and Sindhi, writes of the turban "descending," "succeeded to" and being "aimed at." The Governor General, Lord Ellenborough, in writing to General Napier, commented about the need to support a particular ruler and underlined the substantial nature of the turban: "I have little doubt, that once established in the possession of the turban . . . Ali Murad will be able to establish the more natural and reasonable line of succession to the turban, and clothe the measure with the firms of legality" (Eastwick 1849:277).

For the Mughal rulers of India, the turban and its associated ornaments had the powerful and mystical qualities that crowns had in medieval Europe. The jewels attached to the turban included the *kalghi*, an aigrete of peacock or heron feathers with a jewel attached to it. This was only conferred on the highest nobles. The *jigha* consisted of a cluster of jewels set in gold with a feather. The *sarpech* and *sarband* were strings of jewels or filigree work of gold or silver, stitched onto the turban. There was also a string or diadem of pearls worn as a garland around the turban, the *sirha*. Kings in the medieval Hindu tradition were the controllers of the earth and its products, and in cosmographic terms jewels were the essence of the earth, its most pure and concentrated substance. Thus the cloth turban with its associated jewels brought together all the powers of the earth.

Akbar, the Mughal Emperor, delighted in innovative patterns or designs of clothes and created a new vocabulary for talking about them. Like all rulers of the period, he had special warehouses and treasuries for the maintenance and storage of clothes, arms, and jewels. He also decreed changes in the basic design of some articles of clothes. According to Abu'l Fazl, the author of the "Ain-i Akbari," a general description of Mughal rule during the period of Akbar, the Emperor took an inordinate interest in every aspect of the production of cloth. There were imperial workshops in major cities of the empire which could "turn out many master pieces of workmanship: and the figures and patterns, knots and variety of fashion which now prevail astonish experienced travelers" (Fazl I:94). Akbar collected cloth from other Asian countries and Europe, as well as India.

Cloth and clothes received as presents, or commissioned or bought in the open market, were carefully kept and classified by the day of the week and the day in the month on which they arrived at court, as well as by price, color, and weight. There was a rank order of clothes and cloth: Those received on the first day of the month of *Farwardin* "provided they be of good quality, have a higher rank assigned to them then pieces arriving on other days; and if pieces are equal in value, their precedence or otherwise, is determined by the character of the day of their entry; and if pieces are equal as far as the character of the day is concerned, they put the lighter stuff higher in rank; and if pieces have the same weight, they arrange them according to colour" (Fazl I:97). The author lists 39 colors, most of which refer to the colors of fruits, flowers, and birds. Given the variety of colors and fabrics, the almost infinite variations of design motifs in the textiles, and the great variation possible by folding, cutting, and sewing into garments, one can imagine the possibilities for originality and uniqueness. Some sense of this creativity and great variation was demonstrated in the recent exhibition of Indian textiles organized by Mattiebelle Gittinger (Gittinger, 1982)

Akbar, like his successor, lived in a world of textiles, clothes, and jewels, and created elaborate rules restricting the wearing of some emblems, jewels, and types of clothes to certain ranks in Mughal society. As the British in the nineteenth century steadily extended their control over their subjects and their allied Princes, they ordered and simplified those emblems of sovereignty and began to act as the Sovereign in India.

FROM ROBES OF HONOR TO MANTLES OF SUBORDINATION

The significations entailed in the receipt of *khilats* were not lost on the British from the days of Sir Thomas Roe's visit. In the second half of the eighteenth century, as the Company's military power grew, the British transformed themselves from merchants dependent on the good will and protection of Indian monarchs into rulers of a territorially based state. As part of this process, the British officials of the Company sought to be honored with Mughal titles and *khilats.* In Bengal, as the Company's leaders gradually began to act as Indian sovereigns, they in turn began to grant *khilats* to their Indian subordinates and to use their influence with the Mughal Emperor to obtain titles for their allies and employees. In the early decades of the nineteenth century, a visit to Delhi and the Mughal Emperor and ennoblement at his hands had become a kind of tourist attraction for high-status Europeans. Captain Mundy, who accompanied Lord Combermere, the Commander in Chief of the Army in India, on an inspection tour through North India from 1827 to 1829, visited Delhi. The offering of *nazr* (gold coins) and receipt of *khilat* was on the itinerary. Mundy describes the enrobement, and his reaction to it:

> On receiving Lord Combermere's offering, the King placed a turban, similar to his own, upon his head, and his lordship was conducted, retiring with his face sedulously turned towards the throne, to an outer apartment, to be invested with a khillât, or dress of honour. In about five minutes he returned to the presence, attired in a spangled muslin robe and tunic; salaamed, and presented another nuzzar. The staff were then led across the quadrangle by the "grooms of robes" to the "green room," where a quarter of an hour was sufficiently disagreeably employed by us in arraying ourselves, with the material tastily bound round our cocked-hats. Never did I behold a group so ludicrous as we presented when our toilette was accomplished; we wanted nothing but a "Jacik i' the Green" to qualify us for a May-day exhibition of the most exaggerated order. In my gravest moments, the recollection of the scene provokes an irresistible fit of laughter. As soon as we had been decked out in this satisfactory guise, we were marched back again through the Lâl Purdar and crowds of spectators, and re-conducted to the Dewânee Khâs, where we again separately approached His Majesty to receive from him a tiara of gold and false stones, which he placed with his own hands upon our hats (Mundy 1832:172).

The officials of the East India Company exchanged what they defined as "presents" with Indian rulers and some of their subjects, but changed the nature and signification of this act. Company officials could not accept "gifts" and when protocol required officials to accept a *khilat*, weapons, or jewels, they had to deposit them in the Company's *toshakhana* (treasury). These gifts were recycled, given in turn to some Indian ruler at a durbar or other official meeting when it was deemed appropriate for the Company to exchange gifts with Indians. According to the rule that the Company followed, and which they imposed not only on their own subjects but on the allied Princes when presents were exchanged, it was prearranged that the value offered by each party must be equal. In short, prestation and counter-prestation had become a contractual exchange. The British were aware of the contradiction inherent in the practice in terms of Indian theories of prestation. In India a superior always gives more than he receives, yet as an "economic man," the nineteenth-century Englishman was not about to enhance his honor by giving more than he received.

The basis of British authority in India in the first half of the nineteenth century was ambiguous. In their own eyes they ruled by right of conquest. Yet their own Monarch was not the Monarch of India; the agency of rule was a chartered Company, supervised by Parliament. In the wake of the Great Revolt of 1857–58, the Company was abolished, their Queen was declared ruler of India, and India became part of the Empire in constitutional terms. The Crown of Great Britain became the ultimate source of authority for British and Indians. As part of the signalizing of this new legal arrangement, an Order of Knighthood, "The Star of India," was established (Cohn 1983).

The intentions of the Queen and her advisors in establishing this new Order were spelled out in its "Letter Patent and Constitution" published July 6, 1861:

> . . . It hath been the custom of Princes to distinguish merit, virtue and loyalty by public marks of honor in order that eminent services may be acknowledged and to create in others a laudable emulation, and we being desirous of affording public and signal testimony of our regard by the institution of an order of knighthood, whereby our resolution to take upon ourselves the government of our territories in India (India Office Library and Records, L/P & S/15/1:215).

Initially the Order was restricted to 25 members, British and Indian, the Highest British Officials of Government and the most important of the Indian Princes being invested with the mantle and insignia of the Order. Four years after its establishment, the Order was reorganized into the three ranked classes of Knight Grand Commander (KGCSI), Knight Commander (KCSI), and Companion (CSI), and the numbers who could be awarded the honor were greatly increased.

The light blue mantle of the Order was lined in white silk and fully covered the body. It fastened with a white silk cord decorated with blue and silver tassels. On the left side of the robe, over the heart, was embroidered in gold thread the rays of the sun, and superimposed in diamonds was the motto, "Heaven's light our guide" and a star. The collar was a large necklace made of a gold chain with palm fronds and lotuses; in its center was an emblem of the Crown of Great Britain, from which hung a pendant with a portrait of the Queen of England.

The mantle, insignia, collar, and pendant were distinctly European in their form and content. The recipients of the knighthood had to sign a pledge that the mantle, and its attachments would be returned at the death of the recipient, as the knighthood was not hereditary. This provision offended most Indian recipients, as Indians of all statuses stored gifts and emblems of honor that they received for their posterity. The *toshakana* (treasure room) of a Prince was an archive of objects whose origin and receipt embodied his status and honor. They could be taken out on occasion to be worn, used, or displayed, but they would be held from generation to generation to mark the constitutive events in the history of the family or the State. Shawls, robes, clothes, and pieces of cloth received in ritual contexts embodied those contexts. Even a peasant family will have several trunks full of cloth, saris, dhotis, and piece goods that have been received at weddings or in other ritual contexts, which are seldom worn but are displayed and discussed on solemn occasions. In a very direct way, these objects constitute the relationships between individuals, families, and groups.

The Nizam of Hyderabad, the most important allied Prince of the British, objected strenuously, not to the honor the knighthood bestowed on him by the Queen, but to the mantle and the jeweled insignia. The Nizam through his Prime Minister Salar Jang pointed out to the Viceroy that the "people of this country have a particular antipathy to wearing costumes different from their own." This, Salar Jang stated, was especially true of Princes, "who have always been tenacious of the the costume of their ancestors," and he pointed out that "the wearing of the robe of the new order, would probably be ridiculed by his people." If the robe were made out of velvet or silk it would be in contravention of Mohammedan law. The Nizam also raised an issue about the wearing of the pendant which had a portrait of the Queen, as proper Muslims were "prohibited from wearing the likeness of any created being on their person" (India Office Library and Records, L/P & S/15/3:80–82). The Viceroy sternly informed the Resident at Hyderabad, who had forwarded the objections of the Nizam and his Prime Minister, that the statutes and constitution of the Star of India were not to be questioned. The Nizam had to accept the regalia as is, or refuse to accept the honor.

In 1861, the British in India had yet to develop a formal investiture ceremony for the induction of knights into the order. Hence when the patent and regalia reached the Nizam, although he made proper reverence both to the patent and to the insignia, he did not put the mantle on, and the whole matter was quietly dropped. But by the end of the nineteenth century, the Nizams as well as all other recipients of knighthood seemed pleased enough to wear the robe and associated insignia.

By 1869, at the time of the first visit of a member of the royal family, the Duke of Edinburgh, the pages wore a seventeenth-century cavalier costume. At the Imperial Assemblage of 1877, a full-dress version of Victorian "feudal" was utilized for the design motif of the ceremony at which Queen Victoria was made Empress of India. From 1870 to World War I, the number of occasions at which Indians, depending on their status, roles, and regional origins, had to appear in their assigned "costumes," increased enormously.

With the advent of the railroad, the Viceroy and his suite, the Governors, and other high officials and their retinues traveled more and more frequently. The Central Government and each of the major provinces had a cool-season and hot-season capital. The seasonal trips between these capitals provided occasions for an increasing number of meetings between the top rulers and Princes, landlords, rich merchants, and an army of lower Indian officials. The Monarch's birthday, Jubilees, the crowning of Edward VII and George V King-Emperors of India, all provided occasions for the displaying of Empire at home and in India.

With the opening of the Suez Canal in 1869, the trip to and from India was cut from months to a matter of weeks, facilitating the flow of royalty and aristocrats visiting India, and of Indian princes visiting the Continent and England. Indians as part of their tours would be presented at Victoria's court, at Windsor or at her "cottage," Osbourne House on the Isle of Wight. Here she had a "durbar room" built and decorated for receiving the homage of her loyal Indian feudatories. Indians were required on such occasions to appear in their "traditional" Indian royal dress rather than Western clothes (V.C. Chaudhuri 1980:344).

"ORIENTALIZING" INDIA

The establishment of the Star of India and its investiture evoked in its intent and regalia British Victorian conceptions of a feudal past. It was part of the general process of enhancing the image of the monarchy and the aristocracy to symbolize a simpler past, in contrast to the rapid social, economic, and political change that characterized contemporary reality. This past was seen as the source of Britain's liberties, its legal system, and its natural order, which grew from an organic relationship between rulers and ruled. This was more than mere nostalgia for a past that might have never been. It was a powerful symbolic statement by the ruling classes (who themselves were not necessarily aristocratic) about order, deference, and hierarchy as the prerequisites for maintaining political and social stability during a period of economic and technological change (Burrow 1981; Strong 1978; Hobsbawm and Ranger 1983).

As Britain had a feudal past, so did India, particularly the India of the Princes and the great mass of the Indian peasantry. The application of social evolutionary theories to India by a wide range of British officials and scholars yielded a crucial ruling paradigm: The Indian present was the European past (Maine 1871). This construction of a universal history enabled the British to control the Indian past, as they too had been feudal but were now advanced out of this stage. But since the British were still in a position through their own history to direct the future course for India, it made the British part of India in their role as rulers.

India was seen through British beneficence as being capable of being changed. They had created the conditions for the Indians' advance up the social evolutionary ladder by introducing the ideas of private property and modern education, the English language and its thought and literature, railroads, irrigation systems, modern sanitation and medicine, and authoritarian yet rational bureaucratic government, and the form of British justice. The British also knew the dangers of too rapid a move out of the feudal stage—the unleash-

ing of disorder, dislocation, and potentially dangerous revolution-
ary forces that, if not controlled and checked, could lead to anarchy.
To prevent this dangerous outcome, Indians had to be controlled,
made to conform to the British conception of appropriate thought
and action, for their own future good. India had a future, but its
present had to be an "Oriental one" to prevent a too rapid and hence
disruptive entry into the modern world. What might be thought of
as the Orientalization of the clothes of British rule in India began,
as did the westernization of clothing in the army.

During the Great Uprising, the British quickly shed their heavy,
tight, redcoated uniforms. W.H. Russell, who was sent by the Times
to report on the war, wrote in one of his letters:

> . . . I have often thought how astonished, and something more,
> the Horse-guards, or the authorities, or the clothing depart-
> ments, or whatever or whoever it may be that is interested in
> the weighty matters of uniform, and decides on the breadth of
> cuffs, the size of lace, the nature of trowser-straps, and the cut
> of buttons, would be at the aspect of this British army in India!
> How good Sir George Brown, for instance, would stand aghast
> at the sight of these sunburnt "bashi-bazouks," who, from heel
> to head and upwards, set at defiance the sacred injunctions of
> her majesty's regulations! Except the highlanders . . . not a corps
> that I have seen sport a morsel of pink, or show a fragment of
> English scarlet. The highlanders wear eccentric shades of gray
> linen over their bonnets; the kilt is discarded. . . . Lord Cardi-
> gan, in his most sagacious moments, would never light on the
> fact that those dark-faced, bearded horsemen, clad in snowy
> white, with flagless lances glittering in the sun, are the war-
> hardened troopers of her majesty's 9th lancers; or that yonder
> gray tunicked cavaliers, with ill-defined head-dresses, belong to
> the Queen's bays . . . . Among the officers, individual taste and
> phantasy have full play. The infantry regiments, for the most
> part, are dressed in linen frocks, dyed carky or gray slate colour—
> slate-blue trowsers, and shakoes protected by puggeries, or linen
> covers, from the sun . . . . It is really wonderful what fecundity
> or invention in dress there is, after all, in the British mind when
> its talents can be properly developed. To begin with the head-
> dress. The favourite wear is a helmet of varying shape, but of
> uniform ugliness. In a moment of inspiration some Calcutta hat-
> ter conceived, after a close study of the antique models, the
> great idea of reviving, for every-day use, the awe-inspiring

head-piece of Pallas Athene; and that remarkably unbecoming affair . . . became the prototype of the Indian tope in which the wisest and greatest of mankind looks simply ridiculous and ludicrous. Whatever it might be in polished steel or burnished metal, the helmet is a decided failure in felt or wickerwork, or pith, as far as external effect is concerned. It is variously fabricated, with many varieties of interior ducts and passages leading to escape-holes for imaginary hot air in the front or top, and around it are twisted infinite colours and forms of turbans with fringed ends and laced fringes. When a peacock's feather, with the iris end displayed, is inserted in the hole in the top of the helmet, or is stuck in the puggery around it, the effect of the covering is much enhanced . . . . I have seen more than one pistol in one of the cummerbunds, or long sashes, which some of our officers wear round the stomach in the oriental fashion (Russell, quoted in Ball 1859,II:325–27).

With the reestablishment of social order in Upper India, the army was reorganized. What had been the Bengal Army was in effect dissolved. European soldiers who had enlisted in the Company service were pensioned and/or repatriated to Great Britain, and henceforth all of the European troops serving in the Indian army would be from regular Royal battalions, which were rotated through India. The British officers of the Indian army were now commissioned by the King and would be permanently assigned to units made up of Indians, who were recruited from "the martial races:" Sikhs, who accounted for 20 percent of the army in 1912; Punjabi Muslims (16 percent); Gurkhas (12 percent); Rajputs, mainly from Rajasthan (8 percent); Dogras and Garhwalis (7.5 percent); Pathans (8 percent); Jats (6 percent). The remaining soldiers in the army were made up of Marathas, Brahmans, Hindustani Muslims, and "other Hindus," of whom the only significant number were Telagus and Tamils (GOI, Army in India Committee 1913,IA:156).

In addition to the "class composition" of the new army, its dress was transformed as well, for both Indian soldiers and British officers. Over the second half of the nineteenth century, the service uniform for Europeans and Indians was much the same—cotton khaki trousers and shirt, with a jacket added in cold weather. Indians were given "exotic" headgear, the Sikh turban as previously discussed, and each of the other major martial races had their distinctive turban in terms of wrapping and color. The Gurkhas began to be recruited after the Gurka wars of 1814–15 and took readily to European-style uniforms, which they have continued to wear in the British and Indian army to the present. Their distinctive headdress in the second half of the nineteenth century was the Kilmarnock cap, a visorless, brimless pillbox. For service in the Boxer Rebellion they were issued broad-brimmed felt hats, which they wore up to World War I in the Australian style with one side turned up. Subsequently they have worn it with the brim down and at a "jaunty angle." Their uniforms, with jacket and trousers, have been dark blue or green.

Vansittart, the author of the handbook on the Gurkhas for use by their officers, described them as having a strong aversion to wearing a turban, as they associate it with the Plainsmen whom they "despise." Vansittart goes on to eulogize the Gurkhas, "as delighting in all manly sports, shooting, fishing . . . and as bold, enduring, faithful, frank, independent and self reliant . . . they look up to and fraternise with the British whom they admire for their superior knowledge, strength and courage, and whom they imitate in dress and habits." (Vansittart, quoted in Tuker 1957:92-93; Bolt 1975:57, 63). The Gurkhas had a "traditional" weapon, the kukri, a 20-inch curved knife carried in the waistband which became their trademark.

It was in designing the dress uniforms for the officers and men that the British exercised their fantasy of what an "oriental" warrior should like. As was common in the second half of the nineteenth century, the cavalry units got the most colorful and dramatic uniforms. As was noted, during the Mutiny the British began to add cummerbunds and *puggrees*—linen covers wrapped around their wicker helmets or cloth caps and hats. A few British went all the way and began to wear full turbans, which were recognized as having some protective function. A full turban could be made up of 30 or 40 feet of cloth and, when thickly wrapped over the whole head and down the ears, could protect the head from a glancing sabre blow. General Hearsey, who commanded a division of the Bengal army, came from a family which had long provided officers, and many British thought he had Indian "blood." After the Mutiny, Hearsey had his portrait painted in a long black oriental-style robe, wearing a richly brocaded cummerbund and holding a scimitar. Could he have been seeking to appropriate part of his enemies' powers through using his clothes?

By the end of the nineteenth century, the dress uniform of the

British officers of the cavalry had become fully "orientalized;" it included a knee-length tunic in bright color, breeches and high boots, and a fully wrapped colorful turban. The Indian non-commissioned officers and troopers were similarly attired for dress parades and the increasing number of ceremonial functions.

The change in uniform for both European and Indian emphasized a basic conceptual change. One of the results of the Mutiny was to rigidify the already considerable differences between Indians and British. The Indians, seen by the British in the first half of the nineteenth century as misguided children, had been revealed by their actions in 1857–59 to be treacherous and unchangeable. Outwardly they might conform to the sahib's expectation but they could never be trusted. At any time their deep-seated, irrational superstitions could break forth in violence and overturn all the painful efforts of the conquerors to lead them in proper directions. Policies based on an assumption of change were proven wrong, so what was required was a strong hand capable of smashing any "sedition" or disloyalty, combined with an acceptance of Indians. Henceforth, the British should rule in an "oriental manner," with strength and with the expectation of instant obedience.

For this reason, Indians more than ever should look like Indians; those the British most depended on to provide the strength to keep India, the soldiers, should appear as the British idea of what Mughal troopers looked like, with their officers dressed as Mughal grandees. Another characteristic believed to be quintessentially Indian or oriental was a love of show, of pageantry, of occasions to dress up in beautiful or gaudy clothes. Indians, it was believed, were susceptible to show and drama, and hence more occasions were found where rulers and subjects could play their appointed parts and could act their "traditions" through costume. Hence the insistence that the Chiefs and their retinues should always appear in their most colorful (if outmoded) clothes. The first major demonstration of this new ruling paradigm was during the visit of the Prince of Wales to India in 1876.

The Prince and his large suite traveled widely throughout India, arriving in Bombay, then proceeding to Ceylon and Madras, and reaching Calcutta in November of 1876. There he was treated to a month-long round of entertainments, balls, and levees, culminating in a large investiture ceremony for the Star of India. The trip was well reported in England by correspondents from leading newspapers. *The Graphic* and the *Illustrated London Weekly* sent artists who recorded all the events for the home audience. In their drawings, the artists dwelt upon the exotic quality of Indian life and dress, such as the "wild" Naga tribesmen and women brought down to Calcutta to entertain the Prince and British high society with their barbarous dances. The Prince was also treated to a *nautch*—a dance by young women which was a popular entertainment for eighteenth century Nabobs. The dancers' beautiful and colorful dresses and their sensuous movements were anything but Victorian (Annual Register 1782:36).

At center stage throughout the Prince of Wales' visit were the Princes of India, in all their splendor. Neither the pen of the journalists nor the black-and-white line drawings of the artists could adequately capture the variety and color of the clothes, nor the extraordinary display of precious stones and jewelry with which the figures of the Indian rulers were decked. The intent of the whole visit was to inspire the prince's loyalty by the presence of the eldest son of their English queen, and to affirm their central role in the maintenance of the Empire.

Everywhere he went, the Prince of Wales was showered with valuable gifts by his mother's loyal Indian feudatories. Princes vied to outdo their competitors with the value, ingenuity, and brilliance of jewels, paintings, antique weapons, live animals, richly embroidered brocades, and other art works which they presented to him. What he collected in six months of touring in India literally filled the large converted troop ship, the *Serapis*. When he returned, his trophies and gifts went on traveling exhibition throughout England and eventually wound up in a quasi-museum in London at the Lambeth Palace. In return for their gifts, the Prince of Wales presented the Princes with copies of Max Muller's English translation of the *Rig-Veda*.

It was not only the Princes themselves who enthralled the Prince and his suite as they traveled, but also their exotic retainers, dressed in a dazzling variety of costumes. The editors of *The Graphic* pulled out all stops in trying to describe for their readers the impression that these "military fossils" made on the Europeans.

One of the chief features of the Maharajah of Cashmere's reception of the Prince of Wales was the wonderfully heterogeneous character of the troops who lined the route from the river to the

Palace. Never on record has such a miscellaneous army been collected together. The troops wore uniforms of all countries and all
ages, and carried as many different weapons, ranging from
chain armour and Saracenic javelins to the scarlet uniforms and
muskets of British soldiers half a century ago, the 12th and the
19th centuries being thus, as our artist remarks, face to face.
There were troops in veritable native costume, turbaned, and
carrying blunderbusses or flint-and-steel muskets; next to them
would be a red-coated company, with white, blue, or black
knickerbockers, and striped worsted stockings; then would come
a detachment in chain-mail and breastplates, and steel caps with
high tufts; while others again wore brass helmets, and were clad
in brass breast and back-plates, not unlike our own Household
Cavalry. One corporal particularly attracted our artist's attention,
being clad in a new tunic of cloth, on which the mark "superfine" had been left, a badge of distinction of which the wearer
appeared highly proud. He bore an old trigger gun, with a bayo-
net with a broad-leaved blade. Notwithstanding the semi-
European clothing and armament of many of the troops, however, very little of European discipline, or drill, apparently
existed, and our sketch of "Charge!" will give an idea of the
helter-skelter ruck—so characteristic of Eastern warfare—with
which a squadron of cavalry obeyed the word of command. Our
artist writes: "This regiment wore a green uniform with red
facings—some were shod and others barefoot—their trousers
were reefed up to their knees, while their sleeves were exceed-
ingly lengthy. As for the horses, they had ropes for bridles, and
in appearance were veritable descendants of Rozinants (*The
Graphic*, March 4, 1876:222).

Through the first half of the nineteenth century, the British seemed
to eschew competing with the splendors of Indian royal clothes. Unlike their eighteenth century counterparts who wore vividly colored
silks and satins, they wore fairly informal coats, dark or muted in
color, straight and at times baggy trousers, and plain shirtwaists and
vests. Until the middle of the nineteenth century, when the *sola topi*
(pith helmet) became ubiquitous, their headgear was a beaver stove-
pipe hat or a cap. The white ruling elite must have appeared dowdy
in comparison with their Indian underlings, who dressed in a version of Mughal court dress while carrying out their official functions.
The British appeared to have given up the sartorial struggle of trying
to outdress the pageant of Oriental splendor they sought to control.

It was Queen Victoria herself who suggested that the Civil servants in India should have an official dress uniform, as did their counterparts in the Colonial Service. The administration of India was completely separate from the ruling of the other colonials, one being run through the India Office and the other through the Colonial Office. Although the question of a special uniform was raised several times after the Queen expressed interest, the Council of India decided that prescribing a dress uniform would be an undue expense for their officials (Davies 1937:487).

Lord Lytton, Viceroy from 1876 to 1880 and a great believer in the power of ceremony and display as an integral part of ruling India, complained to his Queen that "official functions" in India looked like "fancy dress balls," because there was no check on the "sartorial fancies of the civil service" (Davies 1937:488). Although no uniform was prescribed for the Indian Civil Service until the early twentieth century, "some civil officers had provided themselves with one which was similar . . . to the levee dress of the 3rd and 5th class civil servants at home and in the colonies" (Earle, India Office Library and Records Memo 1876, Euro Mss. F86/163). The only civilians allowed a "dress uniform" by regulations were those who had "distinct duties of a political kind to perform, and who are thereby brought into frequent and direct personal intercourse with native princes." This uniform included a blue coat with gold embroidery, a black velvet lining, collar and cuffs, blue cloth trousers with gold and lace two inches wide, a beaver cocked hat with black silk cockade and ostrich feathers, and a sword (V.C. Chaudhuri 1980:373).

THE GAEKWAR AND THE KING

An incident occurred during the Imperial Durbar of 1911 that illustrates the official British concern with conformity of dress and manners expected of the Indian Princes. In 1911, King George V and his Queen traveled to India for his formal crowning as the King-Emperor of India. This was to be the only time that a reigning Monarch of Great Britain was to visit India before Independence. All three Imperial Durbars took place at the same site. In the first two, the structure marking the ritual center was a dais on which the Viceroy proclaimed the new titles of the Emperor. In 1911 the focal point of the event was a large platform, covered by velvet awnings and drapery and dubbed the homage pavilion, on which the King and his Princess sat on thrones. In previous Durbars, the Indian Royalty and nobles had been more or less passive bystanders; this time, it was decided that the leading Princes would individually offer "homage" as an expression of fealty and respect to their Imperial majesties.

The Gaekwar of Baroda was highly westernized, and generally considered by the British to be a "progressive" ruler, but too friendly with a number of prominent Indian nationalists. Baroda was ranked second behind Hyderabad in the official order of precedence at the Imperial Durbar established by the Government of India for Indian states. Therefore, the Gaekwar was to follow the Nizam in offering homage. The day before the actual ceremony a rehearsal was held to instruct the Princes in the proper form of offering homage to the King-Emperor and his consort. They were told to walk up the steps of the platform, bow low before each of their majesties, and then walk backwards down the steps in such a fashion as never to show their back to the Royal couple. The Gaekwar of Baroda was unable to attend the rehearsal and sent his brother to take notes for him.

On the day of the offering of homage, the Gaekwar was dressed in a plain white knee-length jacket and his "traditional" red turban. He wore white European trousers and carried an English style walking stick. He did not wear, as was expected, the sash of the Order of the Star of India. The Gaekwar approached the King, bowed once, omitting any obeisance to the Princess, took several steps backward, then turned and walked down the steps swinging his cane. It appears that at the time nothing was said about his behavior; subsequently however, led by the *Times* reporter, his behavior was interpreted as seditious. A major row ensued in the English language Press of India as well as in England itself over what was defined as a studied, purposeful, and seditious insult. The storm was revived three weeks after the event, when the newsreels taken at the Durbar reached England. The *Illustrated London News* of January 29 reproduced a page of sequential stills from the film showing "very clearly the way in which the Gaekwar of Baroda, carrying a stick, entered the Presence, bowed curtly, and walked off with his back to the King-Emperor" (Jan. 29, 1912:67). In addition to the pictures of the Gaekwar they printed pictures of two other ruling chiefs paying homage with deep bows of reverence. The Gaekwar and members of his court protested that, for personal reasons, the Gaekwar was distressed on the day of the ritual, was confused as to what was proper behavior, and intended no insult or lack of manners by what had happened (Rice 1931:16–22; Sergeant 1928:127–41).

The intentions of the Gaekwar are less relevant than his failure to maintain the dress code expected of Indian Princes. The most seditious touch of all would seem to have been the Gaekwar's use of a walking stick, an accouterment of the white Sahibs, military and civilian, which marked the insouciance they displayed in the presence of the Indian masses. It was also used on occasion to thrash Indians whose actions, manners, or appearance irritated them.

In India, the military "orientalized" to overawe the Indian Princes and the heathen masses; at home, the ruling classes archaized their ceremonial dress to overawe the new middle classes and the potentially dangerous lower orders of society. From the middle of the nineteenth century, the British at home increasingly invented or reinvented civic rituals at all levels of the polity. These rituals called for the creation of costumes, regalia, and accouterments to mark them as special and hallowed by tradition. They were designed to evoke in participants and audience, from the Lord Mayors of small cities to wealthy merchants and bankers in London, to the Royal family, to Union officials, a collective conception of the past (Cannadine 1983). The use of costumes and accouterments developed for such civic rituals were transported to India by the British to hierarchize the grandeur of their Indian princes. As a writer in the *Illustrated London News*, summing up what for him was the success of the Imperial Durbar of 1911, explained;

Despite the oft-repeated statement that this age is a very drab one sartorially so far as the West is concerned, there are various occasions on which Europe is able to show the Orient that it, too, can display itself in brilliant plumage. Such instances as the Coronation of King George and Queen Mary and that of King Edward VII and Queen Alexandra jump to the mind at once: and to these memories of glittering kaleidoscopic state pagentry must now be added those of the Great Durbar held so recently at Delhi. There Europeans vied with Asiatics with excellent effect (Jan. 27, 1912:11).

INDIANS IN EVERYDAY CLOTHES

One of the first impressions formed by British travelers to India in the nineteenth century was of the nakedness of most of the Indians whom they encountered on their arrival. Most British travelers to India from the eighteenth century to the early nineteenth century arrived either in Madras or at Diamond Harbour, down river from Calcutta. Madras was an open roadstead where British passengers had to disembark from their ships into open row boats manned by Indian boatment. At Diamond Harbour many travelers transferred to barges or small sailing boats for the remainder of the trip to Calcutta. The boatman was usually the first Indian they were able to observe closely. James Johnson, a surgeon in the Royal Navy who was in India in the late eighteenth century, records his impressions of the dress of the Bengali boatmen (*dandi*):

> The habilment of the Bengal *dandy*, or waterman who rows or drags our *budjrow* (barge), up the Ganges, consists in a small narrow piece of cloth (*doty*), passed between the thighs, and fastened before and behind to a piece of stout packthread, that encircles the waist. In this dress, or undress, corresponding pretty nearly to the figleaf of our great progenitor, he exposes his skin to the action of the tropical sun, a deluge of rain, or a piercing northwester, with equal indifference! (Johnson 1813:420–21).

British women newly arrived in India recorded their shock not only at the seminakedness of lower status Indian household servants, who seemed constantly underfoot, dusting, sweeping, lounging about, or playing with the *babalog* (white children), but also at their free access to the bedrooms of the *Memsahibs* as if they were nonmales. The traveler or sojourner in India quickly adjusted to the near nakedness of the Indian males, which after a while did not shock British sensibilities "owing to the dark colour of the skin, which as it is unusual to European eyes has the effect of dress" (Calcott 1812:2). They then began to discern great variation, based on region, caste, sect, and wealth, in Indian dress.

Indian Hindu male dress consists of three large pieces of cloth. One the *dhoti*, is wrapped and folded in various ways, and covers the lower half of the body. A second piece, worn in cooler weather, is a cotton shawl, or *chadar*. The third piece, a long, narrow strip of cloth which is wrapped around the head, is the turban or *pagri*. The usual textile for these cloths was cotton, but on occasion silk would be worn. There is, however, enormous variation in how parts of the *dhoti* are tucked into the waist and in the length of draping. Such details frequently indicate the occupation or status of the wearer. Most Hindu *dhotis* were white and without seams. Even Hindus whose work required them to wear Muslim-style stitched clothes, and later European jackets or coats of various kinds, would change into a *dhoti* when arriving home.

The basic difference between Hindu and Muslim clothes was that Muslim clothes were tailored, which involved the cutting and sewing of cloth, but Hindu clothes were of uncut pieces, formed into garments by folding, tucking, and draping. Although it was frequently asserted that in ritual and domestic contexts in the nineteenth century, uncut and unsewn clothing was invariably worn, I have found no adequate explanation of this injunction to use only uncut cloth when performing *puja* worship. This is certainly a common habit today among more orthodox Hindu males, who will bathe and then put on a fresh *dhoti*; on most auspicious ritual occasions such a *dhoti* will be of silk.

My speculation is that the use of unsewn cloth or a *dhoti* for males performing *puja*, or the use of *sets* of specified cloth and clothes as prestations, reflects an underlying concept of the necessity of completeness, or unpenetratedness, of totality, which is congruent with Hindu ideas of cosmogony. Parallel to the male wearing only an unsewn garment during *puja* were women who, by the late nineteenth century, had taken to wearing a *choli*, a sewn blouse or petticoat, which they removed while cooking food. Cooking had to be done in a specially designated and ritually cleansed area of the house.

N.C. Chaudhuri has described how males who worked in Mughal courts or in British offices would wear Muslim dress, but followed the rule that such garments were "worn for work only, and never in personal life. . . . Hindus who put on Muslim costume for public appearance scrupulously put them off when going into the inner house, and for religious observances, and they would never dream of wearing anything but orthodox Hindu clothes" (N.C. Chaudhuri 1976:53). The mansions of wealthy Calcutta Hindus in the late nineteenth century frequently had a western-style dressing room, complete with a wardrobe made in England, adjacent to the master's bedroom in the outer apartment of the house. There the master would change into Hindu clothes before entering the inner apartment and courtyard, the province of the women and the deities of the house. (N.C. Chaudhuri 1976:57).

The exception to the rule of eschewing sewn clothing at home in pre-nineteenth-century India was in the Punjab and Rajasthan. The Rajputs appear to have taken to wearing a *jama* (sewn coat) before the advent of the Mughals (Verma 1978:47). What was conventionally thought of as Mughal court dress adapted major elements of Rajput dress during the time of Akbar (Buschan 1958:30). It was also during this period that marking features were established to differentiate Hindu from Muslim attire, even when they were wearing the same type of coat (a *jama* or *angarakha*). The *jama* has ties that fix the flap of the upper half of the garment under the armpit and across the chest; Muslims wear their *jama* tied to the right, Hindus to the left. The *jama* became reduced to a shirt-like garment for cold weather wear among peasants of Upper India in the nineteenth and twentieth centuries, but the custom of tieing continued to follow the old pattern of left for Hindus, right for Muslims (Ghurye 1966:129).

The Mughal rulers prescribed a form of their own dress for Hindus associated with them or employed in their offices and as officials. However, the British tried to have Hindus who worked for them—whether as domestic servants or as clerks, writers, and revenue and judicial officials—continue to wear the Mughal-style dress appropriate to their functions (N.C. Chaudhuri 1976:57–58). Writing about British attitudes toward Indians wearing European clothes, N.C. Chaudhuri trenchantly sums up the situation: "They, the British, were violently repelled by English in our mouths and even more violently by English clothes on our backs" (1976:58).

By the mid-nineteenth century, increasing numbers of urban Indians, particularly in Calcutta and Bombay, began to wear articles of European clothing. In Bombay the lead was taken by the Parsis, a group descended from the Zoroastrians, who had fled from Persia when the Islamic rulers began to persecute them for maintaining their religion. The Parsis settled in coastal areas of Gujarat, and by the eighteenth century were an important component of the population of Bombay, as carpenters, builders, and boat builders. By the early nineteenth century, some had become successful merchants, bankers, and European-style businessmen. Although they maintained a distinctive style of dress, particularly in the caps they wore, trousers, shoes, and an adaptation of a long English frock coat became new elements of their distinctive costume.

By the 1880s many successful, wealthy Indians and Western-educated Indian males had taken to wearing European clothes in public. Even those who normally wore a complete Western outfit, however, did not take to Western headgear. Many Indians continued to wear a turban with European clothes, particularly in the cold season. They also took to wearing a great variety of caps, from military forage caps to a wide range of brimless skull caps. The one type of hat that Indians did not wear was the pith helmet.

By the eighteenth century, the Europeans were aware of rules governing where Indians could wear footcoverings, and before whom they could appear in slippers. During a visit in 1804 to the Peshwa in Poona, the head of the Maratha Confederacy, Lord Valentia, who was touring India collecting botanical specimens, observed the expected behavior. Accompanied by the long-time British Resident Colonel Close and his retinue, he entered the court-yard of the palace in a palanquin, but from there had to continue on foot. He entered the Durbar room, and before stepping on the white cloth covering of the floor, took off his slippers. Lord Valentia was met by the Peshwa's *Dewan* (prime minister), and after a few minutes the Peshwa entered and remained standing by his throne (*gaddi*, literally a cushion). Valentia approached, flanked by the Dewan and the Resident, and was lightly embraced by the Peshwa. Then, after the Peshwa seated himself, Valentia had to sit on the floor crosslegged as "we had no chairs or cushions, and were not permitted to put out our feet, as showing the sole of the foot is considered disrespectful" (Valentia 1809, II:120–21). After formal conversation, done through an interpreter who spoke only to the Dewan, who in turn spoke to the Peshwa, Valentia was invited to have a private conversation with the Peshwa in a small room adjacent to the Durbar. Here, seated on a small "Turkey" rug next to the Peshwa, they spoke more informally for over an hour before returning to the Durbar room for dismissal. Valentia recorded, "I was extremely tired with my position, that it was with some difficulty that I could rise, and for a few minutes was obliged to rest against the wall" (II:122).

In portraits, successful and rich Europeans in India frequently are portrayed in their offices with several of their Indian employees or associates. The crucial Indians for the Europeans were their *Banians*, a title minimally translated as "cash keeper." These were men who ran both official and commercial activities of the British. They secured credit, dealt with most Indians on the *Sahibs'* behalf, kept their books, and were their factotums in all their public dealings. Another employee of high status was the *Munshi*, inadequately described as a "scribe." The *munshi* frequently were highly educated Muslims who acted in the initial phases of a European's career as his teacher of Persian and Urdu, and later as a confidential secretary responsible for his correspondence with Indian officials and rulers. In eighteenth-century paintings, the *Munshi* and *Banian* have their slippers on while the bearer or *hukkah bardar* is barefoot. This is obviously a concession on the part of the European to the high status of these employees. Captain Thomas Williamson spent upwards of twenty years in India in the 1780s and 1790s. His *East India Vade Mecum* (1810), the first guidebook for Europeans to provide detailed instructions on managing a household and observing proper manners, observed that:

> A Banian invariably rides in his palanquin attended by several underlings. . . . He, to a certain degree, rules the office, entering it generally with little ceremony, making a slight obeisance, and never divesting himself of his slippers: a privilege which, in the eyes of the natives, at once places him on a footing of equality with his employer (Williamson 1810:189–90).

In the 1830's F.J. Shore, a judge in Upper India, complained that "natives of rank" walk into the rooms of Englishmen with their shoes on. He attributed this practice to a combination of the bad manners of the natives of Calcutta "who are of an inferior order" and the ignorance and carelessness of Europeans who do not know eastern etiquette (Shore 1837, I:79–80). Shore, who was highly critical of his countrymen's lack of knowledge and their disdain for the people of India, explained to his European readers they should not allow Indians in their presence with shoes. If Indians did so, the *sahib* should explain to them that:

> "Nations have different customs; ours is to uncover the head— yours to uncover the feet, as a token of respect. You would not presume to walk into the sitting-room of another native with your shoes on; why then do you treat me with a disrespect which you would not show to one of your own countrymen? I

am not prejudiced, and it is quite immaterial to me which practice you choose to adopt. You can either take off your shoes or
your turban, but I must insist on one or the other mark of civil-
ity if you wish me to receive your visits." This is unanswerable
by the native; and those English who have acted in this manner,
have been decidedly more respected by the people" (Shore 1837
I:80).

By 1854, so many Indians in Bengal, particularly in Calcutta, had
taken to wearing European shoes and stockings, that the Governor
General in Council passed a resolution allowing native gentlemen
"on official and semi-official occasions . . . to appear in the presence
of the servants of the British government" wearing European boots
or shoes (V.C. Chaudhuri 1980:425). Twenty years later, the rule was
made general throughout India and now included Government
courts, as the practice of wearing European dress had spread up-
country, among "educated native gentlemen accustomed to European habits." The rule was to apply only to the public parts of
courts, and not the chambers of the judge. His rooms were "private"
and hence he could there enforce whatever rules he wished.

There were several issues lurking beneath the seemingly trivial
question of which Indians of what status could wear what kinds of
shoes, and where. Indian Christians always were allowed to wear
their shoes wherever Europeans would normally wear their shoes.
Europeans had long objected to removing their shoes when entering
an Indian temple or when appearing in the durbar of an Indian
ruler. The British construction of the rules governing the wearing
or non-wearing of shoes was that Europeans did not have to conform to Indian custom, but Indians had to conform to European
ideas of what was proper Indian behavior. The Europeans could
also decide when an Indian practice had changed sufficiently to
allow their subjects to follow new rules. The "victory" of the Bengalis, in getting rules regarding the wearing of shoes changed, encouraged some of them to try to have changed the rule that they must
wear turbans while they were in government offices.

A group of Bengali officials in the 1870s petitioned the Lieutenant
Governor of Bengal to allow them "to adopt the European custom
of uncovering the head in token of respect in durbars and courts of
justice, and on all other official occasions and places" (Chaudhuri
1980:429). The petitioners pointed out that the "wearing of the *pagri*

(turban) is at present not a national custom of the Bengalis." Many Bengalis, they wrote, think the *pagri* an unreasonable headdress, as "it does not act as sufficient protection from the glare and heat of the sun," and is inappropriate to "active occupations." As a result of the decline in the use of the *pagri*, they claimed that Indians who work in government offices are forced to keep two headdresses: A *pagri*, which they carry in boxes or store in their offices, and a "light cap" which they actually wear. When a European superior approaches them while they are working in the office, they remove their caps and put on the *pagri*.

The Indians suggested a simple solution to the question: "We think that the best course is to wear caps and to uncover the head as token of respect." They pointed out that this would not prevent those Indians who continued to wear *pagris* from doing so, but those who by inference were more progressive in their dress and manners should not be forced to continue a custom they thought old-fashioned. In making their request, the petitioners felt they were acting in concert with the rulings about shoes, as that question was settled by the acceptance of the fact that Indians could wear shoes while the rest of their dress was "Oriental," and did not require Indians to fully adopt European dress. Hence, substituting the wearing of a cap indoors rather than going bareheaded in the European fashion could seem appropriate. To continue to be forced to wear a *pagri* in the presence of Europeans rather than wearing brimless caps could act "as a cause of moral depression on the people."

The Lieutenant Governor was strongly opposed to the suggested innovation. He did not think the petitioners represented "even the middle class of the natives of Bengal." It was proper for native gentlemen to wear whatever they wanted in private life, he wrote, but the use of the cap "was a very slovenly and unbecoming style of dress for public occasions." The Lieutenant Governor declared that "No European of respectability would appear in such caps." They were not "western" nor were they "Oriental," and hence by implication they were some kind of bastard concoction, which furthered a tendency he abhored towards laxity in dress and manners—and dress and manners were the means by which Indians showed proper respect in the office and on public occasions. Sir Ashley Eden then went on to lecture those Indians seeking to change current dress codes:

If any change in the rules is to be made it should not in the
Lieutenant-Governor's opinion, take the shape of further relaxa-
tion of existing customs. Indeed, the Lieutenant-Governor thinks
that the chief change required, is that some of the Native gentlemen, especially native officials, who attend levees and durbars
should pay greater attention than heretofore to their customs,
and should in this way imitate the European custom of showing respect by not appearing on such occasions in the ordinary
clothes in which they have just left their desks or court-houses.
The new prevailing laxity in this matter may possibly have some
bearing on the want of cordiality in the relations between Europeans and Natives, of which such frequent complaint is made by
those who remember a different state of things. Attention to costume was a form of respect in which the forefathers of the present generation were never deficient. In giving up the customs of
appearing with the head covered on public occasions, Native
gentlemen are adopting neither the customs of the West nor of
the East, and the movement is one which the Lieutenant-
Governor deprecates and which he is certainly in no way prepared to encourage (Chaudhuri 1980:436).

THE UNIFORM OF THE INDIAN NATIONAL CONGRESS

By the last decades of the nineteenth century, there was increasing
documentation of the declining production of fine cotton textiles
in India. Muslins of Dacca, printed cloths of the South of India,
palampores, fine woolen shawls of Kashmir and the Punjab, had all
but disappeared (Havell 1888:18–20; Havell 1890:9–15; Birdwood
1880:244–58); Murkherjee 1888:317–98; Irwin 1973). While the demise of fine weaving and printing was being decried, it was also
noted that cheaper and coarser cotton cloth, frequently woven out
of imported thread, continued to be in demand as it was cheaper
and sturdier than Lancashire-made *dhotis* and *saris*. The effects of
European imports on the production of Indian textiles were highly
differentiated on a regional basis, and reflected ritual imperatives,
changing social statuses, and taste. E.B. Havell, Superintendent of
the School of Arts in Madras and subsequently of the Government
Art School in Calcutta, who was the most influential of the Europeans concerned with the restoration of Indian fine arts and crafts, described the complexities of the situation in regard to Indian textiles
in Madras:

The European goods have their great advantage in point of cheapness, and consequently the native manufacturer who supplies the wants of the low caste and poorer classes has suffered most.

White Cloths - for Male Wear. Two kinds of white cloth for personal wear are produced by the native weaver: first, a plain white cloth with a narrow border of coloured cotton, and sometimes with a broader band woven across each end, which are worn by the low caste poor; and, secondly, superior cloths of fine texture in which the borders are broader and of silk, and generally embroidered with a simple pattern, and the bands at each end either of silk or of silver lace. These cloths, originally intended for Brahmins only, are now indiscriminately worn by the wealthier classes of every caste. The first of these has been almost entirely superseded for general wear by English long cloth, which is cheaper than the native cloth by about one half. Still, the manufacture is carried on throughout the districts on a very small scale, for the native cloth is always worn, by those who can afford it, on occasions of ceremony, and by some it is preferred on account of its superior durability and thicker texture. The manufacture of the finer cloths still occupies a very large proportion of the weavers, and is extensively carried on in and around about Madura and Salem. The prosperity of this industry has also been affected to a less extent by the cheapness of European goods, in a similar way, that whereas a well-to-do native would formerly have four to six country cloths in constant wear, many now reserve the more expensive costume for the religious and domestic ceremonies at which a Hindu would expose himself to ridicule if he appeared in other than his traditional dress. But as these cloths are only within the reach of the wealthier classes, it is probable that the spread of Western ideas and mode of dress has had more prejudicial effect on the industry than the mere cheapness of European goods. Both in the fine, but more especially in the inferior cloths, the profits of the weaver seem to be reduced to a very low margin.

Cloth for Female Wear. The manufacture of cloths for female wear is carried on on a very extensive scale, and has not declined to such an extent as the other, for though the industry has suffered considerably in the inferior kinds by the competition of English and French cheap printed cotton goods, European manufacturers have not hitherto produced anything which can at all compete with the finer cloths of Tanjore, Kuttálam and Kuranád, and other places. While the more gorgeous beauties of

the textile manufactures of the north, such as those of Benares,
Surat and Gujerat, have been fully recognised, it is a pity that
the more sober, though none the less remarkable, artistic
qualities of these fine cloths and their adaptability in many ways
to decorative purposes have not been better appreciated. Artisti-
cally speaking, a decline is only noticeable in the cotton cloths,
most of which have lost their characteristic beauty by the use of
European dyed thread. The Madura cloths, however, are an exception (Havell 1888).

The decline of the craft production of Indian cloth, used for dress,
decoration, and rituals, was caused by a combination of price and
the changing of taste of Indian consumers. In the 1860s European
manufacturers had not yet developed an adequate knowledge of the
varied tastes of Indians or the functions of cloth in India. James
Forbes Watson, Reporter of Economic Products at the India Office
in London and Director of the India Museum, was a lifetime student
of Indian textiles who produced 18 volumes containing 700 samples
of Indian textiles. Twenty sets of what Watson thought of as portable
"textile museums" were distributed in Great Britain and India. His
goal was to acquaint manufacturers with the "tastes and needs of
their Indian customers." In addition to his sample books, he wrote
what remains today the most extensive single-volume study of Indian dress and textiles, *The Textile Manufactures and the Costumes
of the People of India*, London 1866. In this work he explained
that to be successful, the manufacturer producing cloth for the Indian market had to know "how the garment was worn, by which
sex and for what purpose." Above all, he had to grasp "the
relationship between the size of cloth, its decoration and use, if
he were to be successful in selling textiles in India." The European manufacturer might produce a cloth that was correct in size,
length, and breadth for a turban or *lungi* (loincloth) but it might
prove "unsaleable because its decoration is unsuitable . . . or
because it is not in good taste from an Indian point of view"
(Watson 1866:5).

Watson cheerfully stated that increased consumption of European cloth in India would be good for both the Manchester manufacturers and the people of India. Indians were underclothed and
hence cheap textiles would be a boon for them. If the Indian weavers
couldn't compete, it wouldn't necessarily be a bad thing as:

In a great productive country like India it is certain that *she* will gain; for if supplies from Britain set labour free there, it will only be to divert it at once into other and perhaps more profitable channels. It might be otherwise if India were not a country whose strength in raw products is great and far from developed; but as it is, her resources in this direction are known to be capable of a vast expansion and to be sufficient to occupy the energies of her whole people (Watson 1866:8).

As can be seen by the exchange between the Lieutenant Governor of Bengal and his Bengali underlings, Indian tastes in clothes were rapidly changing. The thousands of clerks and functionaries who worked in the Government and commercial offices of Calcutta and Bombay had by the late nineteenth century developed a distinctive form of dress, a mixture of Indian and European. They wore an un-ironed white European shirt with tails out, covering the top of their finely draped white *dhoti*; their legs were bare to midcalf, showing white socks held up by garters, and their feet were shod in patent leather pumps or short boots produced by Chinese bootmakers in Calcutta (Thurston 1906:519).

Some of the wealthier and more flashily dressed Bengalis were described by S.C. Bose as thinking that an adaptation of the European style of dress could bring them the benefit of "modern civilization" by "wearing tight pantaloons, tight shirts and black coats of alpaca or broadcloth." They would top this costume with "a coquettish embossed cap or a thin folded shawl turban" (S.C. Bose 1881:192).

The wealthy of Calcutta sought to modernize not only their dress, but their home furnishings as well. I noted above the separation of the large Calcutta mansions into two sections: A domestic one of the women which was private, and a public set of rooms used by males for entertaining their Indian and occasional European guests. The drawing rooms were furnished in a mixed "Oriental" and "Western" style.

A Canadian visitor, Anna Leonwens, described a visit to the home of a wealthy gentleman, Ram Chunder, in Bombay. She described him as "educated in all the learning of the East as well as in English, but never the less a pure Hindoo in mind and character." The occasion was for an evening of Indian dance, drama, and music. Her host was dressed in a "rich and strikingly picturesque" manner.

He wore deep crimson satin trousers, a white muslin *"angraka"* or tunic, a purple vest with gold embroidery, a fine Cashmere cummerbund, white European stockings, and embroidered antique Indian slippers (Leonwens 1884:175). The entertainment took place in a large room, furnished in the Oriental style, with *kincob* (brocade) wall hangings decorated with peacock feathers. The floors were a fine tile mosaic, and around the walls on tables and shelves were a "melange of European ornaments, clocks, antique pictures, statues, celestial and terrestrial globes and a profusion of common glass wear of the most brilliant colors" (Leonwens 1884:174).

It was not only the wealthy, Western-educated, or urban middle classes whose dress was beginning to change, but more common folk as well. Tribesmen recruited from the hills of Southern India as labor on tea and coffee plantations spent some of their wages on turbans and caps (innovations for them) and woven coats "of English cut" for festival clothes (Thurston 1906:520). An Indian working for Edgar Thurston, Superintendent of the Madras Government Museum and head of the Ethnographic Survey of Madras, appeared wearing a white patchwork shirt, adorned "with no less than six individual and distinct trademarks representing the King-Emperor, Brittania and an elephant, etc." The inclusion of the printed trademarks was generally popular; soldiers of the Maharaja of Kashmir wear jackets blazoned with the manufacturer's identification of "superfine" (*The Graphic*, March 4, 1876:229). European manufacturers were supplying cloth with all sorts of designs, which according to Thurston met the "Indians' love of the grotesque," a taste nurtured by exposure to the "carvings on Hindu temples and mythological paintings" (Thurston 1906:522). One of the most popular patterns in cloth manufactured for use in women's petticoats had a border "composed of an endless procession of white bicycles of ancient pattern with green gearing and treadles, separated from each other by upright stems with green and gold fronts . . ." (Thurston 1906:522).

While a few Europeans were proselytizing for better taste and seeking to "direct progress in a right groove and to prevent the decline of Indian art," some early Indian nationalist writers were developing a critique of the Government of India's policies furthering the destruction of Indian "manufactures," which they claimed advantaged British manufacturers to the detriment of incipient Indian efforts to establish modern industry. The early nationalists also argued that Government revenue policies were contributing to the continued misery of the mass of Indian cultivators (Buck 1886:i; Tarapor 1978, 1980, 1981; Chandra 1966; Sarkar 1973, Ch. III; for a counter-argument see Morris, 1963 and 1968).

Thus there were two streams of thought: the aesthetic and moral concern of Europeans influenced by the art and craft movement in Great Britain and their Indian experience, and the early Indian nationalist critique of government policies leading to the continued impoverishment of India. These two streams of thought provided a major part of the ideology of the *swadeshi* movement in Bengal, 1903–08. The movement's goals were complex, but one aim was to encourage the development and use of indigenously produced goods through a boycott of European manufactures. As the movement developed, there was increasing discussion and propaganda to encourage Indian weavers and to revive the hand spinning of cotton thread (Sarkar 1973:94–108). These ideas were taken up and formalized by Mahatma Gandhi through the next decade. Gandhi had been much influenced by Ruskin's and Morris's critiques of modern industrial society and its destructive and alienating effects on the bodies, minds, and morals of the European working classes (Chatterjee 1984). Gandhi continually articulated and elaborated on the theme that the Indian people would only be free from European domination, both politically and economically, when the masses took to spinning, weaving, and wearing homespun cotton cloth, *khadi*. To give substance to these theories, he created the enduring symbols of the Indian nationalist movement; the *chakra* (spinning wheel), which appeared on the Indian National Congress flag and continues to be ambiguously represented on the Republic of India's flag, and the wearing of a *khadi* "uniform," a white handspun cotton *dhoti*, *sari*, or *pajama*, *kurta* and a small white cap.

In 1908, when he was still in South Africa, Gandhi began to advocate handspinning and weaving as the panacea for the growing pauperization of India. (Decades later, Gandhi could not recall ever having seen a spinning wheel when he began to advocate their use) (Gandhi 1968, II:730). In 1916, after his return to India, he established an *ashram*, where a small group of his followers were to begin practicing what Gandhi had been preaching. The first order of business was to find or develop a *chakra* to implement his call, not only to boycott foreign-made cloth and thread, but to make and wear their own *khadi*. At first they had to make do with cloth which was handwoven, but made of mill-made thread produced by Indian mills. It was not until 1917 or 1918 that one of his loyal followers, Gangabehn Majumdar, located some spinning wheels in Baraoda and encouraged some weavers to spin and weave cloth for the *ashram*. The next step was to try to produce their own cloth at the *ashram*: the first result was a cloth 30 inches wide, which was too narrow for an adequate *dhoti*. The first piece of cloth produced cost 17 annas per yard, grossly expensive for the time. Finally Gangabehn was successful in getting cloth of adequate width, 45 inches, made so that Gandhi was not "forced to wear a coarse short *dhoti* (Gandhi 1968:735–37).

I have been unable to find out when and how Gandhi created the uniform of the Indian National Congress, but it was clearly between 1918 and 1920. During the First Non-Cooperative Movement of 1920–21, the wearing of *khadi* and especially the cap, by now dubbed a "Gandhi cap," was widespread and became the symbolic focus, once again, of the British-Indian battle over headdress. In March of 1921, Gandhi reported that some European employers were ordering that the white *khadi* caps not be worn in the office. Gandhi commented that "Under of rule of Ravana," the villain in the Ramayana, "keeping a picture of Vishnu in one's house was an offence, [so] it should not be surprising if in this *Ravanarajya* [Raj of Ravana] wearing a white cap . . . not using foreign cloth, or plying the spinning wheel came to be considered offences" (Gandhi 1964–65, XIX:482).

A month later, the Collector of Allahabad in Eastern Uttar Pradesh forbade government employees from wearing "the beautiful, light inoffensive caps" (XX:105). A few months later in Simla, Indians in government service said they risked dismissal if they wore *khadi* dress and caps (XX:223). A lawyer in Gujarat was fined 200 rupees and ordered out of court for wearing the cap; when he returned an hour later still wearing the cap, another 200 rupees were added to his fine (XX:204). The campaign, as far as Gandhi was concerned, was highly successful. When an English businessman dismissed a young clerk for wearing the offending hat, he declared "the manager by his simple act of dismissal of a poor Indian employee had given political color to the transaction." The British were falling for Gandhi's symbolic transformation of the *khadi* cap into a sign of rebellion. He urged Indians everywhere, by the simple act of wearing a hat, to bring the Raj to its knees (XX:378–79, 487–88). The British, Gandhi argued, were confusing Non-Cooperation with the use of *khadi*, thereby reinforcing the power of the movement. If they were so frightened by the mere wearing of a *khadi* cap, which was a "convenience and symbol of *swadeshi*," what might happen if he, Gandhi, asked Government employees to stop working, and not just wear *khadi*?

The Chief Justice of the High Court of Bombay issued a letter to all judges under his jurisdiction to bar pleaders in their courts from wearing the Gandhi cap; if they continued to do so, he said, they were to be charged with contempt of court for having been disrespectful to the judge. The Chief Justice went on to state, "No pleader should appear in Court if he wears any headdress *except* a turban" (Gandhi, XXII:15). Gandhi also reported that a Muslim youth was shot by a European youth for selling or wearing a Gandhi cap (Gandhi XXII:175).

HEADS AND FEET: TURBANS AND SHOES

From the eighteenth to the twentieth century, the British and Indians fought out a battle about the proper forms of respectful behavior, centered on heads and feet. But to say that turbans, caps, and shoes were symbolically charged for both groups tells us little. What were the underlying meanings of this battle?

Europeans explained the nature of Indian headdress in functionalist and materialist terms: the turban was for the protection of the head. Watson described the Indian turban as providing "protection from the heat of the sun, it is usually of a fine muslin-like texture, which when folded, is at once bulky and porous—this admirably fulfilling its main purpose . . . [the light cloth] is a good non-conductor" and "allows the free escape of perspiration" (Watson 1866:13). Indians clearly did not share the idea that the turban or other headdresses were primarily for protection from the sun. The elaborate decoration of the caps, the jewel-bedecked turbans of the rulers, and the choice of a hat as a major symbol of the Nationalist movement all indicate that hats are much more than a form of protection from the heat or the rays of the sun.

I can only sketch some of the possibilities that might help explain the significance of head coverings for Indians. Clearly, there is no simple answer to the question of the significance of the head for Indians. Fazl wrote that for Muslims the head is the seat of the senses, (Fazl 1927:167). For Hindus the head is the locus of the eyes, including the third or inner eye in the center of the forehead. Lawrence Babb has persuasively argued that sight is the crucial sense cosmographically for Hindus. "Hindus wish to see their deities" (Babb 1981:387). Today, Hindus live in constant sight of the deities, in the form of ubiquitous colored lithographs, which emphasize and accentuate the face and eyes of the deities. Indians wish to see and be seen, to be in the sight of, to have the glance of, not only their deities, but persons of power. The concept of *darshan*, to see and be seen, includes going to a temple, visiting a holy man or guru, or waiting for a glimpse of a movie star or the Prime Minister.

Babb stresses that the Hindu conception of "seeing" is not "just a passive product" of "sensory data originating in the outer world;" it involves the observer directly with the person or deity seen. Hindus live in a substantive world in which there are constant flows of various forms of matter, among them emanations from "the inner person, outward through eyes to engage directly with objects seen, and to bring something of these objects back to the seer" (Babb 1981:396). Not only is the head the seat of sight, but it is also the part of the body that concentrates positive flows of substances and powers within the body. In the practice of raj yoga, for example, one seeks to concentrate through exercise and meditation the power of the whole body in the head.

As the head is the locus of power and superior forms of knowledge, the feet become the opposite. The feet are "the sources of downward and outward currents of inferior matter" (Babb 1981:395). When a Hindu visits a guru, a parent, a patron, a landlord, a government official, or a god, he or she will touch their feet. This is an "act of submission or surrender" but it is also a reciprocal act, as one is obliged to offer "shelter and protection to the one who has surrendered." By touching the feet one is taking what is ostensibly base and "impure" from a superior being and treating it as valuable and "pure" (Babb 1981:395).

I think Babb's exegesis and analysis, which draws on the work of Wadley and Marriott in their discussions of power and substantive flows, provides an explanation for the significance of the head and feet, and hence their coverings. It explains why Lord Valentia was correct in surmising that his feet, if pointed towards the Peshwa, would have defiled him; they were the source of impurity. Shoes and slippers were dirty, not just from being used to walk around in, but as the repositories of base substances flowing from the wearer's body. This is why it was an Indian custom not only to take off one's dirty shoes or slippers when entering the space of a superior, but more importantly, to sit so that the feet would not imperil the well-being of others.

The solution worked out in Indian courts to accomodate the inability of Europeans to sit for long periods on a rug or a cushion with their feet tucked under them was to allow them to sit on chairs; thus their feet, covered or uncovered, would be facing downward. Today, or at least yesterday—35 years ago when I was doing field work in a village—the few villagers who had chairs would sit on them, particularly if they had provided me with a chair, but with their feet off the ground and tucked up under them.

A painting by Thomas Daniel, based on sketches by James Wales, shows Sir Charles Malet delivering a ratified treaty to the Peshwa in Poona in 1792; we see almost all the Indians and Europeans sitting or kneeling on a large rug, while the Peshwa sits on a slightly raised platform, supported by large cushions. Of the fifty-odd figures depicted, all but two have their feet placed so that they cannot be seen. Some of the English appear to have lap cloths or cummerbunds covering their feet; one English military officer is wearing boots, but the sole of his boot is on the ground. One Indian soldier is kneeling in such a fashion that one bare foot can be seen, but he too has the sole of his foot firmly on the rug (Archer 1979, Pl.261).

The writers of guide books who advised British travelers never to touch an Indian on his turban or head were correct, but this was not merely politeness in observing yet another peculiar Indian custom; because the hands, like the feet and mouth, are sources of impurities, touching the head would threaten the well-being of the Indian being touched.

In the conceptual scheme which the British created to understand and to act in India, they constantly followed the same logic; they reduced vastly complex codes and their associated meanings to a few metonyms. If Indians wore shoes in the presence of *Sahibs*, they were being disrespectful in the early nineteenth century. But to Indians, the proper wearing of slippers or shoes stood for a whole difference in cosmology.

The European concepts of custom and superstition were a means to encompass and explain behavior and thought. They allowed the British to save themselves the effort of understanding or adequately explaining the subtle or not-too-subtle meanings attached to the actions of their subjects. Once the British had defined something as an Indian custom, or traditional dress, or the proper form of salutation, any deviation from it was defined as rebellion and an act to be punished. India was redefined by the British to be a place of rules and orders; once the British had defined to their own satisfaction what they construed as Indian rules and customs, then the Indians had to conform to these constructions. Wearing the Gandhi cap thus was a metonym for disorder. To the Indian this cap was indeed a symbol, but a highly complex one. Involving a cosmological system which set the meaning of the head and its covering, it had as well an ideological referent as a critique of British rule in India, and embodied to its wearer a protest against the insults and deprivations of 150 years of colonial rule.

ACKNOWLEDGMENTS

This paper was written while I was the holder of a fellowship for independent study and research awarded by the National Endowment for the Humanities. The paper is based on my continuing research on the British construction of a colonial sociology and its representations in eighteenth- and nineteenth-century India. This work over the past ten years has been supported by the National Science Foundation, the American Council of Learned Societies and Social Science Research Council Joint Committee on South Asia, the American Institute of Indian Studies, and the Lichtstern Research Fund of the Department of Anthropology of the University of Chicago.

In writing this paper, my greatest debt is owed to the South Asia Collection of the Regenstein Library of the University of Chicago and to its creator, Maureen L. P. Patterson. The paper reflects the influence of Anthony King, of the Sociology Department of Brunel University, whose writings, conversations, and "guided architectural tours," taught me that one can read the past in objects, museum collections, buildings, and landscapes, as well as in documents and books. While I was writing the paper I learned much about the significance of clothes in conversations with my colleague Jean Comaroff. The paper would not have been completed without

Lois Bisek's skill, patience, and uncanny ability to make sense out of my ungrammatical, misspelled, and wretchedly typed draft.

REFERENCES CITED

Archer, Mildred
    1972   Company Drawings in the India Office Library. London: H.M. Stationary Office.
    1979   India and British Portraiture, 1770–1825. New York: Sotheby Parke Bernet.

Babb, Lawrence
    1981   Glancing: Visual Interaction in Hinduism. Journal of Anthropological Research 37:387–401.

Ball, Charles
    1859   The History of the Indian Mutiny, 2 vols. London: London Printing and Publishing Co.

Beetham, David
    1970   Transport and Turbans: A Comparative Study in Local Politics. London: Oxford University Press.

Birdwood, George
    1880   The Industrial Arts of India. London: Chapman and Hall, Ltd.

Bolt, David
    1975   Gurkhas. London: White Lion Publishers.

Buck, E.C.
    1886   Preface. Journal of Indian Arts 1 (1):i-iv.

Burrow, J.W.
    1981   A Liberal Descent: Victorian Historians and the English Past. Cambridge: Cambridge University Press.

Bhushan, J.B.
    1958   The Costumes and Textiles of India. Bombay: D.B. Taraporevala.

Buckler, F.W.
    1927–28   The Oriental Despot. Angelican Theological Review 10 (3):238–49.
    1922   Two Instances of Khilat in the Bible. Journal of Theological Studies 23:197–99.

Callcott, Maria Graham
    1812   Journal of a Residence in India. Edinburgh: A. Constable.

Cannadine, David
    1983   The Context, Performance and Meaning of Ritual: The British Monarchy and the "Invention of Tradition," c. 1820–1977. *In* The

Invention of Tradition, Eric Hobsbawn and Terence Ranger, eds. pp. 101–64. Cambridge: Cambridge University Press.

Chandra, Bipan
1960   The Rise and Growth of Economic Nationalism in India. New Delhi: People's Publishing House.

Chaudhuri, N.C.
1976   Culture in a Vanity Bag. Bombay: Jaico Publishing House.

Chaudhuri, V.C.
1980   Imperial Honeymoon with Indian Aristocracy. Patna: K.P. Jayswal Research Institute.

Cohn, Bernard
1983   Representing Authority in Victorian India. *In* The Invention of Tradition, Eric Hobsbawm and Terence Ranger, eds., pp. 165–209. Cambridge: Cambridge University Press.

Davies, C.C.
1937   India and Queen Victoria. Asiatic Review (n.s.) 33:482–504.

Eastwick, E.B.
1849   A Galance at the Sind Before Napier or Dry Leaves from Young Egypt. Karachi: Oxford University Press.

Falcon, R.W.
1896   Handbook on the Sikhs for the use of Regimental Officers. Allahabad: The Pioneer Press.

Fazl, Abu'l
1927   The Ain-i-Akabari, Vol. I. Calcutta: Asiatic Society of Bengal.

Foster, William ed.,
1899   The Embassy of Sir Thomas Roe to the Court of the Great Mughal. 1615–19, Vol. I. London: Hakluyt Society.

Gandhi, M.K.
1966   An Autobiography: The Story of My Experiments with Truth. Boston: Beacon Press.
1964–65 Collected Works. Dehli: Publications Division, Ministry of Information and Broadcasting, Government of India.

Gascoigne, Bamber
1971   The Great Mughuls. London: Cape.

Ghurye, G.S.
1966   Indian Costume. Bombay: Popular Prakashan.

Gittinger, Mattiebelle
1982   Master Dyers to the World. Washington: Textile Museum.

Gopal, S.
1976   Jawaharalal Nehru: a Biography, Vol. I. Cambridge, Mass.: Harvard University Press.

India, Government of (GOI)
   1913   Proceedings of the Committee on the Obligations Devolving on
           the Army in India, Its Strength and Cost. Vol 1-A, Minority Re-
           port. Simla: Government Central Branch Press.

Hasan, Ibn
   1936   The Central Structure of the Moghul Empire and Its Practical
           Working up to the Year 1657. London: Oxford University Press.

Havell, E.B.
   1888   The Printed Cotton Industry of India. Journal of Indian Art 2(19):
           18–20.
   1890   The Industries of Madras. Journal of Indian Art 3(26):9–16.

Heathcote, T.A.
   1975   The Indian Army: The Garrison of British Imperial India,
           1822–1922. New York: Hippocrene Books.

Hobsbawm, Eric and Terence Ranger
   1983   The Invention of Tradition. Cambridge: Cambridge University
           Press.

Hutchins, Frances
   1967   The Illusion of Permanence: British Imperialism in India. Prince-
           ton: Princeton University Press.

Irwin, John
   1973   The Kashmir Shawl. London: Her Majesty's Stationary Office.

Islam, Riazul
   1970   Indo-Persian Relations: A Study of the Political and Diplomatic
           Relations between the Mughal Empire and Iran. Teheran: Iranian
           Culture Foundation

Iyer, Anantha Krishna
   1935   The Mysore Tribes and Castes, Vol. I. Mysore: Published under
           the auspices of Mysore University.

Johnson, James
   1813   The Influence of Tropical Climates. London: J.J. Stockdale.

Khan, I.A.
   1972   The Turko-Mongol Theory of Kingship. Medieval India: A Mis-
           cellany 2:9–18.

Leonowens, Anna H.
   1884   Life and Travel in India. Philadelphia: Porter and Coates.

Macauliffe, M.A.
   1909   The Sikh Religion: Its Gurus, Sacred Writings, and Authors, VI
           Vols. Oxford: Clarendon Press.

Macleod, W.H.
   1976   The Evolution of the Sikh Community. Oxford: Clarendon Press.

Mereweather, J.W.B. and F. Smith
1919   The Indian Army Corps in France. London: J. Murray.

Moore, Joseph Sr.
1886   The Queen's Empire and her Pearls. Philadelphia: J.B. Lippincott.

Morris, Morris D.
1963   Towards a Reinterpretation of Nineteenth Century Indian Economic History. Journal of Economic History 23(3):606–618.

Morris, Morris D. et at.
1968   Reinterpretation of Nineteenth Century Indian Economic History. Indian Economic and Social History Review 5(1):1–15.
Royal Anthropological Institute Newsletter (RAIN) (56)1983.

Rice, Stanley
1981   The Life of Sayaji Rao III, Maharaja of Baroda, Vol. II. London: Oxford University Press.

Sarkar, Sumit
1973   The Swadeshi Movement in Bengal, 1903–08. New Delhi: Peoples Pub. House.

Sergeant, Philip W.
1928   The Ruler of Baroda: An Account of the Life and Work of the Maharaja Gaekwar Sayajirao III. London: J. Murray.

Shore, F.J.
1837   Notes on Indian Affairs, Vol. I. London: J.W. Parker.

Singh, Khushwant
1953   The Sikhs. London: G. Allen and Unwin.
1963–66 A History of the Sikhs, Vols. I and II. Princeton: Princeton University Press.

Strong, Roy C.
1978   Recreating the Past: British History and the Victorian Painter. New York: Thames and Hudson.

Tarapor, Mahrukh
1978   Indian and the Arts and Crafts Movement. Paper read at the Victorian Studies Conference, Birmingham.
1980   John Lockwood, Kipling, and British Art Education in India. Victorian Studies 23(21):53–81.
1981   Art Education in Imperial India: The Indian Schools of Art. Paper read at the Seventh European Conference on Modern South Asia Studies, July 1981. SOAS, London.

Thurston, Edgar
1908   Ethnographic Notes in Southern India. Madras: Printed by the Superintendent, Government Press.

Tripathi, R.P.
   1956   Some Aspects of Muslim Administration. Allahabad: Central
           Book Depot.

Tuker, Francis
   1957   Gorkha: The Story of the Gurkhas of Nepal. London: Constable.

Uberoi, J.P. Singh
   1967   On Being Unshorn. Transactions of the Indian Institute of Ad-
           vanced Study 4:87–100. Simla: Pooran Press.

Lord Valentia, George Annesley Mountnorris
   1909   Voyages and Travels in India, Ceylon . . . , Vol II. London:
           printed for W. Miller.

Verma, Som Prakash
   1978   Art and Material Culture in the Paintings of Akbar's Court. New
           Delhi: Vikas.

Wallman, Sandra
   1982   Turbans, Identities, and Racial Categories. Royal Anthropological
           Institute Newsletter (October) (52)2.

Watson, J. Forbes
   1866   The Textile Manufacturers and the Costumes of the People of
           India. London: G.E. Eyre and W. Spottiswoode.

Watson, J. Forbes and John Kaye
   1868–75 The People of India, 8 Vols. London:India Museum.

Williamson, Thomas
   1810   The East-India Vade Mecum, 2 Vols. London: Black, Parry and
           Kingsbury.

11. *Gandhi and* Khadi, *the Fabric of Indian Independence*

SUSAN S. BEAN

 Cloth was central to the Indian struggle for national self-government—cloth as an economic product and cloth as a medium of communication. Cloth was officially incorporated into the nationalist program in 1921 when the Indian National Congress resolved to campaign for the boycott of foreign cloth, to require its officers and workers to spin cotton yarn and wear hand-spun, hand-woven cloth (*khadi*), and to adopt a flag with the spinning wheel in the center. Mahatma Gandhi was the force behind the adoption of these resolutions, but they were successful because Gandhi had achieved an understanding of the role of cloth in Indian life, the culmination of decades of experimentation with cloth as a medium of communication and means of livelihood.

Gandhi's changing sociopolitical identity can be traced through his costume changes as well as through his speeches, writings, and activities. As he came to appreciate the semiotic properties of cloth, he learned to use it to communicate his most important messages to followers and opponents and to manipulate social events. Once he had appreciated the economic importance of cloth in India, he made it the centerpiece of his program for independence and self-government. The development of Gandhi's thought and practice, which is explored in the following pages, is illuminated by the historical and cultural context provided in Cohn (this volume) and Bayly (1986). Cohn analyzes the use of costume in the reorganization and management of hierarchical relations during the British Raj. Bayly provides valuable insights into the role of cloth in Indian culture, emphasizing its moral nature—its capacity to embody and transmit social value—a characteristic of cloth which Gandhi appreciated.

LESSONS IN THE SOCIAL MEANING OF COSTUME

When Mohandas K. Gandhi disembarked at Southampton in 1888, he was wearing white flannels given to him by a friend and saved especially for the occasion, because he "thought that white clothes would suit [him] better when [he] stepped ashore" (Gandhi 1957:43). On his arrival at Southampton he realized that white flannels were not worn in late September. Later he replaced his Bombay-style clothing, which he thought "unsuitable for English society" (Gandhi 1957:50), with an evening suit from Bond Street, patent leather shoes with spats, and a high silk hat, "clothes regarded as the very acme of fashion" (Fischer 1982:37). Gandhi was sensitive to the connection between costume and social status, and perceived that changes in social position required changes in costume. His sensitivity became self-consciousness because Gandhi, the student from India, was so ignorant of how Gandhi, the London barrister, should appear.

In 1891 when Gandhi returned home to Rajkot, a barrister, he promoted the westernization of his household, begun for him by his brother, by adding items of European dress (Gandhi 1957:92). Gandhi believed his success was dependent on westernization. Later, in the harsher, more repressive, and openly racist South Africa where he went to work as a barrister in 1893, he confronted his indelible Indianness.

On this third day in South Africa, he visited the Durban court. It was explained to him that Hindus had to remove their turbans in court, though Muslim Indians were permitted to keep their turbans on. Turbans were not like hats: In this context, removal was not deferential, it was demeaning (see Cohn, this volume). Gandhi thought he could solve the problem by wearing an English hat, but his employer warned him that he would be undermining efforts for recognition of the Indian meaning of the turban and for permission to keep it on in court. His employer added, in appreciation of Indian dress: "An Indian turban sits well on your head." Besides, he said, "If you wear an English hat you will pass for a waiter" (Gandhi 1957:108). (Most waiters in South Africa were Indian converts to Christianity who wore English dress.)

Gandhi kept his turban and began to appreciate the limits of his Englishness—limits imposed by the colonial regime and by his pride as an Indian and a Hindu. But still he thought he could make his Indianness compatible with Englishness. He wore a fashionable frock coat, pressed trousers, and shining shoes with his turban (Fischer 1982:57). After he was thrown off the train to Pretoria for traveling first class, he reapplied for a first-class ticket, presenting himself to the station master "in faultless English dress" (Gandhi 1957:116). He succeeded. The station master said, "I can see you are a gentleman" (Gandhi 1957:117).

Gandhi later also succeeded in persuading the railway authorities to issue first- and second-class tickets to Indians "who were properly dressed" (Gandhi 1957:128). He sought to demonstrate that Indians could be as civilized as Englishmen and therefore were entitled to the same rights and privileges as citizens of the British Empire. This belief seemed to be supported by the Empress Victoria herself, who stated that there was a distinction between "aliens and subjects of Her Majesty [and] between the most ignorant and the most enlightened of the natives of India. Among the latter class there are to be found gentlemen whose position and attainments fully qualify them for all the duties and privileges of citizenship" (Queen Victoria, quoted in Erikson 1969:172–3).

When Gandhi brought his family to South Africa in 1896 he believed "that in order to look civilized, our dress and manners had as far as possible to approximate to the European standard. Because, I thought, only thus could we have some influence, and without influence it would not be possible to serve the community. I therefore determined the style of dress for my wife and children. How could I like them to be known as Kathiawad Banias? The Parsis used then to be regarded as the most civilized people amongst Indians, and so, when the complete European style seemed to be unsuited, we adopted the Parsi style. Accordingly my wife wore the Parsi sari, and the boys the Parsi coat and trousers. Of course no one could be without shoes and stockings. It was long before my wife and children could get used to them. The shoes cramped their feet and the stockings stank with perspiration" (Gandhi 1957:186).

Soon the prospect began to fade that one could be an Indian and a full citizen of the British empire by wearing Indian headgear with an English suit. For one thing, it had become clear that the color of one's skin was as much a part of one's costume as a frock coat, and this fundamental Indianness Gandhi would not have changed even if he could. He began to admire Indian dress. In 1901, back in India for a visit, he met some rulers of Indian states at the India Club in Calcutta. Gandhi recalls, "In the Club I always found them wearing fine Bengalee *dhotis* [Hindu garments of seamless cloth, wrapped and folded around the lower body] and shirts and scarves. On the darbar day [Viceroy's audience] they put on trousers befitting *khansamas* [waiters] and shining boots. I was pained and inquired of one of them the reason for the change. "We alone know our unfortunate condition [began the reply]. We alone know the insults we have to put up with, in order that we may possess our wealth and titles. . . .' 'But what about these *khansama* turbans and these shining boots?' I asked. 'Do you see any difference between *khansamas* and us?' he replied, and added, 'They are our *khansamas*, we are Lord Curzon's *khansamas*. If I were to absent myself from the levee, I should have to suffer the consequences. If I were to attend it in my usual dress, it would be an offence'" (Gandhi 1957:230). As in the Durban court, the sartorial dictates of the Empire were demeaning for its Indian citizens (see Cohn, this volume). During the same visit he remarked on his mentor, Gokhale: "In the Congress I had seen him in a coat and trousers, but I was glad to find him wearing a Bengal *dhoti* and shirt [at home]. I liked his simple mode of dress though I myself then wore a Parsi coat and trousers" (Gandhi 1957:234). Gandhi began to experiment with his own costume. Soon he embarked on a tour of India to learn about its people; he traveled third class. For clothing he took a long woolen coat, a *dhoti*, and a shirt. But on his return to Bombay in 1902 he resumed the life of the well-dressed, well-housed barrister riding first class on the trains.

Gandhi's responses to the costumes of others and his experiments with his own attire indicate a growing awareness of the meaning of clothes—their importance as indicators of status, group identity, social stratification, and political beliefs. He had begun to doubt the possibility of being both a dignified Indian and an English gentleman. The sartorial requirements of the Empire forced Indians to humiliate themselves, and revealed the true relationship—of master and slave—between the English and the Indians. Gandhi's experiments with simple, inexpensive Indian garments expressed his growing disdain for possessions and his growing identification with the poor.

By 1908 he had come to believe that Indians could not be Englishmen and that India should be ruled for the benefit of India by Indians. He set forth these views in *Hind Swaraj* (*Indian Home Rule*) (1908), where he also said: "If people of a certain country, who have hitherto not been in the habit of wearing much clothing, boots, etc., adopt European clothing, they are supposed to have become civilized out of savagery" (Gandhi 1922:32). He himself had believed this when in 1893 he appealed to the railroad authorities to allow Indians in European dress to ride first class, and in 1896 when he brought his family to South Africa and insisted on the further westernization of their dress. By 1908, he no longer believed that European garments were an index of civilization and Indian ones of its lack.

In *Hind Swaraj*, Gandhi first articulated the importance for India of the economics of cloth. For fifty years, an economic nationalism (whose roots were in fact much older) had been evolving in India. British rule had not benefited India, as the British maintained. On the contrary, British rule had destroyed the economy of India by taking its wealth back to England, by overtaxing its farmers, and by destroying Indian industries that might compete with English ones, thus causing poverty, famine, and disease. Cloth manufacture had been the premier industry of India and its decline was a chief cause of Indian poverty. These views were set out in detail in R.C. Dutt's two-volume *Economic History of India* (Dutt 1901 & 1903). Gandhi commented in *Hind Swaraj*: "When I read Mr. Dutt's *Economic History of India* I wept; and, as I think of it, again my heart sickens. . . . It is difficult to measure the harm that Manchester [the seat of the English mechanized textile industry] has done to us. It is due to Manchester that Indian handicraft has all but disappeared" (Gandhi 1922:105).

From 1908 on, these two elements—the economics of cloth and the semiotics of cloth—united in Gandhi's thought. By 1921, *khadi* (homespun cloth) had become central to his politics. The intervening years were full of experiments with costume and with the production of handmade cloth.

CLOTH IN ECONOMIC NATIONALISM

Gandhi's campaign for *khadi* was a product of economic nationalism. Gandhi's views on cloth and clothing were unique, but the elements of which they were composed were not. According to the economic nationalists, India's decline was due largely to British destruction of Indian manufactures beginning in the late eighteenth century. Cotton textiles had been India's premier industry. Weavers and dyers so excelled in producing both coarse , inexpensive textiles and fine, exquisitely dyed, luxury textiles that Indian cloth was prized in Rome, China, Egypt, and Southeast Asia.

> As early as 200 B.C. the Romans used a Sanskrit word for cotton
> (Latin, *carbasina*, from Sanskrit *karpasa*). In Nero's reign, deli-
> cately translucent Indian muslins were fashionable in Rome
> under such names as *nebula* and *venti* textiles (woven winds) the
> latter exactly translating the technical name of a special type of
> muslin woven in Bengal up to the modern period. . . .The qual-
> ity of Indian dyeing, too, was proverbial in the Roman world, as
> we know from a reference in St. Jerome's fourth century Latin
> translation of the Bible, Job being made to say that wisdom is
> even more enduring than the "dyed colors of India" (Irwin 1962).

In the fifth century A.D. an Indonesian diplomatic mission carried textiles from India and Gandhara to China. In the eleventh century, "500 Jewish families on their way to settle in the Northern Sung capital of China, bought cotton goods in India to take as gifts" (Gittinger 1982:13). Fifteenth-century fragments of Indian cloth found at Fostat, near Cairo, show that the trade was not exclusively in fine textiles. The fragments are "often lacking in care or precision [in dye crafts-manship] and only occasionally showing exceptional skill. Inescapable is the sense that these were made for a modest clientele and do not represent elements of a 'luxury' trade" (Gittinger 1982:33).

Until the sixteenth century, Indian and Arab merchants dominated the trade in Indian cottons. From the late sixteenth century, Europeans gained increasing control of the world trade in Indian cottons (Chaudhuri 1978). At first European traders were interested in Indian cottons as trade goods which could be exchanged in Southeast Asia for spices. By the middle of the seventeenth century, the traders had discovered that if they supervised the design of the textiles made in India, these could be sold at a reasonable profit in London. At the end of the seventeenth century, the demand for Indian painted cottons had become so great that France banned chintz imports to protect its own silk industry (Irwin and Brett 1970:3,4). England followed suit a few years later. So popular were these fabrics that the prohibitions were ignored. In 1720 "a second prohibition was introduced . . . to forbid 'the Use and Wearing in Apparel' of imported chintz, and also its 'use or wear in or about any Bed, Chair, Cushion, or other Household furniture'" (Irwin and Brett 1970:5).

The great popularity of Indian cottons was due both to the cheapness and to the superiority of Indian products. Indian handspun yarns were superior to those produced in England and were imported for the weaving of fine cloth. Indian dyers were expert in the technology of mordant dyeing, which produced washable cottons in vibrant colors (Chaudhuri 1978:237ff). While the competition from Indian cloth could be fought with duties and prohibitions, the technological superiority remained unchallenged until the industrial revolution.

From the late eighteenth century, with the development and growth of machine spinning and weaving and the adoption and modification of Indian cotton-dyeing technology (Gittinger 1982:19), England began to produce quantities of inexpensive cotton textiles. English political control of India permitted adjustments in tariffs (and import prohibitions) to assure the advantage of Lancashire cottons in trade. English cotton-spinning mills secured supplies of raw cotton from India, and British traders succeeded in competing in India with the local hand-loom industry, thus opening a vast new market for the products of the Lancashire mills. The hand-spinning of cotton yarns had virtually died out in India by 1825. Only the highest counts of cotton yarns could not be reproduced by machinery. Even Indian hand-loom weavers used the cotton yarns produced in Lancashire. During the nineteenth century, exports fell drastically and the world's greatest exporter of cottons became a major importer of cotton yarns and piece goods. "In the first four years of the nineteenth century, in spite of all prohibitions and restrictive duties, six to fifteen thousand bales [of cotton piece-goods]

were annually shipped from Calcutta to the United Kingdom.
. . . After 1820 the manufacture of cotton piece-goods declined
steadily, never to rise again" (Dutt 1906:296). Between 1849 and
1889, the value of British cotton cloth exports to India increased from
just over 2 million pounds a year to just less than 27 million pounds
a year (Chandra 1968:55). At the end of the nineteenth century, the
development in Europe of inexpensive, easier-to-apply chemical
dyes dealt the final blow to Indian technological superiority in textile
production.

The interpretation of these changes has long been a subject of
heated debate among historians and economists. Did British cloth
destroy the demand for Indian hand-looms or supplement it? Did
indigenous production really decline or was it simply consumed in
the domestic market? Did British policy destroy Indian manufactures or was the demise of Indian industry the inevitable result of
the competition between artisans and machines? Did India fail to in-
dustrialize because British policy prevented it or because Indian society was infertile soil for industrialization?

During the late nineteenth century, an interpretation of England's economic relations with India evolved that became the economic basis of Indian nationalism. In this economic nationalism, the
history of cotton production and trade was central. Especially significant was the transformation of India from the world's most advanced producer of cotton textiles to an exporter of raw cotton and
an importer of cloth.

Dadabhai Naoroji was the recognized leader of this movement
and codified the theory of economic nationalism. In his view, "the
continuous impoverishment and exhaustion of the country" (Naoroji 1887) was unquestionably the result of British rule. Wealth was
taken from India to pay the Englishmen in London who ruled India
and to pay large salaries and pensions to English civil servants, who
spent much of this wealth in England. Grinding poverty and severe
famines resulted from the enormous tax burden on the cultivators.
British protection of English industries, through trade advantages
in the structure of tariffs, destroyed indigenous artisanry and prevented the development of machine industry.

Naoroji and other early nationalists (e.g., Ranade, Tilak,
Gokhale) believed that the low tariffs on British yarns and cloth com-
ing into India and the high tariffs on Indian textiles taken out of
India caused the decline of the textile industry, forced more people

onto the land, and created an unbalanced economy that exacerbated the poverty of India. Furthermore, they believed that the tariff structure on cotton goods revealed the true nature of British rule:

> Be that as it may, as regards this question of the cotton duties, the mask has now fallen off the foreign English administration of India. The highest officials in the country, nay the entire official body and the leading newspapers in England, have had to make the humiliating confession—The boast in which we have been so long indulging, the boast that we govern India in the interest and for the welfare of the Indians, is perfectly unfounded; India is held and governed in the interests of the English merchants (*The Bangabasi*, 17 March 1894, quoted in Chandra 1966:235).

The national leadership united on this issue, and on the importance of protection for India's artisans and nascent industries. Moreover, for the first time they united in action, around the issue of cotton tariffs. In 1896 they urged the boycott of foreign goods (Chandra 1966:250). The tactic of appealing to the English government of India to practice what it preached—just government—had begun to give way to active opposition. The seeds of opposition, the idea of *swadeshi* (the promotion of indigenous products), had already been planted:

> In 1872 Justice Ranade delivered a series of public lectures at Poona on economic topics, in which he popularized "the idea of *swadeshi*, of preferring the goods produced in one's own country even though they may prove to be dearer or less satisfactory than finer foreign products." These celebrated lectures so inspired the listeners that several of them including Ganesh Vasudeo Joshi . . . and Vasudeo Phadke . . . enthusiastically "vowed to wear and use only swadeshi articles." Joshi used to spin yarn daily for his own *dhoti*, shirt and turban; he started shops at several places to popularise and propagate *swadeshi* goods, and, at the Delhi Durbar of 1877 and in the midst of pageantry and flamboyancy, he represented the Sarvajanik Sabha dressed in pure self-spun khadi (Chandra 1966:122–3).

Indians could fight the destructive power of the English government by using Indian products in preference to foreign ones. The ideology and practice of *swadeshi* grew among nationalists and then, when the English government of India imposed excise duties on Indian cloth, *swadeshi* promoters turned to their most powerful weapon, boycott. In 1896, many people in Dacca resolved to boycott Manchester cloth and to patronize Indian mills (Chandra 1966:126). The center of activity was the Bombay Presidency, home of the nascent textile industry (the first mill opened only in the 1850s). Indians showed their opposition to English clothing by refusing to buy it or wear it, and by burning it. "According to the *Nyaya Sindu* of 2 March 1896 huge bundles of English clothing were thrown into the Holi fire that year" (Chandra 1966:130,n.167). A *Times* correspondent reported that "It was impossible for a respectable citizen to go with a new English piece of cloth without being asked a hundred perplexing questions" (Chandra 1966:130). Even though agitation subsided in subsequent years, *swadeshi*, the promotion of indigenous products, with cloth as its main platform, became a permanent feature of the nationalist movement.

English cloth had become the most potent symbol of English political domination and economic exploitation. As cloth is used mainly in clothing, the results of English exploitation—the demise of indigenous industry—were constantly there for all to see, on the backs of Indians who wore Manchester cloth made into British-style garments, and on Indians who used Manchester cloth for turbans, *kurtas* (shirts), *saris*, and other Indian garments. *Swadeshi*, an attempt to revive and promote Indian industry, required that each person be counted as a patriot-nationalist or a supporter of English domination and exploitation. An individual's political views, encoded in his or her costume, were exposed to public view.

Indeed, part of the reason for the decline of the *swadeshi* movement was the difficulty in procuring, and resistance to wearing, *swadeshi* costume. In the late nineteenth century, the Indian mills and handloom weavers together did not have the capability to clothe the nation. More significantly, most nationalist leaders, including Gokhale and Naoroji (but not the more militant Tilak), continued to wear English costumes with Indian headgear in public. They still believed that the way to gain a just administration of India was to show the English rulers the errors of their ways, so that English fair play and justice would prevail, Indians would be given a greater voice in the government of their land, and artisanry and industry would be revived. Like Gandhi when he appealed to the railway authorities in South Africa in 1893, they seemed to believe that they had to show their English rulers that they were like the English, that they were

English gentlemen, and were entitled to all that the English government would give to its own people.

Thus a fascinating paradox was generated from the semiotic and economic characteristics of cloth. These early nationalists wanted to revive and modernize Indian manufactures, especially the textile industry. But their political beliefs stood in the way of utilizing its products. Cloth is made to be worn and to express the social identity of its wearer. They expressed their belief in English values and their right to English justice by comporting themselves as English gentlemen in English dress (albeit with a special hat or turban to signify a slight cultural distinctiveness). Because they were still committed to this Englishness of dress, they were incapable of carrying out their own program of *swadeshi*.

Gandhi, following the lead of Tilak, Joshi and others, came to the more radical position that to promote Indian industry, foreign notions of civilization and gentlemanliness would have to be discarded. Economic Indianization was intrinsically connected to sociocultural Indianization. One could not promote the Indian textile industry without wearing its products and one could not wear its products and remain a proper Englishman. And if one gave up frock coats and morning suits, one would no longer be an English gentleman entitled to treatment as such. A new strategy would be required to achieve the nationalists' goals for India, a strategy based more on confrontation and opposition than on persuasion and cooperation.

THE MAHATMA AS SEMIOTICIAN

Gandhi began his conscious experimentation with costume on his trip to India in 1901. He had begun to question the political efficacy of gentlemanly dress. The experiments intensified during the *satyagraha* (truth force) campaign of militant non-violence in South Africa, from the 1906 opposition to the Black Act until his departure in 1914. In 1909, when Gandhi settled at Tolstoy Farm, he is said to have put on "laborer's dress"—workman's trousers and shirt in the European style, which were adapted from prison uniform (Nanda 1958:109). There is a photograph of him during the *satyagraha* campaign wearing *lungi* (South Indian wrapped lower garment), *kurta* and coat. His head and feet are bare; he carries a staff and a bag slung across his shoulders. This costume was similar to the one he wore on his third-class pilgrimage through India in 1901. The transformation was so radical and unfamiliar that the Reverend Andrews, who arrived to join the movement in 1913, did not recognize the "man in a *lungi* and *kurta* with close cropped head and a staff in hand," reported Prabhudas Gandhi who added "probably he took him for a *sadhu* (ascetic holy man)" (Gandhi, P. 1957:176).

That same year, after being released from jail, he attended a meeting in Durban in a *dhoti* (perhaps a *lungi*). His feet were bare and he had shaved his moustache. He was in mourning for the dead coal strikers (Ashe 1968:124). However, when he sailed for England in 1914 he was dressed as an Englishman (Fischer 1982:151), and when he landed in India the following year he was dressed as a Kathiawari (Gujarat) peasant, in *dhoti, angarkha* (robe), upper cloth, and turban, the most thoroughly Indian of his costumes. His *satyagrahi* garb was his own design, and expressed simplicity, asceticism, and identity with the masses. His Kathiawari dress was more formal. It identified his region of origin and presented him as a totally Indian gentleman. In his autobiography he comments on this costume "with my Kathiawadi cloak, turban and *dhoti*, I looked somewhat more civilized than I do today" (1982:374). The costume was an attempt to provide an Indian resolution for the contradiction between being civilized and being Indian.

His colleagues were not sure what to make of him. He "was an eccentric figure, with his huge white turban and white clothing, among the western attired delegates" (Gold 1983:63). By appearing in this eccentric fashion he forced his colleagues to notice and accommodate his view of a truly Indian nationalism. He deliberately used costume not only to express his sociopolitical identity, but to manipulate social occasions to elicit acceptance of, if not agreement with, his position.

Despite the thoroughgoing Indianness of his Kathiawari costume (actually because of it) it was inadequate for Gandhi's purposes because it indicated region, class, and religion. Gandhi's program called for the unity of all Indians throughout the subcontinent, rich and poor, Hindu, Sikh, and Muslim. He needed a costume that transcended these distinctions. His experiments continued. He arrived in Madras in 1915 traveling third class and wearing a loose shirt and pair of trousers (Erikson 1969:279). He was photographed in Karachi in 1916 wearing a dark-colored hat similar in shape to what has become known as a "Gandhi cap" (Gold 1983:59). Again during the Kheda *satyagraha* in 1918 he was photographed in his Kathiawari turban. At the 1919 Amritsar Congress he first wore the white homespun "Gandhi cap." Some believe it was derived from South African prison garb (Ashe 1968:199). The cap also resembles some worn by Muslims and it may be important that Gandhi began to wear it during the campaign to support the Caliph of Turkey, a campaign important to Gandhi for its promotion of Hindu-Muslim unity. The cap, which Gandhi discarded two years later, was to become part of the uniform of Indian nationalists (see Cohn, this volume).

Gandhi's final costume change took place in 1921 when he began his national program for the revival of handmade cloth. *Khadi* (homespun) was scarce and expensive, so he urged his followers to wear as little cloth as possible:

> I know that many will find it difficult to replace their foreign cloth all at once. . . . Let them be satisfied with a mere loin cloth. . . . India has never insisted on full covering of the body for the males as a test of culture. . . . In order, therefore, to set the example, I propose to discard at least up to the 31st of October my *topi* (cap) and vest, and to content myself with only a loin cloth, and a *chaddar* (shawl) whenever found necessary for the protection of the body. I adopt the change, because I have always hesitated to advise anything I may not myself be prepared to follow. . . . I consider the renunciation to be also necessary for me as a sign of mourning, and a bare head and bare body is such a sign in my part of the country. . . . I do not expect co-workers to renounce the use of the vest and the *topi* unless they find it necessary. . . . (29 September 1921, quoted in Jaju 1951:98).

Later recalling the same event, Gandhi added he "divest[ed] [him] self of every inch of clothing [he] decently could and thus to a still greater extent [brought himself] in line with the ill-clad masses . . . in so far as the loin cloth also spells simplicity let it represent Indian civilization" (quoted in Jaju 1951:99). Gandhi had completely rejected the English gentleman and replaced him with the Indian ascetic, the renouncer, the holy man. When he visited the Viceroy in 1921 (and still later, when he attended the Round Table Conference in London in 1931 and visited King George and Queen Mary at Buckingham Palace) wearing his *mahatma* garb, nothing could match the communicative power of a photograph of Gandhi in loincloth and *chadar* sitting among the formally attired Englishmen. He communicated his disdain for civilization as it is understood in the West, his disdain for material possessions, his pride in Indian civilization, as well as his power—an ordinary man would not have been granted entry. By dealing openly with a man in *mahatma* garb, the British accepted his political position and revealed their loss of power.

The communicative power of Gandhi's costume was, however, uniquely Indian. Paradoxically, as his popularity grew, the messages he brought to the Indian public in his speeches and writings had increasingly limited range. Gatherings were huge, running to a hundred thousand or more. Only in the cities were public address systems available to him. Most people who went to see him could not hear him. Even if they could hear him the Gujarati or Hindustani or English in which he spoke could not be understood by many, sometimes most, of his audience. In a nation about three-quarters illiterate, his writings were available to still fewer.

Gandhi needed another medium through which to communicate with the people of India. He used his appearance to communicate his most important messages in a form comprehensible to all Indians. Engaged in the simple labor of spinning, dressed as one of the poor in loincloth and *chadar*, this important and powerful man communicated the dignity of poverty, the dignity of labor, the equality of all Indians, and the greatness of Indian civilization, as well as his own saintliness. The communicative power of costume transcended the limitations of language in multilingual and illiterate India. The image transcended cultural boundaries as well. His impact on the West was enhanced by his resemblance, in his simplicity of dress and his saintly manner, to Christ on the Cross.

In India, visual communication has a unique force. The sight of the eminent or holy blesses and purifies the viewer; the experience is called *darshan*. People came, literally, to *see* Gandhi. Through *darshan*, the power of Gandhi's appearance surpassed his message in words. "For the next quarter of a century, it was not only for his message that people came to him, but for the merit of seeing him. The sacred sight of the *Mahatma*, his *darshan*, was almost equivalent to a pilgrimage to holy Banaras" (Nanda 1958:213).

During this same period, Gandhi was experimenting with the economics of cloth production. Gandhi recalled: "It was in London in 1908 that I discovered the wheel. . . . I saw in a flash that without the spinning wheel there was no *Swaraj* [self-government]. But I did not then know the distinction between the loom and the wheel, and in *Hind Swaraj* used the word loom to mean the wheel" (quoted in Jaju 1951:1). "I do not remember to have seen a handloom or a spinning wheel when in 1908 I described it in *Hind Swaraj* as the panacea for the growing pauperism of India. In that book I took it as understood that anything that helped India to get rid of the grinding poverty of her masses would in the same process also establish *Swaraj*. Even in 1915 when I returned to India from South Africa, I had not actually seen a spinning wheel" (Gandhi 1957:489). By the time Gandhi returned to India in 1915, cloth production had become central to his program.

Like most leaders of the nationalist movement, Gandhi thought the reindustrialization of India to be of paramount importance, but unlike most of them he was opposed to mechanized industry, which he viewed as a sin perpetrated on the world by the West. He wanted to revive artisanry. From the establishment of Phoenix farm in 1904, Gandhi had committed himself to the simple life of labor. Machines were labor-saving devices that put thousands of laborers out of work, unthinkable in India where the masses were underemployed. Factory production facilitated the concentration of wealth in the hands of a few big capitalists, and transformed workers into "utter slaves."

Gandhi selected Ahmedabad, the Manchester of India, as the site for his settlement because this "great textile center was best suited for experiments in hand-spinning and weaving which appeared to him the only practicable supplementary occupations for the underworked and underfed masses in the villages of India" (Nanda 1958:134), and ". . . as Ahmedabad was [also] an ancient centre of hand-loom weaving, it was likely to be the most favourable field for the revival of the cottage industry of hand-spinning" (Gandhi 1957:395). Erikson, who has written so brilliantly on the early years in Ahmedabad, observes that "Gandhi blamed the disruption of native crafts [not only for the poverty of India, but also] for the deterioration of Indian identity. He was soon to elevate the spinning wheel to significance as an economic necessity, a religious ritual and a national symbol . . . Gandhi wanted to settle down where both tradition and available materials would permit him and his followers to build a community around the cultivation of spinning and weaving" (Erikson 1969:260).

By the time he settled at Ahmedabad his goal for India was the achievement, through *satyagraha*, of the reduction of poverty, disease, and immorality, and the restoration of dignity. Spinning offered solutions to all these problems. The English had destroyed the greatest cotton producer in the world in order to protect their own industries from competition, to create a source of raw materials not available in the British isles, and to make a ready market for their finished products. Gandhi sought to restore India's lost supremacy, to revive this "second lung" of India (the first was agriculture). His reasoning was simple: If Indians returned to the production of their own cloth there would be work for millions of unemployed, Indian wealth would not be taken to England and Japan, and Indians would again be their own masters (See Jaju 1915:8). "*Swadeshi* is the soul of *Swaraj*, *Khadi* is the essence of *Swadeshi*" (Gandhi quoted in Jaju 1951:12).

Until its demise in the 1820s, spinning had been a supplementary occupation of women all over the country. Weaving, by contrast, had always been a caste occupation. Though at first Gandhi concentrated on reviving spinning among women, he soon broadened his program. Spinning would become the leisure pursuit of all. The wealthy would spin as service; the poor to supplement their incomes. Through spinning, India would be able to clothe itself, and thereby free itself from foreign exploitation and domination. Through spinning, all Indians, rich and poor, educated and illiterate, would be laborers, equal and united through their labor (see Bean 1988):

> Originally there was one specific objective: to give work and clothing to the half-starved women of India. To this was related from the beginning the larger objective of khadi—the cloth itself as a means of economic self-sufficiency (*swadeshi*) which in turn must inevitably produce self-government (*swaraj*). This progression, *Khadi* = *swadeshi* = *swaraj*, was Gandhi's incessant preachment for the rest of his life. . . . His genius had found a tremendous symbol which was at the same time a practical weapon . . . for the liberation of India. . . . The symbol he had found, the wheel itself, assumed enormous importance with the passage of time: it related itself to the whole of life, to God, to the pilgrimage of the spirit. . . (Sheean 1949:154,157,158, see also Bayly 1986).

Gandhi had returned from South Africa determined to wear hand-made cloth. He brought a weaver to the ashram, but there was no hand-spun yarn available for the loom, so Gandhi began looking for a spinner. It was not until 1917 that his associate Gangabehn located spinners who would produce yarn to be woven at the ashram—if slivers, carded cotton for spinning, could be supplied to them. Until then, Gandhi had relied on machine-spun yarn from Ahmedabad mills for his looms, but he still had to get the slivers for hand-spinning from the mills. Gandhi's *khadi* had to be entirely hand-made, so he asked Gangabehn to find carders who could provide the slivers. Gandhi "begged for [the raw] cotton in Bombay" (Gandhi 1957:492). Finally the entire process of making cloth could be done by hand.

At this time, Gandhi's *dhoti* was still of Indian mill cloth. The *khadi* manufactured at the ashram was only 30 inches wide. Gandhi "gave notice to Gangabehn that, unless she provided . . . a *khadi dhoti* of 45 inches width within a month, [he] would do with coarse, short *khadi dhoti*. . . . well within the month she sent [him] a pair of *khadi dhotis* of 45 inches width, and thus relieved [him] from what would then have been a difficult situation. . . ." (Gandhi 1957:493). Perhaps Gandhi was looking for an opportunity to change to a loin-cloth, a change he accomplished two years later. From 1919 on, he was clothed entirely in *khadi*, and instead of the turban, he began wearing the white *khadi* "Gandhi cap." *Khadi* was much too coarse for wrapping as a Gujarati turban.

In 1920 as part of the Non-cooperation Movement, the leaders of the Indian National Congress endorsed hand spinning and weaving, to supply cloth to replace boycotted foreign cloth and to engage the masses in the nationalist cause. In this they followed Gandhi, but they were by no means in full agreement with him. "Tagore argued that trying to liberate three hundred million people by making them all spinners was like urging them to drown the English by all spitting together: it was 'too simple for human beings.' Complaints came in against *khadi* as a material in the conditions of modern living. It wouldn't stand up to the wear and tear of a factory. It was too heavy. It was hard to launder and therefore unsuitable for children. Gandhi's answer was that with more skill there would be better *khadi*" (Ashe 1968:249).

Most nationalists disagreed with Gandhi's opposition to mecha-

Figure 24. Children dressed in khadi *display a chromolithograph, of the sort used in India for veneration and worship, showing the stages of Gandhi's life expressed in sartorial transformations. Clockwise, starting from the lower left, we see Gandhi as a law student in London and next, still in Western dress, during the early years of his stay in South Africa. For his* satyaghraha *campaign in South Africa, he devised his first non-Western costume. At the upper left, Gandhi wears the turban of the Gujarati peasant as part of the distinctly Indian garb he chose for his return to India. He soon replaced the turban with a non-regional "Gandhi cap," adopted by his followers but abandoned by Gandhi in favor of the ascetic garb he wore from 1921 until the end of his life. Photo by Brian Brake from Magnum*

nized industry. Many, including Jawaharlal Nehru, believed industrialization crucial for India's economic well-being. Few felt Gandhi's love for the purity and simplicity of coarse white *khadi*. Jawaharlal Nehru's sister Vijayalakshmi Pandit thought *khadi* rough and drab. She felt deprived to have to wear a wedding sari of *khadi*, though it had been spun and woven by Kasturbai Gandhi and dyed the traditional Kashmiri pink. Their father Motilal Nehru, at the meeting of the Congress Working Committee in Delhi during November 1921, burst out laughing when he heard Gandhi say that a person must know hand-spinning in order to participate in civil disobedience (Nanda 1958:235). In a letter to his son, the elder Nehru spoke of the *khadi* movement as one of Gandhi's hobbies.

Despite their disagreement, the Nehrus and other nationalist leaders supported hand-spinning and *khadi* because they recognized its symbolic and economic importance in the programs of *swadeshi*, boycott, and noncooperation. Mrs. Pandit noted the effects of wearing *khadi* "Gandhi caps," *kurtas*, and *dhotis*: She could no longer detect the social class of the visitors to her family's home. The uniform was a leveler, all Congressmen were the same (Pandit 1979:82). Accommodations were made for intranational variation: *dhotis* for Hindus, *pyjamas* (trousers) for Muslims, turbans distinctive for Sikhs or southern Brahmins. *Khadi*, the fabric of nationalism, transcended and encompassed these distinctions. Gandhi had taught his followers that costume can transform social and political identities. When Gandhi, clothed in loincloth and *chadar*, was received by the Viceroy Lord Reading in 1921, his followers (and his opponents) also saw that costume can be used to dominate and structure a social event. The most important result of those meetings was that Gandhi, wearing his opposition to English values and representing the people of India, was accepted to negotiate as an equal with the representatives of the British Empire in India. Gandhi forced the Empire to compromise its standards and thus demonstrated the power of the freedom movement he led.

By 1921, all Congressmen were dressed in *khadi*. The Governor of Bombay Presidency, C.R. Das, made *khadi* the uniform of civic employees. From July 1922, no member of Congress was allowed to wear imported cloth, and dues were to be paid in hand-spun yarn instead of cash. Hand-spinning and *khadi* had become a fixture in the freedom movement. Economic revitalization and self-government would be accomplished through mass organization, carried on by *khadi*-clad Congress workers promoting indigenous industries and mass action by teaching spinning to everyone, spreading the boycott of foreign products to the most remote villages, and preparing the way for mass civil disobedience.

Khadi had become, in Nehru's words, "the livery of freedom."

REFERENCES CITED

Ashe, Geoffrey
    1968   Gandhi. New York: Stein and Day.

Bayly, C.A.
    1986   The Origins of Swadeshi (Home Industry): Cloth and Indian So-
            ciety, 1700-1930. In The Social Life of Things. Arjun Appadurai,
            ed. Cambridge: Cambridge University Press.

Bean, Susan S.
    1988   Spinning Independence. In Making Things in South Asia:
            Proceedings of the South Asia Regional Studies Seminar.
            Michael Meister, ed. Philadelphia: University of Pennsylvania.

Chandra, Bipin
    1965   Indian Nationalists and the Drain, 1880-1905. Indian Economic
            and Social History Review 2(2):103-44.
    1966   The Rise and Growth of Economic Nationalism in India. New
            Delhi.
    1968   Reinterpretations of Nineteenth Century Indian Economic His-
            tory. Indian Economic and Social History Review 5:35-75.

Chatterji, Basudev
    1980   The Abolition of the Cotton Excise, 1925: A Study in Imperial
            Priorities. Indian Economic and Social History Review
            17(4):355-80.
    1981   Business and Politics in the 1930s: Lancashire and the Making of
            the Indo-British Trade Agreement. Modern Asian Studies
            15:527-74.

Chaudhuri, K.N.
    1968   India's International Economy in the 19th Century. Modern
            Asian Studies 2:31-50.
    1978   The Trading World of Asia and the English East India Company
            1660-1760. Cambridge: Cambridge University Press.

Cohn, Bernard
    1988   Cloth, Clothes, and Colonialism: India in the Nineteenth Cen-
            tury. (This volume).

Dewey, Clive
    1978   The Eclipse of the Lancashire Lobby and the Concession of Fiscal
            Autonomy to India. In C. Dewey and A.G. Hopkins, eds. The
            Imperial Impact. London: Althone Press.

Dutt, Romesh Chunder
    1968   Romesh Chunder Dutt. Delhi: Government of India, Ministry of
            Information and Broadcasting.
    1901,1903   The Economic History of India, 2 vols. London.
    1906   India Under Early British Rule. London: Kegan Paul

Erikson, Erik
  1969   Gandi's Truth. New York: W.W. Norton.

Fischer, Louis
  1982(1951) The Life of Mahatma Gandhi. London: Granada.

Gadgil, D.R.
  1942   The Industrial Evolution of India in Recent Times. Calcutta.

Gandhi. M.K.
  1922(1908) Indian Home Rule. Madras: Ganesh & Co.
  1941   Economics of Khadi. Ahmedabad: Navajivan Press.
  1957   An Autobiography: the Story of My Experiments with
  (1927-29) Truth. Boston: Beacon Press.

Gandhi, Prabudas
  1957   My Childhood with Gandhiji. Ahmedabad: Navajivan Press.

Ganguli, B.N.
  1965   Dadabhai Naoroji and the Mechanism of External Drain. Indian
           Economic and Social History Review 2(2):85–102.

Gittinger, Mattiebelle
  1982   Master Dyers to the World. Washington, D.C.: Textile Museum.

Gold, Gerald
  1983   Gandhi: A Pictorial Biography. New York: New Market Press.

Irwin, John
  1962   Indian Textiles in Historical Perspective. Marg XV(4).

Irwin, John and K. Brett
  1970   The Origins of Chintz. London: Victoria and Albert Museum.

Jaju, Shrikrishnadas
  1951   The Ideology of Charka. Tirupur.

Masani, Rustom Pestonji
  1939   Dadabhai Naoroji: The Grand Old Man of India. London: Allen &
           Unwin.

Mehta, Ved
  1977   Mahatma Gandhi and His Apostles. New York: Penguin Books.

Nanda, B.R.
  1958   Mahatma Gandhi. Boston: Beacon Press.

Naoroji, Dadabhai
  1887   Essays, Speeches and Writings. C.L. Parekh, ed.
           Bombay.

Pandit, Vijayalakshmi
  1979   The Scope of Happiness. New York: Crown.

Pradhan, G.P. and A.K. Bhagwat
  1958   Lokamanya Tilak. Bombay.

Sarkar, Sumit
    1973   The Swadeshi Movement in Bengal, 1903–1908. Calcutta.

Sharma, Jagadish
    1955,1968   Mahatma Gandhi: A Descriptive Bibliography.

Sheean, Vincent
    1949   Lead Kindly Light. New York: Random House.

Sitaramayya, Pattabhi
    1969   History of the Indian National Congress, vol. 1 (1885–1935).
            Delhi: S. Chand.

Wolpert, Stanley
    1962   Tilak and Gokhale. Berkeley: University of California Press.

12. The Changing Fortunes of Three Archaic Japanese Textiles

LOUISE ALLISON CORT

 This paper traces the history and present uses of three long vegetable fibers[1] in Japanese and Okinawan cloth production, exploring their survival in the poorest and most remote mountain regions, their symbolic value in sacred state rituals, and their current role in nationalist and folkloric revivals. By situating the three fibers in their historical and ecological context, and by describing the labor process through which they are produced, the relationship between their symbolic and their material aspects becomes evident. Central to this relationship are the long traditions of female processors and weavers of such fibers, the honor accruing to women for participation in these tasks, and the belief that, through the textile arts, women mediate the spiritual well-being of the larger communities.

Mention the textiles of Japan, and the fibers that come to mind immediately are silk (an animal fiber) and cotton (a seed fiber), not the long vegetable fibers that will be discussed here. During the heyday of textile production in Japan throughout the Edo period (A.D. 1615–1868), the efforts of professional weavers and dyers, supported by an elaborate system of raw-material procurement and finished-product distribution, created an array of fine silk and cotton fabrics.[2]

NOTE: A glossary of Japanese written forms of critical textile terminology is printed on p. 415.

No less appealing than the sumptuously tinted and patterned silks were the cottons, characteristically dyed with indigo augmented by other vegetable dyes in solids, stripes, and plaids, and patterns produced by ikat-dying (*kasuri*)[3] or stencil-dyeing. While silks were reserved for luxury garments, cottons made up the work clothes and everyday costumes of most Japanese.

Silk had been known in Japan from the bronze age (Yayoi period, circa 200 B.C.–A.D. 250), but cotton began to be cultivated in Japan only in the fifteenth century. Until that time, the staple fiber for commoners' clothing was the bast fiber[4] called *asa*. *Asa* is a generic term, often translated erroneously as "flax" or "linen," that embraces a range of varieties of grass-bast fibers, of which the most common in Japan were hemp and ramie or "China grass."[5] The fiber known as "linen" or "flax"[6] was not brought to Japan until the eighteenth century (Akashi 1976:123). Even *asa* was a relative latecomer to Japan, arriving perhaps by the end of the neolithic period. During the ten millennia of Japan's neolithic age, coarser fibers had been exploited as the earliest material for cords, ropes, nets, baskets and—finally—woven cloth. Those fibers were the bast fibers of various wild trees and vines that grew on the slopes of Japan's abundant mountains. It may be that weaving was practiced only after the introduction of *asa*, the technique and the new fiber arriving simultaneously, and was than applied to the older tree-bast fibers, which had been used until then only in baskets, mats, and nets.[7]

The introduction of *asa* cultivation, processing, and weaving techniques, probably from the Korean peninsula, quickly made the tree-bast fibers less desirable for cloth-making. The grass-bast fibers of the *asa* group could be cultivated from seed in fields and, when harvested, could be split, softened, and spun into thread in a comparatively simple way. The tougher fibers of the tree-bast group required not only the physical effort of gathering them from mountain slopes but also a longer process of soaking, rotting, boiling with wood-ash (lye), and occasionally beating before the tough fibers could be extracted.[8] At that stage, moreover, the truly time-consuming task began: As the stiff fibers could not be spun into a continuous thread, the individual fibers had to be split and then joined end to end, by twisting or tying, to make a thread. (An individual fiber might, however, be as much as twelve feet long.) When the tree-bast fibers could at last be woven, they produced fabrics that were usually darker in color and rougher to the touch than *asa*.

Logically, the tedious processing of tree-bast fibers should have been abandoned at the earliest possible moment. Yet, some two millenia after the introduction of *asa* to Japan, tree-bast fibers are still used. While *asa* and then cotton replaced them as clothing for commoners, the tree-bast fibers and related leaf fibers survived in two extreme situations. At one extreme, they were retained for their symbolic value in the most sacred state rituals, especially the rites for installing a new emperor. At the other, they continued to serve in clothing for inhabitants of the poorest and most remote mountain regions, where restricted land area and severe climate precluded cultivation of other fibers, where hard labor required rough, durable garments, and where wild materials were important sources of cash income. In recent decades, just as they seemed about to lose even those tenuous identities, their use has been revived in contexts that recall the association of certain long vegetable fibers with the most ancient core of Japanese culture. Their symbolic power has revived amid a widespread prosperity that has obliterated their last claim to practical usefulness.

In this paper, I will focus on three of these traditional long vegetable fibers.[9] I have selected these three fibers because I have had field contact with the people who still gather, process, and weave them. The first fiber I consider is that produced either from *kōzo* (*Broussonetia kazinoki*) or from *kaji* (*Broussonetia papyrifera*). From a very early time the two fibers, both from plants of the mulberry family, were considered to be interchangeable, especially as sources of fiber for the utility cloth called *tafu*, meaning simply "thick cloth." Yet mulberry-plant fibers were indispensable for imperial rituals as well.

The second fiber I discuss is *kuzu* (*Pueraria hirsuta*), a vine yielding a lustrous fiber that became important for use in various ceremonial garments.[10] The third fiber is *bashō* (thread banana, *Musa liukiuensis*). Properly speaking, thread-banana fiber is not a tree-bast but a leaf fiber, although the two types of long vegetable fibers are closely related on the basis of morphology.[11] In the hierarchy of Okinawan textiles, thread-banana cloth occupied the same low position with regard to *asa*, cotton, and silk as did the mulberry-plant fibers in Japan. After a long period under Japanese trade influence, the independent kingdom of Okinawa became a Japanese domain in the seventeenth century, and thread-banana cloth became tribute cloth. The post–World War II revival of this fabric has a specifically political

context: Reassertion of the independence of Okinawan culture from
that of Japan.

MULBERRY-PLANT FIBERS AS SACRED THREADS
AND SACRED CLOTH

Japanese mythology and early literature show a range of conceptions concerning bast fiber and cloth that were embodied in early
patterns of worship. The contrasting properties of the various tree-
bast and grass-bast fibers, and the various stages of processing the
fibers as thread and as cloth, were expressed in ritual pairings of
white (mulberry-fiber) and blue-green (asa) "cloth offerings" or of
mulberry-plant thread and woven cloth. The two-color "cloth offerings" adorned the Shinto altar and were indispensable components
of imperial accession rituals. The latter pair, held during private
worship performed by women for their households, suggests that
both thread and woven cloth from the humble tree-bast fibers were
understood as essential to human welfare.[12]

Of the two plants in the mulberry family, botanists believe that
kōzo is indigenous to Japan, since it grows wild throughout the islands. Kaji, however, seems to have been introduced at some point,
since it is found wild only in the two southerly islands of Kyushu
and Shikoku. (Kaji grows wild throughout Southeast Asia and the
Pacific Islands.) The Kogoshūi ("Gleanings from Old Tales"), a document written in A.D. 807 by an advocate of the Imbe (Imibe) family
of hereditary court ritualists, alleges that both asa (hemp, ramie,
etc.) and kaji were introduced to Japan by the founders of the Imbe
clan; presumably the clan ancestors migrated from the continent
into Kyushu toward the end of the neolithic period (Okamura
1977:251). Since the fibers of both kōzo and kaji can be used for both
weaving and papermaking, from an early date they were thought
of as interchangeable, and the term kōzo is often used to indicate
both.

The most informative early source on the uses of textiles in
Japan is the Manyōshū, the first anthology of Japanese verse, completed around A.D. 759 and containing some 4500 poems, mostly
from the seventh and early eighth centuries. The Manyōshū poems,
rich in allusions to details of everyday life, indicate that silk,
whether imported or locally made, had become the desired luxury

cloth. *Asa*, not to mention other bast-fibers, had been relegated to commoners' clothing and papermaking.[13] Yet the *Manyōshū* also shows that bast-fiber fabrics were far from unimportant, whether as ordinary clothing or in special ritual use. The complex of textile- and garment-related terms that appears in the *Manyōshū* suggests that *asa* and the tree-bast-fiber cloths were often paired and were thought of as complementary elements of a set.

Fabric woven from the mulberry-plant fibers was called "*taku* cloth," (*takununo*; in compound words, pronounced *tae*), from the early term for the fiber, *taku*. One *Manyōshū* poem (XVI:3791–3) describes a man wearing "the cloth of *tae* tissue" and "the handwoven cloth of sun-dried hemp" wrapped "like a double skirt" that proved attractive to "many a country lass from her lowly cottage"[14] (whereas his imported silk garments attracted the notice of the court ladies).

Manyōshū poems mention various kinds of *taku* fabrics, cords and ropes, caps, and bedding. Through the literary device called the pillow word,[15] all such *taku* products were associated with the word "white" or with other white objects. Bleached mulberry-fiber cloth was known more specifically as *shirotae*, "white *taku* cloth," and was likened in poetry to snow, clouds, waves, and feathers. At the other end of the spectrum was *aratae* or "rough *taku* cloth." In fact *aratae* designated tree-bast fibers other than mulberry, such as mountain wisteria, which even with bleaching did not lose their brownish cast (Okamura 1977:118).

A second pair of opposites emerging in *Manyōshū* usage consisted of *nigitae*, "smooth cloth," and *aratae*, "rough cloth." The word *nigitae* was written with the character meaning "peace" or "harmony"—the same character that also appeared in Yamato, the name of the state that developed by the seventh century through the "harmonization" of various rival clans. The similarity of the two terms is probably not coincidental. *Nigitae* signifies finely-woven fabric made soft and lustrous by fulling—prolonged beating with a wooden mallet (the "pacification" of the cloth?). According to the *Kogoshūi* of A.D. 807, *nigitae* could be woven from either *asa* or mulberry fiber, and it was used specifically for sacred garments (Okamura 1977:252).

Closely related to *nigitae* is the term *nigite*, meaning folded fiber or cloth offerings. *Nigite* offerings were an indispensable element in the basic form of the Shinto altar. An altar was constructed on any site that was to be used to perform a sacred act. A coarse mat was spread over the clean-swept ground and a special eight-legged table placed upon it. A branch of a glossy-leaved evergreen tree was stood upright on the table, enclosed by a rope tied to posts at the four corners of the table, and draped with the cloth offerings, or *nigite*. These offerings were of two types, white and blue-green.[16]

The *Kogoshūi* makes clear that the white cloth offerings were made from mulberry fiber (*kaji*), while the blue-green cloths were made of *asa*.[17] It seems probable that at first both types of "cloth offerings" were made out of unwoven strands of fiber, although later they came to be made of woven cloth or of paper made from the same fibers (Okamura 1977:86–89). The paired fiber offerings appear on the archetypal altar, the one described in one of the most important Shinto myths. After the unruly male deity Susanoō disrupted with various acts of desecration the work of his sister, the sun goddess Amaterasu—planting the rice fields, performing the harvest festival, and weaving the garments for all the gods—the angry goddess retreated into a cave, plunging the world into darkness. The efforts of the other gods to placate her wrath began with setting up a great altar using a five-hundred-branched evergreen tree ornamented with a necklace of sacred jewels, a sacred mirror, and the special white and blue green cloth offerings. The cloth offerings are said to have been supplied by the god Ama no Hiwashi, divine ancestor of the Imbe clan which became associated with ritual production of sacred cloth for the imperial court (Tsunoda, de Bary, and Keene 1958:30–31).

Yet another term found in *Manyōshū* verses is *yū*, literally, "tree batting."[18] Like the term for "cloth offerings," *yū* seems to have designated not woven cloth but thread—specifically, according to the *Kogoshūi*, the thread of the mulberry fiber *kaji* from which *nigitae* cloth was produced. The term *yū* meaning "tree batting" is related to a character with the same pronunciation meaning "pure, sacred" (sometimes used to write the name of the Imbe clan, hereditary producers of *nigitae* cloth as detailed in the *Kogoshūi*). *Yū* is also related to another homophone meaning "to tie," which was not only the function of a length of fiber or thread, but also a term appearing in the names of gods associated with growth and fecundity (Okamura 1977:66). *Manyōshū* poems indicate that a loop of this mulberry-fiber thread was always worn to tie back garment sleeves when worshipping the gods.[19] One poem (III:443) tells of a woman worshipping while holding the thread in one hand and the woven cloth in the other. The presence of the thread may indicate at once her "pure" state as she performs the worship and the nature of her ritual request.

Other *Manyōshū* poems confirm that household worship was a responsibility of the senior woman of the house. When the first fruits were offered on the night of a special harvest ritual (*Niinamesai*, "Festival for the First Tasting"), men were shut outside (Ellwood 1973:72). (By contrast, worship at the state level was conducted by hereditary male priests.) To hold up thread and cloth for worship was to offer the fruits of women's work. Various tribute laws of the early Yamato state exacted a certain quantity of woven cloth—varieties of bast-fiber cloth—and a certain amount of rice from each household, and the "loom duty" was specifically the woman's (Toyota 1965:249). (Again, by contrast, luxury silks for use in the court were woven by male weavers at government-operated provincial or central workshops.) Just as the goddess Amaterasu wove to make garments for all the gods, so each woman wove to clothe her family (and to pay the tax).

HARMONIZING OF OPPOSING ELEMENTS IN SACRED CLOTH

The various pairings of tree-bast and grass-bast fibers in early literature and in religious ritual show a conscious mingling of ancient and recent, indigenous and continental elements in the material culture. At the political level, the unification of Japan was achieved by a clan known as Yamato. The Yamato state, arising in western Japan and strengthened by close contact with continental technology, succeeded in winning the allegiance of several dozen independent tribal groups. The special accession ritual performed by each new Yamato emperor incorporated the pairings of cloth fibers and other materials in a manner that underscored the emperor's power to unify those disparate cultural elements.

Women's responsibility for both household weaving and household worship reflected an ancient order—the order of the neolithic period. This same encapsulation of neolithic patterns appeared at the state level, in the harvest festivals that were part of the cycle of annual rituals performed for the welfare of the Yamato state. The most important was the annual offering of the first fruits (*Niinamesai*). At the beginning of each emperor's reign, however, the first-fruits ritual was replaced once only by the *Daijōsai*, "Great Offering Ritual," wherein the new emperor asserted his authority by undertaking the ritual usually performed by priests. Cloth figured importantly in the items that were offered. The *Kogoshūi* claimed that the Imbe clan's responsibility for providing sacred cloth began with the god Ama no Hiwashi's hanging the two kinds of cloth offerings on the lower branches of the archetypal altar. Subsequently, according to that text, certain Imbe-clan descendants of Ama no Hiwashi were charged with the responsibility of producing cloth from mulberry-plant fiber and *asa*. As fertile ground on which to cultivate the plants, those clan members were given the province of Awa (now Tokushima Prefecture, on the island of Shikoku). In the years when the imperial accession ritual occurred, they supplied cloth to the court (Okamura 1977:253).

In this manner the *Kogoshūi* of A.D. 807 asserted the ancient prerogatives of the Awa branch of the Imbe clan. That text was written, however, to defend the family rights against the rise in stature of the other major priestly house, the Nakatomi, following reorganization of the government by the Taihō code of A.D. 702. The Nakatomi clan and the Imbe clan supposedly shared responsibilities in the Department of Worship, the members of the Nakatomi clan reciting prayers and the members of the Imbe clan providing all materials for ritual use. But by the time of the accession ceremony of A.D. 927, the Imbe clan was supplying only mulberry-fiber cloth, while the Nakatomi clan was providing the cloth woven from *asa*. By the time of that ceremony, moreover, a shift in terminology had occurred, reflecting a further loss of status by the Imbe clan and the cloth that they produced. The term *aratae*, "rough cloth," had come to include mulberry-fiber cloth together with other coarser cloths made from tree-bast fibers, while *nigitae*, "smooth cloth," excluded mulberry-fiber cloth and referred to *asa* alone.

The *Daijōsai* ceremony took place during one night in late autumn, following months of preparation.[20] Two identical buildings were constructed within the imperial palace grounds, using unpeeled logs and thatch recalling ancient forms of architecture. They were the Yuki Hall to the east and the Suki Hall to the west. Meanwhile, two ritually-designated fields (the eastern Yuki Field and the western Suki Field) were used to grow the offertory rice and other grain. Some of the rice was offered as grain; the rest was fermented to make rice wine. Of the wine, half was left white and half was tinted black with ash of a certain bitter wood. Elsewhere, craftspeople chosen by divination prepared the mulberry-fiber thread and woven cloth to be provided by members of the Imbe clan[21] and the *asa* to be sent by the Nakatomi clan.

Before the ceremony, within the inner chamber of the Yuki and Suki Halls, couches were constructed of piled mats. At the head of each couch stood two lamps, one black and one white, and two baskets of cloth, a black one containing "rough cloth" and a white one holding "smooth cloth." A dais held offerings of cooked rice and millet (a major foodstuff prior to the introduction of rice at the close of the neolithic period), placed on oak leaves, and of white and black sake. The emperor performed identical rituals of offering within each hall, but he went first to the Yuki Hall as night was deepening, then to the Suki Hall when dawn was approaching.[22]

The new emperor's offering of paired "rough cloth" and "smooth cloth" suggests a multilevel symbolism at work in the ritual for the harmonizing of the contrasting worlds of rough and smooth, dark and light, east and west, even native and continental.[23] The ultimate purpose of the *Daijōsai* was to "pacify" through harmonizing the "rough spirit" (*aramitama*) and the "smooth spirit" (*nigimitama*), whether those counterbalancing forces were interpreted as resting within an individual, or within the nation, or in the characters of the major gods, the rough male deity Susanoō and the serene sun goddess Amaterasu. Each of the two types of cloth belonged to a cluster of associated objects and concepts. *Aratae*, coarse tree-bast cloth, was linked to black rice wine, millet, black basket, black lamp, the Yuki Hall, night, the east, the unruly Susanoō, the rough spirit. In the context of Japan, where advanced clans spread from west to east, the east always connoted the holdout of unconverted barbarians. Contrasting images were associated with *nigitae*, fine bleached and fulled grass-bast cloth: white rice wine, rice, white basket, white lamp, the Suki Hall, morning, the west, the calm and radiant Amaterasu, the smooth spirit. The Yamato state, personified in the emperor, owed its power to having harmonized two groups of opposing elements: The older indigenous elements of the neolithic society (rough tree-bast fibers, millet) and the advanced continental elements (including rice and *asa*) brought by the Yayoi cultural invasion, which spread over Japan from west to east.

While the *Daijōsai* ceremony served, on the ritual level, to reestablish the desired balance, on the cultural level it continued the process whereby the old elements were gradually overwhelmed and obliterated by the new. By the time of the accession ceremony held in A.D. 927, the members of the ancient Imbe clan had already lost their right to present *asa*, as we have seen. Eventually the Imbe clan lost even its right to offer "rough cloth" of mulberry fiber; the last presentation of *aratae* from the Imbe of Awa is recorded for the *Daijōsai* ceremony of 1339. Thereafter all offertory cloth came from the Nakatomi (by then known as the Fujiwara) domain.[24]

In 1915, and again in 1928, the *Daijōsai* ceremony was enacted according to the ancient records, and the old Awa province was called upon once again to supply the appropriate "rough cloth." A special weaving shed was constructed on the grounds of the shrine honoring the ancestral deity of the Imbe clan, Ama no Hiwashi, and unmarried girls were selected as weavers.

Apparently no effort was made to weave with mulberry fiber, however: in 1915 bleached hemp (coarse *asa*) was supplied, and in 1928 the warp had to be changed to finer *asa* in the form of spun ramie, because the hemp was unmanageable for the young weavers whose experience was limited to silk and cotton (Okamura 1977: 263–68).

"THICK CLOTH" AND RURAL SURVIVAL

At the other extreme from its incorporation into imperial ritual, mulberry-plant fiber continued to be processed and woven in the most mountainous and resource-poor areas of Japan. Production of utilitarian "thick cloth" was women's work. In this century, mountain women have found "thick cloth" to be a means of participating in an engulfing cash economy and, more recently, a way to cope emotionally with the gradual depopulation and economic devaluation of mountain communities.

Despite the gradual disappearance of mulberry-fiber cloth from ritual use, the need for it never disappeared entirely from everyday life. Even the court required a copious supply of what is simply termed "cloth" (*nuno*) in records of tribute being sent from the sixty-two provinces. Thirty provinces sent "cloth" (presumably indicating tree-bast fibers, since *asa* is listed separately), and those provinces lay mainly in the east, far from the capital of Kyoto and relatively backward in economic development (Toyota 1965:248–51). By the

Edo period the standard term for such cloth was "thick cloth".[25] The actual fiber used to make this "thick cloth" depended upon the region, and even coarse *asa* or coarse cotton cloth was sometimes designated by the term (Yanagida 1976:24; Gotō 1976). One characteristic common to all varieties of "thick cloth" was that it was woven on a simple body-tension or backstrap loom, whereas commercial weaving carried on in urban workshops used the floor loom. The floor loom was less tiring to the weaver and more efficient, but it was unsuited to weaving "thick cloth" because the loom's constant tension and the long distance between beams tended to pull apart twist-joined warp threads.

The rustic "thick cloth" attracted the attention of local scholars of the late eighteenth and early nineteenth centuries who traveled extensively to document regional rural culture.[26] The Shinto scholar Motoori Norinaga (1730–1801), aware of ancient ritual uses of the fiber called *yū*, was pleased to find the same fiber still being used to make "thick cloth" in the province of Awa. He wrote admiringly, "The color is white and the thread is strong. When the cloth is washed, it does not need starching, and with every washing it becomes whiter" (Gotō 1974:122). In the mid-nineteenth century, a local Awa scholar elaborated on the cloth's virtues:

> . . . [T]*afu* is made from mulberry bast and is not a kind of *asa* cloth. It is woven in [several counties in Awa province] and is also produced in quantities within Tosa province. In my youth it was bleached and dyed with family crests and was used commonly for clothing, but the taste of today's world has turned to gorgeousness, and "thick cloth" is worn by young people only when they are learning fencing. One does not see people wearing it regularly. It is used only for bags to hold rice and barley, or for edgings on tatami mats, or for doorway banners. . . .
>
> In the mountain district of Iya, people who are now elderly wore "thick cloth" both summer and winter in the days of their youth. An extremely cold winter was expressed by the fact that one had to layer five or seven "thick cloth" garments for warmth, and in the dialect of that area occur references to "six-layer chill" and "seven-layer chill." On my visit to those mountains in the ninth month of 1842, I saw that most people have now changed to cotton garments. . . .(Gotō 1974:122).

Such texts show that, by the early nineteenth century, the use of cotton for commoners' garments had become so commonplace that the very name "thick cloth" was unknown to most people. One of the last areas where "thick cloth" continued to be woven for garments was the mountainous interior of Awa province (now Tokushima prefecture). One such locale was the Kitō district, comprised of small, isolated hamlets lining the narrow valley of the Naka river which flows around the south flank of Shikoku's tallest peak, Mount Tsurugi. Out of Kitō's present area of 232.08 square kilometers, only 0.7% is arable land. Mountain products, including timber and charcoal, have always been the main items for tribute or cash income.

Throughout the Edo period, the Kitō district was controlled by the Hachisuka domain, based in the coastal city of Tokushima. Aside from the meager area set aside for slash-and-burn cultivation to support the local population, the land was domain-owned forest, and the residents lived in extreme poverty. Over half were landless, and their numbers increased as the domain steadily attempted to turn more land into forest. In addition, mulberry fibers were claimed by the domain for use in papermaking and were collected as a tax item from every household. An undated document from Kitō local officials warned the domain that any further increase in demand for mulberry fiber would deprive the residents of fiber even for essential clothing, without which they could not work in the domain forests (Takeuchi 1982:8).

Gotō Shōichi (1897–1980), the noted textile historian born in Tokushima, remembered during his childhood—when all urban commoners wore indigo-dyed cotton garments—seeing the "strange sight" of mountain men coming to town in their stiff brown costumes (Gotō 1976). Cotton could never replace "thick cloth" for work clothing in the mountains, where the costume of "thick cloth" jacket tied at the waist with a straw rope and "thick cloth" trousers or leggings repelled brambles and twigs. Much-washed "thick cloth" became soft and felted; the older fabric was used for inner garments, and examples are known of "thick cloth" loincloths passed down for three generations (Kawabata 1982). Mulberry fiber was also used for all other fabric requirements of the mountain household, including bedding and mosquito nets (urban households used indigo-dyed asa mosquito nets). Perhaps most important were the "thick cloth" bags used to transport precious grain and seed on foot, using shoulder poles, over steep, slippery mountain paths. Grain bags were the last "thick cloth" items used in the mountains.[27] The ability to process and weave "thick cloth" was a

*Figure 25. Mountain work clothing from Tokushima prefec-
ture, made of mulberry (kōzo) fiber in the early twentieth
century. Photo by Mary Dusenbury*

prerequisite for marriage. Girls began learning to prepare thread
around the age of ten, and by the age of fifteen they were weaving
(Horiuchi 1982:98).

Statistics for "thick cloth" production in the Kitō area are available from the mid-nineteenth century onward; they show that, from
the turn of the century, the production of the cloth actually increased, despite the decline in its use for garments.[28] This increase
in "thick cloth" production was caused, paradoxically, by the introduction of cotton cloth to the area by itinerant merchants, who were
willing to trade cotton (produced in workshops in Tokushima) for
"thick cloth." The merchants sold the "thick cloth" to urban consumers for use as storage and food processing bags and as indigo-
dyed tatami edging. At certain times, "thick cloth" was worth more,
measure for measure, than cotton, so that the women who wove it
received in exchange not only the equivalent length of cotton but
also a few coins as well. The opportunity of earning cash held a powerful attraction for the residents of the resource-poor mountain villages. The entire recorded production for 1912, 1800 bolts of "thick
cloth," was sent out of the region (Takeuchi 1982:11). The women

used the cotton mainly for their own clothing, while continuing to weave sturdy "thick cloth" workclothes for the men in the household.[29] Not vanity but poverty forced them to do so.

Sakakibara Asa, a Kitō woman born in 1891, grew up in the era when "thick cloth" production was increasing. Like many other girls of the region, she was sent to town to work as a nanny for the children of a middle-class family. A year's service netted her only twenty yen, and Asa realized that she would never prosper through such work. She used her twenty yen to buy bolts of striped cotton from a merchant in a coastal town, and then she peddled the cotton in the mountain villages through which she passed on her way back to Kitō. With the cash earned in that way she bought "thick cloth" in Kitō and sold it to the same merchant.[30] After three years of trading, she had saved 360 yen (Takeuchi 1982:17–18).

Asa also wove "thick cloth" herself. The thread was prepared at night, by the light of the fire in the open hearth, or in spare moments between daytime chores. Some women were even able to twist the thread while walking the mountain paths on their way to the fields. Working steadily every night, it took two weeks to prepare enough thread to weave one bolt of cloth, and two or three days more to weave it (Takeuchi 1982:18–19).

Trading of "thick cloth" for cotton continued into the 1920s; thereafter, women continued to weave it for their own household use, primarily for bags. But production was dying out when World War II created acute shortages of mill cloth and brought "thick cloth" garments back into use. With the return of prosperity in the mid-1950s, "thick cloth" weaving in Kitō seemed to end altogether. But in the 1970s, Sakakibara Asa—whose son was now the mayor of Kitō—was instrumental in reviving the craft one last time. This revival took the form of a village-sponsored social-service program "to make life worth living" for elderly people had lost their integral role in household-based economies, since most of the male heads of households went into the towns and cities to work. Asa and other people old enough to remember the process gathered at the new Hall of Creative Crafts built at the edge of the Naka river. Their students were housewives in their forties and fifties who were also idle now that their children were grown (Takeuchi 1982:12).

At the same time that "thick cloth" weaving was reviving in its original mountain context, it was also transmitted for the first time to an urban setting by the Tokushima weaver Kawabata Fumi (born

1928). Trained in western-style tailoring, Fumi happened to read about Kitō "thick cloth" while recuperating from a serious accident. Once she regained the use of her hands, she went to Kitō to learn mulberry-fiber processing and weaving from one of the elderly women in the village. Fumi's husband became involved in cultivating both *kaji* for fiber and indigo for dye. Fumi weaves mainly *obis*, finding the stiff cloth well suited to use for the wide kimono sash. She exhibits her ikat-dyed pieces in the annual Traditional Crafts Exhibitions sponsored by the Ministry of Cultural Affairs. Her customers are middle-class women who enjoy the occasional luxury of wearing a kimono instead of Western garments and who take an interest in patronizing traditional crafts. Some of them are also her students (Kawabata 1982). Thus it seems likely that the "thick cloth" tradition will continue as a curiosity practiced by a few studio weavers. The poverty of its mountain weavers forced it out of use there; the affluence of urban housewives may underwrite its continuation.[31]

SILKEN *KUZU* CLOTH: FROM LUXURY FABRIC TO WALLPAPER

Similar in appearance to silk, cloth made from bast fiber of the *kuzu* vine was produced, like silk, on a commercial rather than household scale, although the labor was done by women. For centuries tied to the economy of the warrior class, *kuzu* cloth producers made a successful transition to the modern economy, only to falter when they could not compete with Korea because of the cost of labor-intensive raw-materials processing. Even the discovery of *kuzu* cloth by the Folk Craft Movement has not managed to secure its survival.

Whereas mulberry-fiber textiles never escaped their association with a primitive standard of living—even when incorporated into the *Daijōsai* ritual of imperial accession—the cloth woven from *kuzu* (called *kuzufu*, *kappu*, or *kuzununo*) was identified early on as a luxury fabric. When finely split, using a needle, the fiber looks almost like raw silk. It shows to best advantage when used as weft only and allowed to lie flat within a fine warp of silk, grass-bast fiber, or cotton. (At an early time *kuzu* was used for both warp and weft,[32] but that technique soon died out, as *kuzu* does not lend itself to the spinning necessary for strong warp threads.)

Crisp and lustrous *kuzu* cloth was the desired fabric for tailoring

Figure 26. An Edo-period warrior's parade jacket made of
kuzufu, *from the mid-nineteenth century; the family crest
of a domain leader is outlined in black silk cord, overlapping
the back seam. Photo by Louise Allison Cort*

special skirt-like trousers (*sashinuki*, gathered at the ankles with silk
cords) worn by male courtiers when playing a kind of kickball called
kemari. The game was a social grace in the court of the Heian period
(A.D. 795–1185), and it continued to be popular among the Kyoto nobility. *Kuzu* cloth was also used by warriors for hunting costumes,
as lining for chain-mail armor jackets, and for trousers to be worn
on horseback. *Kuzu*-cloth trousers worn for travel were dyed with
a special black dye that made them water-repellent. *Kuzu* cloth was
ideal for the straight-lined silhouette of the sleeveless jacket and
trouser combination (*kamishimo*) worn by warriors on formal occasions (grass-bast fibers could also be used for such garments) and
for the crisp, crest-emblazoned jackets worn in summer processions.

Kuzu cloth became associated centuries ago with the town of

Kakegawa in ancient Tōtōmi province (now Shizuoka prefecture). The first known mention of the fabric in connection with the place occurs in a poem by the courtier Fujiwara no Tamesuke (1260–1328): 00.7501.25

> This too is a skill of the place—
> In every gateway they are preparing *kuzu* cloth:
> The town of Kakegawa.

The mere availability of *kuzu* was not a deciding factor, as the vine grows wild throughout the Japanese Islands. However, the town of Kakegawa lay along the coastal trunk road (*Tōkaidō*) connecting the imperial capital of Kyoto to the eastern provinces—to the important city of Kamakura, headquarters for the military government (A.D. 1185–1333), and later to the capital at Edo. Tamesuke was on his way to Kamakura when he composed his poem. Kakegawa was a "station" along the highway where travellers could expect to find food and shelter. They could also find protection. At the beginning of the fifteenth century, a powerful local warrior built a fortified residence there. It was replaced by a larger scale castle erected at the end of the sixteenth century. During the Edo period, the castle was occupied by a succession of warrior families (Takahashi 1975:5).

Under the policy of the Tokugawa government, designed to keep its rivals off guard, all domain leaders were obliged to spend fixed periods of time in Edo. On their journeys to and from the capital many used the *Tōkaidō*. Commoners going on pilgrimages also traversed the road. In Kakegawa they replaced their worn-out traveling trousers or bought bolts of cloth as souvenirs and distributed them throughout the country. *Kuzu* cloth is listed as a noteworthy Kakegawa product in the 1712 compendium of famous local products from various provinces, *Wakan Sansai Zue* (Kodama 1965:240–41). Woodblock prints of the early nineteenth century show *kuzu*-cloth shops lining both sides of the road through Kakegawa; those shops are still there, although the cloth business has diminished.

Production of *kuzu* cloth during the Edo period was controlled by the Kakegawa domain as an important source of income, as well as for use in regular presentations to the government and to other domain leaders. An economic survey of 208 villages within the domain, carried out in 1805–06, listed as the sources of *kuzu* fiber the villages of Kamisaigō and Kurami. Both villages lay in the mountainous interior. The *kuzu* harvested there was sent to Kakegawa, where townswomen prepared the fiber and wove the cloth (Saida 1973:56–57,74).

The *kuzu* plant with all its uses was the subject of a special study, *Seikatsuroku* ("Record of Processing *Kuzu*"), published in 1828 by the agricultural advocate Ōgura Nagatsune. While Ōgura recorded the use of *kuzu* fiber for cloth, he focused on the edible starch processed from the root as an emergency food in famine years. *Kuzu* starch had long been a staple in Japanese cooking, especially for sweets, since it did not become gummy when cold and, according to principles of Chinese medicine, its yin root nature was believed to counteract the yang acidity of sugar.[33] A sweet made from *kuzu* had been a famous product of the station-town of Nissaka, not far from Kakegawa, since the sixteenth century.

Ōgura's tract gives detailed instruction for processing *kuzu* fiber for weaving, as it was done in Kakegawa, noting that fiber preparation is the key to the quality of the finished cloth. Cotton was the usual warp fiber. Cloth of different weaves and grades was woven in lengths suitable for trousers, for formal jacket-and-trouser sets, for procession jackets, and for other specialized garments, and it could be purchased plain or dyed. Lavender was the popular color in 1828, but nineteenth-century sample books show that blue-green, gray, brown, and beige were also available. *Kuzu* cloth intended for children's summer trousers was woven in a striped pattern. Cheap grades of *kuzu* cloth were dyed with stencils to imitate the woven stripes.

The abolition of the warrior domains in 1871 had disastrous effects on the *kuzu*-cloth industry as it was so dependent upon the warrior class. Many merchants went out of business, some selling their remaining stock to lacquerers for use as undercoating on lacquered wooden objects, a function usually served by cheap coarse cloth. The few merchants who hung on tried desperately to discover new uses for their product.

Someone remembered the traditional use of *kuzu* cloth to reinforce the area around the handles of the paper-covered sliding door (*fusuma*) used as room divider and closet door, and had *kuzu* cloth woven in bolts wide enough to cover the door itself. The idea was successful, and cloth for these doors sustained the Kakegawa workshops until around 1900, when the wide cloth was further adapted to use as wallpaper—"grass cloth"—for export to Europe and North

America. That enormously popular product was the mainstay of production until 1960. Experiments with dyes developed methods for using powdered mineral pigments that would not fade. In the prewar years, and again after the war, annual production reached 100,000 bolts.

After the Japanese occupation of Korea in 1910, the *kuzu* plant had been introduced to check erosion on deforested slopes, and Korea also began processing the fiber and supplying it for use in Kakegawa. A booklet printed in 1954 by the Kakegawa *kuzu*-cloth merchants' association reflects uneasiness at being dependent upon Korea to supply the bulk of *kuzu* fiber (Anon. 1954:3). The booklet was designed to instruct farmers who wanted to undertake *kuzu* processing as a side-business, with the hope of increasing the numbers of local producers. The move came too late, however, for Korea had already begun producing its own "grass cloth," and a strike by Korean fiber suppliers against the Kakegawa merchants dealt a fatal blow to the Japanese grass-cloth business. Only a handful of Kakegawa shops continue to operate, producing *kuzu* cloth for obis, handbags, and souvenir items in the "folk craft" idiom.[34]

Kuzu fiber is still processed in the villages mentioned in the survey of 1805. The work is done by elderly farm women who receive extremely low pay. (In 1976 the women who split and knotted the fibers into threads received only 20 yen per bundle, but one kilogram of treated *kuzu* fiber—perhaps one hundred bundles—cost 18,000 yen from the retail merchant.) The merchant is responsible for organizing the production process: He hires women to gather and prepare the fiber, purchases it and distributes it to other women who prepare the thread,[35] pays for the thread, and has it woven in his workshop.

In the 1930s, the beauty of *kuzu* cloth came to the attention of the small group of connoisseurs of traditional Japanese "folk crafts" known as the Folk Craft Movement. Their leader, Yanagi Sōetsu (1889–1961), eulogized *kuzu* cloth as follows:

> There are few fabrics in which nature itself appears so artlessly. One must acknowledge that people prepare it and people weave it, but human strength is only a small part of it. This cloth was born precisely because *kuzu* has a character that cannot easily be controlled. People do no more than lend their skills in order to articulate its beauty. As a result, one might say that their work

commemorates nature's beauty. In weaving, value is determined by the extent to which the qualities of the given fiber can be brought to life. The work of the weaver is to serve that effort. The most respectful weaver makes the best *kuzu* fabric.

Everyone remarks on the special luster of *kuzu* cloth. It is this luster that identifies the cloth as *kuzu* cloth. It differs from the luster of silk or *asa*. In that respect *kuzu* has more integrity. It dislikes being twisted. The woven cloth has an essential straightness, and it is somehow masculine. It is different from supple silk. It does not roughen like cotton. For these reasons, it was welcomed for garments that required a well-defined line, such as *hakama* trousers or *kamishimo* outfits. For the same reasons, it was also fitting as the covering of a flat, vertical *fusuma* panel or even more so for the wall of a Western-style room. Few people have yet discovered how appropriate it is for bookbinding. There must be many new ways to use its particular beauty and firmness to the best advantage.

. . . Pieces made in the past tell us how beautifully *kuzu* grew, was dyed, was woven, and was tailored. Nowadays, unfortunately, demand has fallen off, and only *fusuma* coverings continue to be made. Those fabrics are plain white for the most part, and since they are inexpensive the weaving is hasty and coarse. One cannot expect to find anything that bears comparison with the work of the past (Yanagi 1981:271–72).

A number of issues of Yanagi's monthly magazine *Kōgei* (Craft), issued from 1931 to 1951, were bound with varieties of striped and plaid *kuzu* cloth especially woven by Yanagi's nephew, Yanagi Yoshitaka, who took a particular interest in that cloth among the many traditional types that he wove. No one has yet emerged, however, to take a role comparable to that of Kawabata Fumi for "thick cloth." Unless such a person appears and generates new interest in the cloth, its production will probably die out naturally with the generation of elderly women who presently process the fiber.

BANANA-FIBER CLOTH AND OKINAWAN CULTURAL IDENTITY

In the earliest Okinawan hierarchy, different grades of cloth produced from thread-banana fiber served as royal garments, ritual robes, and utilitarian clothing. When Okinawa became a Japanese tributary, silk and grass-bast cloths replaced the finest banana-fiber cloth in a superimposed hierarchy of desirability. In this century, the Folk Craft Movement has helped identify banana-fiber cloth as a "National Treasure," whose production now sustains the sense of identity of Okinawan weavers resisting a new wave of Japanese cultural dominance.

The cloth known as *bashōfu* in Japanese, *haji* in Okinawan, is woven from leaf fiber of the thread-banana plant.[36] This species of banana differs from the two others also found throughout the Ryukyu archipelago, one producing ornamental flowers and the other edible fruit. Specialists disagree as to whether the thread banana is native to the Ryukus or was introduced from the outside and—if so—from where (Walker 1976:324).[37] No one knows when Okinawan banana-fiber cloth began to be produced, but until the mid-twentieth century it was being woven throughout the islands.

The Ryukyu archipelago is a chain of some 140 small islands stretching between the Japanese island of Kyushu to the northeast and Taiwan to the southwest. Okinawa, lying midway along the chain, is the largest island. The islands further south, known collectively as the outer islands (Sakishima), are closest to Taiwan. The island of Okinawa has always been the center of development in the Ryukyus, and its name is often used to designate the entire archipelago. Its location, roughly equidistant from Taiwan, the South China coast, and the Philippines, made it a key transfer point on maritime trade routes, and its culture was influenced by a complex intermingling of various outside cultures. The process of unifying rival, independent clans that led to the formation of the Yamato state in Japan by the seventh century A.D. was echoed on Okinawa beginning in the twelfth century and in Sakishima about two centuries later. In 1429, Shō Hashi unified three independent feudal states and established a kingdom closely patterned on Chinese models, with its capital on Okinawa at Shuri, adjacent to modern Naha. The Chinese cultural influence continued to predominate even after the Ryukyus were conquered in 1609 by the Shimazu domain, based in Satsuma province at the southern tip of Kyushu. With Japan closed to outside contact by government decree, Satsuma exploited the Ryukyus as an avenue for illegal trade. After the fall of the Tokugawa government and the dethronement of the last Shō king, the Ryukyus became the Japanese prefecture of Okinawa in 1879. The islands were lost to Japan at the close of World War II and remained under United States jurisdiction until they reverted to Japan in 1972.

Most of the early documentary evidence regarding banana-fiber cloth occurs in Chinese records. The earliest mention is found in a document dated 1372, which notes banana fiber and grass-bast fibers as the plant fibers being woven into cloth and sewn into garments by the local population (Akashi 1976:373). Another Chinese document, from 1532, specifies that banana-fiber garments were worn in summer and the grass-bast fiber ramie (called *bu* in Okinawan) was preferred for winter (Akashi 1976:373). The same fibers were reported as being woven by women and sold in the market-places by a Japanese document of 1603 (Akashi 1976:372).

While these records seem to indicate that neither cotton nor silk was being processed or woven in the Ryukyus prior to the early seventeenth century, a Chinese text of 1534 lists a variety of silks and cottons being sold in the Shuri markets (Akashi 1976:372). Presumably those textiles were trade goods brought from India or China. Japanese tradition insists that techniques for raising silkworms and cultivating cotton were introduced from Satsuma in the seventeenth century, but local lore maintains that both silk and cotton had been brought from China about a century earlier (Miyagi 1973:115,122).

Whatever the source of the silks and cottons, they figured importantly in the strict Chinese-style hierarchy of costumes and colors that was established by the beginning of the sixteenth century as a corollary to the ranking system, and revised in 1639. According to that system, members of the royal family and the court wore lined silk garments in winter and on all formal occasions and unlined ramie garments in summer. Warriors wore cotton for ordinary use and lined silk for formal occasions in winter; in summer, they wore banana-fiber cloth for ordinary dress and unlined ramie for formal occasions. Commoners wore cotton in winter and banana fiber in summer; they were not permitted to wear silk (Tsujiai 1973:20–23).

The classification system implies that ramie was considered superior to banana-fiber cloth, but the unequal status of the two fabrics may not have been established until the seventeenth-century revision and may reflect a Japanese viewpoint. Earlier records showing the use of banana-fiber cloth as tribute cloth suggest that it was highly desirable. In the late sixteenth century, the finest grade of

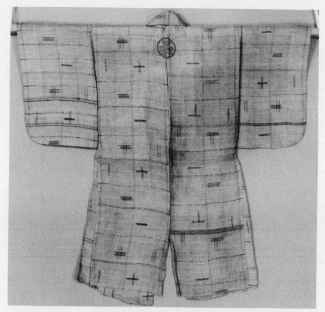

Figure 27. A seventeenth-century summer jacket of banana-fiber cloth from Okinawa, probably made of tribute cloth tailored in Japan. It is believed to have been worn by the third head of the Owari Tokugawa house, Tsunanari (1652–99). Tokugawa Reimeikai collection: Tokyo

banana-fiber cloth (*niigashi,* "boiled skeins," for which the thread was boiled with lye before weaving in order to increase its pliability and luster) was being sent to China together with horses, mother-of-pearl inlaid lacquer, conch, and sulphur (Tsujiai 1978:4). The 1616 record of the estate of the first Tokugawa shogun, Ieyasu (1542–1616), lists thirty-three bolts of banana-fiber cloth (Tokugawa 1977:644). Another Japanese document shows that, on the occasion of the birth of a Japanese imperial prince in 1644, King Shō Ken sent gifts of a sword, a horse, thirty rolls of velvet, thirty bolts of *niigashi* banana-fiber cloth, fifty bolts of "ribbed" (gauze-weave?) banana-fiber cloth, thirty bolts of thin banana-fiber cloth, one hundred bundles of cotton, and five vats of wine (Tokugawa 1977:690). The 1644 list also indicates the diversity of banana-fiber cloths.

However, ramie predominates in tribute records from the seventeenth century on.[38] The annual tribute established by the Shimazu clan in 1611 included six thousand bolts of fine ramie and ten thousand bolts of coarse ramie but only three thousand bolts of banana-fiber cloth (Tonaki 1977:36). Quality control of ramie production was assured by the establishment in every village, in 1619, of a supervised workshop for fiber preparation and weaving (Miyagi 1973:121). Except for the banana-fiber cloth woven in Shuri, that cloth does not seem to have been subject to the same restrictions. Later tribute records suggest that most banana-fiber cloth was replaced by unwoven banana-fiber (Miyagi 1973:121), but how that was used is not clear.

The rise of ramie's importance may be directly related to the needs of Japan. Banana-fiber garments with their stiffness and porosity were ideally suited to summer wear in hot, humid Okinawa, since they stood away from the body and allowed moisture to evaporate, but the Japanese climate is more temperate.[39] Fine-textured, bleached ramie was more appropriate for the softer drape of Japanese garments, and it was better suited than most grades of banana-fiber cloth to the subtle dye colors and hand-painted and stencil-dyed decoration fashionable in Japan. For some time, ramie had been established in Japan as the most desirable fabric for summer wear.

Within Okinawa itself, however—despite the implication of the official dress rules—certain kinds of banana-fiber cloth seem to have maintained a high status. A 1711 dictionary of the Ryukyuan language relates that "in the past" the formal garment for women had been the *hiranuki*: It was made from either banana fiber or ramie, was dyed blue-black with indigo, and was lined (Tsujiai 1973:22). The stipulation of lining recalls the formal winter dress of the upper classes and hints that before silk became available, banana fiber was an equal alternative to ramie for formal garments. (Indeed, it was customary, upon the birth of a princess to the Shō family, to assign to her use a specially-cultivated grove of thread-banana plants or field of ramie [Okamura 1977:398]). The same dictionary also describes a dark-blue indigo-dyed robe called *chōginu* ("court robe") or *kurochō* ("black court") worn by noblemen on formal occasions (Tonaki 1977:36). An 1829 administrative report from Amami Oshima, north of Okinawa, describes the painstaking process by which the *chōginu* robe was made:

The best-quality banana fiber is split as finely as possible, and the thread is dyed numerous times in indigo, over a five-day period, until it is saturated. The family members take turns fulling the woven cloth over two or three days. The finished cloth is lustrous. . . . It is sewn into wide-sleeved garments and worn with a wide sash (Shigeno 1976:98).

The term *kurochō* was also given to a dark blue robe worn until recently by women at weddings, although the cut differed from that of the man's robe worn at court (Okamura 1977:399). The woman's *kurochō* would appear to be the descendent of the ancient *hiranuki*.

The description of using the "best-quality fiber" for fabricating the man's *chōginu* robe implies a high degree of refinement in techniques of preparing banana fiber, a further indication of the importance of both the fiber and the cloth. As early as 1546, a Korean document recorded that three different grades of cloth were made from the varying qualities of fiber in the inner and outer section of the trunk: "The finest grade is white as snow, smooth and flawless as a beautiful woman's skin" (Tonaki 1977:36). Each piece of the thread-banana stalk—formed of leaf sheaths wrapped tightly in concentric layers, opening into "leaves" only at the very top— has fiber on both surfaces, sandwiching a pulpy center, but only the long fibers on the outer surface are used for weaving (the short fibers of the inner surface formerly were used by papermakers). Furthermore, the quality of the fiber is best on the innermost layers, where it is protected from the elements. An 1872 report on banana-fiber cloth production differentiated six grades of fiber altogether. The three outer grades were used only for heavy thread, cords, and ropes. The fourth layer from the outside was used for work clothes, the fifth for everyday garments, and the sixth for garments for formal occasions (including all the garments mentioned above). Only three leaf sheaths of the finest grade occurred on a given plant.

The qualities of the different grades of fiber were expressed in terms of the quantity of rice for which they could be traded; work-clothing grade was called "3 *shō*" (5.76 quarts), whereas the finest grade was called "1 *tō* 3 *shō*" (almost 25 quarts). The relative fineness of the grades of cloth was expressed in terms of *yomi*, a unit of eighty warp ends. In a standard width of slightly more than one foot, work-clothing cloth would have seven to nine *yomi*, cloth for everyday wear ten to twelve *yomi*, and the finest cloth twenty *yomi* (1600 warp ends) (Tonaki 1977:35; Tsujiai 1973:25). Finally, the overall quality of fiber was improved by careful trimming of the plant to make it grow straight and branchless. Thread-banana plants intended for twenty-*yomi* garments were usually grown inside the walled courtyard that surrounded the Okinawan dwelling, protected from the wind until they reached their ideal thickness after three years.

Regional differences—including subtle variations in soil and climate—created further levels of distinction. The finest quality of banana-fiber cloth—the *niigashi* mentioned above—was woven in the royal capital, Shuri, a center for all types of textile production. Shuri banana-fiber cloth was not traded on the market but sent to the court. The Japanese scholar Arai Hakuseki, visiting Okinawa in 1719, acknowledged that the finest banana-fiber cloth was "better than hemp or ramie" (Uemura 1971:67). Shuri banana-fiber cloth was dyed in brilliant colors; one surviving garment is striped with dark and medium blue, rust-red, and white on a mustard-yellow ground. It is a man's robe; women's garments usually had red grounds. Various ikat patterns were employed, as were complex woven designs—gauze weaves and floating-warp patterns—probably borrowed from Chinese silks. Plain-weave banana-fiber cloth was patterned colorfully with the Okinawan stencil-resist technique called *bingata*, "red pattern."

In contrast to the gorgeous variety of the banana-fiber cloth from Shuri, the commoners' banana-fiber cloth was severely restricted. Only plain-weave cloth was permitted. Only simple stripes (narrower for men than for women and for elders than for young people), dyed in blue or reddish-brown, could be worn. Women were allowed to wear dark, small-figured printed patterns for formal occasions. The effect of such rules was to make status distinguishable at a glance (Nihon Minzoku Gakkai 1973:114–15). Only after the end of Tokugawa rule were commoners free to use the full range of Okinawan textile-decorating techniques, and they developed their own hierarchy: ikat for formal garments; simple ikat, checks, and stripes for everyday ware; and stripes or plain cloth for work clothes (Tonaki 1977:34).

With the demise of Shimazu control and the end of the tribute-cloth system in 1903, the ramie textiles from the southern Ryukyus (Sakishima) became important commercial goods on the open market. They were already famous as "Satsuma ramie" in the Japanese market, and they became a major source of income. Banana-fiber cloth, however, was not well known outside the Ryukyus. In 1923, for example, out of 81,000 bolts produced, only 251 were sent to Japan. With cheap mill cloth available in Okinawa, and with the growing popularity of Western-style garments, production of banana-fiber cloth declined steadily: 135,000 bolts had been woven in 1895, but only 27,000 were woven in 1940.

An exception to the overall decline occurred in the village of Kijōka, one of the two areas in northern Okinawa (Yambaru) that had long had a reputation for its commoner-class banana-fiber cloth, known as "Yambaru banana-fiber cloth." In Kijōka, ikat-dyed banana-fiber cloth was redeveloped and the Japanese-style floor loom was introduced by a local man, Taira Shinshō. Shinshō's son Shinji, as mayor of the village, continued the effort to improve quality by inviting specialists to give instruction. In 1939 he arranged for the first exhibition of banana-fiber cloth at a department store in Tokyo (Tonaki 1977:37).

At just that moment the leader of the Folk Craft Movement, Yanagi Sōetsu, published an article in praise of banana-fiber cloth in his monthly magazine *Kōgei*. Yanagi had first become familiar with the cloth when he made several study trips to the Ryukyus in the 1920s. Yanagi was deeply sympathetic to the cause of Okinawan cultural identity, and he championed such issues as the campaign to allow Okinawan language to be used alongside Japanese. In his article, Yanagi praised banana-fiber cloth because it had to be prepared from beginning to end by hand and did not lend itself to mechanization, and because it was worn by all classes from high to low. He said that banana-fiber cloth presented an opportunity to approach the very "wellsprings of beauty" (Yanagi 1954:188).

Only a few years after Yanagi wrote, the destruction of war swept over the islands, bringing the weaving of banana-fiber cloth to a halt. However, a number of Kijōka girls had been sent to the Japanese city of Kurashiki to work in an airplane factory. Among them was Taira Toshiko (born 1921), eldest daughter of Shinji. With the war's end, the plant closed, and its owner—Ōhara Sōichirō, an ardent supporter of Yanagi's Folk Craft Movement—became concerned about the Okinawan girls. When he heard that they had some familiarity with weaving, he arranged for them to be trained by the weaver Tonomura Kichinosuke (now director of the Kurashiki Folk Craft Museum, established with Ōhara's backing).

Toshiko returned to Okinawa in 1946 with exhortations from Yanagi and Ōhara to preserve Okinawa's textile tradition. She started by recruiting war widows and gradually developed a group of women that called itself the "Society for the Preservation of Kijōka Banana-fiber Cloth." At first the society's income was so meager that Toshiko operated a general store to support herself, but with the backing of influential women among the American occupation forces and of the Folk Craft Movement members in Japan, the group's work gradually became known. In 1974 the society, with Toshiko as its representative, was designated an Important Intangible Cultural Property ("Living National Treasure") by the Japanese government (Tonaki 1977:37–38). This honor guarantees financial support for the society so long as it conforms to strictly-defined standards of the "traditional" procedures within the production of banana-fiber cloth.[40]

Production of banana-fiber cloth continues elsewhere in Okinawa, with similar cultural motives but without the official support of the Japanese government. On the island of Iriomote, in the western Yaeyama group, women under the guidance of a young Kyoto-trained weaver named Ishigaki Akiko process and weave thread-banana fiber as part of a movement to preserve the economic and cultural independence of their island in the face of increasing dependence on the Japanese economy and intensive development of Okinawa as a Japanese resort. Their concern for perpetuating the production of banana-fiber cloth is part of a larger concern for preserving the cultural fabric of which it is a part, including the songs that accompany its processing and the festivals and rituals in which it is meant to be worn. At the same time, the Iriomote weavers are ready to modernize their product in order to make it economically viable. Unlike the women of Kijōka, they are not committed to following certain rules defining the nature of banana-fiber cloth. Their goal is to experiment with new dyes, designs, and uses, allowing the cloth to keep step with an affluent modern culture that appreciates and searches out "traditional" materials.

The accomplishment of the women of Kijōka and Iriomote is admirable, but it is supported by a long tradition that not only required women to weave but also endowed that activity with primary importance. A Japanese visitor to the Ryukyus in 1876 remarked that "there is no woman—even in the royal family—who is ignorant of the skills of spinning, reeling, weaving, and stitching" (Miyagi

1973:275). That complex of skills was further urged upon women by Japanese government edicts such as the one of 1834 that proclaimed: "A woman's foremost accomplishment is not to purchase a single garment for either summer or winter but to prepare them all by her own hands" (Miyagi 1973:116).

Behind the edict lay, of course, the obligation to submit cloth in payment of annual taxes as well as to clothe all the members of the family. But various traditions, no doubt older than the edicts, encouraged the production of banana-fiber cloth and even made it pleasurable. In the arduous task of preparing the banana fiber, women were supported by the community custom of gathering in the evenings at a bonfire-lit crossroads to sing and talk as they worked together. Since young men tended the bonfires, such gatherings were opportunities for matchmaking. The young woman about to marry, faced with the responsibility of weaving twenty-*yomi* banana-fiber garments for herself and her groom, was aided by her friends, who contributed their thread to her (Tonaki 1977:36).

The Okinawan woman weaving for her lover or her family expressed affection through her work. Folk songs from every village record the deep emotion that underlay the work: "I wind on the skeins of twenty-*yomi* thread to make my beloved a formal robe like a dragonfly wing" (Miyagi 1973:184). But the work of weaving also had another powerful symbolic meaning: The woman did not just adorn her family and keep them warm, she also protected them spiritually. According to Okinawan belief, the living person is activated by the presence of a spirit located in the chest, called *mabui*. That spirit withdraws from the body at the time of death, but it can also be stolen or lost. When the *mabui* is thought to have escaped, a woman member of the victim's family is responsible for performing the rites that will reinstall it. The ritual for returning the *mabui* begins with collecting three pebbles from a particular place and binding them inside the garment behind the neck (Lebra 1966:22,25,61). The body of the standard Okinawan garment is formed by two narrow loom-widths of banana-fiber cloth joined by a central back seam; the well-sewn back seam keeps the *mabui* in place. (A corpse is dressed in a kimono having the back seam slightly opened, so that the *mabui* may exit [Tonaki 1977:34].)

Both affection and spiritual power are embodied in the capacity of the banana-fiber or cotton towel called *tisaji* to protect the man for whom it was made. Women wove elaborately-worked *umui* (remembrance) towels for their lovers. Sisters wove *uminai* towels for their brothers to take on long sea voyages, reflecting the Okinawan belief in a sister's unique power to protect her brother. This belief sprang from the founding myth involving a sister and brother and was incorporated in the custom of having a sister and brother share leadership of a kingdom (Lebra 1966:101; see also Weiner, this volume).

The Okinawan woman's role as leader was centered in the spiritual realm, while the man's role was political. At every level—state, community, kin group, and household—it was the responsibility of senior women to enact the rituals. Priestesses at the higher levels of society were chosen for their manifest ability, believed to be an inborn aspect of their character, to attract and secure the favor of the gods (Lebra 1966:26). By tradition they remained unmarried, and they lived on the grounds of the main village shrine. Their badge of office was a white robe, now of ramie or cotton but formerly of banana-fiber cloth (Tonaki 1977:36). When not in use, the robe was kept in the shrine. In some places it was the custom to burn the robe every twelve years (Lebra 1966:76).

In Okinawa, where dark indigo-dyed garments were the customary garb for formal and auspicious occasions, white was worn only by priestesses or by participants in funerals. The mourning garment was woven with stripes of white cotton within the banana fiber warp, and at the funeral it was turned inside out and draped over the head (Tonaki 1977:34), marking the exceptional occasion by a reverse of usual practice. So too the precincts of village shrines or other sacred places were marked off by ropes twisted to the left rather than to the right, as was usual (Lebra 1966:53). So too did the priestess's white robe—the robe of banana-fiber cloth— set her apart from ordinary society, as someone who operated in a realm of special spiritual power.

CHANGE AND SURVIVAL

The three long vegetable fibers, and the elements of ancient material culture they represent, have survived within drastically altered contexts by fulfilling specific needs in sacred ritual, trade and commerce, or isolated peripheral economies. In each tradition, women have always contributed the intensive labor necessary to collect, process, and prepare the fibers, although both their positions within the economy of production and their rewards for participation have varied. Mulberry-fiber cloths were used both for imperial accession rituals and for utilitarian purposes in remote mountainous regions. In the royal courts, the cloth contributed to the ritual perpetuation of the state; in the mountains, the woman's skill in producing such cloth was vital to the survival of her household. From an early date, *kuzu* cloth was produced as a commercial product, and the labor of women was an invisible element controlled by the merchant who sold the cloth. Banana-fiber cloth was both produced by women (whether for household, royal court, or trade) and worn by women in their roles as religious authorities. The role of women as processors and weavers of the fiber was honored and supported by community custom.

In recent decades, just as all three fibers have seemed about to be abandoned for good, they have drawn the attention of groups concerned with defining and preserving elements of Japanese traditional culture, especially the Folk Craft Movement led by Yanagi Sōetsu. But this attention has helped to assure the continuing survival of only one kind of cloth. In 1974, after Okinawa had reverted to Japanese control, the Japanese government claimed banana-fiber cloth as a Japanese "National Treasure" and began to give economic support to the group of women that still produces it. Simultaneously, however, another group of Okinawan weavers began producing banana-fiber cloth as part of an effort to resist Japanese cultural and economic dominance.

Cloth of mulberry-plant fiber is still produced, thanks to the determination of mountain women to resist the boredom of enforced idleness resulting from a transformed economy—and thanks also to the curiosity of an urban weaver (with her students, resisting the boredom of middle-class urban life). *Kuzu* cloth survives because the lifetime habits of hard-working, elderly farm women, who continue to gather and process the fiber, allows *kuzu* cloth production to continue. For both kinds of cloth, survival is tenuous, but it is significant. Sheer sentimentality does not have the power to perpetuate fiber cloths known and used continuously since the late neolithic period, now that they are no longer economic necessities; but stronger emotions may yet preserve them.

NOTES

1. The designation "long vegetable fibers" is used to distinguish the bast or stem fibers (such as the mulberry-plant fibers *kōzo* and *kaji*, and the fiber of the *kuzu* vine, to be discussed in this paper) and the structural or leaf fibers (such as *bashō*, the third fiber to be discussed) from other, shorter fibers or nonfibrous plant components, including wood, seed fibers, and the soft tissues of leaves, pith, and green bark (Weindling 1947:13–15). Thanks to Amanda Mayer Stinchecum for introducing me to this term as being more precise than the commonly-used "bast fibers."

2. Much cotton fabric was also produced on a noncommercial basis for home consumption, but the distinctive feature of Edo-period textile production was the range of fine-quality commercial goods.

3. The resist-dye process generally known by its Indonesian name, ikat, is called *kasuri* in Japanese. The process involves wrapping bundles of warp and/or weft threads before dyeing in such a way as to produce patterns that become visible when the cloth is woven.

4. Based upon the cellulose polymer (empirical formula $C_6H_{10}O_5$) as are all vegetable fibers, bast or stem fibers are the fibrous bundles occurring in the inner bark (bast or phloem) of the stems of dicotyledenous plants. The cells are typically long and thick-walled and overlap one another; they are cemented together by noncellulosic materials to form continuous strands that may run the entire length of the plant. The bast fibers are released from the cellular and woody tissues of the stem, and are broken down into constituent cells, by the process of controlled rotting called retting (Weindling 1947:15; Cook 1968:3–4).

5. *Taima* (*Cannabis sativa*) and *choma* or *karamushi*.

6. *Ama* (*Linum usitatissimum*).

7. Almost no fiber objects survive from the neolithic period, but their traces appear as impressions left on pottery, the famous "cord-patterned" (*jōmon*) earthenware that gives its name to Japan's neolithic period (?–ca. 200 B.C.). Twisted cords were coiled around sticks and rolled over the pot's damp surface to consolidate and decorate it; baskets and cloth were spread under the pot as it was being constructed. There is no way of detecting which fibers might have left their marks on the pots.

8. To be precise, the processing of hemp and ramie was far from easy, and the chief advantage of these plants over the tree-bast fibers was that they could be cultivated and harvested within four or five months. Ramie in particular required scraping or pounding to remove the outer bark before the retting process could be effective, although the resultant fiber was a natural white comparable to bleached cotton, as contrasted to the darker hue of hemp (Weindling 1947:276 and 293).

9. Other wild tree-bast fibers still used in Japan and the Ryukyus include

yamafuji ("mountain wisteria," *Wisteria brachybotrys*), *shina* (*Tilia japonica*), and *atsushi* (*Ulmus laciniata*) (Gotō 1964).

10. Although *kuzu* is commonly translated as "arrowroot," the Japanese plant is not identical to the arrowroot plant, which comes from the tropical West Indies. *Kuzu* was introduced to the United States at the Philadelphia Centennial Exposition of 1876 and now flourishes throughout the Southeast, where it is known—and cursed for its invasive qualities—as kudzu (Shurtleff and Aoyagi 1977:9 and 12ff.).

11. Like the bast or stem fibers, the leaf fibers are long, strong, and firmly bound into filaments by a natural gum. They traverse the leaves, forming their supporting and strengthening structure (Weindling 1947:13–14).

12. Yanagida remarked upon the ancient Shinto concept that the proper offerings to the gods are not luxury goods but the best of each person's everyday necessities (Yanagida 1976:31).

13. *Asa* paper was used for inscribing imperial edicts and, dyed various colors, for copying Buddhist sacred texts. The reddish-brown paper called *kokushi*, made from either one of the mulberry plant fibers, was used for ordinary documents (Toyota 1965:272).

14. Translations from Nippon Gakujitsu Shinkōkai 1965:75.

15. A "pillow word" is a conventional epithet used in Japanese poetry to modify certain fixed words.

16. *Shironigite* and *aonigite*.

17. The Japanese term *ao* can mean either "green" or "blue". It is not clear whether the term indicates in this case that the *asa* cloth offerings were dyed blue with indigo or that they simply had the greenish cast of freshly-cut vegetation. I tend to feel the latter was meant, since in modern shrine usage the strands of *asa* are undyed.

18. The same characters used to write *yū* were later read as *momen*, the word for "cotton".

19. The loop of thread was called *yūdasuki*. The custom persists in the Ryukyus, where a loop of fiber is slung over the right shoulder of the priestess who approaches the shrine, to invoke the protection of the gods. The general term for the sleeve-loop, *tasuki*, is related to the verb *tasukeru*, "to aid" (Okamura 1977:89).

20. The description of the ritual that follows is based on Ellwood 1973, although the interpretation is my own.

21. The Imbe clan members were responsible for sending one bolt of mulberry-fiber cloth (*aratae*) and six *kin* (almost eight pounds) of mulberry-fiber thread (*yū*) (Okamura 1977:257).

22. The terms for the offertory cloth, *yū* and *asa*, here allude to their homophones meaning "evening" and "morning."

23. Ellwood notes that the formulation of the ritual was influenced by continental (Taoist and Confucian) ideas regarding the necessity of the proper adjustment between contrasting opposites, yin and yang (Ellwood 1973:155).

24. Records of subsequent *Daijōsai* ceremonies even indicate that the baskets of *aratae* actually contained bleached *asa* cloth (Okamura 1977:263).

25. *Tafu*, written with the characters meaning "thick cloth" but possibly simply a colloquial corruption of the ancient term *tae*.

26. Production of "thick cloth" was documented in the interior of Shinano province (modern Nagano prefecture) (Gotō 1974:122).

27. Motor vehicles entered the district only in the 1930s (Takeuchi 1982:9). All rice—a luxury item reserved for festival days—used in Kitō had to be carried in from the coast, as did salt. The local diet, typical of mountainous regions, was based on millet or barley and greens. In the mid-1950s, Gotō collected twenty-two "thick cloth" items from Kitō: fifteen were grain bags, two were lunch-box bags, two were bags for storing bedding, only one was a garment. Three of the grain bags had been dyed with persimmon tannin to waterproof them (Gotō 1974:126).

28. Production for 1896 was 450 bolts; for 1900, 750 bolts; for 1904, 800 bolts; for 1912, 1800 bolts. A Kitō village office report of 1905 mentions that some three hundred households were involved in "thick cloth" production, with an average of one woman per household weaving the cloth (Takeuchi 1982:11).

29. A survey of 1897 noted that, whereas in the past both men and women had worn "thick cloth" jackets and trousers as their usual costume, it was now rare to find women wearing "thick cloth" (Gotō 1974:123).

30. Around 1910, a bolt of striped cotton sold for 1 yen 60 sen, while a bolt of "thick cloth" was worth 1 yen 70–80 sen (Takeuchi 1982:17).

31. In the summer of 1988 I visited Kitō and met three of the women who have chosen to carry on the skills they learned from the preceding generation of mountain women. Having mastered the basic skills, they are now intent upon finding new designs and uses for the *tafu* that they weave on both backstrap and frame looms (the latter using cotton warps). Although they say that most Kitō citizens do not understand what they are doing or why, they find inspiration from occasional meetings with women in other mountainous areas of Japan who are attempting to continue their own regional traditions of tree-bast fiber cloths.

32. The oldest example of *kuzu* cloth known in Japan was found adhering to the front of a bronze mirror excavated from a tomb in Fukuoka Prefecture, northern Kyushu, dating to the third or fourth century A.D. Both warp and weft threads were of S-twisted *kuzu* fiber (Nunome 1983:46–47).

33. The manifold uses of *kuzu* starch as food and medicine are outlined in Shurtleff and Aoyagi 1977:10–12, 52–56.

34. In 1987 I was surprised to encounter a display of handsome "sunshades,"

distributed by a San Francisco importer, made with *kuzu* fiber wefts (although the publicity did not name it as such). The importer's color brochure illustrated Kakegawa women—some of whom I had met—gathering, processing, and weaving *kuzu* fiber.

35. Collecting the *kuzu* vines in the mountains and removing the fiber by soaking the coiled vines and washing them in running stream water requires physical stamina and can only be done by women in good health, although the women I met doing such work were in their seventies. Preparing the thread tends to be done by women of frailer health, who work indoors while sitting.

36. Japanese *bashō*, Okinawan *bashaa*.

37. The Okinawan plant is closely related to the cultivated species, *Musa textilis*, that is indigenous to the Philippine archipelago and is the source of the textile fiber known as Manila hemp or abaca (Weindling 1947:38–43).

38. The bulk of tribute was sent as rice, reflecting standard practice in Japan, but the rice-poor islands of Miyako and Yaeyama were permitted to send a portion of their due as cloth. Okinawan ramie was distributed throughout Japan as "Satsuma ramie" (Tonaki 1977:36).

39. An unlined jacket for mid-summer use, tailored from striped and ikat-patterned banana-fiber cloth of exquisite quality, is said to have been worn by the third head of the Owari branch of the Tokugawa house, Tsunanari (1652–99). It may be one of the oldest surviving examples of banana-fiber cloth. The Japanese name for a jacket with this cut and fabric was *shimabaori*, which may mean either "striped jacket" or "island jacket"—referring to the source of the fabric (Tokugawa *et al.* 1983: catalogue no. 245; see Fig. 27 here).

40. The impact of the system of designating "Living National Treasures" upon textile production is examined at length by Amanda Mayer Stinchecum in an unpublished paper, "Growth, Continuance or Decline: Japan's Traditional Textile Arts," presented to the University Seminar on Modern Japan, Columbia University, November 14, 1986.

REFERENCES CITED

Akashi Kunisuke
    1976   Senshoku Monyōshi no Kenkyū (Research on the History
    [1931] of Design Motifs). Kyoto: Shibunkaku.

Anoymous
    1954   Kuzuō Seizō no Tebiki (Handbook on Kuzu Processing).
            [Kakegawa: not given].

Cook, J. Gordon
    1968   Handbook of Textile Fibers—Natural Fibers. Watford, Herts:
            Merrow. 4th ed.

Ellwood, Robert S.
1973   The Feast of Kingship: Accession Ceremonies in Ancient Japan.
         Toyko: Sophia University.

Gotō Shōichi
1964   Asa Izen (Before Asa). *In* Nihon Minzoku Gakkai Kaihō 32:43–47.
1974   Awa no Tafu wo Kataru (Speaking of Awa Tafu). *In* Senshoku to
         Seikatsu 5:122–26.
1976   3 April: interview
1979   24 March: interview

Horiuchi Toshiko
1982   Genshi Sen'i (Primitive Fibers). *In* Senshoku no Bi 16:97–105.

Kawabata Fumi
1982   9 July: Interview.

Kodama Kota, ed.
1965   Sangyōshi II (History of Industry II). Taikei Nihonshi Sōshō 11.
         Tokyo: Yamakawa Shuppan.

Lebra, William P.
1966   Okinawan Religion: Belief, Ritual, and Social Structure. Hono-
         lulu: University of Hawaii Press.

Miyagi Eisho
1973   Okinawa Joseishi (History of Okinawan Women). Naha:
[1967] Okinawa Taimuzusha.

Nihon Minzoku Gakkai
1973   Okinawa no Minzokugakuteki Kenkyū (Ethnographic Research
         on Okinawa). Tokyo: Minzokugaku Shinkōkai.

Nippon Gakujutsu Shinkōkai
1965   The Manyōshū. New York and London: Columbia University
         Press.

Nunome Yoshio
1983   Shōbugaura Kofungun Daiichigofun Shutto no Hiraginu to
         Kuzufu ni Tsuite (Concerning the Plainweave Silk and Kuzu
         Cloth Excavated from Tomb No. 1 in the Shōbugaura Tumulus
         Group). *In* Kodaigaku Kenkyū 99:46–47.

Ōgura Nagatsune
1944   Seikatsuroku (Record of Processing Kuzu). *In* Nihon
[1828] Kagaku Koten Zenshū 11. Tokyo: Asahi Shimbunsha.

Okamura Kichiemon
1977   Nihon Genshi Orimono no Kenkyū (Research on Japanese Primi-
         tive Weaving). Tokyo: Bunka Shuppankyoku.

Saida Shigetoki, ed.
1973   Kakegawa Shikō (Kakegawa Records). Tokyo: Meicho
[1811] Shuppan.

Shigeno Yuko
1976   Amami Senshoku Kō (Thoughts on Amami Textiles). *In*
        Senshoku to Seikatsu 13:98–101.

Shurtleff, William and Aoyagi, Akiko
1977   The Book of Kuzu; A Culinary and Healing Guide. Brookline,
        Mass.: Autumn Press.

Takahashi Nobutoshi
1976   Tōtōmi Kakegawajō (Tōtōmi Kakegawa Castle). Fujiidera: Nihon
        Kojō Tomonokai.

Takeuchi Junko
1982   Ki no Nuno, Kusa no Nuno (Cloth from Trees, Cloth from
        Grass). *In* Aruku-miru-kiku 184:4–31.

Tokugawa Yoshinobu
1977   Sumpu Onwakemonocho ni Mirareru Senshokuhin ni Tsuite
        (Concerning the Textiles Recorded in the Sumpu Record of Be-
        quests). *In* Kinko Sōsho 4:607–716.

Tokugawa Yoshinobu et. al.
1983   The Shogun Age Exhibition; From the Tokugawa
        Art Museum, Japan. Tokyo: The Shogun Age Execu-
        tive Committee.

Tonaki Akira
1977   Kijōka no Bashōfu (Banana-fiber Cloth of Kijōka). *In* Kijōka no
        Bashōfu. Ningen Kokuhō Shiriizu 41:34–40. Tokyo: Kōdansha.

Toyota Takeshi ed.
1965   Sangyōshi I (History of Industry I). Taikei Nihonshi Sōshō 10.
        Tokyo: Yamakawa Shuppan.

Tsunoda, Ryusaku; Wm. T. de Bary; and Donald Keene
1958   Sources of Japanese Tradition. New York: Columbia University
        Press.

Tsujiai Kiyotarō
1973   Ryukyu Bashōfu (Banana-fiber Cloth of the Ryukyus). Kyoto:
        Kyoto Shoin.
1978   Ryukyu no Bashōfu (Banana-fiber Cloth of the Ryukyus). Kyoto:
        Tambaya.

Uemura Rokurō
1971   Okinawa no Shikisai oyobi Senshoku to Minzoku (Okinawa's
        Color Sense and its Textiles and People). Tokyo: Iseikatsu
        Kenkyūjo.

Walker, Egbert H.
1976   Flora of Okinawa and the Southern Ryukyu Islands. Washington,
        D.C.: Smithsonian.

Weindling, Ludwig
1947   Long Vegetable Fibers. New York: Columbia University Press.

Yanagi Sōetsu
1954   Bashōfu Monogatari (Tale of Banana-fiber Cloth). *In* Yanagi
        Sōetsu Senshū V:147–90. Tokyo: Nihon Mingei Kyōkai.
1981   Watashi no Nengan (My Resolve). *In* Yanagi Sōetsu Shūshū
        Mingei Taikai 3:271–72. Tokyo: Chikuma Shobō.

Yanagida Kunio
1976   Momen Izen no Koto (Before Cotton). Tokyo: Ōbunsha.
(1939)

GLOSSARY OF JAPANESE WRITTEN FORMS

ama	亜 麻
aramitama	荒 御 魂
aratae	荒 妙
asa	麻
bashō	芭 蕉
choma	苧 麻
imbe	斎 部
kaji	構
karamushi	苧
kōzo	楮
kuzu	葛
kuzufu (kappu, kuzununo)	葛 布
nigimitama	和 御 魂
nigitae	和 妙
nigite	和 幣
shirotae	白 妙 白 栲
tafu	太 布
taima	大 麻
taku	栲
takununo	栲 布
yamato	大 和
yū	木 綿 or 斎 or 結

Index

Abortions, 150, 167
Adolescence, 165, 199
Africa, 73–74. *See also* Sakalava
Afterlife: Kuba dress for, 135–37; in Trobriand Islands, 38–39. *See also* Mortuary practices
Agricultural production; cotton, 180, 282, 378; flax, 13, 14, 182, 183, 187, 198–99, 201–204; and linen production, 202–206, 228; in San Antonino, 247, 257–58, 260–71
Ahmedabad: cloth production in, 369–70
'*Aiga*, 41, 48, 65n.9
Akbar, 18, 312, 314, 315–16
Almagristas, 288
Amaterasu, 382, 385
Ampanjaka, 75, 78(fig.)
Ampisikina, 82
Ampzing, Samuel, 233, 234
Ancestors, 139n.12; authority of, 73–74; Kodi, 146, 147; Mughal, 306; Sakalava, 74–75, 86–90, 94–95, 96–97, 109nn.13, 14, 112n.27
Andes: textiles of, 275–78; uses of cloth in, 279–80. *See also* Inka
Angarkha, 366
Appliqué, 121
Aqlla, 17, 24; role of, 289–91
Arabs, 91, 354. *See also* Muslims

Arachne, 219
Aratae, 381, 384, 385
Architecture: as weaving, 278
Army, 17; *aqlla* and, 290, 291; Sikhs in, 307–310; textile use by, 287–89. *See also* British Army
Arnold, C., 232
Arriaga, Pablo José de, 280–81
Art, 2, 14, 148, 338–40. *See also* Handicrafts; Paintings; Prints
Artisans: Indian, 363; Japanese, 390–91, 395–96, 403–404; Mexican national, 246, 255, 257
Asa, Sakakibara, 390
Asa, 378, 382, 409nn.13, 17; offerings of, 380, 384, 385, 386
Asante, 16
Ashram, 343–44
Assenheim, Henricum Oraem, 226
Aualuma groups, 48
Authority, 21, 318; clothing as, 312–14; Yamato state, 383–84. *See also* Power
Awa, 384
Awasqa, 278

Bags: thick cloth, 388, 389, 409n.27
Baldung, Hans, 219, 220
Banana-leaf bundles, 37, 47(table), 54; distribution of, 48–50, 55–56; manu-

417